The Beat Generation

and

The Angry Young Men

THE BEAT GENERATION

and

THE ANGRY YOUNG MEN

edited by GENE FELDMAN

and MAX GARTENBERG

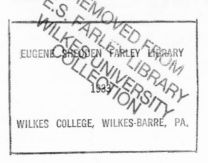
Essay Index Reprint Series

BOOKS FOR LIBRARIES PRESS

FREEPORT, NEW YORK

PS 536
F45

INTERNATIONAL STANDARD BOOK NUMBER:
0-8369-2354-5

LIBRARY OF CONGRESS CATALOG CARD NUMBER:
71-156639

PRINTED IN THE UNITED STATES OF AMERICA

CONTENTS

ACKNOWLEDGMENTS

The Beat Generation

"Sunday Dinner in Brooklyn" by Anatole Broyard, published in *Avon Book of Modern Writing No. 2* (Copyright 1954 by Avon Publications). Permission to reprint granted by the author.

"Fracture" by R. V. Cassill, published in *Epoch*, Summer, 1950 (Copyright 1950 by Epoch Associates). Permission to reprint granted by the author.

"The Beckoning Sea" by George Mandel, published in *American Vanguard 1950* (Copyright 1950 by Cambridge Publishing Company). Permission to reprint granted by the author.

"Go" by Clellon Holmes, selections from the novel of the same name (Copyright 1950 by Clellon Holmes). Permission to reprint granted by Music Corporation of America, agent for the author.

"The Time of the Geek" by Jack Kerouac, selection from *The Town and the City* published by Harcourt, Brace and Company (Copyright 1950 by Jack Kerouac). Permission to reprint granted by the publisher, Harcourt, Brace and Company.

"Swinging" by Jack Kerouac, selection from *On the Road*, published by The Viking Press (Copyright 1955, 1957 by Jack Kerouac). Permission to reprint granted by the publisher, The Viking Press.

"Redemption" by Chandler Brossard, selection from *The Bold Saboteurs*, published by Farrar, Straus and Young (Copyright 1952, 1953 by Chandler Brossard). Permission to reprint granted by the author.

"My First Days on Junk" by "William Lee," selection from *Junkie*, published by Ace Books, Inc. (Copyright 1953 by Ace Books, Inc.). Permission to reprint granted by the publisher, Ace Books, Inc.

"Report from the Asylum" by Carl Solomon, published in *Neurotica*, Spring, 1950 (Copyright 1950 by Neurotica Publishing Co., Inc.). Permission to reprint granted by the author.

"Howl" by Allen Ginsberg, in *Howl and Other Poems*, Pocket Poets Series No. 4, published by City Lights Books, San Francisco (Copyright 1956 by City Lights Books). Permission to reprint granted by the publisher.

The Angry Young Men

"I Can't Marry Robert!" by John Wain, selection from the novel *Hurry on Down*, published in the United States as *Born in Captivity* by Alfred A. Knopf, Inc. (Copyright 1953 by John Wain). Permission to reprint granted by the publisher, Alfred A. Knopf, Inc.

"Merrie England" by Kingsley Amis, selection from the novel *Lucky Jim*, published by Doubleday & Company, Inc. (Copyright 1953 by Kingsley Amis). Permission to reprint granted by the publisher, Doubleday & Company, Inc.

"Country of the Blind" by Colin Wilson, selection from *The Outsider*, published by the Houghton Mifflin Company (Copyright 1956 by Colin Wilson). Permission to reprint granted by the publisher, the Houghton Mifflin Company.

To reprint material extensively quoted in the above selection, additional permissions have been granted, as follows:

Quotations from Henri Barbusse, *Under Fire*, published by E. P. Dutton & Co., Inc. (Copyright 1947 by J. M. Dent—renewal), by the publisher, E. P. Dutton & Co., Inc., New York;

Quotations from H. G. Wells, *Mind at the End of Its Tether*, published by William Heinemann, Ltd., by Mfrs. A. P. Watt & Son, for the Executors of the Estate of H. G. Wells; also by William Heinemann, Ltd.

Quotations from Jean-Paul Sartre, *Nausea*, published by New Directions. (Copyright 1949), by the publisher, New Directions.

"The Choice" by John Braine, selection from the novel *Room at the Top*, published by the Houghton Mifflin Company. (Copyright 1957 by John Braine). Permission granted by the publisher, Houghton Mifflin Company.

"The Interview" by J. P. Donleavy (Not previously published). Permission granted by the author.

"Pity Not the Sheep" by Thomas Hinde, selection from the novel *Happy as Larry*, published by Criterion Books, Inc. Permission granted by MacGibbon & Kee, London, England.

"Time and Place" by George Scott, selection from the autobiography *Time and Place*, published by Staples Press, Ltd. (Copyright 1956). Permission granted by Staples Press, Ltd., London, England.

Socialism and the Intellectuals by Kingsley Amis, published by The Fabian Society. Permission granted by Curtis Brown, Ltd., Agent for the Proprietor.

"Sex and Failure" by John Osborne, published in the London *Observer*, January 20, 1957 (Copyright 1957 by John Osborne). Permission granted by Harold Ober Associates, Inc., agent for the author.

Criticism and Commentary

"Disengagement: The Art of the Beat Generation" by Kenneth Rexroth, published in *New World Writing* No. 11 (Copyright 1957 by New American Library of World Literature, Inc.). Permission to reprint granted by the author.

"Review of *Lucky Jim*" by Walter Allen, published in the *New Statesman and Nation*, vol. 47, January 30, 1954. Permission to reprint granted by the New Statesman, London, England.

"The White Negro" by Norman Mailer, published in *Dissent,* Summer, 1957 (Copyright 1957 by Dissent Publishing Associates). Permission to reprint granted by the author.

"Tank in the Stalls: Notes on the 'School of Anger'" by John Holloway, published in *The Hudson Review,* Vol. X, No. 3, Autumn 1957 (Copyright 1957 by The Hudson Review). Permission to reprint granted by The Hudson Review, Inc.

"The Perils of Hypergamy" by Geoffrey Gorer, published in the *New Statesman and Nation,* vol. 53, May 4, 1957. Permission to reprint granted by the New Statesman, London, England.

Introduction

Contemporary history writes itself in nouns: Fascism, Nazism, Communism, Spain, imperialism, Hitler, Stalin, nonaggression pact, Pearl Harbor, Dachau, Hiroshima, Moscow, Yalta, Hungary, Suez . . . names of violence and disaster, of guilt, betrayal, spiritual exhaustion. And superimposed on the experiences these words evoke is a formula whose awful significance may never be washed away: $E = mc^2$, the key to the Atom.

Man, having found the means to release the natural force imprisoned in matter and thereby to obliterate himself, his heirs and the sum total of his racial inheritance, has created the most pervasive fact in his history: one must learn to breathe, eat, make love in its presence; it is a part of every living consciousness.

On the surface of life it seldom obtrudes: the cop blows his whistle, the street crowds move, business goes on from nine to five in a hundred thousand offices. But, the facade of this present seeming normalcy shows signs of weathering; each day the mortar crumbles a little more. Man, behind the masks with which he plays his daily roles, can not be totally blind to the continuing collapse; the consequence is an increasing self-division. He glimpses the portents of chaos everywhere and correspondingly grows aware of his own nakedness and impotence—his nothingness. His fate—survival or extinction—bears less relation to his personal moral bookkeeping than to the scarcely audible assents and dissents of power figures almost too fear-stricken to make decisions. He senses that time is shrinking into itself, the past losing its relevance and the future receding further and further from his control. Only the present seems to hold the possibility of his meaningful participation, for he can still possess the moment.

By choosing to live only in the present, however, he cuts himself off from those values which have propped up his vision of himself as the hero of history. The sense that he is part of an unfolding design (the religionist's belief in increasing good, the positivist's faith in progress) is no longer accessible to him. Even those institutions which have maintained their strength because they have enabled man to achieve desired ends are put to severe tests; for long-term goals have lost their relevance. Marriage, made and perpetuated in order to provide for family continuity, becomes form without substance in an age where tomorrow has a horizon darkened by a mushroom cloud. Work, with its myriad rewards in status and well-being, becomes time spent in thrall. For the individual who steps off the trolley in the conviction that there is really no place to go, all things, persons and beliefs which serve as *means* tend to lose their validity. All of life becomes an accumulation of ends, with all goals immediate.

Should man live a slave to illusions he knows to be untrue? Or should he tear down the false front that masks itself as his dignity and thereby enter into an existence wherein, through acceptance of his lone-ness and of the ever-present possibility of sudden death, he can find the potential for freedom and authentic identity? This is how the question poses itself to many young people on both sides of the Atlantic.

In the United States of America, those "new barbarians" who have chosen the present as the compass of their lives are the Beat Generation. In England, with certain differences, they are the Angry Young Men. Both the Beat Generation and the Angry Young Men are social phenomena which have found increasing literary expression. Because both represent a significant adaptation to life in mid-twentieth century, the writings they have engendered possess an immediate value to us all. In the long run, they may well be the advance columns of a vast moral revolution, one which will transform man from a creature of history to a creature of experience—deriving as their rationale an existentialism that suggest Heidegger and Sartre. For they too, as their philosophic predecessors, accept life as a state of continuing anxiety; they too see man as thirsting for and demanding meaning, even if in the flight from banality they approach the essence of horror.

2

Jack Kerouac, former Columbia University football player who decided that only Squares hit the line for old Alma Mater, coined the phrase Beat Generation. He meant it to apply to himself and his circle of friends who, he felt, represented a complex of attitudes which existed among the youth across the face of America. In his first novel

The Town and the City, he gave the phrase a definition in depth, bringing to life an underground world he had come to know in New York, peopled by a strange breed of American determined to pursue experience to its furthest reaches.

The fiction had its counterpart in reality. There was Allen Ginsberg, a poet whom Kerouac had met at Columbia, who spoke impassionedly of William Blake; "William Lee," an older man and a junkie, who had a Buddha-like awareness of the horror of existence; Clellon Holmes, sober, dedicated, not quite given to the extravagances of mood and gesture of the others; Neil Cassidy, whose mad exuberance and hunger for sensation was a constant goad; Carl Solomon, brilliant and introspective, searching for the fragmentation of perception which had been achieved by the French surrealists.

There were others, too, who moved in and out of this demonic circle which comprised the Beat Generation in the early post-war years, who talked together, sought experience together, and published together (notably in G. Legman's *Neurotica,* which described itself as a journal "for and by neurotics"). But as time passed, the label began to outgrow the group. For *beatness* was not an exclusive condition, and the term Beat Generation came more and more to fit an actual generation that was responding in certain ways to existence in mid-century.

Its attitudes—the rejection of the past and the future, the rebellion against organized authority, the revulsion felt for the Square (the man who played it safe, who stuck to his rut and his illusions and thought that his own life embodied all decent moral values)—these found increasing expression in the works of writers such as Norman Mailer, Vance Bourjaily, Nelson Algren, Herbert Gold, Chandler Brossard, Anatole Broyard, George Mandel and R. V. Cassill.

In a recent issue of *Esquire,* Clellon Holmes defines Beat as being "at the bottom of your personality, looking up." If the generation of which these authors write is Beat, it is because the individuals who compose it have pulled themselves out of an increasingly meaningless rat race rigged up by and for Squares. Not only do the prizes to be won seem worthless, but effort, that most precious of human commodities, seems to be wasted in a game which kills time, deadens awareness and brutalizes feeling. Role-playing, an essential adjunct to making one's mark, demands one mask too many; the Beat Generation in throwing off all masks enters into the inescapable truth and squalor of its own being. In being Beat, it seeks to go beyond the possibility of defeat. It digs everything, likes everything because it has moved beyond reach of the compulsions which drive the Square. In being Beat, it gives up all desire to control nature, events or people. Rather, it wishes to flow with the real tides of existence, those which reach into an underground beyond guise, hate or love.

Too many liars, too many blowhards—this is the sum of its experience. The credo of the Beat Generation therefore becomes simple, direct: the only way to come to terms with life on this planet careening to its doom is to face reality as it is, as one meets it in all moments of agony and joy. Everything else is a hoax or a deception. The Square has his suburbia with a picture window looking out over a graveyard, or he kids himself by chalking political slogans on subway stations. But the man who is Beat knows that he is alone, and that his problem is to learn to live with this knowledge.

As a consequence, his concern is primarily one of self-exploration, of perceiving the self in terms of its connection with immediate experience. Not capable of the act of faith required by a belief in tomorrow, the Beat Man values relationships only as they tend to reveal the truth of his present existence. For him, individuals and places are means whereby he can trace his own shadow and plumb his own nature. All of his contacts are immediate and intense. He has no future which rests on a connection with some person or group. Therefore no other human being can be important to him outside of the moment, and his relationships with others take on the form of a dialogue with a shifting *dramatis personae,* a dialogue always carried on in the present. To the full-blown hipster, the most advanced Beat Generation type, all men are the generic "man," all women the manipulatable "chick."

Politically, of course, the Beat Generation is a cipher. It regards politics as an arena in which Squares juggle words in a gigantic hoax based on the premise that two follows one. The Beat Man knows better: one is one, two is two; sometimes they seem to like going together. But wise in the ways of perversity, he understands full well that words are the colors by which the lie is hidden and the fraud made to appear truth. Because he is an underground form of life, pressured into creating for himself a mythology in which he can play a vital part, the Beat Man accepts but one responsibility: to sharpen his own senses so that he can continue and improve his dialogue with existence.

The language of this dialogue is crude. It includes words whose denotation is vague. Beat, cool, hip, swinging—these are but attempts at description of moods and insights that by their very nature can not be totally pinpointed or defined. Here too the Beat Man stands apart from the Square, whose every move must be within clearly marked limits; in applying rigid names to phenomena, the Square exorcises his fear of the void, of chaos. His Book of Books is the catalogue, the namer and the prop to his illusions. The Beat Generation accepts chaos as being the real world—shifting, changing, perpetually slipping out of his grasp and his attempts to engage it.

What the conclusion of its dialogue is to be, none can tell. But the hope is that it will crack the undersurface of appearance and finally arrive at the meanings which are beyond experience. In this sense, as Kerouac has said, the basic impulse of the Beat Generation is a religious one: to find oneself is to find God. And if it must finally be acknowledged that God is too weak to show His face and that the Beat Generation is a generation of orphans, cut off from the past and its earthly fathers, severed from the future and the Kingdom of God, then the predatory heart of man himself, Satan, will be enshrined the Father. In the wilderness which is life without God, without meaning, God becomes manifest even in his antithesis, who also provides a center, a source, a sliver of certitude.

3

In England, World War II, which leveled tenement and manse in the common rubble of the night raid, produced the psychological leveling which made possible the victory of the Labor Party in the first peacetime election. Although the pressures of socialization, higher income and inheritance taxes weakened the upper classes, the Socialists were generally blamed for the high cost of the war which, by necessity, had been borne into the years of reconstruction. Lacking leadership possessing the boldness to overcome the disadvantage, the Labor Party was swept out of office. In its place came the Tories, wearing the badges of accent, name and tie which have always symbolized rule to the English people. So there came into being

—and remains today—the social anomaly of a Welfare State ruled by a class which must perpetuate itself on privilege.

It is against this background that the phenomenon of the Angry Young Men appears. In origin, they are sons of the lower middle and working classes who came of age with Socialism, had their bodies cared for by the government health program and their minds nourished through government scholarships in red brick universities (though, now and then, at Oxford). Prepared to seek their places in the new England that had been created by parliamentary revolution, they found they had nowhere to go.

Because they recognized themselves to be the very sons for whom their fathers had fought for a better life, they raised their voices in protest. They did not, like the Beat Generation, seek to create their own subterranean world, but wanted entrance into the very real one on the surface where fortunes were made and power wielded. But despite the discomfort they aroused in Establishment circles, it became clear that they were not organizing a new revolution. They had no common goal. Their chief literary spokesmen made their division apparent. John Osborne resembled, most of all, the militant Socialist of the thirties, but Osborne was not advancing any programs of action. Kingsley Amis declared himself also to be a Labor Party man, but his radicalism was so riddled with scepticism as to be untenable. George Scott, despairing for the Socialists, formed a temporary alliance with the Tories. Thomas Hinde, viewing Socialists and Tories as two sides of a bad coin, eschewed politics altogether. Colin Wilson, whose Outsider philosophy begins with the rejection of humanism and rationalism, tried to develop a deeply subjective religious existentialism.

The arrival of these writers on the British literary scene was accompanied by much shouting and bombast. But though their books sold extraordinarily well, they found few friends outside of their own generation, the generation they spoke for. Because they tended to use literature (chiefly the novel) as a means to express discontent rather than as a pure art, they were ignored by most of the academics. An older generation of writers, including men such as V. S. Pritchett and Somerset Maugham, was repelled by the barbaric directness and lack of refinement which characterized much of the work of these Angry Young Men.* Because they persisted in carrying with them working-class attitudes of suspicion and hostility toward an inbred upper-class culture, they made enemies of the Tories. And because they refused to commit themselves to the causes of the Left, even the Laborites eyed them suspiciously.

What did this new generation of Englishmen want? In one sense, they wished what the Socialists had led them to expect: the opportunities from which the class structure of England had excluded their ancestors for centuries. Up to a point, the Welfare State had given them these opportunities; but in the main areas of life where they desired the chance at personal advancement, they found themselves on treadmills heading nowhere. Although they were not required to give up the positive advantages which had been made available to them, they could not escape the sordid triviality that had become the substance of their lives. Educated away from their class roots, they could look only toward a future of mediocrity and inconsequence. Like the Beat Generation, they found themselves forced to seek meaning in the present, and they proceeded to forge their identities in the smithy of the here and now.

The phrase Angry Young Men does not truly describe them. It is a Fleet Street coinage which has stuck because of its dramatic flavor rather than its accuracy. In England, to speak of the Angry Young Men in some literary circles is to invite laughter or derision—even from some of the writers to whom the label has been applied. For the truth is that the Angry Young Men, with the possible exception of Osborne, are too alienated from contemporary British society to be capable of sustained anger.

The term itself, according to John Holloway, derives from the title of Leslie Paul's *Angry Young Man*. The irony is that Paul's memoir deals with a different brand of "angry young man," that of the 'twenties and 'thirties seeking to create a better world through leftist "good causes." If the Angry Young Men of the 'fifties have any attitude in common, it is that they all reject the "good cause" per se. Also, by their implicit, sometimes explicit, attacks on Marxism, they place themselves at a considerable distance from socialist idealism.

One may more satisfactorily speak of The Movement if one bears in

---

* "They have been given great advantages," Pritchett wrote, "but there is no opportunity to exploit them. Hence, they are rude, unreliable, with eyes wide open to the main chance." Said Maugham: "They are scum."

mind that they, in common with their generation, are responding to the same kinds of problems rather than banding together to write and act in accordance with a program. All labels tend to falsify. Perhaps a clearer approach to understanding is afforded by Walter Allen's now classic review of Kingsley Amis' *Lucky Jim*. Allen recognized that, first in John Wain's *Hurry on Down* and then in Amis' earliest venture into fiction, "a new hero" was emerging: the tough intellectual who questioned everything accepted by the society of his time. He was not an esthete floating off to his ivory tower of pure expression (he recognized the phoniness of estheticism), nor the Marxist type of intellectual warrior (he recognized the flatulence of political symbols); he was a man bred by existence in the twentieth century to suspect everyone and everything.

Picking up where Allen left off, George Scott defined the "new hero" in depth, using his own experience as a base. In *Time and Place* he exposed the forces which had shaped him: the collapse of normalcy in the 'thirties, the war and its terrors, the moral failure of British socialism, and the cold war with its foreshadowings of catastrophe impossible to imagine. The consequence was a dilemma in which he found himself hardened toward all abstract values.

This dilemma lies at the heart of the problem facing the Angry Young Man. He has seen too many good causes end up as grotesque mockeries; the result is he distrusts all causes, even those that seem to rise out of his own life—his scepticism includes himself. He cannot ordinarily belong to any party, group or institution, for his mind instinctively revolts against organized cant. Because he lives in the present, his existence is all he can believe in.

He is the man alone to whom Colin Wilson has given the name Outsider. Though the Angry Young Man does not show any overwhelming inclination to follow Wilson down the path of a religious reawakening, he is most pathetic when he thinks, as does John Wain's Charles Lumley or Kingsley Amis' Jim Dixon or John Braine's Joe Lampton, that he can become an Insider merely by donning the proper masks. As Wilson says, the Outsider stands for truth; the life of the bourgeois Insider—the Square—is built upon illusions which keep out the truth. Though the New Hero wills himself to be deceived, truth searches him out in the ultimate insulation of love, money, or status.

And yet, though he distrusts the future because of his awareness of the past and will commit himself to nothing, the Angry Young Man yearns for commitment. It is as if he were possessed of some vestigial memory of once having been a social animal. John Osborne's Jimmy Porter, for all his shrill nay-saying, keeps faith with his working-class friends; Thomas Hinde's Larry Vincent sacrifices everything to find a pornographic picture which might embarrass a friend; and love does penetrate the skepticism of Joe Lampton. To say no to everything is death. Like all young men, these demand life. "How I long for a little human enthusiasm," Jimmy Porter cries for them all. "I want to hear a warm thrilling voice cry out Hallelujah! I'm alive!" There is the longing, but as yet there has been nothing the mind can accept for fulfillment.

4

The crucial difference between the Angry Young Men and the Beat Generation is that the former still care, the latter are beyond caring. The former seek some connection with the world of Insiders, for within that world of false appearances is a truth of social reality. The latter completely abjure the Square's world and seek to create a new reality, one in which vivid experience is everything.

But in the Beat Generation's most underground depths, despite the continuousness of the search for meaning, there is no growth or accumulation of experience which is knowledge. For one moment is devoid of contact with another; it stands an island of felt emotion, soon to disappear leaving no ripple. And so the Beat Generation may well suggest a generation of rag pickers looking for Mystery, Magic and God in a bottle, a needle, a horn.

In stepping out of the competitive arena which custom has marked as the proving ground of manhood, it is forced back into the marginal existence of the adolescent. Because the Beat Generation digs everything, it implicitly wants nothing. In making the capacity to respond to experience the most crucial test a man must face, it denies him the power to shape and transform experience, thereby separating him from the essential source of his vitality. Exuberance takes its place, propped up by artificial stimulants that conceal the real inertness. Even sex becomes just another kick. The Beat Man cannot take because he has nothing to give.

To truly respond, to make the necessary projection of self, would destroy his Beat condition—once again he would care. Once the Beat Man cares, he can no longer dig everything—and this is always his goal. For to the man who is hip, there is nothing more cool than breaking through and swinging, moving in harmony with the way of the world—feeling everything, liking everything and going beyond the need for choice, for acceptance or rejection; he will have entered the nirvana of sheer existence, where there is no pain, no remorse.

And yet, despite the seeming nihilism implicit in the goals and values of the Beat Generation, its rise into literary expression has been one of the most positive developments in American letters in the last two decades. By refusing to attack the same themes so overworked by the authors who had preceded them, the writers who reflect the Beat Generation have brought forth a new subject matter: man himself—bereft of illusion, standing in the dark midnight of existence. They have brought new vigor to American writing, giving it, despite the occasional dips into extremes, a vivacity and power much of it had lacked. Most importantly, in a time where conformity has become the Eleventh Commandment, they have dared stand, begrimed and insolent, and describe with accuracy the Emperor's clothes of splendid nakedness.

So, too, the Angry Young Men have by their continual criticism of the present become, inadvertently, social critics bringing to bear both wit and candor distorted neither by theory or special pleading. In being loyal only to the demands of self-realization, they fire their salvos wherever conscience dictates.

Though the Beat Generation and the Angry Young Men have yet to produce a major literature, they most assuredly have created a significant one, bringing to our awareness certain essential truths about existence in this decade of the twentieth century. Whether they succeed in breaking out of the limitations within which they live and work is not only a function of their developing talents and insights. It is also related to the world and the climate generated by its men and institutions. Their achievement is that in a time of spiritual blackness, they have brought the attention of mankind back to the only source of hope in an exhausted world: the beating, real, existent heart of man.

part one

THE BEAT GENERATION

ANATOLE BROYARD

Sunday Dinner in Brooklyn

> *This generation which has turned its*
> *back on the eternal rat race, desiring*
> *not to change the world but rather to*
> *deaden the pain of having to live in it*
> *—can't these young people return to*
> *their roots, find sustenance and shel-*
> *ter in the homes and towns from*
> *which they came? This story gives the*
> *answer—and also the regret.*

I TOOK A ROUNDABOUT route to the subway, and because I was going to Brooklyn the Village seemed to have at that moment all the charm of a Utrillo. It was only at times like this, in contrast to something else, that this neighborhood became attractive. Ugly in itself, it was a relief from certain kinds of beauty. To most of those like me who lived there, it was as inviting as a view of a squalid village would seem to a princess imprisoned in an ivory tower.

Since it was summer, the Italians were all outside on stoops and chairs or standing along the curb in their Sunday clothes, the old men in navy blue and the young men in powder blue suits, as though their generation was more washed out than the last. The mothers with their hair pulled back and their hands folded in their laps looked like Neanderthal madonnas, and they were dressed, of course, in black, since it was a miracle if someone in their families had not died within the year. The girls wore long pegged skirts which made their feet move incredibly fast. All of their movements seemed to be geared to this same tempo, and their faces were alert with the necessity of defending the one prize they had against mother and brother alike.

On the corner squatted their church—a huge casserole, fat, heavy, and plain as the women who prayed in it. Looking through the open doors as I passed, I saw the arches bending downward like a laborer under a heavy load. Even the bells of this church—presumably the voice of their god—were sour, and every Sunday morning I cursed them together with the priest who played some sort of chopsticks tune over and over on them.

On Thompson Street, a block and a half from where I lived, there was a stable, and here a horse's head poked through the window on the second floor. Above him, on the windowsill of the top floor, a geranium grew out of a rusty one-gallon can. Near the corner, a drunk slept in the sun against the wall of the Mills Hotel, and another drunk stood over him, holding out his hand, saying, "Shake, pal. Shake."

The waterless wading pond in the center of Washington Square, the bull's eye of the Village, was overflowing with guitar players, folk singers, folk dancers, conga drummers, communists, anarchists, voyeurs, frotteurs, fairies, dogs, children, Negroes, sightseers, psychotics, anthropology professors, heroin pushers, tea pushers, carriage pushers, lesbians, *New York Times* readers, people with portable radios, adenoidal girls looking for interesting boys, the uninteresting boys they would eventually wind up with, older girls between affairs, older boys on the lookout for younger girls, and so on. Where they stood, Fifth Avenue dribbled to its conclusion after penetrating Washington Arch.

Looking around, I didn't see any of my crew, so there was nothing else to do but head for the subway. At the entrance on Sixth Avenue and Waverly Place, I took a long breath like a deep-sea diver and went reluctantly underground.

The subway's roaring and screaming in the darkness, the passing under the river with the pressure in my ears—these were such a classical overture to going back home that I was weary of the joke. Riding the wrong way like that, I felt I had left Brooklyn for Manhattan only to discover on arriving that I had forgotten something I needed. Now, retracing my steps, I found the ride an endless torture, as it always inexplicably is under these circumstances, although when I was going in the other direction the distance passed unnoticed.

Of course it was my mother and father I'd forgotten, and I'd do it all over again next time too, but by now I accepted this as in the nature of things. They could hardly forget me though, because they had my picture on the mantle next to the clock. It was ten years old, that picture, but they never asked for a new one, and I was convinced that this was the way they still saw me. Like a criminal, I might alter my appearance, but they were not to be fooled. Each time I arrived, I could see their moist eyes washing away my disguise.

I was holding a book open on my lap—I always carried a book to Brooklyn, as an amulet or charm, a definition of my delicate ego—but for all the reading I did I might just as well have put it into the seat of my pants. My mind kept dropping down the page like a marble in a pinball machine until I finally gave it up, conceding that no book could successfully compete with my favorite fiction, my mother and father.

The train stopped, and a man who had been sitting across from me got out. He had been occupying the seat next to the window, at a right angle to the wall. Now a woman placed alone on the seat parallel to the wall and in front of the one he had vacated, quickly changed to his empty seat. Whereupon a man sitting on the outside of the seat corresponding to the one she now occupied but on my side of the train, jumped up to take her former seat, and the man next to me on the seat parallel to the wall shifted to the seat at his left knee just vacated. All of this was done dead-pan, but when I looked again at the woman to see how she was enjoying her new seat, I found her staring at me. She was sour and middle-aged, and her eyes, which were very small, were brooding deeply on me, full of a very personal distaste, as if she were imagining me as her own son. Something about me displeased the hell out of her—the way I was dressed, my haircut, or the expression on my face, which wasn't businesslike enough to spell security for her in her old age.

I didn't feel like answering this look, so I avoided her by staring myself at a man standing a few feet away from me. This man was very visibly chewing gum, and the movements of his bony jaws were so elaborate and so regular that they reminded me of printing presses. I noticed that he was studying himself in the window glass. Arresting his jaws in a position in which all the complications of structure were particularly conspicuous, he observed himself with the close and scientific attention of a Leonardo. Then the machine resumed its hypnotic movements. Now, shifting the gum this way and that, he worked out a wonderful variety of effects. Anyone watching him would have thought he was chewing over a problem. He began by taking it up languidly, indifferently, disarmingly, chewing with his front teeth, his mouth relaxed to the point where it was half open, when suddenly, without warning, he shifted the wad to the left side and began to work it over systematically between his molars. Very businesslike, he gave it an evenly paced pulverizing, and then, just before all the life ebbed out of it, he shifted it again to the center, where his teeth barely dented it, and his tongue turned it over and over in a revivifying massage.

As the train entered another station, without interrupting this ruminating, he stuck his hand through the rubber lip of the door in a Napoleonic attitude, and when the door drew back he flung his hand after it.

I could never chew gum like that, I was thinking, and then I saw the name of my own station through the open door and I jumped up and ran through it barely in time, absolutely confirming the lousy impression I had made on the sour-faced woman.

At the top of the stairs the sun hit me in the eye. It seemed to me that the sun was always shining in Brooklyn, drying clothes, curing rickets, evaporating puddles, inviting children out to play, and encouraging artificial-looking flowers in front yards. Against my will, it warmed over an ineffable melancholy in me. I felt that it was a great democratic source of central heating for this big house in which everyone lived together.

The streets were almost deserted, since everyone ate dinner at the same time in Brooklyn. I knew these streets so well I could have walked them with my eyes shut. There wasn't a tree I passed into which I hadn't thrown my knife, a wall against which I hadn't bounced my ball, a crack I hadn't avoided lest I break my mother's back. Now I saw them in slow motion; everything stood out in a kind of heavy-handed symbolism, as though I were the camera eye in an arty documentary film. When I was a boy, these streets had quickness and life for me, each detail daring me to do something, to match my wits, my strength, my speed, against them. Then I was always running. I saw things on the run and made my running commentary on them without breaking my stride, hurdling, skipping, dodging, but still racing forward . . . until one day I ran full tilt into myself and blocked my own path.

The scene was made even more sententious by the fact that it was Sunday. There was a tremendous vacuum left behind by God. In contrast to the kitchenlike intimacy of the church on Thompson Street —which in its ugliness succeeded in projecting its flock's image on the universe—the spiky shells on these blocks had a cold, punitive look, and seemed empty except for those few hours in the morning when people came with neutralized faces to pay their respects to a dead and departed deity.

From the corner, I could see my mother in the front yard. Her face was turned toward me, although I knew she couldn't see me at that distance. I had the feeling that wherever I was, her face was always turned toward me. Now she saw me, she was waving and talking. In a moment she would begin to shout. I was already smiling and gesticulating too. I modified my walk, making it playful. "Hello, Paul!" she was shouting. "How are you?" I was still too far to talk. I wanted to run, I always wanted to run those last few yards. I hated the last few steps, the final enormous gap, between us. Once we were close enough, like lovers in an embrace, we wouldn't be able to see each other so clearly.

I seized her by the shoulders and bent to kiss her. As usual, each of us offered a cheek. Quickly we turned our heads, and somehow miraculously avoided kissing each other on the lips, our heads turning just far enough so that each kissed the other with half a mouth in the middle of the cheek, making three or four smacks for good measure. My father was inside. He would have liked to come out too, but he felt he would be a spectacle, and besides he seemed to think that she ought to greet me alone, as though she were giving birth to me again.

He met me at the doorway, and we clogged up there, gesticulating and embracing. We always gesticulated too much, we distrusted language and thoughts. And all the while we were shouting, as if we were singing an opera. "Take off your coat!" they were shouting, "Take off your tie!" Sometimes I almost expected them to ask for my belt and shoelaces, but I suppose they knew that, after all, there was no way of disarming the dagger of the mind.

"Wait, I'll make you a martini!" my father shouted, and he ran off into the kitchen. "Sit down!" my mother shouted. "Make yourself comfortable!" Shoving me into my father's chair, she pressed the button on the arm and I was suddenly in a horizontal position. She switched the radio to WQXR, and one of the more familiar symphonies poured out like coal out of a chute.

This chair had been a gift to my father on one of his birthdays. My mother was delighted by the idea of the button. I never liked it. It always struck me as uncanny. I felt myself straining in it, trying to keep my head up a little. My father came in with the martini. I saw that it was amber. He never thought to make himself one. Like a servant.

The martini was sweet. Suddenly I realized that I loved them very much. But what was I going to do with them?

"Here's the Book Review," my mother said, handing me the paper. They both sat down, waiting for me to read it. How could I read it with them sitting there watching me as if I were performing a great feat? I was a spectacle, they assumed I didn't want to talk to them. I understood too that, in a way, they liked to believe I wasn't there just for a visit, and it was perfectly natural for me to be reading the Book Review of a Sunday afternoon.

I put the paper down, reassuring them that I'd read it later. We looked at each other for a moment, smiling. I felt that I was stretched out on a bier. Pressing the button, I allowed the back of the chair to come up. I smiled at my mother to show her I didn't mind the chair. I liked it, but I just felt like sitting up, I was such a bundle of energy.

"Well, how's everything, Paul?" she said. From the time I had been two years old, they had called me Bud, but somewhere in the last few years they began calling me Paul the way the outside world did. "Everything's fine," I said, realizing of course that they had no idea what that everything embodied. This vagueness was our tenderness.

They'd have loved to know, but they were afraid of finding out something which might have offended not them, but me.

The dinner was ready. It was always ready when I arrived. Sometimes I had the fantasy of just walking by the house: my mother would be in the front yard, holding a box lunch in her hands. I would take the box without stopping. My face would be expressionless, hers grieving but controlled. My father would stand just inside the doorway. . . .

My mother brought in the roast and my father carved it with great concentration, as if he were carving out our destiny. He placed on my plate the portion he had always desired for me. My mother heaped potatoes, gravy, vegetables on my plate. "I know you like to eat," she said, smiling and heaping my plate still more. This was a fiction. I never ate heartily, but nevertheless I exclaimed, "You know me, Mom!"

Pretending I could scarcely wait, I attacked the roast with knife and fork, while my mother held back to observe this. "Home cooking," I mumbled around a mouthful, these two words speaking volumes to her. I wondered what she thought I ate every day, whether she ever speculated for a moment that I might have liked it better. As a matter of history, the first time I ate in the Automat, when I was about twelve, I discovered that my mother was not an especially good cook, and this had hurt me as much as anything in my childhood. I could hardly swallow the food for years after that, but practice makes perfect, and I had learned to chomp with the histrionic absorption of a movie hero on a picnic.

As we ate, we regressed in time, reingesting all the events that had separated us. We retraced our steps to the very beginning, and there, joining hands, we advanced again from the birth of the soft-eyed boy to my embarrassing and unassimilable prodigality there at the table. To their great surprise, it always came out the same. We always bumped up against the present. Each time we raised our eyes from the plate, we were startled to discover each other, so camouflaged by time. As soon as our eyes met, we jumped back, as from an abyss. In these encounters, we resembled two forever inhibited people who press against each other in the subway: both want the contact, but neither dares admit it.

It was like my friend Andrew's description of the first analyst he went to. This one was not a Freudian, he belonged to a group which held our difficulties to be "interpersonal," and so instead of having Andrew lie on a couch while he sat behind him, they faced each other across a table. There Andrew would lay out all the disgusting things he had done, avoiding the analyst's eye for fear of showing shame or triumph, but sneaking furtive glances now and then, while the analyst, on his side, had his hands full dissembling disapproval or any other sign which might conceivably have disturbed Andrew's flow. Occasionally, however, in darting about the room and briefly lighting on the table like flies, their eyes would collide, and in that split second shockingly copulate in a deep obscene surmise.

Our conversation consisted of answerable questions and unquestionable answers. As usual, my mother found that I looked thin. All my life, I had managed to stay thin as a reproach to her, and on her side, as if a mother's role were that of a fanatic taxidermist, she had done her best to stuff me. She asked me where I took my laundry. "Aren't the prices outrageous? And the way they boil your clothes in all that acid, a shirt doesn't last six months." She was working around to suggesting that I bring my laundry to her. Maybe those dirty shirts would tell her what she was so anxious, and so ashamed, to know. A smear of lipstick, a smell, a stain, might paint a Japanese picture.

My father discussed the last month's boxing matches. Since I occasionally watched televised bouts in a bar, this had become a regular gambit. With an old man's memory, which clings to things as a child clings to its mother, for fear of being abandoned, he recalled every blow. If I happened to disagree with him—by mistake, or because I wasn't following him—he revised his version accordingly. We fought those fights side by side.

When he wasn't talking about boxing, his remarks were designed to show me that he was a liberal, a man who understands. Yesterday he gave up his seat in the subway to a Negress. Jews are smart. Everybody does things without knowing why. Nobody can say who's right and who's wrong. There are two sides to every question.

I remembered him when he was ten feet tall and his every statement was a revelation of the absolute order of things. I tried to steer him around to himself, to push him gently back into his own indistinctly remembered convictions, but this only succeeded in panicking him. He tried to believe that the only difference between us was that I was "modern." He was going to be "modern" too, by denying everything he felt, and forgetting the few lessons life had taught him. He thought of my modernity as relentless and inescapable, a march of history which would let nothing—parents least of all—stand in its way.

My mother was smiling, and as I watched her over a forkful of mashed potatoes I realized that she was still pretty. I knew that smile from way back, I remembered how it had once outshone the sun in heaven. Only, it had had more of a Mona Lisa character then, an ambiguity that gave it a special quality of romance. Where was that romance now? I wondered. Which of us was unfaithful, and why? Each was caricatured by a love we didn't know how to express. Afraid to feel, we were condemned to think, and at the same time not to think. When—and how—had our oneness become three? What ingredient was added to my mixture to turn it to poison? What alchemy isolated my substance beyond their—and my—understanding? There we were, playing a painful game of blindman's buff. We began by bandaging our eyes; then the bandages had fallen away and we had realized that we were blind.

At last I judged that I had eaten enough, an exemplary amount. With all my blood and nerves busy in my stomach, I relaxed, I became flatulent with affection. My mother saw my face go blank and she beamed. Belly to belly, that was the only true way to talk.

My father was describing how, on the job, he had solved a problem that had stumped even the architect. He had just 'scribed a plumb line on the floor. "Well I'll be god-damned," the architect had said, "if old Pete hasn't gone and done it again!" As I listened to this story, I never doubted it for a moment, and I was proud of him. That was his reality, and in it he was still magnificent, just as my mother could calculate better than the Secretary of the Treasury, how much it would cost a newlywed couple to set up housekeeping. It was in these attitudes, like an old-fashioned photograph, that I thought of them most fondly, and although I had long since exiled myself from that Garden of Eden, it was something I could not root out of my feelings. This homely love was my history. Like a navel, it was a reminder that I hadn't been struck fully formed from my own brow. I remember a story an Army doctor told me, about a Negro soldier whose belly was ripped open in a fight. They sewed him up in time and saved his life, but when they pulled off the adhesive tape, his belly button—he had the old-fashioned protruding kind—came away with it. When he saw what had happened, the soldier was beside himself, in the full sense of that expression, and they couldn't calm him down until the doctor sewed his belly button back on.

I knew how he felt. Although I liked to imagine myself unfettered by human history, faced only by free choices, exquisitely irresponsible, it was still comforting to know that I hadn't been born in a bad novel like most of the people who spent their evenings in Village bars. Although they too probably came from Brooklyn or the Bronx, I couldn't imagine them with families. They seemed to have risen spontaneously from rotting social tissues, the way flies were thought to generate in filth, or in a wound.

I admit that whenever I considered my parents for any length of time, I generally arrived at a feeling of incredulity there too, but at least this is some kind of an emotion, and after all, how else can you look at a mother and father who hatched you like a plot and then couldn't read their own writing? They, too, were inevitably incredulous, always wondering. I could see them right there in that moment struggling with this puzzle which was hidden in the back of their minds the way people you read about now and then in the newspapers hide their children in a closet or a windowless room for twenty years. Always, without realizing it, they were wondering what I was, whether to be proud of me or ashamed, whether my strangeness was genius, sickness, or simply evil, whether I had sold my soul like Faust or was still learning to walk, whether I was a hero or an abortion. In the familiar terms, I was a failure. I had neither money, fame, nor any immediate prospect of either. At least if I had been an idiot, lurching up and down the sidewalk in front of the house, they could have lavished all their pent-up love on my helpless heart, but as it was they were never sure.

My father was still talking about the job. He seemed very proud to have a hand in this particular building, which had been given a lot of publicity and which was apparently expected to become a world-famous monument on Broadway. As superintendent, he had a set of plans, and he brought them out for me to see. I recognized the name of a large low-priced clothing chain which sold standard stuff on installments. Feigning a show of interest, I studied the plans. Besides some very ill-adapted functionalist architecture, the building boasted two tremendous figures—a male and a female nude—above its façade, on either side of the store name like parentheses. They were over fifty feet high, my father assured me, and would be draped in neon lights. "They're like the Statue of Liberty on Broadway," he said, and I knew by the tone of his voice that he was quoting somebody. "What are they supposed to stand for?" I asked, in spite of the feeling I had that this question was all wrong. He looked at me, surprised and a little embarrassed. He was searching his mind for an answer, and although by now I didn't want an answer, I didn't know how to stop what I had started. I looked at the plans again. The figures were sexless, without even the pretense of drapery or a fig leaf. I knew what they stood for. The Statue of Liberty, since it was a French gift, may be presumed to have something under her robes, but these were American-made, this was the naked truth.

My father moved his lips as if to speak, but said nothing. In spite of myself again, I turned on him inquiringly, and he dropped his eyes. "It seems like a mighty big job, Pop," I said. "They must have a lot of confidence in you." "You said a mouthful," he said quickly, plainly relieved. "The architect himself asked for me."

Primitive tools—a saw, a hammer, nails, a square rule, a leveler—these were not enough. I looked at my father, at his innocent face which had been chiseled into homely, heart-rending lines by the simplest kind of considerations, at his jaw made square by practical decisions, his mouth made thin by everyday resolutions, his eyes kept clear and alert with estimations of length, breadth, and height . . . and it struck me then that his head might have been done by a sculptor with a warm feeling for texture and no talent for portraiture, a craftsman with no idea of art.

Suddenly I felt a mushrooming urge to blurt out something—I don't know what—"I think you're great, Pop," or "I'm with you," or "To hell with them all," and this made me very nervous, so nervous I could hardly sit still. In desperation, I abruptly decided to leave. With my mouth still full of lemon meringue pie, I announced apologetically that I had an unbreakable appointment for which I was already late. I had been on the point of calling them up, I improvised, for that very reason, but I felt that even a short visit was better than none. I would come again soon and we would have a nice long talk.

They immediately fell into a frenzy of reassurances. Talking both at once, drowning each other out, they assured me that I didn't have to give explanations to them, they certainly understood how busy I was, and they had not the most infinitesimal wish to interfere with these quintessential commitments. Perish the thought—perish, in fact, the mother and father who would interrupt for a thousandth of a second their son's glorious onrush toward his entelechy. . . .

Caught up in their extravagance, I reiterated my determination to come again soon with all the fervor of MacArthur vowing to return to the Philippines. I again congratulated my mother for having served up a truly historic feast and made ready to leave, avoiding my own eyes in the mirror as I knotted my tie.

My father left the room for a moment and reappeared in his coat. He would walk me to the subway, he said. I was on the point of protesting, but I knew I shouldn't, so I said "O.K., Pop, let's go." I kissed my mother, and she walked out to the gate with us.

Closing the gate behind me, I said, "So long, Mom," and she answered, "So long, Bud," slipping unconsciously into my old nickname again. The sound of it moved me more than I would have thought possible, and I impulsively kissed her again before my father and I faded from her sight.

At the corner I looked back to see her still standing there, her features erased by distance, and I waved, although I knew she couldn't see me. To my astonishment, she waved back. I caught the movement of her arm in the corner of my eye just as I was turning my head. I couldn't believe I had actually seen it—I knew she couldn't see across the street without her glasses. I stopped and took a step back—she was gone. Had I imagined it? It seemed very important to me to find out, and then I realized that I believed she *knew* when I turned the corner, she *sensed* it. No, no, I expostulated with myself, she only knew how long it took us to reach the corner, and then she waved. . . .

"What's the matter?" It was my father, asking why I had stopped. "I was wondering how Mom could see this far," I said. "She just waved at us." "Yeah, she waves three, four times," he said indifferently, and we started off toward the subway again.

I was trying to dismiss a vague fear that he wouldn't stop at the subway entrance, that he would go all the way with me, then I reflected that he rarely came to visit me. My mother had never been to my place. "I can't climb all those steps," she would say, as if I lived on top of Parnassus. Once my father and I had walked, just as we were walking now, through the Village. He didn't remember the neighborhood very clearly—he said the last time he'd been there was before I was born—and he had looked around him like the sightseers who go through the streets in plastic-topped buses. On Fourth Street, we had passed a big fat lesbian dressed in men's clothes and with her hair cut like a man. My father favored her with a disapproving glance as she went by. "Put a dress on that bastard and he'd be a woman," he said, wholly unaware that it was.

A few minutes later, as we were walking through Waverly Place, he swept his arm over half a century's changes and said "You know, this used to be all sportin' houses around here. . . ." and I could see that he was wondering how the simple, old-fashioned sportin' house— where you knew what you wanted and got what you paid for—had given way to this, had borne a brood of Hamlets and hermaphrodites whose sport was an ambiguous affair in which you never knew who was getting the f——ing or what unheard-of infections you risked in the bargain, and where you paid with your life. . . .

We had reached the subway entrance and I stopped, but he began to descend the steps. I seized him by the arm. "You don't have to walk me down, Pop," I said.

He was surprised. "That's all right," he said. "I haven't got anything else to do."

"Yeah, but what's the use of your breathing all those fumes and then having to come all the way up again?" I said, still holding his arm.

He was disappointed, I could see that he wanted to walk me down. "O.K., Pop," I said, letting go of his arm and starting down, "I guess a few steps don't faze you, do they?"

"No," he said, "I'm used to them," and we went down together and he came back up alone.

R. V. CASSILL

Fracture

There have always been the bohe-
mians, the odd-ball characters, the
bearded eccentrics holed up in grimy
tenements and cold-water flats. In the
past they were merely vivid, carefree
relics, a part of "the sights" for the
tourists from uptown. Now there's a
change: the square is no longer so certain. Suddenly the Rebel Without a
Cause has assumed a new role, one
fraught with urgent meaning . . .
and danger.

I WON'T HAVE HIM in the house any more," she
said. "I know that sounds like I'm getting old and mean
and middle class and all that. But I simply don't want him
here again. Is that unreasonable, hon?"

And the odd, characteristic thing about Margaret's ultimatum was that it didn't climax a discussion with her husband, who sat among the papers he had brought from the
office, quiet as a well-fed Buddha. They didn't argue. Had
they ever argued seriously? He couldn't remember a time.
The ultimatum came at the end of an interior discussion

so detailed that one suspected a regular little courtroom inside her head, where the advocates of conflicting views were allowed to confront, scowl, and grimace at each other.

So Worth thought. He had mentioned Harold at dinner. "Don Carpenter had a time with Harold yesterday," he said. "Seems Harold was coming over to his place for something. Well, Harold called to say that he'd got stuck in a bar on 83rd and wondered if Don would pick him up. When Don got there Harold was out in front heckling a parade of schoolchildren. I guess he was in wild shape—not shaved and you know how he looks with a beard on that green depraved face of his. Everytime a bunch of kids in costume would pass him he'd say loudly, 'Ain't that gawd dam cute?' Don says that there was a big circle around him, an empty place where women had pulled back away from him with their babies, kind of watching him uneasily out of the corners of their eyes."

"Oh good Lord," Margaret said.

"Then—this is the rich part—Don took him home and it seems that Don's uncle had just dropped in too. Don went out to the kitchen to mix a drink. Harold followed him out and said in a very loud voice, 'Where'd you get that ugly ball headed sonofabitch? Uncle, huh? Uncle Shmunkle.' Don's mother came tearing out and made Don get Harold out of the house."

"I admit," Margaret said, "that I don't see what's funny about it. Harold's just pathological. He ought to be locked up. There's nothing funny about a sick man. Harold is disgusting."

"Oh well," Worth said. The matter seemed to drop, but he knew it was being argued further in her mind. Since they had left the table and come to the living room, sitting with Margaret had been like sitting in a theater where the curtain for some reason is not yet raised. The action has evidently begun and sometimes the curtain is bulged or fretted by the movement of the actors. There is suspense but no sound until suddenly the stage manager resolves the conflict, says, "I won't have him in the house," banishes the contentious pleader so that when the curtain does go up the stage is vacant—but very orderly. Reason has swept it clean. The closed session has found results which may be published. Margaret has made up her mind.

"Whatever you want," Worth said. "I can take Harold—usually I can take him—or leave him alone. If you don't want him here . . ."

He shifted in his chair to settle back in contentment with her and the life they worked out together. She makes up her mind, he thought, just the way she set about fixing up this apartment, considering each of the rather drab possibilities and finally imposing sweet reason on what had been a hodge-podge of dowdiness when they moved in. Two years ago when they came to the city they had no choice but to take this fantastically old-fashioned apartment in a gone to seed neighborhood. And now look at it. The brown and purple drapes were gone. The lighting was rearranged. Painting the walls in the best modern way, working their furniture into place so it seemed to fit not only the dimensions of the room but the very habits of their living together had transformed the grotesqueness that seemed, God knows, to have been built into these rooms to a gray, white, and ivory order in which their large Braque reproduction fitted as smoothly as the parts of a gyro compass. When he came home in the evening there was a kind of soothing each time he passed from the battered street to the precision of their apartment. This orderliness was Margaret's way with all things. His comfort was all her doing.

Of course it was all her doing, and yet it was an important part of her orderliness that she should ask, when the question had really been tied up and disposed of, "Is that unreasonable?" Her arrangements would be incomplete without his approval. And of course he gave it.

"It isn't at all, darling. There is no point in injuring ourselves trying to be courteous to Harold. He doesn't live in a mental world where courtesy makes any difference anyhow." Worth yawned. "You're the one to say. It's your home. He's your family friend."

"Well," she said, and obviously this was a point she had dispatched far back in her silent debate. "I don't think his coming from the same town makes an obligation at all. No . . . there are so many things about him that I can't stand. Like the change he picked up in the bar the other day. I don't think he was so drunk he didn't know whose it was. I would have called him to book for that."

"I should have," Worth said. "My fault, dear. I could have pointed out to him quietly that it was ours. It didn't seem worth mentioning at the time."

"How much was it?"

"Seven or eight dollars. I should have . . ."

"I won't have you blame yourself," Margaret said. "It simply isn't your fault. You always act in a good sane way. But there goes Harold with our seven or eight dollars. So . . . Then his harping at the Courtneys. 'The Courtneys are sonsofbitches, the Courtneys are sons-ofbitches.' I think I told him rather stiffly that the Courtneys are friends of ours. He didn't pay any attention to me. That's too much. He says the same things about us to other people, for no reason. Did we ever give him any reason? I admit nobody believes him, but it scares me to know he's talking like that about us."

"I doubt if he talks about us," Worth said.

"How can you be sure?"

"I think he likes us. Poor Harold."

"O.K., Worth. There's no way to be sure. Let's drop that point. But about a month ago—I didn't tell you this—I caught him stealing a bottle out of the closet right there. He looked like a mean little kid. I thought he was going to hit me when I caught him. I was truly scared. You were in the kitchen and I almost screamed."

"Oh not Harold. Harold wouldn't hurt a fly."

She came over and sat on the arm of his chair. Her plaid wool skirt rubbed his arm. He smelled the briskly clean smell of the wool. "Is it really all right with you if we don't have Harold here again? I mean not let him in if he comes? He'll be here knocking at our door some-time and we'll have to tell him he can't come in. I'll do it. I wouldn't expect you to because you're so softhearted. But is it really O.K. if I tell him NO he can't come in?"

"Sure." He smiled, pulled her down to him so he could rub her forehead with his nose. "After all, our marriage would be a poor partnership if we couldn't talk and arrange things like this. Let Harold go."

"You're so good," Margaret said. "You're good to everyone and I'm not like that. I'm just not made that way," she said in a childlike voice. He pecked happily at her cheek.

Presently when she had gone to the kitchen he had a pleasant vision of her in this part of her self-created setting, her blade-slender figure among the gray and white planes of the kitchen furniture. The warm brown gray of the walls was one of the colors that Margaret had mixed herself. A real triumph of taste.

Thinking of her in her simple and spotless kitchen and thinking how much the simplicity and severity of it pleased her, he wondered what had got into him that evening when he had thought of buying her the bracelet. Her thirtieth birthday was not very far off. This year he had not known what to get her. Since he'd come back from the ETO, birthday presents had been quite simple for her. Clothes that she had halfway picked for herself—pausing just far enough short of actual selection so he'd have an area of choice to make it his gift— or something for the apartment. They were settled now and her wardrobe was well-rounded. It would have to be something different this year. Still the bracelet had been a wild impulse, clear off the track.

The jewelry she liked was the sort which had the plain beauty of a microscope or a camera or some other instrument of precision. Her jewel box looked like an instrument case. Silver went with her clothes. He supposed the cool color of silver was really meant for her.

The bracelet fitted none of these conditions. He had noticed it in the window of a shop just at the edge of their neighborhood. The shop window was stuck full of junk, bracelets and rings and necklaces that were completely tasteless. At first glance this bracelet was the same kind of thing. There were spars of gold angling out of the band like the grains in a head of barley. It was oddly made. There were three coils of gold wire ending in the spars and the clasp fastened by wrapping these coils together like a spring. When his eye had stopped on it among the other junky pieces it had occurred to him that it had a quality of its own. It looked genuinely like a savage ornament, and it seemed to him Margaret might like it for its outright contrast to the other jewelry she owned.

Now that seemed a bad idea. Still he would not make up his mind. A bit of contrast quite unexpectedly given might please Margaret more than he knew.

Later that evening they talked more about Harold. She had passed judgment and even the specter of him should have been banished out of the apartment. It hadn't gone yet. She was restless. She might have been feeling that in her efforts at justice something had been overlooked. At last she said, "About Harold. Do you really agree with me? I can't be sure of myself. I knew Harold when he was a little boy, and I used to remember that I thought—after I left home, I mean—that he wasn't like the rest of the Parsons, not so stuck up. Maybe now that I have the chance to be nasty to him I'm paying back the Parsons family for the way they used to be. And if he's the only good one in the lot . . . He is awfully poor, don't you suppose?"

"I suppose."

"And he is an artist."

"Not really. I don't think he works at all. He talks big about a book he's writing. Nobody has ever seen a page of it."

"I don't want to hurt him because there's something malicious in me," she said. "I want to be right."

"Now, darling, you gave your reasons like a little lawyer. They seem adequate. You could probably find more if you thought longer."

"Only, am I sure?" she said.

"Hon, it's all settled. Goodbye to Harold."

She sighed her contentment, twisted down in the couch so the breeze from the window would not touch her head any more.

"Thank you for keeping me straight, friend. I couldn't stand to have him come here any more," she said.

II

Thursday evening on their way home from the movies they stopped in the neighborhood bar and found Harold there. He had been waiting for them, it turned out, after he had called their apartment and got no answer.

They had not noticed him when they came in; they had taken their usual table back by the empty dancefloor and had been served their drinks. They sipped and then there was a moment of silence. Worth was wondering if he ought to give his wife the bracelet which he had, after all, bought for her birthday. That odd gold bracelet was right now in his inside coat pocket, wrapped in a tissue paper parcel. There were only two more days until her birthday and they had never made much of waiting to show the presents they had for each other. Now he was feeling that he might be able to explain well his reasons for buying something so out of character—so garish—for her. He might make a few amusing observations on the subject which she would remember and which would associate themselves ever after with the gift.

Then all at once Harold was standing over them. His shocking face peered down at them woefully. "Hello. I know I made a big ass out of myself the last time I saw you," he said. "Gawd. I can't drink decently and I know it. What's that got to do with it? No excuse. I made an ass out of myself. Period. See? I don't even know how to apologize decently. Oh forget it. Jesus." His face in the barlights looked decayed and his clothes smelled with a combination of wet wool, urine, and tobacco smells. "Can I sit down?" he asked. "Or do you want me to get the hell away from you?"

Worth threw a smile to his wife and said, "Sit down, please. What will you drink?"

"Listen," Harold said doggedly, like a child who drives himself to say something which is not only painful but which seems to him to verge on nonsense as well. "May I sit down, Margy? I know what I did, too. I know I got some of your money the other night. God. I don't know how I did it. Did I . . . ? I guess not. Forget it. I know I didn't have any and then the next morning right in my breast pocket I found six dollars. How much was it now? I want you to tell the truth." He pushed a handful of dollar bills across the table, fifteen or twenty of them, wrinkled so much the pile stood an inch thick. "Please now, tell me."

"Never mind," Margaret said sharply. "We've forgotten about it."

"No, no, Please tell me."

He's going to cry, Worth thought, and that isn't necessary.

"Here's the whiskey. Drink up, everybody. It was change from a ten, Harold, about eight and a quarter," he said.

After he took the money they drank in silence. A boy and girl left their stools at the bar and came back to the dance floor. The boy put a quarter in the jukebox, turned to the girl with an almost imperceptible shrug of invitation. Her body rose to meet him as the music began. She went on tiptoe against him. The music had been chosen for the season—to say it was April, to make it blatantly clear what the wind on the streets was all for.

"Jesus," Harold said. "Too much noise. We can't talk here. I hate to ask . . . Forget it. Can we go up to your place for a nightcap? Here's the pitch. I've got to talk to you people tonight. That's not a joke."

"Well . . ." Margaret seemed to be deliberating.

"I know what you must think of me," Harold said.

"We'll do it this way," Worth said. "Margaret's tired, but you and

I will run down to your place for a while. For one drink. I've got to be at the office tomorrow and that's no joke either."

The street, when they went out with Harold, seemed by accident or miracle to have changed from what it was twenty minutes before. Perhaps because the bar was so dark, there seemed to be a luminosity in the air that they had not noticed, as if the air were full of a million sequins. When they had come from the theater the street was empty. Now a whole parade of boys and girls moved up the block—not exactly conjured by magic, because it was time for intermission at the Y dance, but magically making the night big and disquieting.

"I'll be home by twelve," Worth said; and at that moment as he looked around he was startled by his wife's face, her look of frightened determination.

"If it's only for that long"—she laughed—"I'll come too. If I may, Harold?"

Why? It was too silly, Worth thought, to believe that she was afraid Harold would lead him astray. He could not account for it.

"Please," Harold said. "I'm glad you're coming. The two of you together is what I need to get me out of my rut. I mean you people are such a team. Nuts. I mean I like you sooo." Delighted now, he made them hold the cab while he went back inside to get an extra pint.

III

They had been fooled and taken in, there was no doubt of that. In their moment of compassion in the bar Harold had made a demand on them they could not refuse. Who could tell what desperate thing he might do if they would not help him? He had looked so terribly wasted and shaky. Now, climbing the stairs to his apartment, his drunken unbearable arrogance was loose again. The taxi ride had given him time to drink half the pint like a happy child drinking pop.

"You might know them sonofabitching Courtneys," he said to Margaret. "You know what that bitch Alice Courtney said to me the other day? 'Harold, you're malodious,' she said. I ought to let her have it right in the mouth. So she thinks I'm a bum, so what? Forget it." He had grabbed Margaret's arm—his black fingernails pinching into the cloth of her coat—and was dragging her up the stairs at his own headlong pace, thrusting his ugly happy face toward her, ignoring her anger. "Yeah. That bitch. You know who she's playing around with while that fag husband of hers goes out with his fag pals? I'll tell you . . ."

"Oh!"—the convulsive, revolted sigh of Margaret's breath.

It seemed to Worth that his wife would turn at any moment and march righteously toward home; and he thought later that she might have done so if they had not come then to Harold's door and into what he had always referred to as his apartment.

The shock of seeing it—the immediate acid shock—must have restored anyone from the notion that Harold was more to be blamed than pitied. There was a studio couch unfolded in the room with a brown blanket rumpled across it, crumbs and grease spots on the blue couch upholstery and no sign of any linens. In front of the couch was a long coffee table crowded with beer cans from which the roaches poured as the light went on. Among the cans were crusts and slivers of meat. There was a chair in the room. There were three skillets and some dirty plates in the opposite corner on the floor. Something that looked like an egg had been trampled into the linoleum.

"It's lovely, Harold, lovely," Margaret exclaimed. Her voice rang with triumph. After all, her excursion over here was not in vain. To see this den of corruption was revenge for the embarrassments he had caused her. "Maid's day off?"

He stood blinking in the harsh light from the ceiling fixture. He had not counted on the room's being this way. His befuddled face suggested that gnomes must have come in while he was gone and lived the hell out of his room. "It's kind of messy," he said in a diminished voice. "Glasses. We've got to have glasses. You see any?"

"I'll look under the couch," Margaret said. While he went out to get some she asked Worth, "Are you going to sit *down* here?" She pulled her wool skirt against her hips as if it were iron that she was fitting close for protection. She moved away from the couch. It might have jumping bugs.

Worth said, "Kilroy was here. Before that Raskolnikov had this suite, I suppose. What the hell? Let's sit down and have a drink anyway. Maybe he does have something on his mind he needs to talk about. You take the chair. I'll sit on the couch."

"He doesn't need us."

"We'll see."

"Worth, doesn't this bother you? I don't understand you."

"I wouldn't want to live here. It's interesting."

"If you could tell me why . . . It's just filthy."

Down the hall they heard Harold speaking and heard a woman's voice—a bawdy, bubbling, fat-woman's voice—answer him with a joke.

"Don't needle him about it," Worth said.

The glasses Harold brought were greasy. Beads of cold water huddled on their surfaces. He divided the whiskey and took an armful of the beer cans from the table so they would have a place to set their drinks.

"It's a mess," Harold said. "But let me explain something—it's always this way." When he laughed very heartily at his joke the laughter turned into prolonged coughing. He rubbed his lips with his fist after he coughed and rubbed his fist on the cover of the studio couch. Margaret set her glass down hard. After seeing the slime on his lips she had no intention of drinking from any of his glasses.

"Have you been doing any work, Harold?" Worth asked. "We hardly know what you're doing these days. The novel you were . . ."

"I haven't committed it yet," Harold said. "I been thinking about it. I may make it oral." His eyes were swinging to cover every detail of the room, as though some arrangement of the papers piled on the floor, the cans, the skillets, and the milk cartons behind the door might hold a pattern which he did not yet know. "Needs a woman's touch, don't it? But nothing like I do. Pretty Sarah is the girl. That's what I have to talk to you Joes about." Again he coughed and rubbed his mouth. "Women, shmimmen. I had a babe and now she's gone."

"Sounds like a blues number," Worth said.

"Don't it? Listen I wrote some song lyrics yesterday. Tell me what you think of this." He began humming the tune of Night and Day. "Hell, I don't remember. It was about a guy whose girl left him and it's spring, see?"

"Never mind," Worth said. "Tell your story. You had a girl and she's left you."

Margaret's face tightened even more. She had never looked colder, more like a disapproving schoolteacher. She was carried by the intensity of her disapproval to a foolish question. "Here?"

"Here, shmere," Harold said. He was jolly drunk enough to ignore what Margaret might think of him. "You know her, Worth old boy.

You ought to know her. Found her when I came to hunt you one day. Never did find you. Found her. She works at your office. Out in the pen in front where they got this acre of pretty girls. Pounds a typewriter. Pretty Sarah LeRoy is the one I mean."

"You're joking," Worth said. "LeRoy's a kid. She can't be more than . . ."

"Well, she's seventeen."

"Good God, Harold."

"Now wait. I ain't so old myself. Relative matter of course. I'm only twenty-seven and the baby of the family. Right, Margaret? Margaret knew me when I was a baby at the breast."

He kept on talking, a harsh croon intended obviously for himself, but pointless and perhaps impossible to him unless he had them there to sit as though he were telling them something. Worth did not listen. He was thinking about Sarah LeRoy. Such a pretty little kid. The starched white of her blouses every morning, the skin that kept fluctuating in color whenever he talked to her, her pleasant eagerness to get work done just right for him, "Yes, Mr. Hough. Yes," the hands that looked so clean and creamy but not yet shaped like a grown woman's hands, the smooth fall of her hair brushed neat for school, he thought, a pretty little maid from school. His idea of her had been so fixed that what he was hearing from Harold stabbed at him like the discovery of a betrayal.

". . . damn near three months," Harold was saying. "Through the winter when it was cold. Happy as little old puppies. Bang, slam, one day she hits me right in the mouth. 'Only reason you want to marry me is you think you ought to.' 'Right,' I said. I was real smart. Whatta quick comeback that was. So bang, slam, she let me have it while I was lying flat on my back in bed. Out the door she goes without even waiting to pack her douche bag. I shouldn't have said that to her because this weather is so nice. I sure need her because . . ."

"Please," Margaret said. "You have no right to tell us things like that. Oh come on, Worth. I can't stand any more of this."

"Sure wish I could coax her back," Harold said. "She was so pretty, so beautiful, so lovely." He lay over against the arm of the studio couch, breathing heavily through his mouth. His tongue lay for a second against his ugly lips. "Listen, Worth old boy, she won't even let me come near to her. I chased her on the street one day and she ran up to a big fat meanlooking cop. That's a fact. You hear me, Worth? Here's what I want you to do . . ."

Margaret was at the door, her gloved hand resting on the frame and her whole body inclined for immediate exit. "Worth . . ." she said. "Coming."

Harold said, "What I want you to do is talk to her for me."

"I'm sorry, Harold."

"Now listen, Worth, I know what I'm talking about. She thinks you're brains from the belly up. That's a fact. She told me. You're her boss. Now listen, you talk to her. Tell her old Harold's cleaned up and quit drinking. If you get a rise out of her I will, too. Anyway talk to her sensible. Tell her . . . I mean she's an adult. Don't give her any Sunny School guff. Just tell her old Harold . . ." Then gently his voice stopped. His hand with the fingers spread and cupped moved caressingly over the arm of the couch. His face in their last glimpse looked sick and moldy as the room, but young, like a debauched child's face.

IV

Their taxi moved for what seemed a very long time through streets of velvety darkness. Over and over Worth thought Not Sarah LeRoy. It seemed impossible to him and then impossible that he should have been so wrong about her. He had been thinking of her as he would have thought of a daughter and she was living with a man almost his own age.

Once when they stopped at a traffic light and the cab was lit from the store windows on the corner, he noticed Margaret watching him distantly. "You're not going to, are you?" she said.

"Going to what?"

"Going to talk to this tramp about Harold?"

"No. Of course not, darling. She's not a tramp, though. We mustn't jump to any judgments."

"Living with *Harold* in that sty? Oh no." He could not see her face but he felt her shudder.

He smiled to himself. He had the melancholy and lonely notion that he was assailed from all sides by the grotesque emotions of other people. "Now, darling," he said, "love and cleanliness are not necessarily mutually dependent, whatever the soap ads say." As he spoke it seemed to him that the cab might as well be the basket of a balloon carrying him miles above the earth while down below the earth was twinkling with the thousand garrulous lights of April. How comic and melancholy to ride at that height saying reasonable things to the empty air.

"Love!" Margaret said. "I've heard everything now."

She went to bed as soon as they got home. "Don't stay up too late," she said.

When he saw the light go out in the bedroom he got a small glass of whiskey from the cupboard. Something soft that the wind carried beat twice against the window. He went to the window and looked down. It was too late now for anyone to be on the street. The upreaching branches of the trees below him swayed as though they were a scaffold that might sometime—soon—collapse all at once to show him the secret and filthy processes of Spring among the roots. In the meantime it seemed that this fragile scaffold was supporting him at a lonely height. If the wind rose more he might hear the snap of branches giving way, letting him drop.

"Margaret," he called. "Margaret? Tonight *was* goodbye to Harold. Never again." He called this out jovially. He went to the bedroom door, wanting to talk to her. If the two of them could really agree and think together they might keep their lofty and precarious perch above the mess that the Harolds and LeRoys made of their lives. He peered toward the dark bed. "Margaret?"

"All right," she said. "I heard you. Please. I'm too tired to talk about it tonight any more."

But I have to talk about it, dear Margaret, he thought. Tonight all this has jarred me loose. He went back toward the window and this time as he approached it was sharply aware of his own reflection emerging on it—the reflection of his white shirt; his head, hands, and trousers being darker hardly registered on the transparent pane. The white animate shape jiggled on the glass. Then in a trick of vision it seemed to be moving against the cover on Harold's couch, an immaculate substance on that dirty blanket. As though it were one of Sarah LeRoy's white blouses he was staring at.

Sarah LeRoy—how wrong could he be about someone? For a long time he thought he had her figured out perfectly and he was quite wrong. From his height in the air he had never seen her as a woman at all. He had missed the simplest fact in the world. A surge of self-pity struck him, the realization that his cleverness had someway cheated him.

He drank and then without thinking lifted his hand to the pocket where the bracelet lay wrapped in its soft paper. His fingers tightened on it and he felt its spring give under the pressure. Margaret's bracelet for her thirtieth birthday. No. He saw now why he had bought this gaudy bit of jewelry. It was not for Margaret.

He was pinching the bracelet together as though he were already fitting it to someone's wrist.

"Sarah LeRoy," he whispered in amazement. "I'll be damned."

Harold seemed to him, just then, very lucky. He envied Harold everything—his enemies, his dirty room, his mammoth drunks, his cough, his Sarah. He saw now why Margaret had wanted so much to get Harold cleanly out of their way. She had been afraid sometime he might envy Harold. She had known what that envy would mean to him; she had known what he was just beginning to grasp—that envy would never lead him to imitate Harold, nor even actually give the bracelet to Sarah, but that it would swing a cold light on his own incompleteness. He saw—or thought he saw—how every limitation in Margaret's life had been placed carefully, like a spar to shore over and hide from him his own matching frailty, and his heart was stung with a treacherous wish to wake her and tell her he understood. At the same time he knew that the time itself for such communication had been spent as ransom against his terrible need.

He opened the window a little as if the stable air of the room were choking him. A flat tongue of wind came in, sliding its secret dampness and urgency against him with a tremor, and on its motion he heard the crackle of branches breaking.

GEORGE MANDEL

The Beckoning Sea

Hallucination or nightmare—the pervasive sense of defeat derives from a very real world. In the context of a time that has lost belief, neither fear nor anger is a suitable response. Defeat imposes its own course of action: live, somehow return to the primary, known emotions. They do not spell salvation but they may provide existence with a content, with ballast, where all other values are empty self-parodies. Originally written as a student exercise, "The Beckoning Sea" evokes a world of desperation and terror in which truth no longer wears the rhetoric of reason.

A STARK MORNING fell upon him, challenging and deriding with stinging hail and an endless emptiness of wet, sticky beach. Gritting his teeth helped somewhat. Running (he ran) was like nightmare-running, when spiteful, sucking ground limits the feet to weighted slow-motion that sends the debility throughout the rest of the body till one cannot even scream. He tried a scream. The sound was lost in the whir and clatter of hail.

With a roar the ocean came up and bit at him with its foam-teeth which then disintegrated into bubbles and trickling highlights, withdrew in skittering haste, reassembled, and bit again. In anger he ran at the breaker to kick it, but, like a blind, bloodless monster, it overcame him with an icy wallop that rolled him over and over, finally dropping his breathless form to the mud. He scurried to his feet and ran upshore till he was out of the ocean's reach, then turned to face it, slapping his bicep in a defiant vulgar gesture.

The hail pinched his face.

Trembling and gasping for air, he sat in the mud and proceeded to build a monument of grime to his scars; a spire for every stigma, a buttress for each frustration.

The scars, he thought, multiply like rabbits, but each new lesion becomes progressively harder to treat.

Letting mud ooze through the clenched red fingers formed the turrets and crude gables of his castle, his memorial to the torture of his being. Now each pain was canonized.

He came to his feet rubbing the gritty sand on the side of his coat, listening to the hail tap on his teeth, wondering whether it hurt or froze. The rest of his body demanded consideration and he found, helplessly, that no distinction between cold and pain was possible to define. He threw out his hands and whirled about, moaning at the hostile sky.

A flicker of movement in the distant emptiness caught his eye, and he watched a speck grow into life.

Falling upon his back, he closed his eyes and subdued his breathing, affecting, as nearly as he could, the inertia of death. The hail fell like aimed needles on his face. Perhaps he might bleed slightly, thereby appearing more convincingly unapproachable. He snickered. Then he shuddered as the vision of his probable grotesqueness crossed his mind: his sand-colored hair blended with, lost in the equally wet sand; his face livid with cold and agitation; his grimy, knob-knuckled hands jutting out of the nondescript coat which accentuated the formlessness of his skin-and-bones frame . . . the big, sad shoes.

Once sunlight rebounded from pink buildings that were bucolic in their affinity with the sprightly sky, and free air cascaded, stimulated, pinched, tickled, made one a part of its eternity and its unshakable kinship with all that was alive.

Too many dim views.

He felt cold hands on his face. They shook him vigorously and he

heard a repressed sob. He opened one eye, then shut it quickly, re-
taining in his mind the image of flesh, feature and expression, of color
and sensitivity. Then the voice, a hybrid of chime and claxon: "Ugh!
Just a drunk. Sick, I thought he was."

*I never urinated in the hallway near the roof. That was rain-water
dropped through a chink in the door or I don't know what. Doris Baum
whose face is lost in the cloudy years was to come and meet me and
I never went there to urinate but I couldn't tell on Doris.*

Lurching to his elbows he shook back his hair, felt cold bugs sneak
down his back. "I'm being pushed into the sea. I'm not drunk at all."

The girl—beautiful, clean, snugly wrapped against the elements—
backed away, her face tensing with fear. As he came to his feet she
began to move away in a run that was embarrassed down to a jerky
pace, spasmodically glancing back under her little violet umbrella.

A grin fortified his wanting features, undid the frozen mask.

He went toward her slowly at first and then in a travestied rush of
anxiety. She stopped, tensed, quickly collapsed the umbrella and
brandished it, losing her countenance to the warpings of panic. Her
slash at him, its accuracy thwarted by hysteria, he easily avoided. It
swung her completely around into his ready grasp. She fought, but
he held her powerless.

"I'll scream!" she shrieked stupidly.

"You're not silly enough."

Just gray sky and mud and horizons of indifferent waters.

"An Indian girl," he said, holding her firmly, "being chased across
a stretch of western desert by a prospector, squatted suddenly as the
man gained ground, and packed sand into the object of his pursuit.
Now why couldn't you have been as ingenious?"

Releasing her, he freed her hand of the dangling umbrella, opened
it and, bowing with flourish, offered it. "You'll not be brutalized today,
little heroine. There are too many transgressions recorded against my
benighted soul as it is."

"You . . . you're not depraved?" she said eagerly "I mean you—"

"I didn't mean to convey anything like that. I'm properly depraved,
but not arbitrary."

"Oooooh," she said, turning her face into the hail, "glory be, I've
got to sit."

She plopped to her seat and raised thankful eyes to the sky. Kneeling, he again presented the umbrella. She took it and sprang to her feet, closing the contraption on the way up. Bracing herself, she pounded him mercilessly, getting in several solid blows before he resumed his feet and withdrew to a point of safety.

He ran upshore, then turned and found her convulsed with laughter.

"Who in heck are you, anyway?" she called, spreading the violet shield above her head and at once becoming composed.

"I'm not anybody in particular," he ventured, taking a cautious step forward. "I'm being forced into the sea. That's my mark of identity."

"Forced into the sea? By whom?"

"By stone and by steel. By noise and odor and platitude. By a dearth of joyousness."

"Woo-ee. Hold it. Come here. . . . I won't batter you any more. You don't look quite like an ogre now, keeping your distance that way. You look more like a . . . like a little boy."

He approached in a shuffle that pressed out of her a burst of absolving mirth. A hearty sigh punctuated her final release of tension. When he met her she handed him the umbrella and, taking his arm, led him down the hail-hazed beach. Her tidy gloves and diverted attention kept her from noticing the grit on his sleeve. She read the face taut with feverish cold and, eventfully, did not suffer the silence that fell between them magnifying the clatter of hail on the umbrella.

"Supposing we have some fun," she said, giving his arm a tug. "The tide is good for crabbing. We could catch some and eat them somewhere. That could be fun."

He considered fun.

"We could roast crabmeat," he said finally. "I'll show you how to do it in the hail."

He left the umbrella with her and approached the surf. In a moment he was tossing crabs over his shoulder, snatching them up with careful alacrity, as if they were hot chestnuts. The girl assembled them in her inverted umbrella, becoming intent upon the gathering of them. Suddenly he stiffened and whirled to face inland, heaved a huge crab yards over her head, and splashed wildly into the sea. She saw him rise out of the foam he had stirred up and hang suspended for a trick instant, then splash and disappear.

Dropping the umbrella, she dashed to the edge of the shore.

"Johnny! Johnny!" she screeched.

He reappeared. In a frenzy she called the improvised name again. Mournful eyes looked at her from the dripping head. The face was livid.

"Come tell me, Johnny," she called through sobs. "Come tell me what's forcing you into the sea."

Standing shoulder-deep in the cold waste of water, he shouted: "Shellfish!"

"Come out," she howled pitifully. "The sea is full of them."

"That bastard was ashore."

"Come out and tell me what. Tell me what's forcing you into the sea."

"Insects," he moaned. "Bugs. Pests of all sorts."

"I can't hear you." She sat in the mud and cried. Slowly he kicked his way out of the water. Quaking with cold, he helped her to her feet.

"Dogs," he said softly. "Beasts."

She looked at him and wept bitterly. Water ran down his purple face. He blinked out the salt drops. "Smoke," he said.

"What else, Johnny?" she sobbed, sniffling and choking back the tears.

"Soot," he said.

"Dirt.

"Warts.

"St. Vitus Dance and almost hallucinations.

"Clerks, commitments.

"Jerks.

"Ticket-takers.

"Boundaries.

"Walls.

"Stalls.

"Classes.

"Castes.

"Misinformation!" he shrieked.

"Nobility, sterility.

"Pride and rigid faces.

"And sugar.

"Greed.

"Priests.

"Ministers.

"Intimidation," he moaned.

"Police.

"Tradition.

"Moral inquisition.

"Teachers, position.

"Lousy schools.

"Sunday schools.

"Escape," he hissed.

"Dancing schools.

"Movies.

"Playing Cards.

"Crowded bars.

"Radios.

"Stagnation," he cried.

"Television.

"Parents.

"Grandparents.

"Uncles and aunts.

"Neighbors in the street. Wings on the house."

He was completely without expression. The girl, transfixed, held the umbrella above him, listened as if to poetry.

"Decay," he said, trembling.

"Jokes.

"Amenities.

"Projections.

"Lies, lies.

"Garbage. And assorted odors.

"Death!" he shouted, shaking violently.

Moaning, the girl took his arm and placed the umbrella in his hand, which was rather stiff. She began to walk him so that his blood might circulate more freely.

"Unproduction is death," he whispered. "Insensitivity and cruelty are death. Inhumanity is death." He began to shout. "And hate is death, and injustice, black calamity, futility, senility—"

He straightened his arm abruptly and ran holding the umbrella high, tripping here and there, but darting to his feet and continuing down the beach.

"Rocks!" he screamed. "Rocks are the last high place. Run, lady, run, run!"

She pursued him, wailing into the relentless hail. Reaching a rock breakwater, he turned and awaited her. He passed her the umbrella and led her by the hand over the jagged heap of stone, assisting her across treacherous footing to the dreary end of the breakwater where the waters lashed the weedy stone, threw saline spray high, and roared like captured beasts.

The hail hammered, crackled, bit.

He steadied the girl as she sat on the gleaming rock, then hugged her to his legs. He pushed his face into the hail and roared at the sky, his head trembling with the strain of his attempt at an impossible audibility. Strident and incoherent, his words wasted away into the meaningless distance where even the turbulent sea lost itself in the static grey cloak of sky. The panicky girl, weeping passionately, tugged at his trousers till he sank down beside her.

A burst of water washed over them, leaving a salt after-spray in their hail-battered faces as they clung to each other. Lowering to their sides, they pulled close to one another, the girl, in her delirium, managing to retain her grasp on the umbrella. He roared again and kissed through the fullness of lips till he could taste her teeth, accepting the intervening hailstones as though they were a special yield of her womanhood, some anomalous creation of her passion. Through her sobs she kissed his neck and jaw, clinging to him for her only assurance of life. He tore open her raincoat and forgot the hail and grew deaf to the sea, caressing her and handling her clothes as if they were in the sanctuary of a bed. Automatically she took him with her hips and limbs, never once lowering the violet parasol that hovered in ludicrous defense between the elemental onslaught and the finality of their contact.

CLELLON HOLMES

Go

> *Always there is the party—unprepared for, feverish. For the Beat Generation, while severing itself from the web of personal relationships that attach to job and home, makes a new fabric of human intercourse. The party, pervasive as ritual, with each "cat" and "chick" out to dig the most from the moment, is of necessity climax without culmination. There are the props for heightened intimacy and perception: bop, weed, sex, booze. But contact between persons, though freighted with intensity, is brief, intangible.*
>
> *Following are two representative selections from Go, a novel which did much to set the literary boundaries of the new youth.*

PERFORMANCES, assortments, resumés: the weekend of the Fourth was made of these. Everyone's enthusiasm rose continually during the two days, as if they all cherished in their heart's privacy some extraordinary memory of the holiday, long since considered infantile but still capable of evoking for each the hot, lost forenoons in all their American hometowns.

Then, the box of fireworks had been carried out into the street to be set off in a lavish squander, which consumed everything before the day lengthened into green

afternoons and parades, and forced them to be content thereafter with
what hungry ecstasy could be gained from the detonations of others.

These buried memories rose in everyone's mind, and as though each
was secretly intent on recapturing or reducing the recollection, the
simplicities of noise and chatter invested them, and they became as
babbling and foolish and imaginative as children.

There was something fortuitous in their gathering, without previous
arrangement, on the fretful, rainy Friday night when they tore up to
Verger's in the Cadillac. Hart dashed about, helping Kathryn into
her raincoat; and then grasping Dinah about the shoulders gruffly
and ogling her, he exclaimed: "Lotsa weed tonight and crazy music!
You dig that, woman?"

She laughed with an intimate twinkle in her large blue eyes, with
a glance that assured him of her appreciation of his attention, but his
words meant nothing to her; in fact, neither of them believed in words,
and only used them to hint at some inexpressible thought. Then Dinah
turned to Kathryn, establishing a secretive, womanly air as easily as
she had just acknowledged Hart's masculine joy, and said:

"You fix up your hair like that all the time? It looks real cute on you.
But, you know, I feel all funny in this ol' dress. It's all we brought
along though. They kidnapped me out of Denver without giving me
even a chance to pack anything!" Then they were off into the wet
lights and snarlings of the midtown streets.

Verger's damp, bare rooms were permeated with his feeling of ex-
clusion from possible celebrations that were going on elsewhere. He
lay, sprawled weakly on one of his cots, among bookish refuse. The
others with him, Ketcham and a brittle, arrogant girl called May who
lived next door, could not raise him from his depression, and, as if to
remind them of their continuing failures, he would cough raspingly
every few minutes, hunching his thin body and then falling ex-
haustedly into the pillows again, and say no word.

The sudden influx of Hart, Dinah, Kathryn, Hobbes, Pasternak and
Ed Schindel who, because of the excitement of the dash uptown, did
not recognize his mood, brought him to his feet with a self conscious,
hacking laugh to rustle among plates and tin cans in the kitchen for
glasses.

The radio was turned on, angular shadows danced in the top
corners near a chipped place in the ceiling through which the ribs of

the building shone whitely; laughter echoed, then filled the crowding silence.

Kathryn sank down beside Ketcham, who said: "Thank God, you've come! It was getting awful and I was just about to leave. She's been insulting him for an hour, and he wouldn't say a word. He's like a lovesick schoolboy with her. Yes, with May! . . . But you know, I called you two yesterday, thinking the three of us could have dinner, but I couldn't get you in." His relief made him unusually warm.

Dinah stood, between kitchen and living room, eyeing not so much the furnitureless apartment with its creaking, worn floors and its dreary unpainted walls that were scarred with old holes in which decades of portraits, calendars, snapshots and saints' pictures had hung, but surveying with watchful, pleasant interest the first clusterings of the others. Hart, who somehow usurped the hostly functions wherever he went, was speaking excitedly to Verger at the encouragement of Pasternak, while Ed, who dwarfed the room, smiled with self effacing benignity nearby.

Dinah, a slim, fresh, pale eighteen, was pliant and yet fragile, a self-possessed bluebell of a girl who gave those around her a certain intangible security by her presence. She had a comradely, direct gaze that was bestowed impersonally on all but Hart. She seemed a wise child, without confusions, utterly wrapped in the moment's developments but distrusting analysis of them, and aware only of the look and gait and mood of others. Her oval face glowed with a feeble girlish flush, and her wide eyes calculated upon life attentively.

Now she chatted with the affected May, who answered in a shrill voice:

"Oh, yes, I'm living next door with a girl friend, you know. I really don't mind the neighborhood because I think everyone should have their year of bohemianism—although, of course, my mother would be horrified if she knew I was living in Spanish Harlem. But I suppose all mothers are that way, don't you think?"

"We're looking for a place," Dinah replied with an affable calm as though she had somehow evaded May's affectations. "Do you happen to know of one? We're staying with David right now, down on York Avenue . . . David Stofsky. But we can't stay in his pad permanently. I've got a job in a Rexall's starting on Tuesday, so we'll have enough cash."

Verger brought whiskey, which Dinah declined sweetly with this: "Oh no, thanks, I never drink any more. Two years ago I was real lush and drinking a quart a day, but I don't pick up now. I even tried to kill myself once." It was no confession, no effort to impress, but simply a friendly remark as she said it. Verger hovered near May for a moment, watching her with sad tenderness, blind to her foolish words and flighty gestures, a patient sorrowful adoration on his face which she ignored expertly.

At that moment, announcing themselves with a muffled rumbling through the halls, Agatson and a disconsolate crowd appeared, only half of them coated against the rain. The others were soaked and Agatson, in the tattered, shrunken pair of blue jeans and turtle neck sweater, looking as unshaven and fierce as a thirsty Portuguese fisherman, shouted: "Is everyone drunk around here? Who are all these people? Who lives in this joint? . . . Ketcham, what are you doing *here* of all places? Bianca was asking about you just last night, yes, yes! I told her to shut up and stop being sincere! . . . Is anyone real drunk? . . . I just walked up the street on the car-tops, and hit only one convertible!"

He was with a Village crowd which, like so many others that night, had come together accidentally and set out restlessly wandering to find themselves in Verger's desolate neighborhood by the river. Now they straggled in and out of his rooms, poking suspiciously into everything, grabbing unguarded glasses and going at the liquor.

Verger was overwhelmed, and as nervous as he always was when Agatson was around, and sat on the floor amid the feet, drinking and coughing. Then, pushed into a corner by their comings and goings, he huddled with an old, rusty long-sword which leaned there like the emblem of some deflated ideal he was reluctant to finally bury. He stabbed at the floorboards with an ironical fervor, not caring how they cavorted among his precious books, but only peeping at May occasionally and, finding her intent upon the tousled and raucous Agatson, returned to his chipping with renewed introspection.

Time withdrew and their excitement flourished. Hart gathered Hobbes, Kathryn and Pasternak together and herding them into the bathroom with Dinah, extracted a stick of marijuana from his hip pocket.

"O.K.," he exclaimed as though someone had ventured a question.

"We'll pick up in here, see. There isn't enough for anybody else so there's no use broadcasting it, is there? You dig what I mean? Just cut back in here once in a while and we'll light up real cozy, okay?"

He lit the cigarette, giggling and laughing and talking between puffs, then held it to their mouths one after the other. Dinah closed her eyes ecstatically and sucked deeply three long times, holding her breath after each.

"Yes!" Hart broke out. "Yes, yes! Again, baby! Go ahead, another one! That's right!"

Outside, May was being pulled about by Agatson, his eyes burning viciously, in a formless dance. The music came from the same all-night program of wild jazz that midnight unleashed to all the city's hidden, backstairs pads where feverish young people gathered over their intoxicants to listen and not to listen; or hipsters woke, like some mute and ancient dead, to have their first cigarette of the "day." The night hours vanished before this music's bizarre imagery, until it finally evaporated into news reports at dawn like a demon turning into a tree.

Across the room from where Hobbes sat on a cot drinking, Kathryn drifted into Pasternak, who was bobbing regularly to the music.

"My God, Pasternak, don't you ever get tired of this noise?"

"What do you mean? Listen, that guy's actually *laying* his horn! You don't listen to it!"

"How the hell can I help but listen to it!" and she laughed scornfully and had some of his drink. They lingered together awkwardly, unable to speak in any but crude, sparring words, yet perilously joined by an unwilling curiosity and awareness concerning each other.

But now Hart and Dinah had started to dance, she clinging about his neck lithely with both bare arms, her head averted into his shoulder. He gripped her hips with large hands and moved her to him and away as though he had tapped a world of grace and abandon inside her and could direct it at will. Their feet hardly moved, but the rest of their bodies weaved rhythmically; she, lidded, trance-like as though in a swoon of dreamy surrender; he, unyielding, compulsive and yet also precise as he pressed her against his chest tighter and tighter.

The room's attention pivoted to them: Ed and Verger watching complacently; Agatson as though it was a clever diversion; Kathryn and Pasternak with an intent, yet somehow dispassionate interest.

May, however, frowned with disgust, shaking her head, and mut-

tered: "Good God!" She searched the faces of the others for agreement,
sure they would feel that the mysterious antagonism between the
sexes, which she found exhilarating and necessary, should not be so
willingly and simply dispensed with.

When it was over, and the others resumed their shuffling about in
the weird light, Hobbes found Pasternak beside him, saying eagerly:
"Isn't Hart terrific? And he's like that all the time! He doesn't care
about anything! He yells 'go!' to everything, everything!"

"Sure, Gene, but the word for that is 'come!' not 'go!' Ha-ha! . . .
Come!"

If this was the wrong sort of answer, Pasternak gave no explanations, but lurched immediately away.

Time withdrew before the tide of saxophones that taxed the radio,
now rising over the lunging drums in banshee screams which brought
shouts from the dimmer corners, then skittering pell mell down some
slope of melody as the rhythm broke on a wild, hard phrase. Trips to
the bathroom and the weed, which never seemed to run out, made all
sensation more fragmentary, bizarre, grotesque. People lay knotted
together grimly, while others danced in stumbling gaiety, or fought
their way to glasses. Talk capsuled into exclamations and laughter;
the sense of having watchers around vanished from everyone's mind,
and they wandered about, paired off, retired to corners, started conversations and abandoned them unfinished.

Hobbes hovered alone by a wall, dizzy from the drinking and the
marijuana, and snagged in the senseless return of an old inferiority,
cherishing a fond sadness as though he had perceived in all the chaos
a deep vein of desperation which everyone else refused to notice. "Out
of what rage and loneliness do we come together?" he thought drunkenly, certain some obscure wisdom lurked in the question. "Don't you
ever ask yourselves why?" And he fancied, through his dizziness, that
he was speaking aloud.

"What's wrong? Are you feeling all right?" a voice said in the din,
piercing his monologue. "Is anything wrong?" It was Kathryn, face
flushed with a half smile, half frown. "You've been scowling for hours,
and I'm drunk as all hell!"

"Oh, *you* know," he replied thickly. "The ridiculous questions.
What about me! How do I fit into this! . . . Humph! You know."

"Jesus Christ, why do you always have to get like that?"

"Well, go away then and have another drink. Go ahead. Where's the end of the night? That's all I was thinking. The whole long night! But go have a drink."

"We can leave whenever you want, but I thought you were having a good time. It was your idea." And she went away with irritation, before he could say that that was not what he had meant at all. So he sat there, knowing that the thoughts had risen in his head because he was dizzy and felt like vomiting, but not realizing that he had skillfully prevented both of them from recognizing this fact.

A commotion suddenly broke out near the windows. Verger, risen from the floor where he had been immobile most of the evening, stood, like a wheezing Golem, brandishing his sword wildly, and was methodically pouring the only remaining bottle of whiskey out the window into the rain. Agatson leapt up from the mattress where he had been thrusting with a disheveled May, and tried to rescue the bottle; but Verger, who endorsed temperance when he was drunk, let it go and there was a distant explosion of glass in the backyards below.

"Now why did you have to do that?" May was moaning thickly. ". . . very childish when you get stinking that way . . ."

As if to fight away some Calvinist Satan of his imagination represented by the tottering figure of Agatson, Verger started swinging the sword crazily, eyes aflame and a strange laugh twisted on his lips. Somebody roared above the radio, laughter screeched in the darkness somewhere, like the mocking of sharp beaked, unblinking birds; and then, at a furious swing which Agatson made no effort to keep away from, the sword crashed through the window nearby, throwing Verger off his balance. As though a trap had been sprung, he thudded stiffly to the floor among the shattered glass, still weakly clutching his rusty weapon.

"O. B.! O. B.! O. B.!" Agatson chanted over his prone body, making a wild sign of the cross.

"A window's broken," Kathryn yelled in the kitchen. "Let's get the hell out of here before the cops come!"

And, as if this charade had brought something to an end, Hart gathered them all together around the sink and said: "We're out of liquor and weed, see, but there's this friend of Ketcham's here that knows a connection up in Harlem, so we'll cut up there to this after-hours joint he knows!"

So they all slipped away, joined by Ketcham and his friend, Ben, a smiling fellow with a smell of benzedrine about him, who loped down the stairs with them, making vague jokes in a midwestern drawl. As they went through the halls, the indifference of the colorless doors and the emaciated cats they found on every landing, and of all physical things, to their very presence, drove them further into their hilarity

As though they were the creations of that night, it drove them, drunk and sober, towards the dawn, through a jumble of dreary streets to still drearier precincts, conglomerate with derelict houses where no light showed, that were fronted by bent iron railings, crusted and awry. The steady drenching of the rain made this Acheron of tenements appear more miserably squalid, and the car careened onward, Hobbes muttering, each time Hart swerved around a torturous corner: "Go! Go!"

They jerked to a halt just off One Hundred and Thirty-eighth Street and, leaping out, Ben leading the way, approached a darkened brownstone no different than its neighbors, where, gathering at the top of the stairs, they were greeted by a large, grave Negro, who smiled distantly as he held the door wider for them to enter, saying: "Good evening, gentlemen. Step right inside, just through that door . . ."

Beyond a room of sofas and ash-stands which had once been the front parlor, was a high ceilinged, drab hall, its windows tacked over with dusty black velvet, a bar built on one side and a scattering of circular tables filling the other. The room was crowded with people, mostly Negroes; the single drinkers at the bar, the parties squeezed around the tables. In the heavy yellow glow from a dim, crystal chandelier—a light as flickering and unreal as if it had come from tapers—an opulent Negro woman was singing, accompanied by a grinning guitarist in a sports shirt, and by an intense pianist, whose cocked head seemed tuned in on some wild poetry within the music which his dark fingers, spidering along the keys, endeavored to draw from the prosaic upright.

Amiably, Ben collected four dollars, managing to edge into a space at the bar, and ordered four drinks, all they could afford. No one seemed to notice them; the faces lining the walls were hot, placid, distracted.

The singer, stamping her foot three times, led off into a fresh burst of song, raising her arms in graceful supplication. "All of me-ee-ee . . . Why . . . not . . . take . . . all of me-ee-ee!" She started sliding between the tables, head thrown back, pausing at each with her hands expressively outstretched in appeal. The guitarist shuffled along behind her, muttering encouragements. Her dusky eyes leveled knowingly at each customer and, as though each saw there and heard in the music the memory they all must have attached to this rebellious and wistful American jazz which was somehow most expressive of the boiling, deaf cities and the long brown reaches of their country, at every table a dollar was pressed into her hand, and with a swing of generous breasts she would move on.

Hobbes, caught up in the living music, gravitated to the piano she left behind. At every fresh chorus, the ascetic Negro there released greater ringing chords, as though the increasing distance of the voice brought the inner melody closer to his poised ear. Hobbes, leaning toward him, was, through his giddiness, suddenly possessed by the illusion of emotional eloquence and started to chant softly, improvising broken phrases. The Negro glanced up for an instant, nodding abstractly, long gone, and with no resentment at the intrusion.

It was a room which day, and the things of the day, had not entered, perhaps for decades; and everyone there was aware of where they were, and of the illegality of it, and yet because of this and the sensual voice of the woman, still moving like some buxom priestess among them, they were caught up together.

Pasternak, against a wall where he and Kathryn stood close sharing a drink between them, exclaimed: "But it's all the same! Everything's the same as everything else! Every one! . . . Baydo-baydo-boo-ba! Can you hear it? . . . But look, look at Hart go!"

The singer was moving across the open space toward the bar and Hart, his head bobbing up and down and his eyes narrowed, was shuffling to meet her, stooped over and clapping his hands like an euphoric savage who erupts into a magic rite at the moment of his seizure. She watched him coming toward her, with dark experienced eyes, and for an instant sang just for him, her shoulders swinging on the deep strums of the guitarist who tarried behind, watchful and yet also appreciative. Hart stopped before her, bobbing, ecstatic, and then, falling down on his knees, he cried: "Y-e-s! Blow! Blow! . . . You know who you are!"; for this was his offering, all he could give. And, as if she accepted it in lieu of money, with a wave of her head, a bright wink at the crowd, and a great display of heaving bosom, she strutted on.

Dinah was smiling faintly, all this and much more being usual for her, allowing him to have it without a word as proof of her commitment to him at that moment. He could say nothing, but laughed hoarsely and took her about the shoulders. There was one more prolonged, incredible chorus, and with a last smile, the singer disappeared and the music was over. Having no more money and having come to some consummation, they all straggled out and into the car again.

Ben's connection had not showed; the sweet cologne fragrance of benzedrine about him and the discoloration of his lips suggested that there may have been no marijuana connection at all, but somehow that did not matter. Continuance was what concerned them, and where to go next. After a number of improbable ideas (places that would not be open, people who would not be up), they settled on a friend of Ben's who lived on One Hundred and Twenty-third Street and Amsterdam Avenue, who would "surely have liquor." Although at another moment this would have seemed unlikely to them all, now they believed it with bland innocence as though all discord in the universe had been resolved by their harmony, which, in any case, did not depend on such details.

They rode as in a sunken city whose life is frozen in watery silence, they alone capable of breath and words, and finally pulled up before another dead house on another bleak street. But as if a morning premonition had touched them, and all felt for the first time a slackening, they groped down a long corridor in a centerless throng. They reached the end of it and went down a treacherous stairway into a dismal backyard, empty of all but garbage cans collecting rain, up two more steps and then, like movie spies taking absurdly circuitous routes, through a window with a broken sash, to find themselves in a chilly, enameled kitchen where people were blankly sitting, drinking coffee. Sensing hostility and leaving the amenities to Ben, they dispersed into the dark echoing rooms beyond, which were filled with incongruous furniture (the rightful refuse of country attics), and where a battered, caseless radio was buzzing softly. Refusing cold coffee coldly offered, Kathryn and Dinah locked themselves into the tiny bathroom, while Pasternak and Hobbes crouched outside. Hart and Ed, wordless and wet, played darts down a narrow hallway connecting these chambers, and finally, with only Ketcham and Ben feeling any embarrassment, they trooped out the window again, Hart calling back from among the cans:

"Sure, we understand, sure. You know, we just thought you'd be up, that's all. But say, if you see his connection, see, get an ounce or so for me. We'll cut by again!", all the time sniffing and chuckling to himself, until his words seemed almost a taunt.

They headed for Ketcham's, and the night and the rain had gone. Hobbes and Kathryn left them there, without excuses, withdrawing from exhaustion, while the others went on to the Magnavox, the quart of beer Ketcham hoped might still be there, and a continued resistance to their own sweet fatigue.

The wisdom of their search for some end of the night (the night that was a corridor in which they lurked and groped, believing in a door somewhere, beyond which was a place from which time and the discord bred of time were barred), the wisdom of this seemed to Hobbes, whose mood had changed again, one answer to the reason for being on which Stofsky had once impaled him. But his avowal, even of this strange thought, was motiveless and without intensity.

On the subway, Kathryn slept unashamedly on his shoulder as they sat among the denimed workmen with lunchpails and fresh newspapers, the hurrying, brisk little secretaries who would get their coffee and a Danish downtown and come fully awake only then, and all the other early riders who opened offices, relieved night porters and prepared machines for the first great, groggy wave of the rush hours.

At Seventy-second Street, a merry troup of Girl Scouts, on a hike that would bring them to a picnic's joy, filled the car with their eagerness and their starched scamperings from seat to seat. Some sat, large eyed, hand in hand; others chattered, craning about, open legged, reading all the advertisements to each other; and a little white socked Negro girl was laughing happily as she fiddled with her neighbor's pigtails. In his almost pleasant dullness, Hobbes thought suddenly:

"To be like them or like us, is there another position?"

*   *   *

That night Stofsky finally left Bianca's at one-fifteen. On top of his bewilderment regarding Verger, Hobbe's failure to return to the apartment after the phone call had plunged him into dark speculations. Though he should have been certain that the incident had nothing to do with him, nevertheless he made a dozen imaginary connections, most of which he voiced to Ketcham and Bianca. They became more and more irritated at him, until he was sure their retorts were only thinly disguised insolence. This threw him into consternation, and made him babble on the more, as if he might outwit his growing depression by courting their assurances that it was unfounded. Eventually it became evident to him that they wished to be left to themselves, and with nervous apologies, he fled.

The gloom and emptiness of the dank subways did not help. He felt utterly alone beneath the sleeping city, and even riffled through his address book in the hope of finding someone who would be glad to see him. Then, walking up York Avenue, he thought of Pasternak, somewhere adrift between New York and the glittering, nightless California of his imagination. There, with Hart and perhaps other strange and exciting people, Pasternak was (he thought) whirling in the center of life, from which loneliness, doubt and conflict were banished.

For a moment, as he paused at the entrance of his building and surveyed the empty street, Stofsky was reminded of the hours after the visions. In that bar, just across there, he had tried all his keys, and like tonight, they had fit no door. But then he had known (or thought he had) that all was love, that behind all indifference lay the fear of powerlessness which love alone could allay. But now he felt embittered, almost unable to recall the simplicity of those emotions, and only aware of the way in which his earnest interferences had all, unaccountably, gone wrong.

He climbed the stairways, lost in thoughts of Hart, Verger, Pasternak, and the others, and it was not until he was almost at his door that he discerned that there was somebody lying crumpled up against it. It was so dark that he could not see this figure clearly, but when he drew nearer, and bent forward, he seemed to remember that sunken chest, those wasted legs. Hurriedly, he lit a match and held it forward, until a dim, ghastly glow enveloped the man, who was pressed against the door in a heap and seemed hardly breathing, but was only asleep.

To his complete surprise and joy, he recognized him. It was Ancke.

"Albert, Albert! . . . Come on, get up! How long have you been lying there? . . ."

Ancke woke suddenly, as Stofsky shook him, with no intermediate period of confusion. He was totally immobile one moment and the next instant wide awake, and getting stiffly to his feet, but not, somehow, alarmed.

"Hello," he said with a faint smile. "I've been meaning to come around. What time is it?"

"It's . . . it's about— Heavens, I don't know . . . I've been expecting you; I mean, I knew you'd turn up eventually! And I dawdled all the way up the street just now, *dawdled!* But come in, come in!"

Ancke shuffled after him, stood about with curiosity while Stofsky snapped on lights, and then, choosing the couch, he laid himself down on it carefully, and breathed a heavy sigh of relief.

"I must have been out there a couple of hours . . . Whew! My back's throbbing . . . A very cozy pad, David, yes, yes . . . But then, of course, it's my feet more than anything."

He looked down at his feet as though they were not part of him at all, but he felt a distant sympathy for them nevertheless. His shoes were battered and cracked and he was without socks. His ankles were grimy and there were scabby sores along both insteps where the patent leather had rubbed against the flesh. And, indeed, the rest of his attire was just as miserable. The sports shirt that hung around his drooping shoulders was unwashed, wrinkled, out at the elbows. His trousers were torn on one leg, baggy about his lean shanks, and spotted with mud around the cuffs. He surveyed himself with a sort of sorrowful amusement.

Ancke was only thirty-three, but everything about him seemed worn and faded. His head was large for the emaciated, almost girlish body, and his lank brown hair gave the appearance of being dry, even dusty. His skin was puffy, yellowish, and in his whole heavy face, with the wide, soft mouth, the small nose, and the pallid cheeks, only his eyes, that were large, dark and luminous, gave any sign of life. They burned fitfully under thick eyebrows. His thin arms and legs were scarred with the countless wounds of the hypodermic needle which had poured morphine into him for years, and the flesh seemed to have shrunk in upon his brittle bones. He quivered involuntarily every few minutes, as though he had chills. He was extremely dirty and smelled of sweat and decaying teeth. He was, in fact, the wrinkled little hustler that Hobbes had seen in The Go Hole with the "cool" man a few weeks before.

"It's so remarkable that you should have come tonight, tonight of all times!" Stofsky was exclaiming. "It's almost prophetic! But where have you been? Do you realize I've been searching for over a month? I had to see you. Tremendous things have been happening . . . But what's this about your feet? Here, let me—My God, what have you been doing to yourself?"

Stofsky had started to remove Ancke's shoes, but paused in horror at the sight of his bare feet. They were covered with hideous corns and running sores that were black with dirt. His toes were bloody and swollen.

"They've been dragging me for a week or so," and Ancke laughed feebly at his own pun. "I've been walking, you see. I haven't had any junk for ten days, that's why, I imagine. I couldn't seem to score with anyone, not even my usual connection on One Hundred and Third Street. Remember that corner? So I've been getting around, looking . . . But don't bother with them, man. You'll only make yourself sick . . . I just have to rest."

"No, no," Stofsky cried with dismay. "Wait a minute, maybe I have some boric acid or . . . No, I don't . . . But I'll wash them . . ." He rushed from cluttered cabinet to sink. "Really, Albert, it's terrible! You must have been walking around for weeks, even months . . . Watch out now, the soap may sting . . ."

Ancke smiled weakly, almost paternally, as Stofsky knelt at his feet, washing them gently with an old rag, and asking endless questions:

"But where have you been? Do you realize Hart's been here and gone again? Just flew in and flew out . . . like an albatross! And Gene went with him. But we looked for you, almost every night we dug the whole square. What about Winnie? Have you seen her? And oh, I've had visions . . . actual manifestations! . . . But quick, tell me everything."

And so Ancke began to talk with patient weariness, gazing now at the ceiling, and now at the eager, intent face before him.

He had been released from Riker's Island almost two months before, and had picked up a few dollars steering second-story men to a friend of his from Chicago days, a fence. This enabled him to get enough morphine to keep "grooved" for several weeks. Jail had, as always, forced him to "throw his habit," and so small amounts were sufficient in the beginning. But gradually he became "hooked" again, and had to hustle about Times Square and Harlem to set up more deals. He bumped into Winnie and "her boy," Little Rock, and they helped him out. Winnie, true to rumors Stofsky had heard, had thrown her morphine habit and, but for a little heroin now and again "just for a lift," was on nothing, and living with Little Rock in a house in Astoria. Ancke "cut around with them once in a while," the evening at The Go Hole had been one such occasion, but preferred staying permanently in Manhattan, where he could keep in touch with all the passers, connections, addicts, homosexual prostitutes, petty crooks and musicians who made up the underground of drugs, crime and craziness which he frequented.

These were his friends from other days in L.A., Chicago, or New Orleans, from numerous jails, tea pads, freighters, bars and cheap hotels; or customers from the year he had peddled stolen prescription blanks on One Hundred and Twenty-eighth Street. Through them he got all the news: who was in and who was out, who was hooked and who was off, what was available and what was going to be hard to get; all the rumors, speculations, gossip, warnings and messages that traveled from mouth to mouth and city to city among the restless, continually circulating fraternity and to which he belonged.

Then his money had run out, those few connections who might advance him a little "M" had vanished or been arrested, and for a week and a half he had walked fruitlessly up and downtown, fighting nausea, and the ache and jitter of his body demanding the drug. He had partially thrown his new habit on this trek, slept in bus stations wrapped in newspapers, begged money for coffee and sandwiches, gone from place to place, run down a hundred empty leads, and finally given up, and with the last of his failing strength, come to Stofsky.

"So now I've got to rest. Maybe for quite a while. Take the strain off myself. Perhaps just sleep. Are you alone here?"

"Yes, yes. Hart and Dinah were staying with me, but they've all gone now. All of them. You couldn't have come at a better time. You don't know how I needed you . . . just tonight. You'll stay here, of course, won't you?"

"I'll have to say 'yes' . . . Could I have a cigarette?"

He took it, raised himself only slightly to receive the light, and inhaled deeply, a look of heavy contentment flushing over his features.

"As long as there's no one else around, I'll stay. Because, you know, everyone drags me now. I mean just everyone, anyone, just people. I really prefer to sit quietly alone. Or even sleep. It's not because I'm afraid, of course . . . nothing like that. You understand? It's all just a drag for me now." And his lids fluttered closed.

"But we must talk," Stofsky said eagerly. "I've got to tell you everything! My visions, and Waters . . . Waters went crazy, you know, and had shock treatment and . . . But, that's right, you don't know Waters. And I've huge tidings from Hart, and . . . oh, so much else! Oh, Albert, you couldn't have come at a better time! I must tell you everything.'

"All right," Ancke replied with patient forbearance. "Maybe for a little while, and then I'll sleep."

"Oh, and Verger! I wanted to talk to you about Verger . . . Now, Albert, what's this about books? You don't know how I've been involved with those books . . . But first, do you realize Verger's the only one who's seen you since you got out? The only one! Why didn't you come here? I could have given you money. You must have known that. I'm working now; yes, a big job, and . . . But, listen, about the books: now, he *pretended* to understand why you took them. But he didn't really. I mean, not *why* he pretended to understand! It wasn't crucial to him, of course, he didn't really get angry. In fact, I'm sure he's even anxious to see you again, so he can prostrate himself or something like that. But, really, it only set him off on more self punishing thoughts. You know how he is. He doesn't want to believe that he's really very proud, he wants to humiliate himself, to suffer, and your stealing his books played right into that . . . But, actually, he does care a great deal, and struggles with his vanity . . ."

"I'd almost forgotten them. I only took three or four, didn't I? You know, I can't even remember . . . But *you* understand about them."

"Yes, but that's my point, because, you see, *he* doesn't!"

"Oh, man, *don't* drag me about those books, not now." Ancke all but clapped his forehead, but there was no annoyance in his exclamation, only weariness, as though he had been pleasantly slipping into a thick inertia until Stofsky had brought up his theft.

But he went on patiently all the same: "I needed the money to score, you see. I had this load all set up, three fresh caps, stuff right out of Bellevue . . . I knew he wouldn't really mind."

"But, don't you see, really he does! Oh, I know he pretends—"

"But I know all that, man! Don't you think I know all that? What I mean is I knew he wouldn't *do* anything. You see? He wouldn't *do* anything. I had to get enough to function, that's all."

He breathed heavily, taking a deeper pull on the cigarette, but there was in his manner the still watchful relief of a man who had righted himself after almost falling from a tight-rope, but knows he still has a long way to go.

"Just don't put me down about *those* things now. I can't make conversation about those things. I mean, we know all about them. You *know* that I understand that it's just Verger's ego, that he really *wants* to be taken advantage of, that he likes to fester on all that . . . You see, I know about that level. But it just drags me now. Really, I would like to sleep."

"But wait," Stofsky exclaimed. "Of course, I knew you understood Daniel, in that sense. That's all it really is with him, of course. But, you see, I've been tilting with everyone's ego recently . . . like a Saint George! Ever since my visions . . . but I must tell you all about my visions! Do you realize, Albert, that I've had revelations, I've been spoken to, called . . . Don't sleep yet, just a little while longer. I must tell you! . . . Everything is love, love . . . But let me explain it all to you, from the very beginning. Don't sleep yet, you must hear this!"

Ancke seemed willing enough to listen, as long as he did not have to speak. He settled down into the pillows, his large eyes half-lidded, his breathing hardly perceptible, his head wreathed in blue smoke curling lazily in the motionless air.

Stofsky proceeded to tell him everything with minute detail, appending exaggerated comments, and giggling at his own exaggerations. As his account widened to include everyone, as one story overlapped into another and the whole narrative became infinitely complex with his elaborate relations with Verger, Ketcham, Hart, Pasternak and Hobbes, he grew sadder, his voice terse, his gaze fixed and yet bewildered. Ancke only lay nodding dreamily, as if he had heard it all many times before, and it was an old, unfortunate, and yet predictable tale that could have but one ending.

"So something has really gone terribly wrong," Stofsky concluded. "They all mock me, or write these letters. But not that alone, I'm used to that, of course; people have always mocked me, I used to like it you know, even play up to it . . . But they are afraid of me too. And repulsed! Can you possibly know what I mean? . . . But, of course you do, of anyone. That's why I can tell you these things. I've told no one else . . . But, just tonight, Arthur, Bianca, even Hobbes . . . no, you don't know him . . . but they all seemed annoyed with me, and then look what happened with Hart and Dinah! Just because I wanted to love them, to be honest. The truth, the truth! For even now, when it's earned me nothing but contempt, I *do* believe it. Heavens, do they think I—"

Ancke sighed sympathetically, but also with such heaviness that Stofsky broke off.

"Just accept it, man. Don't get all hungup that way."

"Well, maybe you're right. I won't listen to them anymore." Stofsky continued, taking this as the assurance he had courted unsuccessfully earlier. "It's only because they don't understand that they . . . shrink from me. That's really what it is you know. They can't bear me, they pass looks. Oh, I see them doing it!"

"But you shouldn't get hungup on all that, man," Ancke said in such barely audible tones that Stofsky moved closer. "You know how people are. Now, you've got eyes for making things better, for making people get along, and accept one another. That's your trouble. You get all worried about it. You rush around, 'tilting with egos' perhaps, as you said. But that's probably all ego too . . . your ego! . . . Now, don't get angry. Oh, I know when you're getting angry, so come on now . . . But that's just putting other people down, you see what I mean? I mean, that's what they do to you in return."

He smiled benignly and his voice subsided to little more than a weary murmur: "Now don't get all hurt. I really know about all this . . . It's all such a drag. I don't mean that it's unimportant, caring for people, all that concern . . . but you shouldn't get hurt, you know. I wouldn't hurt you, and I understand why you feel the way you do . . . You know, *I* feel sometimes like I'm dying . . . every minute of the day a little more. You see what I mean? I'm being smothered . . . all these relationships, hangups, conflicts, all that business . . . it stifles me."

He heaved another sigh that seemed to shiver his whole frame.

"I've been so tired this time, for instance. Since getting out. Listless, horrified. By the hangups with people. Just anyone. The public. You know, even people you like. You have to smile, talk, arrange to get somewhere. There's hassles about food, where to sleep, news, all that. I used to be able to walk along the street—meeting the people—and get by, laugh, take my time . . But now it all drags me terribly. I really prefer to sit quietly alone, just to rest . . . And, you know, I really think I'll sleep right now. Why don't I just sleep?" His lids met. "*You* understand."

"Ego? Is that all it is?" Stofsky uttered, asking himself, though speaking aloud. "Is that what it's been all along? Just like psychoanalysis. Maybe that's all it was, even the visions, although I didn't feel that way . . ."

He gazed at the limp figure before him, and there was a wounded brightness in his dark eyes.

"It was probably madness then, as my father said. I should have kissed everyone's feet, or screamed at them. Is that what you mean, Albert? Crushed them for feeling repelled by me? By my very face? Or been absolutely crushed by them. Is that what you mean? . . . Why has it got to be that way? Tell me, suddenly I don't seem to know at all, is that the way things really are?" His stare was more fixed than before, but his lips were trembling. "What if that's the way they really are," he muttered to himself. "Tell me."

"Now look, man, don't be hurt. Don't be crushed . . . and don't crush anyone else either. Don't you see? Don't care about all that."

Ancke had come back once more, as if from the dead. He took another cigarette resolutely, and touched Stofsky's shoulder abstractedly. "But, look, I'll tell you something that happened to me, just a week or so ago. And then I'll sleep."

He cleared his throat, breathed deeply once or twice, took a long drag on the cigarette, blinked his eyes, smiled wanly at the ceiling, and began speaking softly and slowly, with a certain careful solemnity as though to avoid any excitement.

"I was on the Fifth Avenue Bus. You see, I was cutting up to Harlem to see a junkie that Little Rock used to know in Atlanta. It was early evening, and I thought the river might be nice, so I decided to take the bus up the Drive, instead of getting all hungup in the subways. I really just wanted to watch the water and get a look at the George Washington Bridge . . ."

There had been a drunken old woman four seats ahead of him, it seemed. It was crowded, hot, and sitting next to her was a perfectly-coifed young matron with net gloves, in an expensive print dress, and carrying several small parcels from fashionable stores. The drunken woman was fifty or so, ratty, even wizened, and she had a dirty, white linen tam clapped askew a bird's nest of badly dyed hair. Her lean, wrinkled fingers were smudged, her nails bitten and cracked. Her clothes had been youthful fifteen years before, but now they were mournfully jaunty on so withered a figure. There was an underfed scrawniness to her cheeks which made the crude touches of rouge resemble a mortician's handiwork.

"She might have been one of those whores that used to work Columbus Circle in the old days, only since then she's gone to pieces fast . . ."

The young matron pointedly turned away from her into the aisle, but the old woman seemed oblivious of this, and sat picking her nose, mumbling absent-mindedly to herself, and primping her hair as though somehow flattered to be on that bus among all those combed, polished, and dignified ladies. Finally the young matron got up, and with a meaningful look at the other young matrons in the other seats, moved toward the center door. Something in this action infuriated the old woman, for she began to cackle, swear and even spit in her seat. She grumbled to herself, to passing cars, and finally to the others in the bus:

"They're taking over everything! The sonsabitches think they can run everything . . . even the transit system! Well, not while I'm around, the bastids!"

She could not restrain this mounting rage, and went on sputtering and swearing until she had worn herself out, and, noticing the way everyone had drawn away from her and sat peering at her covertly, hopelessness and embarrassment overcame her anger. She was separated, by several seats, from everyone else, for they had edged away as though on the suspicion of disease. She sat on, not daring to look around for fear she would see the pitiless, disapproving glances, and realize that she had cut herself off from the feeling of security and personal worth that being there on the bus amid the colorful frocks, subdued conversations and contented faces, had given her. She sat, flushed and hurt, fidgeting with her clothes, fishing for nothing in her miserable handbag, muttering, and wiping away small, angry tears from her old eyes, while everyone watched and looked at one another with that slight understanding shake of the head that signified all had realized that they had, at least, their disapproval of her in common; and this made them closer to each other, even a little more good-natured than before.

"Everyone was suddenly very sympathetic with everyone else, because they all felt that they might have been rejected, humiliated, anxious or unsuccessful the rest of the time, but now they were the same, for this one moment, simply *because* they weren't like her. You see? . . . But she got all hungup being angry with that woman, and then on being humiliated by everyone else . . . I kept saying to myself: 'What does she care? Why does it matter to her?' I even thought of going up to her and telling her that, but it was too much trouble."

"How terrible! . . . And perfect too, in a way!" Stofsky exclaimed. "But that's what I mean. Why didn't they understand *why* she was injured—I mean, everything you perceived in it—instead of crushing her that way. Why didn't they accept her? Instead of thinking of themselves, their idea of themselves!"

"But, listen, man," Ancke replied, as though he was long-suffering but intended to endure. "Why didn't *she* accept them? . . . They were acting the same way toward *me*! All that time! I'm sure they knew I was completely saturated with narcotics, and had this disgusting skin disease and everything. Why, I had the whole back of the bus to myself! Don't you see? . . . Now, I know that's just the way the public is. I realize they think I'm revolting, abhorrent . . . but not only that, I know *why* they think that . . . and more important, I *accept* the fact that they do . . . They're disgusted because they've got to save their own egos, you see? But I haven't got one, I mean I don't care about all that anymore, so it doesn't matter to me . . . I just accept it, so as not to get hungup . . . By the way, do you have a pair of shoes you can lend me?"

Stofsky was stunned and unable to decide on his reaction.

"What a strange idea!" he cried. "The end of the ego, the death of the will!" He was clasping and unclasping his hands. "Maybe that's what I really meant by 'die, give up, go mad.' But what a provocation this is! Do you realize? We should expect people (and ourselves mainly, of course) not only to understand why other people think us abhorrent, unbearable, a contagious disease . . . but to accept it as well! Not even to *feel* humiliated . . . even in the heart!"

Meanwhile Ancke had collapsed from the effort of telling the story, and would only murmur: "It's just a drag, as I've said. Once you know why anyone rejects you or judges you, that it's for themselves and not you, it doesn't matter anymore. But more important, it becomes a terrific, stifling, really death-like drag to care about it . . . And finally you just prefer to sit quietly alone . . ."

He peered at Stofsky, as though checking a final time, and found him lost in calculations there on the floor, his lips drawn, and then breaking into sudden, incredulous giggles. His depression of an hour before had vanished.

"Yes," Stofsky reflected after a moment. "It's a weird perception, almost frightening . . . But it raises many problems. The end of self . . . what a thought!" He turned towards Ancke, his brows pulled together with questions. "But how do you tell people *this?* How can you make them understand *this?* It was hard enough before . . . on the other level. Or is all that—wanting to make them see it—is all that ego, too?" and he mumbled this last to himself, and then looked back at Ancke whose lids had drifted together. "But I've kept you talking too long, eh, Albert? . . . Albert?"

But Ancke was asleep, and had been for the last few minutes; that deep, impregnable sleep that is like a trance, that is almost a rehearsal for death, and from which one cannot be called, but must call oneself.

Stofsky gave a forlorn little laugh under his breath, and getting up, pulled a blanket over Ancke with a careful tenderness of which he would have been ashamed if anyone had been there to see.

"And now I am alone," he whispered.

But that night he had a dream, without trappings, without symbols; a dream of extraordinary clarity while he dreamt it, but which he could not remember at all clearly when he awoke.

He walked down an inky corridor, much like one of those in Water's building or in his own, and he was out of breath, as if he had come up many long and tiring flights. The door at the end of that corridor did not surprise him, nor, when he opened it without knocking, did the large, shadowy hall beyond it; a hall such as one can rent for fifteen dollars a night in Harlem brownstones; long, the fancy moldings and dusty crepe streamers giving it a pathetic and abandoned appearance. Nor was he surprised by the throne at one end of it, a throne that was not surrounded by an ambient light, or even very clean and polished, but still somehow regal and entirely proper to the figure sitting there: an aging man of once powerful physique, now vaguely weary, His untrimmed beard fanned out in white folds upon His chest, His eyes shining with muted brightness as only an old man's eyes can shine out of the limpid stillness of an old face. God.

Stofsky approached, without fear or excitement, and found himself on his knees, looking up, still conscious of his breathlessness. He paused for an instant, peering at the face, realizing an old, skeptical curiosity concerning it which he somehow knew would be tolerated; noting the wrinkles, the faint pink glow of the cheeks, the expression of weary passivity.

Then he began to tell all that had happened since the visions, endeavoring to stick close to the facts and keep the report brief and accurate. All the same, it seemed to him to take an inexcusable time to go through it all. Finally, reaching Ancke and mentioning his worry over his future, he came to the end.

"I should have had you here before, I know," God said with an audible sigh. "But then . . ." And He looked down at Stofsky with an expression of such sadness and such resignation that Stofsky was actually embarrassed to have been the cause of such a look on God's face.

"But what am I to do next, Sir?" he managed to say.

At that, he thought that God might lean forward and touch his head with one of those large, veinless hands, so gentle and sorrowful was the light which bathed His Face. But He did not.

"How shall I help them now? You see, I'm so confused and tired—," forgetting that God must know everything.

"You must go back, and even doubt," God said after a moment's pause, "and remember none of this. There's an end which you shall discover. It waits there for you. Without you, it cannot happen. And it must."

"But what shall I do?", wanting, with childlike earnestness, some sign to guide him, to make acceptance easier.

"Being saved is like being damned," God said with thoughtful simplicity, as though it was one of the unutterable secrets of the universe given to Stofsky now because he had been patient, because he had come so far.

Then God did lean forward until His beard fell straight down into his lap and Stofsky could see the wet brilliance of His large eyes. "You must go," He said, "Go, and love without the help of any Thing on earth."

For a second, Stofsky seemed to recall the words; then remembered a line like that in Blake, and thought that perhaps this was not God at all, but Blake himself. But then, looking closer, he knew it *was* God, and thought it wonderful and just that God should quote Blake too.

As he was about to rise, however, a question rose in his mind, something almost irreverent and certainly mortal, and even though he suspected that he had no right to ask it, he could not let the opportunity pass somehow.

"Things are so terrible," he began. "The violence, misery, the hate . . . war and hopelessness . . . I wonder," and he gave one fearful and yet challenging glance into Those Eyes. "Why can't *You* help all that? Do you know how human beings suffer? . . . Can't You help them, Sir?"

God's face grew dim and drawn, as though the question gave Him pain He knew there was no sense to feel, but pain He took upon Himself in spite of that. He seemed for that moment a majestic and lonely man in His rented hall, on His dusty throne, who had received too many petitioners, too long, and understood too much to speak anything but the truth, even though it could not help.

"I try," He replied simply. "I do all I can."

Then Stofsky woke, and it was still dark. He could remember most of it, as though it had just happened, and felt a kind of heavy peace. But very soon he fell off to sleep again, and dreamt no more, and had forgotten when the morning came.

JACK KEROUAC

The Time of the Geek

It was Kerouac who named his generation "beat." In two novels, The Town *and* The City *and* On The Road, *he gave it also its Creed—DIG EVERYTHING—and its Trinity: Poet, Hoodlum and Junkie—an interlocked trio fused by a continuing dialogue. Kerouac's characters are not impinged upon by the society around them: they have fully succeeded in making their own world, with places to go to, things to do. And when they're not on the move, there's always the big kick: the jazz combo whose beat is beyond mind or reason, the hell-bent party that promises there'll be no end, or the stick of tea that will bring one back to the lap of God.*

HE WANDERED into Times Square. He stood on the sidewalk in the thin drizzle falling from dark skies. He looked about him at the people passing by—the same people he had seen so many times in other American cities on similar streets: soldiers, sailors, the panhandlers and drifters, the zoot-suiters, the hoodlums, the young men who washed dishes in cafeterias from coast to coast, the hitchhikers, the hustlers, the drunks, the battered lonely young Negroes, the twinkling little Chinese, the dark Puerto Ricans, and the varieties of dungareed young Americans in leather jackets who were seamen and mechanics and garagemen everywhere.

It was the same as Scollay Square in Boston, or the Loop in Chicago, or Canal Street in New Orleans, or Curtis Street in Denver, or West Twelfth in Kansas City, or Market Street in San Francisco, or South Main Street in Los Angeles.

The same girls who walked in rhythmic pairs, the occasional whore in purple pumps and red raincoat whose passage down these sidewalks was always so sensational, the sudden garish sight of some incredible homosexual flouncing by with an effeminate shriek of general greeting to everyone, anyone: "I'm just *so* knocked out and you *all* know it, you *mad* things!"—and vanishing in a flaunt of hips.

And then the quiet men with lunchpails hurrying off to work across these blazing scenes, seeing nothing, stopping for nothing, hurrying for busses and trolleys, and vanishing. The occasional elderly gentleman wearing a look of fear and indignation at having to endure the proximity of such "riff-raff." The cops strolling by with nightsticks, stopping to chat with newsvendors and cab-drivers. The dishwashers who leaned in steamy kitchen doorways, all tattooed and muscular. The occasional crooks and thieves and murderous hoodlums who passed in silent, arrogant, gum-chewing groups.

This was the way Peter had seen it everywhere in these years of the war, but nowhere was it so dense and fabulous as on Times Square. All the cats and characters, all the spicks and spades, Harlem-drowned, street-drunk and slain, crowded together, streaming back and forth, looking for something, waiting for something, forever moving around.

Through all this passed occasional out-of-town visitors, in gaping happy families, the father and the mother grinning expectantly because "it's Times Square," and the young daughter clinging to her brother's or her fiancé's arm with gleeful excitement, and the young man himself glaring defiantly about because he burned at the thought of the word "hick" or the word "square" that must be on the minds of a thousand hoodlums.

Peter knew all these things. By this time he was on familiar terms with many of the young drifters who haunted Times Square day and night. Some of them he had met in other cities thousands of miles away but he was always certain of running into them again at Times

Square in New York, the sum and crown of every marqueed square and honky-tonk street in America. It was the one part to which all the "characters" eventually migrated across the land at one time or another in their lone-wolf scattering lives. On Times Square he could meet a Norwegian seaman he had drunk with in the alleys of Picadilly, or a Filipino cook who had borrowed ten dollars from him in the Arctic Sea, or a young wrangler-poolshark he had gambled with in some San Francisco poolroom. On Times Square he would suddenly see a familiar face he had seen somewhere in the world for dead certain. It was always a wonder to see such a face and hauntingly expect to see it again years later in some other night's-market of the world.

To Peter the course of his life now seemed to cross and re-cross New York as though it were some great rail-yard of his soul. He knew that everything on earth was represented within the towering borders of New York. It thrilled his soul: but at the same time it had begun to mortify his heart.

He could stand on Times Square and watch a Park Avenue millionaire pass in a limousine at the same moment that some Hell's Kitchen urchin hurried out of its path. The gay group of young Social Register revelers piling into a cab, and some young bitter-fierce John Smith tempered by Public School No. 16 standing at a hotdog stand watching them, before going into an all-night movie to see them on the screen. The trio of influential businessmen, fresh from the convention dinner, strolling by absorbed in high conversation, and the tattered young Negro from 133rd Street dodging meekly out of their way. The meditative Communist committeeman brushing shoulders with the sullen secret Bundist from Yorkville. The Greenwich Village intellectual looking down his nose at the Brooklyn machinist reading the *Daily News*. The Broadway weisenheimer-gambler glancing at the old farmer with bundles wrapped in newspaper who gapes and bumps into everyone. The sartorial First Nighter frantically trying to hail a cab while the crowds swarm out of the second-run double-feature movie. The mellow gentleman in the De Pinna suit headed for the Ritz bar, and the mellow gentleman staggering by and sitting down in the gutter, to spit and groan and be hauled off by cops. The young Bohemian writer who couldn't pay his rent, always arguing about his art, and the sleek, smoothly-attired zooter twirling his key chain and eying the girls on the corner. The robust rosy-

cheeked young priest from Fordham, with some of his jayvee basket-
ballers on a night of "good clean fun," and the cadaverous morphine-
addict stumbling by full of shuddering misery in search of a fix. The
plug-ugly thuggish panhandler with the beery breath bumming a
nickel from the embarrassed Methodist preacher waiting for his lug-
gage in front of the Dixie Hotel. The hairy old Babylonian gliding
lecherously towards an evening of pleasure in the Turkish Baths, and
the trim little shopgirl hurrying home from work to take care of her
aged father. The lissome blonde Hollywood "starlet" in dark glasses
and mink in a Cadillac with her bald-headed "producer," and the two
Vassar girls from Westchester with best-seller novels. Then the bleak
young Negress who swept floors, in an old coat and cotton stockings,
shambling along. The sad young soldier-boy, Private John Smith,
U.S.A., wearing campaign ribbons, lonely and haunted, and the Lieutenant Commander, Third Naval District, Navy "E" for excellence in
procurement, glancing at his watch impatiently, then waving at his
blonde (he met her last month at the Waldorf bar) as she arrives in a
cab, calling, "Here I am, darling!" Private Smith watched all this
from the sidewalk in front of the White Rose bar and grille.

Peter watched too: he knew all these things and they were impressed in his heart, they horrified him. These were only some of the
lives of the world, yet all the lives of the world came from the single
human soul, and his soul was like their souls. He could never turn
away in disgust and judgment. He could turn away angrily, but he
would always come back and look again.

As Peter stood there, he recognized three young men strolling up
the street. They were a strange trio: one was a hoodlum, one was a
dope addict, and the third was a poet.

The hoodlum—Jack—was a sleek, handsome youngster from Tenth
Avenue, who claimed that he was born "on a barge in the East River"
eighteen years before. He was well-dressed, seemingly composed in his
bearing and quiet, almost dignified, in his manner. It was only that
he could never concentrate; he was always looking around as though
anticipating something. His eyes were hard and blank, almost elderly
in their stony meaningless calm. He talked in a swift, high-pitched,
nervous voice, and kept looking away stonily, twirling his key chain.

The dope addict, whose only known name was Junkey, was a small, dark, Arabic-looking man with an oval face and huge blue eyes that were lidded wearily always, with the huge lids of a mask. He moved about with the noiseless glide of an Arab, his expression always weary, indifferent, yet somehow astonished too, aware of everything. He had the look of a man who is sincerely miserable in the world.

The poet—Leon Levinsky—had been a classmate of Peter's at college, and was now a merchant seaman of sorts, sailing coastwise on coalboats to Norfolk or New Orleans. He was wearing a strapped raincoat, a Paisley scarf, and dark-rimmed glasses with the air of an intellectual. He carried two slim volumes under his arm, the works of Rimbaud and W. H. Auden, and he smoked his cigarette stuck in a red holder.

They came along the sidewalk, Jack the hoodlum swaggering slowly, Junkey padding along like an Arab in the Casbah, and Leon Levinsky, lip-pursing, meditative, absorbed in thought, twinkling along beside them with his Charley Chaplin feet flapping out, puffing absently on the cigarette-holder. They strolled in the lights.

Peter walked up and greeted them.

"So you're back finally!" cried Levinsky, grinning eagerly. "I've been thinking of you lately for some reason or other—actually I guess it's because I've so much to tell you!"

"Why don't we go and sit down?" proposed Junkey wearily. "Let's sit in the cafeteria window there and we can talk and keep an eye on the street."

They went in the cafeteria, got coffee, and sat down by the windows, where Junkey could resume his pale vigil of Forty-Second Street—a vigil that went on a good eighteen hours a day, and sometimes, when he had no place to sleep, twenty-four hours around the clock. It was the same with Jack—the same anxious vigil of the street, from which the watchers of the Street could never turn their eyes without some piercing sense of loss, some rankling anguish that they had "missed out" on something. Junkey always sat facing the street, and when he talked, sometimes with intense earnestness, his eyes kept nevertheless going back and forth as he combed the street sweepingly under drooping eyelids. Even though Peter and Leon Levinsky sat with their backs to the window, they could not help turning now and then just to see.

Leon Levinsky was about nineteen years old. He was one of the strangest, most curiously exalted youngsters Peter had ever known. He was not unlike Alexander Panos, in a sense, and Peter had been drawn to him for this reason. Levinsky was an eager, intense, sharply intelligent boy of Russian-Jewish parentage who rushed around New York in a perpetual sweat of emotional activity, back and forth in the streets from friend to friend, room to room, apartment to apartment. He "knew everybody" and "knew everything," was always bearing tidings and messages from "the others," full of catastrophe. He brimmed and flooded over day and night with a thousand different thoughts and conversations and small horrors, delights, perplexities, deities, discoveries, ecstasies, fears. He stared gog-eyed at the world and was full of musings, lip-pursings, subway broodings—all of which rushed forth in torrents of complex conversation whenever he confronted someone. He knew almost everyone Peter knew, a few thousand others Peter did not know. Like young Panos, Leon Levinsky was also likely to show up suddenly morose and brooding, or simply disappear from the "scene" for months and Peter liked that too. He lived alone in some rooming house downtown. Before that he had lived with his family in the Lower East Side, where he had read a thousand books late at night and dreamed of becoming a great labor leader someday. That was all over with now, that was his "poor little Jew's past," as he put it.

"But just one thing, Pete," said Levinsky now, holding his chin judiciously and gazing at Peter with glittering eyes, "I wanted to talk to you about that Alexander friend of yours, the poet in the Army who sends you his social conscience bleatings about the brotherhood of man. I wanted to ask you not to class me with that—that sentimental fool, you might say. Don't be offended. As a matter of fact I understand and even appreciate your reverence for him—which is so *gone* for a person like you, really. On top of that I'm even honored that you should consider me an Alexander. But there are things so much more important now, at least more complex and interesting and illuminated you see, really, things going on right now, more penetrating and more intelligent somehow than your Alexander, your smalltown Rupert Brooke, your joy-and-beauty poet of the hinterlands—"

But Peter was about three years older than Levinsky and therefore he listened to all this with smiling indulgence. The young hoodlum Jack never had any idea what Levinsky was talking about, he just sat and looked around. Junkey, with his eyes sarcastically lidded, his mouth turned down at the corners in a mask-like expression of weary indifference and misery, listened to everything with earnest attentiveness and knowledge. He was wise in his own right.

Ever since Peter had known Levinsky, it was a matter of listening to his gentle torrential chastisements about his own ignorance and blindness to things. Levinsky was always urging him to "get psychoanalyzed" or to "come down" from his "character heights" and so on—a continual attempt to convert him to his, Levinsky's, point of view, for what reasons Peter could never understand.

"I do admit that there's a certain dignity to your soul," said Levinsky, jiggling his knee, "but it's not a sadness of understanding, it's really a neurotic failure to see yourself clearly. One more thing, Pete, I wanted to ask when I can meet your family, I'd like to meet your father again and some of your brothers . . . especially Francis.

"And now," he went on in the same breath, sticking a fresh cigarette in the holder, "I must tell you everything." He lit the cigarette avidly. "A lot of things have been happening since you've been gone. I see quite a bit of Judie—your Judie—and sometimes she is most charming to me, although for the most part she is not. I've had many long conversations with Kenneth Wood—yes, I know him now, I met him through Dennison: and of course I've got so much to tell you about Dennison, but first we'll talk of Kenneth Wood. In the first place I wanted to ask you a few questions about him: you met him in the merchant marine, didn't you? I want to know what kind of family he has."

After months at sea Peter was only too pleased to supply the necessary fuel for Levinsky's talk. "I've been to Kenny's house only once and I met his father and great-grandmother. The old lady is close to a hundred years old and she still remembers old Abilene—"

"What is that?" demanded Levinsky, impatient and curious.

"That's where they made their fortune, way back. It's an old cowtown in Kansas . . . it was very wild in those days."

"Oh, never mind that nonsense. I want to know about *them*—I want something intelligent—"

"I'm telling you! His father is a handsome sort of man-about-town who's in some business on Wall Street. His mother's divorced and remarried to an Austrian count. How's that?"

"Hmm," mused Levinsky. "Then they still have money. Where do they live, what kind of a place is it?"

"It's an apartment towers on the East River, swanky as hell."

"What's his father like? What does he *think?*"

"How should I know!"

"The grandmother, the grandmother!" cried Levinsky—"what's *her* value, what's her vision, give me *information!*"

"Man, how annoying you do get!" spoke up Junkey suddenly with an earnest glance at Levinsky. "Give him a chance to get his bearings, the guy's been at sea, he's trying to relax and enjoy himself, ever since we've been sitting here you've been telling him what's wrong with him"—and with this Junkey returned his agonized gaze to the window.

"That's true," admitted Levinsky, deeply absorbed, "but it's somehow beside the point." And he suddenly giggled again, but in a moment fixed Peter with his beady glittering eyes. "I don't suppose you've ever heard of Waldo Meister?"

"A little . . . not much."

"Waldo Meister is a dilettante. It seems that he is a friend of Kenneth's family, a friend of his father's through some old business matters. They're *all rich,* don't you see!"

"Who?"

"Kenny and his family, Waldo Meister, and, of course, Dennison— all these evil figures of decayed families."

"What's evil about them?"

"I shall tell you, but first:—it seems that Waldo is a rare and curious person. He has only one arm. He's ugly, quite horrible, but impressive sort of. That is, impressive to everyone but Kenny Wood, who is eviler than Waldo somehow."

"What are you raving about!" cried Peter, frowning. "I shipped out with Kenny Wood, he's just a happy-go-lucky kid. What are you trying to say?"

"Don't give me that simple stuff. Nothing is simple, everything is complex and evil and audacious too . . . and that goes for your Kenny Wood. And let's not start arguing about simple normal happy-go-lucky Americans. Let me talk. Waldo is an execrable man straight out of some fin-de-siècle romance, a decaying Dorian Gray, a monster, and finally, a magician of darkness.—I'm using these symbols in a poem incidentally—an evil magician surrounded by the decline of

the West on all sides . . . despised like Philoctetes, avoided, yet
hypnotic and compelling . . . a doctor of horror, an organ-grinder of
the angels surrounded by the vulgar pigeons of the West."

"What's all this?"

"I'm just amusing myself. To continue: out of the pure madness
of his position in the world, this amazing Waldo Meister has turned
right around to foist an even greater madness upon the world. There
being only one person in the world who openly berates him for his
physical disability, who openly despises him, mocks him, taunts him—
your so-called simple-kid Kenny Wood—Waldo turns right around
and refuses the company of anyone else but Kenny himself. A really
sordid yet angelic situation. Strange angels."

"Kenny wouldn't mock a cripple. Who *is* this man?"

"I was coming to that. Before Waldo lost his arm in an automobile
crackup, he was a close friend of Dennison's, they went to the same
private school together, later to Princeton, they knew Kenny through
his father, who was a gay blade and was everywhere, and when
Kenny began drinking as a youngster he went out on binges with
them. He was driving the car one night drunk, only about fourteen
years old, and cracked it up somewhere in Long Island, and one of
the girls in the party almost died from injuries."

"I never knew about that crackup. I knew Kenny was a wild guy
but I never knew about this Waldo guy," uttered Peter vaguely.

"Can't you see what an amazing situation it is?—Kenny is responsible for Waldo's physical defect, and he mocks him for it, and Waldo
accepts his mockery with gratitude almost. It's the most evil and symbolic and decadent situation!—amazing! But I have a million other
things to tell you, it all fits into the picture, a great canvas of disintegration and sheer horror. Right across the street from here there's an
amusement center—see it there?" he pointed eagerly. "It's called the
Nickel-O, see the big sign?—and there you have, at around four in the
morning, the final scenes of disintegrative decay: old drunks, whores,
queers, all kinds of characters, hoods, junkies, all the castoffs of
bourgeois society milling in there, with nothing to do really but just
stay there, sheltered from the darkness as it were.

"You see how bright the lights are?—they have those horrible bluish
neons that illuminate every pore of your skin, your whole soul finally,
and when you go in there among all the children of the sad American

paradise, you can only stare at them, in a Benzedrine depression, don't you see, or with that sightless stare that comes from too much horror. All faces are blue and greenish and sickly livid. In the end, everyone looks like a Zombie, you realize that everyone is dead, locked up in the sad psychoses of themselves. It goes on all night, everyone milling around uncertainly among the ruins of bourgeois civilization, seeking each other, don't you see, but so stultified by their upbringings somehow, or by the disease of the age, that they can only stumble about and stare indignantly at one another."

"A mad description of the Nickel-O if I ever heard one," remarked Junkey with approval.

"But there's more to it than that!" cried Levinsky, almost jumping up and down. "Under the bluish lights you're able to see all the defects of the skin, they all look as though they're falling apart." He giggled here. "Really! You see monstrous blemishes or great hairs sticking out of moles or peeling scars—they take on a greenish tint under the lights and look really frightful. Everybody looks like a geek!"

"A geek?"

"The drunkards or addicts or whatnot who eat the heads off live chickens at carnivals . . . didn't you ever hear about geeks? Oh, the whole point's there!" he cried happily. "Everybody in the world has come to feel like a geek . . . can't you see it? Can't you sense what's going on around you? All the neurosis and the restrictive morality and the scatological repressions and the suppressed aggressiveness has finally gained the upper hand on humanity—everyone is becoming a geek! Everyone feels like a Zombie, and somewhere at the ends of the night, the great magician, the great Dracula-figure of modern disintegration and madness, the wise genius behind it all, the Devil if you will, is running the whole thing with his string of oaths and his hexes."

"I don't know," said Peter. "I don't believe I feel like a geek yet. I don't think I'll buy that."

"Oh, come, come! Then why do you have to mention it, why do you have to deny it?" grinned Levinsky slyly. "Really, now, I know you, I can tell that you have horrible guilt-feelings, it's written all over you, and you're confused by it, you don't know what it is. Admit it at least. As a matter of fact you told me once yourself."

"Admit what?"

"That you feel guilty of something, you feel unclean, almost diseased, you have nightmares, you have occasional visions of horror,
feelings of spiritual geekishness— Don't you see, everybody feels like
that now."

"I have a feeling like that," stammered Peter, almost blushing, "that
is . . . of being guilty, but I don't know, it's the war and everything,
I think, the guys I knew who got killed, things like that. And well,
hell!—things aren't like they used to be before the war." For a moment
he was almost afraid that there was some truth in Levinsky's insane
idea, certainly he had never felt so useless and foolish and sorrowful
before in his life.

"It's more than *that*," pursued Levinsky with a long, indulgent,
sarcastic smile. "You yourself have just admitted it now. I've been
making a little research of my own, I find that everybody has it. Some
hate to admit it, but they finally reveal that they have it. He-he! And
it's amazing who discovered this disease—"

"What disease?"

At this, Levinsky and Junkey exchanged secret smiles, and turned
them upon the bewildered Peter. "It's the great molecular comedown.
Of course that's only my own whimsical name for it at the moment.
It's really an atomic disease, you see. But I'll have to explain it to you
so you'll know, at least. It's death finally reclaiming life, the scurvy
of the soul at last, a kind of universal cancer. It's got a real medieval
ghastliness, like the plague, only this time it will ruin everything,
don't you see?"

"No, I don't see."

"You will eventually. Everybody is going to fall apart, disintegrate,
all character-structures based on tradition and uprightness and so-
called morality will slowly rot away, people will get the hives right on
their hearts, great crabs will cling to their brains . . . their lungs will
crumble. But now we only have the early symptoms, the disease isn't
really underway yet—virus X only."

"Are you serious?" laughed Peter.

"Perfectly serious. I'm positive about the disease, the real physical
disease. We all have it!"

"Who's we?"

"Everybody—Junkey and me, and all the cats, more than that,

everybody, you, Kenny, Waldo, Dennison. Listen! You know about molecules, they're made up according to a number of atoms arranged just so around a proton or something. Well, the 'just-so' is falling apart. The molecule will suddenly collapse, leaving just atoms, smashed atoms of people, nothing at all . . . as it all was in the beginning of the world. Don't you see, it's just the beginning of the end of the Geneseean world. It's certainly the beginning of the end of the world as we know it now, and then there'll be a non-Geneseean world without all that truck about sin and the sweat of your brow. He-he! It's great! Whatever it is, I'm all for it. It may be a carnival of horror at first—but something strange will come of it, I'm convinced. But these are my own ideas and I'm deviating from the conception we've all reached about the atomic disease." He mused with perfect seriousness.

"Listen, Leon, why don't you go back to becoming a radical labor leader," laughed Peter.

"Oh, it all ties in. But wait, I wasn't finished. The Nickel-O has become a great symbol among all of us, it's the place where the atomic disease was first noticed and from which it will spread, slowly and insidiously, that place there across the street!" he cried gleefully. "You'll see great tycoons of industry suddenly falling apart and going mad, you'll see preachers at the pulpit suddenly exploding—there'll be marijuana fumes seeping out of the Stock Exchange. College professors will suddenly go cross-eyed and start showing their behinds to one another. I'm not explaining it properly . . . but that doesn't matter, you'll begin to see it yourself, now that you're back. And now," he resumed gravely, "I wanted to tell you about Dennison. Incidentally he wants to see you, he heard your ship was back, go see him tomorrow. Dennison, I must tell you, has dropped his old habits of going to a psychoanalyst and idly biding his time learning jiu-jitsu and so on, and has begun an active participation in the phantasmagoria of modern life."

"What's he done?"

"He's got a morphine habit. He's moved to a new apartment now, down on Henry Street, right under the Manhattan bridge, a dirty old cold water flat with peeling disintegrating walls. His sister Mary's there with him taking care of the baby. Junkey sometimes lives there too"—and he bowed to Junkey graciously—"and the whole place is

mad day and night, overrun with people who dash about getting morphine prescriptions from dishonest doctors. Mary takes Benzedrine,
there's a mad character called Clint who comes around all the time
with marijuana, and the whole place is a madhouse. You've got to see
it—especially Dennison with his baby son in one hand and a hypo
needle in the other, a marvelous sight."

"You don't really think it's marvelous. Incidentally, how's Dennison's wife coming along?"

"No—it's more than marvelous, really, and besides I've been talking
to you almost maliciously all this time, insincerely in a way, of course.
Oh, his wife's supposed to be dying now . . . she's still in that sani-
tarium in California or someplace. We've got to have a long serious
talk, alone. That's another thing. Where are you going now, what
are you going to do tonight?" Levinsky demanded eagerly.

"I'm going right up to Judie's."

"But we must talk. When? when?—and remember, I want to meet
your family. Can't I go to dinner there sometime? There are so many
things to settle, everything's happening, everything's changing—and
also I want you to read some of my new poetry, and I want you to
come in the Nickel-O with me some night so I can point everything
out to you in its proper order."

"Well, all right," agreed the amenable Peter. He got up to go, but
Levinsky jumped up solicitously.

"You're not leaving now, are you?" he cried.

"Yeah, I'm going to see my gal now. . . ."

"Ah! I knew something like that was coming, something about
peace and normalcy and whatever else you may call it. . . ."

Peter looked gravely at him.

"Oh, never mind," snickered Levinsky. "So you're going to see
Judie and forget all about the atomic disease in her arms. Actually,
don't you see, I'm all in favor of it, I still believe in human love at the
ends of the night. But may I ride on the subway with you?" he asked.

"It's okay with me," said Peter, who was growing more and more
sullen at these sly manipulations. On the other hand, Levinsky had
been like this ever since Peter had known him, and he understood
somehow.

"You *do* feel like a geek, don't you?" Peter smiled. "But you know
all the things you're talking about, people don't want them! They want

peace and quiet . . . even if those things don't exist. Everybody's trying to be decent, that's all."

Levinsky was aroused with interest. "Let them *try!*" he brought out with an imitation of a snarl, and a malicious-looking smile—a smile he had learned from Dennison.

"There you go imitating Will Dennison again!" Peter taunted.

"Nonsense, my days of sitting at Dennison's feet are over—the position is almost reversed, in a sense. He listens to my ideas now with great respect, where it used to be just the other way around. Pete," said Levinsky eagerly, "wait for me just a minute while I make a phone call. I'll ride on the subway with you for a very specific reason— I want to prove to you that everyone is mad on the subway. Everybody's radioactive and don't know it." And with this he rushed off eagerly.

At that moment someone went by on the sidewalk. Junkey, starting with a jump, suddenly vanished from the cafeteria, almost before Peter noticed it.

The young hoodlum Jack leaned forward to Peter confidentially. "Junkey's connection just went by outside, the guy he buys the dope from. I don't go for that stuff, it costs too much, you get all hung up on it, then you're sick all the time when you can't get it." There was almost a note of conspiracy in these words, the first he had spoken all night. Now that they were alone at the table, the young hoodlum had grown quite voluble. "I tried it once, it gave me a good kick, but then I got sick and I puked. I like to drink myself, to get lushed . . . don't you?' he demanded anxiously, peering at Peter blankly. "Listen, you know? I got something on the fire that if it comes out right I'll never have to worry about money again, I'll be all set, man. A plan, you know?"

"Uh-huh," said Peter vaguely.

Jack gave him a significant look, paused awhile looking over his shoulder. Then he leaned forward, almost whispering. "I know a guy, see, and, well, last week I picked up on a sap from him, a blackjack unnerstand? So then I—well, you know what these guys are always talking about, that kid Levinsky, that's all right, you know?—sit around and talk and pass the time of day. But I believe in doin' something, you know? Action! They talk all the time, him and Junkey. But I met this guy in a bar, this is the plan I'm telling you, and this guy claims he's got all his money stashed in his room up in the Bronx, money and lots of suits and shoes and everything. The guy was drunk, and he's from out of town, lonesome, a shipyard worker, all that. Shipyard workers are always lonesome," he added vaguely. "I used to work in a shipyard myself, but I don't like to work, you know? . . . I don't dig guys tellin' me what to do all the time. I told him, this shipyard worker, I could fix him up with girls, see?" He paused significantly.

"Can you?" grinned Peter—who had never seen him with a girl. He was always standing around the street ruefully looking at girls swinging by under the lights.

"Well, sure, man—I know hundreds of 'em," Jack cried almost resentfully. "Girls! I know a guy who's got a way with 'em, you know?—a pimp this guy is. Well, on Saturday night I'm gonna go up there to this shipyard worker's house, with a girl I know, and beat him up and walk out with all his money and clothes. I won't even bring the blackjack. I'll just crack him a couple with my fists"—and he bared his fists from under the table and showed them to Peter. "That's all, man, that's the way I'll do it, I'll belt him a couple! wham! wham! I got it all figured out, one in the solar plexus, one on the point of the chin. Then I can kick him in the neck too . . . that knocks out a guy, you know?" he whispered earnestly. Then, confidentially: "Did you ever fight a guy? Did you ever knock out a guy? My brother's a great fighter, you know? How about comin' up there with me tomorrow night?" he concluded nervously, looking around the cafeteria over his shoulder.

Before Peter could muster up any sort of reply, Levinsky came rushing back. They left Jack sitting alone, worrying and brooding anxiously, and went out to take the subway.

"Everyone's mad around here," commented Peter sullenly, with a sense of foolish loneliness.

"But that's not the half of it! Just *wait* till you see my subway experiment which proves conclusively that the atomic disease has already made great headway!"

"You're not serious about all this, Leon! What the hell's happened to you?" cried Peter, exasperated.

For the first time that evening Levinsky grew serious, or seemed to, pursing his lips judiciously, glancing at Peter gravely and nodding his head. "Yes, I'm serious, but only in a way you see—"

"Only in a way—bull!"

"But no. Actually, you see, in a sense it's the invention of Dennison's sister Mary. There's no doubt about the fact that Mary Dennison is mad, but that's only because she wants to be mad. What she has to say about the world, about everybody falling apart, about everybody clawing aggressively at one another in one grand finale of our glorious culture, about the madness in high places and the insane disorganized stupidity of the people who let themselves be told what to do and what to think by charlatans—all that is true! All the advertising men who dream up unreal bugaboos for people to flee from, like B.O. or if you don't have such-and-such a color to your wash you're an outcast from society. Listen!—all the questionnaires you have to fill out in this bureaucratic system of ours asking all kinds of imaginary questions. Don't you see it, man? The world's going mad! Therefore it's quite possible there *must be* some sort of disease that's started. There's only one real conclusion to be drawn. In Mary's words, everybody got the atomic disease, everybody's radioactive."

"It's a dumb conclusion," muttered Peter. "I wish you'd be serious."

"The amazing thing is this!" cried Levinsky gaily. "All the horror that Mary Dennison sees, and incidentally participates in—and there's more horror in that girl and in her view of the clawing world than Dennison himself ever dreamed in his greatest heroic moments—the amazing thing is that it all might be *awfully* true. Now I'm serious. Supposing it were! supposing it were! what then?"

"That's silly," muttered Peter again.

"But wait! There's a lot more to it!"

They were in the subway station. Levinsky picked out an old newspaper from a trash barrel and began folding it and tearing out sections, with a grave air, glancing slyly at Peter as he did all this.

"What does this remind you of?" he demanded.

"What?"

"This!—tearing and folding this old newspaper, haven't you ever seen mad people, how they behave?"

"Yes," laughed Peter, suddenly inexplicably amused by the performance, "that's pretty good."

When a train pulled in, they got on, and Levinsky stationed Peter at the door to keep a sharp eye on everyone in the car. "Remember," he instructed gleefully, "you watch closely anybody I pick on with

my . . . my magical newspaper performance. With both you and I
staring at the victim, he'll begin to feel vibrations of paranoid persecu-
tion. You'll see how everyone has become essentially mad—the whole
insane world." He flung his arms around with a look of rapture. "Now
watch."

Levinsky sat down, wild-eyed and fantastic in his military raincoat
and flowery scarf, and the train got underway on the express run up
to Seventy-Second Street. He sat opposite a distinguished-looking old
man who had a little boy of four with him—a melancholy severe old
man staring meditatively into space, full of stately thoughts, and a
gleeful little child looking around at everyone with curiosity. They
sat there holding hands as the train rocked along.

Levinsky opened up his newspaper and seemed to begin reading it,
but suddenly Peter realized with horror that there was a hole torn in
the middle of the page, through which the incredible Levinsky was
intently studying the old man across the aisle. At first no one noticed
anything. But gradually, of course, the old gentleman's eyes roved to
Levinsky's newspaper. There, with an awful shock, instead of headlines he saw a great living picture, the beady glittering eyes of a madman burning triumphantly into his through a hole in the page.

Peter saw the old man flush. He himself had to turn away, blushing
furiously with mortification. Yet at the same time he felt a wicked and
delightful sense of pleasure. He had to watch, and he peeked around
the door in a convulsion of horror and glee. What was most incredible
and funny was that Levinsky himself continued to stare—through the
hole—intently at the old man with perfect gravity and seriousness, as
though he believed with his whole heart in the full significance of his
experiment.

To cap everything, just as everyone across the aisle was beginning
to notice Levinsky's stupendous act—and indeed, just as they began to
fidget nervously, and look around furtively, sometimes glancing over
to Peter as though they sensed his conspiracy in the matter (though he
tried to look innocent and unconcerned), just as they were beginning
to look to each other for confirmation of the fact that it was Levinsky
who was mad, not *they*—the madman himself with delicate propriety,
pleasure, and gentle absorption, began tearing strips out of the newspaper and dropping them to the floor one by one from gentle fingers.
Meanwhile he smiled fondly at the page, never looking away, but

eager, intense, pleased, and preoccupied with what he was doing, alone in the joys of pleasant perusal.

It was the maddest thing Peter had ever seen. Levinsky was perfect in his performance, solemn and serious. For just a moment he looked up from what he was doing to stick his forefinger in his ear and hold it there in deep thought, as if his brains might come spilling out if he didn't hold them in.

It was even more horrible to realize the small pitiable truth in his statement that everyone in the subway was somewhat insane. Some who noticed what Levinsky was doing looked away nervously and preferred to imagine that nothing at all was happening; they were perfectly stolid in their refusal of the situation, they sat like stones and brooded. Others were irritable and undertook every now and then to glance suspiciously at the performance; they seemed indignant and refused to look any more, they would not "be tricked" as Levinsky considered it. And there were those in the car who simply did not notice; they were coming home from work too tired to notice anything. Some were reading the paper, others were sleeping; some were chatting eagerly, others were just brooding without having looked, and others thought that he was some harmless nut and paid no attention.

There was one element Levinsky had not bargained for—the people in the car who had a profound curiosity and everlasting concern with things and a sense of funniness. All these elements, including the old gentleman's little companion, a Negro coming home from work, an eager young student, and a well-dressed man carrying a box of candy, stared with delight at Levinsky's antics. The old gentleman, who was the direct victim of the performance, was too painfully involved in the personal aspects of the matter to make up his mind whether it was funny, or absurd, or horrible: he was fixed by a pair of mad burning eyes and could only look away with deep embarrassment.

Meanwhile he held on to the little boy's hand, almost frightened for his sake now, and certainly confused, while the little boy stared gape-jawed at Levinsky.

"What's he doing?" he cried, turning to the old man.

The old man shook his head warningly, tightening his grip on the little hand. The little boy was fidgety, and sat with his feet up on the seat gazing almost solemnly at Levinsky.

Suddenly the little boy unleashed a crazy screaming laugh and bounced off the seat across the aisle and stuck his face in the hole in the newspaper and began staring pop-eyed at Levinsky with huge delight, knowing it was a game, jumping up and down and clapping his hands and giggling with glee, and crying: "Do some more, mister, Hey, do some more!"

And at this, the eager young student, the Negro man, and the man with the box of candy all smiled and chuckled heartily, even Peter doubled up laughing helplessly—and then it was altogether too much. Levinsky himself became embarrassed, looked bashfully around the car at all the faces, blushed, stared sad-eyed at the mess he had made on the floor, snickered, and looked helplessly towards Peter. The whole experiment became disorganized. Others in the car who had been frightened or indignant a moment before began to laugh also. Everybody was grinning and craning and looking around and sensing something funny. Peter, like the rat deserting the sinking ship, hurried into the next car and hid himself in a corner and tried to keep from exploding. Once he peeked back to see Levinsky sitting there among all those people, absently musing.

He met the sad, subdued Leon Levinsky on the platform when they got to Seventy-Second Street.

"But don't you see, Pete, it all worked out the way I told you," he said, fingering his lips, "except for the little kid. Actually though," he reflected seriously, "it was in a way beautiful, because it showed that children cannot recognize madness. That is, they understand what is mad and what is not mad, they simply *understand*. And finally—they haven't had time to burden themselves with character structure and personality armors and systems of moral prejudice and God knows what. Therefore they're free to live and laugh, and free to love—like those few other men in the car."

Peter gazed at him with amazement.

Levinsky went back to the downtown side of the platform—while Peter had to go uptown to see Judie. When he last saw him, Levinsky was standing there among the subway crowds, gaping around and musing darkly about the puzzle of himself and everybody else, as he would always do.

JACK KEROUAC

Swinging

"You've got to go, man, go." This was a new breed: car thieves, hop-heads, bop cats linked by an intensity that transformed them into seekers after Revelation on the superhighways of the U.S. This selection is from On the Road, *which gave the Beat Generation its first chance at respectability, making the movement itself more than a form of "immature exhibitionism." With the publication of this novel,* Rebels Without a Cause *became fashionable, worthy of the attention of literary-minded fashion magazines and other professional guardians of our culture.*

HE CAME TO THE DOOR stark naked and it might have been the President knocking for all he cared. He received the world in the raw. "Sal!" he said with genuine awe. "I didn't think you'd actually do it. You've finally come to *me*."

"Yep," I said. "Everything fell apart in me. How are things with you?"

"Not so good, not so good. But we've got a million things to talk about. Sal, the time has *fi-nally* come for us to talk and get with it." We agreed it was about time and

went in. My arrival was somewhat like the coming of the strange
most evil angel in the home of the snow-white fleece, as Dean and I
began talking excitedly in the kitchen downstairs, which brought
forth sobs from upstairs. Everything I said to Dean was answered with
a wild, whispering, shuddering "Yes!" Camille knew what was going
to happen. Apparently Dean had been quiet for a few months; now
the angel had arrived and he was going mad again. "What's the
matter with her?" I whispered.

He said, "She's getting worse and worse, man, she cries and makes
tantrums, won't let me out to see Slim Gaillard, gets mad every time
I'm late, then when I stay home she won't talk to me and says I'm an
utter beast." He ran upstairs to soothe her. I heard Camille yell, "You're
a liar, you're a liar, you're a liar!" I took the opportunity to examine
the very wonderful house they had. It was a two-story crooked, rickety
wooden cottage in the middle of tenements, right on top of Russian
Hill with a view of the bay; it had four rooms, three upstairs and one
immense sort of basement kitchen downstairs. The kitchen door
opened onto a grassy court where washlines were. In back of the
kitchen was a storage room where Dean's old shoes still were caked
an inch thick with Texas mud from the night the Hudson got stuck
on the Brazos River. Of course the Hudson was gone; Dean hadn't
been able to make further payments on it. He had no car at all now.
Their second baby was accidentally coming. It was horrible to hear
Camille sobbing so. We couldn't stand it and went out to buy beer
and brought it back to the kitchen. Camille finally went to sleep or
spent the night staring blankly at the dark. I had no idea what was
really wrong, except perhaps Dean had driven her mad after all.

After my last leaving Frisco he had gone crazy over Marylou again
and spent months haunting her apartment on Divisadero, where every
night she had a different sailor in and he peeked down through her
mail-slot and could see her bed. There he saw Marylou sprawled in
the mornings with a boy. He trailed her around town. He wanted
absolute proof that she was a whore. He loved her, he sweated over
her. Finally he got hold of some bad green, as it's called in the trade
—green, uncured marijuana—quite by mistake, and smoked too much
of it.

"The first day," he said, "I lay rigid as a board in bed and couldn't
move or say a word; I just looked straight up with my eyes open wide.

I could hear buzzing in my head and saw all kinds of wonderful technicolor visions and felt wonderful. The second day everything came to me, EVERYTHING I'd ever done or known or read or heard of or conjectured came back to me and rearranged itself in my mind in a brand-new logical way and because I could think of nothing else in the interior concerns of holding and catering to the amazement and gratitude I felt, I kept saying, 'Yes, yes, yes, yes.' Not loud. Just 'Yes,' real quiet, and these green tea visions lasted until the third day. I had understood everything by then, my whole life was decided, I knew I loved Marylou, I knew I had to find my father wherever he is and save him, I knew you were my buddy et cetera, I knew how great Carlo is. I knew a thousand things about everybody everywhere. Then the third day I began having a terrible series of waking nightmares, and they were so absolutely horrible and grisly and green that I just lay there doubled up with my hands around my knees, saying, 'Oh, oh, oh, ah, oh . . .' The neighbors heard me and sent for a doctor. Camille was away with the baby, visiting her folks. The whole neighborhood was concerned. They came in and found me lying on the bed with my arms stretched out forever. Sal, I ran to Marylou with some of that tea. And do you know that the same thing happened to that dumb little box?—the same visions, the same logic, the same final decision about everything, the view of all truths in one painful lump leading to nightmares and pain—ack! Then I knew I loved her so much I wanted to kill her. I ran home and beat my head on the wall. I ran to Ed Dunkel; he's back in Frisco with Galatea; I asked him about a guy we know has a gun, I went to the guy, I got the gun, I ran to Marylou, I looked down the mail-slot, she was sleeping with a guy, had to retreat and hesitate, came back in an hour, I barged in, she was alone—and I gave her the gun and told her to kill me. She held the gun in her hand the longest time. I asked her for a sweet dead pact. She didn't want. I said one of us had to die. She said no. I beat my head on the wall. Man, I was out of my mind. She'll tell you, she talked me out of it."

"Then what happened?"

"That was months ago—after you left. She finally married a used-car dealer, dumb bastit has promised to kill me if he finds me, if necessary I shall have to defend myself and kill him and I'll go to San Quentin, 'cause, Sal, one more rap of *any* kind and I go to San

Quentin for life—that's the end of me. Bad hand and all." He showed me his hand. I hadn't noticed in the excitement that he had suffered a terrible accident to his hand. "I hit Marylou on the brow on February twenty-sixth at six o'clock in the evening—in fact six-ten, because I remember I had to make my hotshot freight in an hour and twenty minutes—the last time we met and the last time we decided everything, and now listen to this: my thumb only deflected off her brow and she didn't even have a bruise and in fact laughed, but my thumb broke above the wrist and a horrible doctor made a setting of the bones that was difficult and took three separate castings, twenty-three combined hours of sitting on hard benches waiting, et cetera, and the final cast had a traction pin stuck through the tip of my thumb, so in April when they took off the cast the pin infected my bone and I developed osteomyelitis which has become chronic, and after an operation which failed and a month in a cast the result was the amputation of a wee bare piece off the tip-ass end."

He unwrapped the bandages and showed me. The flesh, about half an inch, was missing under the nail.

"It got from worse to worse. I had to support Camille and Amy and had to work as fast as I could at Firestone as mold man, curing recapped tires and later hauling big hunnerd-fifty-pound tires from the floor to the top of the cars—could only use my good hand and kept banging the bad—broke it again, had it reset again, and it's getting all infected and swoled again. So now I take care of baby while Camille works. You see? Heeby-jeebies, I'm classification three-A, jazz-hounded Moriarty has a sore butt, his wife gives him daily injections of penicillin for his thumb, which produces hives, for he's allergic. He must take sixty thousand units of Fleming's juice within a month. He must take one tablet every four hours for this month to combat allergy produced from his juice. He must take codeine aspirin to relieve the pain in his thumb. He must have surgery on his leg for an inflamed cyst. He must rise next Monday at six A.M. to get his teeth cleaned. He must see a foot doctor twice a week for treatment. He must take cough syrup each night. He must blow and snort constantly to clear his nose, which has collapsed just under the bridge where an operation some years ago weakened it. He lost his thumb on his throwing arm. Greatest seventy-yard passer in the history of New Mexico State Reformatory. And yet—and yet, I've never felt better and finer and happier with the world and to see little lovely children playing in the sun and I am so glad to see you, my fine gone wonderful Sal, and I know, I *know* everything will be all right. You'll see her tomorrow, my terrific darling beautiful daughter can now stand alone for thirty seconds at a time, she weighs twenty-two pounds, is twenty-nine inches long. I've just figured out she is thirty-one-and-a-quarter-per-cent English, twenty-seven-and-a-half-per-cent Irish, twenty-five-per-cent German, eight-and-three-quarters-per-cent Dutch, seven-and-a-half-per-cent Scotch, one-hundred-per-cent wonderful." He fondly congratulated me for the book I had finished, which was now accepted by the publishers. "We know life, Sal, we're growing older, each of us, little by little, and are coming to know things. What you tell me about your life I understand well, I've always dug your feelings, and now in fact you're ready to hook up with a real great girl if you can only find her and cultivate her and make her mind your soul as I have tried so hard with these damned women of mine. Shit! shit! shit!" he yelled.

And in the morning Camille threw both of us out, baggage and all. It began when we called Roy Johnson, old Denver Roy, and had him come over for beer, while Dean minded the baby and did the dishes and the wash in the backyard but did a sloppy job of it in his excitement. Johnson agreed to drive us to Mill City to look for Remi Boncœur. Camille came in from work at the doctor's office and gave us all the sad look of a harassed woman's life. I tried to show this haunted woman that I had no mean intentions concerning her home life by saying hello to her and talking as warmly as I could, but she knew it was a con and maybe one I'd learned from Dean, and only gave a brief smile. In the morning there was a terrible scene: she lay on the bed sobbing, and in the midst of this I suddenly had the need to go to the bathroom, and the only way I could get there was through her room. "Dean, Dean," I cried, "where's the nearest bar?"

"Bar?" he said, surprised; he was washing his hands in the kitchen sink downstairs. He thought I wanted to get drunk. I told him my dilemma and he said, "Go right ahead, she does that all the time." No, I couldn't do that. I rushed out to look for a bar; I walked uphill and downhill in a vicinity of four blocks on Russian Hill and found nothing but laundromats, cleaners, soda fountains, beauty parlors. I came back to the crooked little house. They were yelling at each other as I slipped through with a feeble smile and locked myself in the bathroom. A few moments later Camille was throwing Dean's things on the living-room floor and telling him to pack. To my amazement I saw a full-length oil painting of Galatea Dunkel over the sofa. I suddenly realized that all these women were spending months of loneliness and womanliness together, chatting about the madness of the men. I heard Dean's maniacal giggle across the house, together with the wails of his baby. The next thing I knew he was gliding around the house like Groucho Marx, with his broken thumb wrapped in a huge white bandage sticking up like a beacon that stands motionless above the frenzy of the waves. Once again I saw his pitiful huge battered trunk with socks and dirty underwear sticking out; he bent over it, throwing in everything he could find. Then he got his suitcase, the beatest suitcase in the USA. It was made of paper with designs on it to make it look like leather, and hinges of some kind pasted on. A great rip ran down the top; Dean lashed on a rope. Then he grabbed his seabag and threw things into that. I got my bag, stuffed it, and as Camille lay in bed saying, "Liar! Liar! Liar!" we leaped out of the house and struggled down the street to the nearest cable car—a mass of men and suitcases with that enormous bandaged thumb sticking up in the air.

That thumb became the symbol of Dean's final development. He no longer cared about anything (as before) but now he also *cared about everything in principle;* that is to say, it was all the same to him and he belonged to the world and there was nothing he could do about it. He stopped me in the middle of the street.

"Now, man, I know you're probably real bugged; you just got to town and we get thrown out the first day and you're wondering what I've done to deserve this and so on—together with all horrible appurtenances—hee-hee-hee!—but look at me. Please, Sal, look at me."

I looked at him. He was wearing a T-shirt, torn pants hanging down his belly, tattered shoes; he had not shaved, his hair was wild and bushy, his eyes bloodshot, and that tremendous bandaged thumb stood supported in midair at heart-level (he had to hold it up that way), and on his face was the goofiest grin I ever saw. He stumbled around in a circle and looked everywhere.

"What do my eyeballs see? Ah—the blue sky. Long-fellow!" He swayed and blinked. He rubbed his eyes. "Together with windows—

have you ever dug windows? Now let's talk about windows. I have seen some really crazy windows that made faces at me, and some of them had shades drawn and so they winked." Out of his seabag he fished a copy of Eugene Sue's *Mysteries of Paris* and, adjusting the front of his T-shirt, began reading on the street corner with a pedantic air. "Now really, Sal, let's dig everything as we go along . . ." He forgot about that in an instant and looked around blankly. I was glad I had come, he needed me now.

"Why did Camille throw you out? What are you going to do?"

"Eh?" he said. "Eh? Eh?" We racked our brains for where to go and what to do. I realized it was up to me. Poor, poor Dean—the devil himself had never fallen farther; in idiocy, with infected thumb, surrounded by the battered suitcases of his motherless feverish life across America and back numberless times, an undone bird. "Let's walk to New York," he said, "and as we do so let's take stock of everything along the way—yass." I took out my money and counted it; I showed it to him.

"I have here," I said, "the sum of eighty-three dollars and change, and if you come with me let's go to New York—and after that let's go to Italy."

"Italy?" he said. His eyes lit up. "Italy, yass—how shall we get there, dear Sal?"

I pondered this. "I'll make some money, I'll get a thousand dollars from the publishers. We'll go dig all the crazy women in Rome, Paris, all those places; we'll sit at sidewalk cafés; we'll live in whorehouses. Why not go to Italy?"

"Why yass," said Dean, and then realized I was serious and looked at me out of the corner of his eye for the first time, for I'd never committed myself before with regard to his burdensome existence, and that look was the look of a man weighing his chances at the last moment before the bet. There were triumph and insolence in his eyes, a devilish look, and he never took his eyes off mine for a long time. I looked back at him and blushed.

I said, "What's the matter?" I felt wretched when I asked it. He made no answer but continued looking at me with the same wary insolent side-eye.

I tried to remember everything he'd done in his life and if there wasn't something back there to make him suspicious of something

now. Resolutely and firmly I repeated what I said—"Come to New
York with me; I've got the money." I looked at him; my eyes were
watering with embarrassment and tears. Still he stared at me. Now
his eyes were blank and looking through me. It was probably the
pivotal point of our friendship when he realized I had actually spent
some hours thinking about him and his troubles, and he was trying to
place that in his tremendously involved and tormented mental categories. Something clicked in both of us. In me it was suddenly concern
for a man who was years younger than I, five years, and whose fate
was wound with mine across the passage of the recent years; in him
it was a matter that I can ascertain only from what he did afterward.
He became extremely joyful and said everything was settled. "What
was that look?" I asked. He was pained to hear me say that. He
frowned. It was rarely that Dean frowned. We both felt perplexed
and uncertain of something. We were standing on top of a hill on a
beautiful sunny day in San Francisco; our shadows fell across the
sidewalk. Out of the tenement next to Camille's house filed eleven
Greek men and women who instantly lined themselves up on the
sunny pavement while another backed up across the narrow street
and smiled at them over a camera. We gaped at these ancient people
who were having a wedding party for one of their daughters, probably
the thousandth in an unbroken dark generation of smiling in the sun.
They were well dressed, and they were strange. Dean and I might
have been in Cyprus for all of that. Gulls flew overhead in the spar-
kling air.

"Well," said Dean in a very shy and sweet voice, "shall we go?"

"Yes," I said, "let's go to Italy." And so we picked up our bags, he
the trunk with his one good arm and I the rest, and staggered to the
cable-car stop; in a moment it rolled down the hill with our legs
dangling to the sidewalk from the jiggling shelf, two broken-down
heroes of the Western night.

*   *   *

First thing, we went to a bar down on Market Street and decided
everything—that we would stick together and be buddies till we died.
Dean was very quiet and preoccupied, looking at the old bums in the
saloon that reminded him of his father. "I think he's in Denver—this

time we must absolutely find him, he may be in County Jail, he may
be around Larimer Street again, but he's to be found. Agreed?"

Yes, it was agreed; we were going to do everything we'd never done
and had been too silly to do in the past. Then we promised ourselves
two days of kicks in San Francisco before starting off, and of course
the agreement was to go by travel bureau in share-the-gas cars and
save as much money as possible. Dean claimed he no longer needed
Marylou though he still loved her. We both agreed he would make
out in New York.

Dean put on his pin-stripe suit with a sports shirt, we stashed our
gear in a Greyhound bus locker for ten cents, and we took off to meet
Roy Johnson who was going to be our chauffeur for two-day Frisco
kicks. Roy agreed over the phone to do so. He arrived at the corner
of Market and Third shortly thereafter and picked us up. Roy was
now living in Frisco, working as a clerk and married to a pretty little
blonde called Dorothy. Dean confided that her nose was too long—
this was his big point of contention about her, for some strange reason
—but her nose wasn't too long at all. Roy Johnson is a thin, dark handsome kid with a pin-sharp face and combed hair that he keeps shoving
back from the sides of his head. He had an extremely earnest approach and a big smile. Evidently his wife, Dorothy, had wrangled
with him over the chauffeuring idea—and, determined to make a
stand as the man of the house (they lived in a little room), he nevertheless stuck by his promise to us, but with consequences; his mental
dilemma resolved itself in a bitter silence. He drove Dean and me all
over Frisco at all hours of day and night and never said a word; all
he did was go through red lights and make sharp turns on two wheels,
and this was telling us the shifts to which we'd put him. He was mid-
way between the challenge of his new wife and the challenge of his
old Denver poolhall gang leader. Dean was pleased, and of course
unperturbed by the driving. We paid absolutely no attention to Roy
and sat in the back and yakked.

The next thing was to go to Mill City to see if we could find Remi
Boncœur. I noticed with some wonder that the old ship *Admiral
Freebee* was no longer in the second-to-last compartment of the shack
in the canyon. A beautiful colored girl opened the door instead; Dean
and I talked to her a great deal. Roy Johnson waited in the car, reading
Eugene Sue's *Mysteries of Paris*. I took one last look at Mill City and

knew there was no sense trying to dig up the involved past; instead we decided to go see Galatea Dunkel about sleeping accommodations. Ed had left her again, was in Denver, and damned if she still didn't plot to get him back. We found her sitting crosslegged on the Oriental-type rug of her four-room tenement flat on upper Mission with a deck of fortune cards. Good girl. I saw sad signs that Ed Dunkel had lived here awhile and then left out of stupors and disinclinations only.

"He'll come back," said Galatea. "That guy can't take care of himself without me." She gave a furious look at Dean and Roy Johnson. "It was Tommy Snark who did it this time. All the time before he came Ed was perfectly happy and worked and we went out and had wonderful times. Dean, you know that. Then they'd sit in the bathroom for hours, Ed in the bathtub and Snarky on the seat, and talk and talk and talk—such silly things."

Dean laughed. For years he had been chief prophet of that gang and now they were learning his technique. Tommy Snark had grown a beard and his big sorrowful blue eyes had come looking for Ed Dunkel in Frisco; what happened (actually and no lie), Tommy had his small finger amputated in a Denver mishap and collected a good sum of money. For no reason under the sun they decided to give Galatea the slip and go to Portland, Maine, where apparently Snark had an aunt. So they were now either in Denver, going through, or already in Portland.

"When Tom's money runs out Ed'll be back," said Galatea, looking at her cards. "Damn fool—he doesn't know anything and never did. All he has to do is know that I love him."

Galatea looked like the daughter of the Greeks with the sunny camera as she sat there on the rug, her long hair streaming to the floor, plying the fortune-telling cards. I got to like her. We even decided to go out that night and hear jazz, and Dean would take a six-foot blonde who lived down the street, Marie.

That night Galatea, Dean, and I went to get Marie. This girl had a basement apartment, a little daughter, and an old car that barely ran and which Dean and I had to push down the street as the girls jammed at the starter. We went to Galatea's, and there everybody sat around—Marie, her daughter, Galatea, Roy Johnson, Dorothy his wife—all sullen in the overstuffed furniture as I stood in a corner, neutral in Frisco problems, and Dean stood in the middle of the room with his balloon-thumb in the air breast-high, giggling. "Gawd damn," he said, "we're all losing our fingers—hawr-hawr-hawr."

"Dean, why do you act so foolish?" said Galatea. "Camille called and said you left her. Don't you realize you have a daughter?"

"He didn't leave her, she kicked him out!" I said, breaking my neutrality. They all gave me dirty looks; Dean grinned. "And with that thumb, what do you expect the poor guy to do?" I added. They all looked at me; particularly Dorothy Johnson lowered a mean gaze on me. It wasn't anything but a sewing circle, and the center of it was the culprit, Dean—responsible, perhaps, for everything that was wrong. I looked out the window at the buzzing night-street of Mission; I wanted to get going and hear the great jazz of Frisco—and remember, this was only my second night in town.

"I think Marylou was very, very wise leaving you, Dean," said Galatea. "For years now you haven't had any sense of responsibility for anyone. You've done so many awful things I don't know what to say to you."

And in fact that was the point, and they all sat around looking at Dean with lowered and hating eyes, and he stood on the carpet in the middle of them and giggled—he just giggled. He made a little dance. His bandage was getting dirtier all the time; it began to flop and unroll. I suddenly realized that Dean, by virtue of his enormous series of sins, was becoming the Idiot, the Imbecile, the Saint of the lot.

"You have absolutely no regard for anybody but yourself and your damned kicks. All you think about is what's hanging between your legs and how much money or fun you can get out of people and then you just throw them aside. Not only that but you're silly about it. It never occurs to you that life is serious and there are people trying to make something decent out of it instead of just goofing all the time."

That's what Dean was, the HOLY GOOF.

"Camille is crying her heart out tonight, but don't think for a minute she wants you back, she said she never wanted to see you again and she said it was to be final this time. Yet you stand here and make silly faces, and I don't think there's a care in your heart."

This was not true; I knew better and I could have told them all. I didn't see any sense in trying it. I longed to go and put my arm around Dean and say, Now look here, all of you, remember just one thing: this guy has his troubles too, and another thing, he never complains and he's given all of you a damned good time just being himself, and if that isn't enough for you then send him to the firing squad, that's apparently what you're itching to do anyway . . .

Nevertheless Galatea Dunkel was the only one in the gang who wasn't afraid of Dean and could sit there calmly, with her face hanging out, telling him off in front of everybody. There were earlier days in Denver when Dean had everybody sit in the dark with the girls and just talked, and talked, and talked, with a voice that was once hypnotic and strange and was said to make the girls come across by sheer force of persuasion and the content of what he said. This was when he was fifteen, sixteen. Now his disciples were married and the wives of his disciples had him on the carpet for the sexuality and the life he had helped bring into being. I listened further.

"Now you're going East with Sal," Galatea said, "and what do you think you're going to accomplish by that? Camille has to stay home and mind the baby now you're gone—how can she keep her job?—and she never wants to see you again and I don't blame her. If you see Ed along the road you tell him to come back to me or I'll kill him."

Just as flat as that. It was the saddest night. I felt as if I was with strange brothers and sisters in a pitiful dream. Then a complete silence fell over everybody; where once Dean would have talked his way out, he now fell silent himself, but standing in front of everybody, ragged and broken and idiotic, right under the lightbulbs, his bony mad face covered with sweat and throbbing veins, saying, "Yes, yes, yes," as though tremendous revelations were pouring into him all the time now, and I am convinced they were, and the others suspected as much and were frightened. He was BEAT—the root, the soul of Beatific. What was he knowing? He tried all in his power to tell me what he was knowing, and they envied that about me, my position at his side, defending him and drinking him in as they once tried to do. Then they looked at me. What was I, a stranger, doing on the West Coast this fair night? I recoiled from the thought.

"We're going to Italy," I said, I washed my hands of the whole matter. Then, too, there was a strange sense of maternal satisfaction in the air, for the girls were really looking at Dean the way a mother looks at the dearest and most errant child, and he with his sad thumb and all his revelations knew it well, and that was why he was able, in tick-tocking silence, to walk out of the apartment without a word, to wait for us downstairs as soon as we'd made up our minds about *time*. This was what we sensed about the ghost on the sidewalk. I looked out the window. He was alone in the doorway, digging the street. Bitterness, recriminations, advice, morality, sadness—everything was behind him, and ahead of him was the ragged and ecstatic joy of pure being.

"Come on, Galatea, Marie, let's go hit the jazz joints and forget it. Dean will be dead someday. Then what can you say to him?"

"The sooner he's dead the better," said Galatea, and she spoke officially for almost everyone in the room.

"Very well, then," I said, "but now he's alive and I'll bet you want to know what he does next and that's because he's got the secret that we're all busting to find and it's splitting his head wide open and if he goes mad don't worry, it won't be your fault but the fault of God."

They objected to this; they said I really didn't know Dean; they said he was the worst scoundrel that ever lived and I'd find out someday to my regret. I was amused to hear them protest so much. Roy Johnson rose to the defense of the ladies and said he knew Dean better than anybody, and all Dean was, was just a very interesting and even amusing con-man. I went out to find Dean and we had a brief talk about it.

"Ah, man, don't worry, everything is perfect and fine." He was rubbing his belly and licking his lips.

*   *   *

The girls came down and we started out on our big night, once more pushing the car down the street. "Wheeoo! let's go!" cried Dean, and we jumped in the back seat and clanked to the little Harlem on Folsom Street.

Out we jumped in the warm, mad night, hearing a wild tenorman bawling horn across the way, going "EE-YAH! EE-YAH! EE-YAH!" and hands clapping to the beat and folks yelling, "Go, go, go!" Dean was already racing across the street with his thumb in the air, yelling, "Blow, man, blow!" A bunch of colored men in Saturday-night suits were whooping it up in front. It was a sawdust saloon with a small bandstand on which the fellows huddled with their hats on, blowing over people's heads, a crazy place; crazy floppy women wandered around sometimes in their bathrobes, bottles clanked in alleys. In back of the joint in a dark corridor beyond the splattered toilets scores of men and women stood against the wall drinking wine-spodiodi and spitting at the stars—wine and whiskey. The behatted tenorman was blowing at the peak of a wonderfully satisfactory free idea, a rising and falling riff that went from "EE-yah!" to a crazier "EE-de-lee-yah!" and blasted along to the rolling crash of butt-scarred drums hammered by a big brutal Negro with a bullneck who didn't give a damn about anything but punishing his busted tubs, crash, rattle-ti-boom, crash. Uproars of music and the tenorman *had it* and everybody knew he had it. Dean was clutching his head in the crowd, and it was a mad crowd. They were all urging that tenorman to hold it and keep it with cries and wild eyes, and he was raising himself from a crouch and going down again with his horn, looping it up in a clear cry above the furor. A six-foot skinny Negro woman was rolling her bones at the man's hornbell, and he just jabbed it at her, "Ee! ee! ee!"

Everybody was rocking and roaring. Galatea and Marie with beer in their hands were standing on their chairs, shaking and jumping. Groups of colored guys stumbled in from the street, falling over one another to get there. "Stay with it, man!" roared a man with a foghorn voice, and let out a big groan that must have been heard clear out in Sacramento, ah-haa! "Whoo!" said Dean. He was rubbing his chest, his belly; the sweat splashed from his face. Boom, kick, that drummer was kicking his drums down the cellar and rolling the beat upstairs with his murderous sticks, rattlety-boom! A big fat man was jumping on the platform, making it sag and creak. "Yoo!" The pianist was only pounding the keys with spreadeagled fingers, chords, at intervals when the great tenorman was drawing breath for another blast—Chinese chords, shuddering the piano in every timber, chink, and wire, boing! The tenorman jumped down from the platform and stood in the crowd, blowing around; his hat was over his eyes; somebody pushed it back for him. He just hauled back and stamped his foot and blew down a hoarse, baughing blast, and drew breath, and raised the horn and blew high, wide, and screaming in the air. Dean was directly in front of him with his face lowered to the bell of the horn, clapping his hands, pouring sweat on the man's keys, and the man noticed and laughed in his horn a long quivering crazy laugh, and everybody else laughed and they rocked and rocked; and finally the tenorman decided to blow his top and crouched down and held a note in high C for a long time as everything else crashed along and the cries increased and

I thought the cops would come swarming from the nearest precinct. Dean was in a trance. The tenorman's eyes were fixed straight on him; he had a madman who not only understood but cared and wanted to understand more and much more than there was, and they began dueling for this; everything came out of the horn, no more phrases, just cries, cries, "Baugh" and down to "Beep!" and up to "EEEEE!" and down to clinkers and over to sideways-echoing horn-sounds. He tried everything, up, down, sideways, upside down, horizontal, thirty degrees, forty degrees, and finally he fell back in somebody's arms and gave up and everybody pushed around and yelled, "Yes! Yes! He blowed that one!" Dean wiped himself with his handkerchief.

Then up stepped the tenorman on the bandstand and asked for a slow beat and looked sadly out the open door over people's heads and began singing "Close Your Eyes." Things quieted down a minute. The tenorman wore a tattered suede jacket, a purple shirt, cracked shoes, and zoot pants without press; he didn't care. He looked like a Negro Hassel. His big brown eyes were concerned with sadness, and the singing of songs slowly and with long, thoughtful pauses. But in the second chorus he got excited and grabbed the mike and jumped down from the bandstand and bent to it. To sing a note he had to touch his shoetops and pull it all up to blow, and he blew so much he staggered from the effect, and only recovered himself in time for the next long slow note. "Mu-u-usic pla-a-a-a-a-ay!" He leaned back with his face to the ceiling, mike held below. He shook, he swayed. Then he leaned in, almost falling with his face against the mike. "Ma-a-a-ake it dream-y for dan-cing"—and he looked at the street outside with his lips curled in scorn, Billie Holiday's hip sneer—"while we go ro-man-n-n-cing"—he staggered sideways—"Lo-o-o-ove's holi-da-a-ay"—he shook his head with disgust and weariness at the whole world—"Will make it seem"—what would it make it seem? everybody waited; he mourned—"O-kay." The piano hit a chord. "So baby come on just clo-o-o-ose your pretty little ey-y-y-y-yes"—his mouth quivered, he looked at us, Dean and me, with an expression that seemed to say, Hey now, what's this thing we're all doing in this sad brown world?—and then he came to the end of his song, and for this there had to be elaborate preparations, during which time you could send all the messages to Garcia around the world twelve times and what difference did it make to anybody? because here we were dealing with the pit and

prunejuice of poor beat life itself in the god-awful streets of man, so
he said it and sang it, "Close—your—" and blew it way up to the ceiling
and through to the stars and on out—"Ey-y-y-y-y-y-es"— and staggered
off the platform to brood. He sat in the corner with a bunch of boys
and paid no attention to them. He looked down and wept. He was the
greatest.

Dean and I went over to talk to him. We invited him out to the car.
In the car he suddenly yelled, "Yes! ain't nothin I like better than
good kicks! Where do we go?" Dean jumped up and down in the seat,
giggling maniacally. "Later! later!" said the tenorman. "I'll get my boy
to drive us down to Jamson's Nook, I got to sing. Man, I *live* to sing.
Been singin 'Close Your Eyes' for two weeks—I don't want to sing
nothin else. What are you boys up to?" We told him we were going
to New York in two days. "Lord, I ain't never been there and they tell
me it's a real jumpin town but I ain't got no cause complainin where
I am. I'm married, you know."

"Oh yes?" said Dean, lighting up. "And where is the darling tonight?"

"What do you *mean*?" said the tenorman, looking at him out of the
corner of his eye. "I tole you I was *married* to her, didn't I?"

"Oh yes, oh yes," said Dean. "I was just asking. Maybe she has
friends? or sisters? A ball, you know, I'm just looking for a ball."

"Yah, what good's a ball, life's too sad to be ballin all the time,"
said the tenorman, lowering his eye to the street. "Shh-eee-it!" he said.
"I ain't got no money and I don't care tonight."

We went back in for more. The girls were so disgusted with Dean
and me for gunning off and jumping around that they had left and
gone to Jamson's Nook on foot; the car wouldn't run anyway. We saw
a horrible sight in the bar: a white hipster fairy had come in wearing
a Hawaiian shirt and was asking the big drummer if he could sit in.
The musicians looked at him suspiciously. "Do you blow?" He said
he did, mincing. They looked at one another and said, "Yeah, yeah,
that's what the man does, shhh-ee-it!" So the fairy sat down at the
tubs and they started the beat of a jump number and he began strok-
ing the snares with soft goofy bop brushes, swaying his neck with that
complacent Reichianalyzed ecstasy that doesn't mean anything except
too much tea and soft foods and goofy kicks on the cool order. But he
didn't care. He smiled joyously into space and kept the beat, though

softly, with bop subtleties, a giggling, rippling background for big solid foghorn blues the boys were blowing, unaware of him. The big Negro bullneck drummer sat waiting for his turn. "What that man doing?" he said. "Play the music!" he said. "What in hell!" he said. "Shh-ee-eet!" and looked away, disgusted.

The tenorman's boy showed up; he was a little taut Negro with a great big Cadillac. We all jumped in. He hunched over the wheel and blew the car clear across Frisco without stopping once, seventy miles an hour, right through traffic and nobody even noticed him, he was so good. Dean was in ecstasies. "Dig this guy, man! dig the way he sits there and don't move a bone and just balls that jack and can talk all night while he's doing it, only thing is he doesn't bother with talking, ah, man, the things, the things I could—I wish—oh, yes. Let's go, let's not stop—go now! Yes!" And the boy wound around a corner and bowled us right in front of Jamson's Nook and was parked. A cab pulled up; out of it jumped a skinny, withered little Negro preacher-man who threw a dollar at the cabby and yelled, "Blow!" and ran into the club and dashed right through the downstairs bar, yelling, "Blow-blowblow!" and stumbled upstairs, almost falling on his face, and blew the door open and fell into the jazz-session room with his hands out to support him against anything he might fall on, and he fell right on Lampshade, who was working as a waiter in Jamson's Nook that season, and the music was there blasting and blasting and he stood transfixed in the open door, screaming, "Blow for me, man, blow!" And the man was a little short Negro with an alto horn that Dean said obviously lived with his grandmother just like Tom Snark, slept all day and blew all night, and blew a hundred choruses before he was ready to jump for fair, and that's what he was doing.

"It's Carlo Marx!" screamed Dean above the fury.

And it was. This little grandmother's boy with the taped-up alto had beady, glittering eyes; small, crooked feet; spindly legs; and he hopped and flopped with his horn and threw his feet around and kept his eyes fixed on the audience (which was just people laughing at a dozen tables, the room thirty by thirty feet and low ceiling), and he never stopped. He was very simple in his ideas. What he liked was the surprise of a new simple variation of a chorus. He'd go from "ta-tup-tader-rara . . . ta-tup-tader-rara," repeating and hopping to it and kissing and smiling into his horn, to "ta-tup-EE-da-de-dera-RUP!

ta-tup-EE-da-de-dera-RUP!" and it was all great moments of laughter and understanding for him and everyone else who heard. His tone was clear as a bell, high, pure, and blew straight in our faces from two feet away. Dean stood in front of him, oblivious to everything else in the world, with his head bowed, his hands socking in together, his whole body jumping on his heels and the sweat, always the sweat, pouring and splashing down his tormented collar to lie actually in a pool at his feet. Galatea and Marie were there, and it took us five minutes to realize it. Whoo, Frisco nights, the end of the continent and the end of doubt, all dull doubt and tomfoolery, good-bye. Lampshade was roaring around with his trays of beer; everything he did was in rhythm; he yelled at the waitress with the beat; "Hey now, babybaby, make a way, make a way, it's Lampshade comin your way," and he hurled by her with the beers in the air and roared through the swinging doors into the kitchen and danced with the cooks and came sweating back. The hornman sat absolutely motionless at a corner table with an untouched drink in front of him, staring gook-eyed into space, his hands hanging at his sides till they almost touched the floor, his feet outspread like lolling tongues, his body shriveled into absolute weariness and entranced sorrow and what-all was on his mind: a man who knocked himself out every evening and let the others put the quietus to him in the night. Everything swirled around him like a cloud. And that little grandmother's alto, that little Carlo Marx, hopped and monkeydanced with his magic horn and blew two hundred choruses of blues, each one more frantic than the other, and no signs of failing energy or willingness to call anything a day. The whole room shivered.

On the corner of Fourth and Folsom an hour later I stood with Ed Fournier, a San Francisco alto man who waited with me while Dean made a phone call in a saloon to have Roy Johnson pick us up. It wasn't anything much, we were just talking, except that suddenly we saw a very strange and insane sight. It was Dean. He wanted to give Roy Johnson the address of the bar, so he told him to hold the phone a minute and ran out to see, and to do this he had to rush pellmell through a long bar of brawling drinkers in white shirtsleeves, go to the middle of the street, and look at the post signs. He did this, crouched low to the ground like Groucho Marx, his feet carrying him with amazing swiftness out of the bar, like an apparition, with his

balloon thumb stuck up in the night, and came to a whirling stop in
the middle of the road, looking everywhere above him for the signs.
They were hard to see in the dark, and he spun a dozen times in the
road, thumb upheld, in a wild, anxious silence, a wild-haired person
with a ballooning thumb held up like a great goose of the sky, spinning and spinning in the dark, the other hand distractedly inside his
pants. Ed Fournier was saying, "I blow a sweet tone wherever I go and
if people don't like it ain't nothin I can do about it. Say, man, that
buddy of yours is a crazy cat, looka him over there"—and we looked.
There was a big silence everywhere as Dean saw the signs and rushed
back in the bar, practically going under someone's legs as they came
out and gliding so fast through the bar that everybody had to do a
double take to see him. A moment later Roy Johnson showed up, and
with the same amazing swiftness. Dean glided across the street and
into the car, without a sound. We were off again.

"Now, Roy, I know you're all hung-up with your wife about this
thing but we absolutely must make Forty-Sixth and Geary in the incredible time of three minutes or everything is lost. Ahem! Yes!
(Cough-cough.) In the morning Sal and I are leaving for New York
and this is absolutely our last night of kicks and I know you won't
mind."

No, Roy Johnson didn't mind; he only drove through every red
light he could find and hurried us along in our foolishness. At dawn
he went home to bed. Dean and I had ended up with a colored guy
called Walter who ordered drinks at the bar and had them lined up
and said, "Wine-spodiodi!" which was a shot of port wine, a shot of
whisky, and a shot of port wine. "Nice sweet jacket for all that bad
whisky!" he yelled.

He invited us to his home for a bottle of beer. He lived in the tenements in back of Howard. His wife was asleep when we came in. The
only light in the apartment was the bulb over her bed. We had to get
up on a chair and unscrew the bulb as she lay smiling there; Dean did
it, fluttering his lashes. She was about fifteen years older than Walter
and the sweetest woman in the world. Then we had to plug in the
extension over her bed, and she smiled and smiled. She never asked
Walter where he'd been, what time it was, nothing. Finally we were
set in the kitchen with the extension and sat down around the humble
table to drink the beer and tell the stories. Dawn. It was time to leave

and move the extension back to the bedroom and screw back the bulb. Walter's wife smiled and smiled as we repeated the insane thing all over again. She never said a word.

Out on the dawn street Dean said, "Now you see, man, there's *real* woman for you. Never a harsh word, never a complaint, or modified; her old man can come in any hour of the night with anybody and have talks in the kitchen and drink the beer and leave any old time. This is a man, and that's his castle." He pointed up at the tenement. We stumbled off. The big night was over. A cruising car followed us suspiciously for a few blocks. We bought fresh doughnuts in a bakery on Third Street and ate them in the gray, ragged street. A tall, bespectacled, well-dressed fellow came stumbling down the street with a Negro in a truck-driving cap. They were a strange pair. A big truck rolled by and the Negro pointed at it excitedly and tried to express his feeling. The tall white man furtively looked over his shoulder and counted his money. "It's Old Bull Lee!" giggled Dean. "Counting his money and worried about everything, and all that other boy wants to do is talk about trucks and things he knows." We followed them awhile.

Holy flowers floating in the air, were all these tired faces in the dawn of Jazz America.

We had to sleep; Galatea Dunkel's was out of the question. Dean knew a railroad brakeman called Ernest Burke who lived with his father in a hotel room on Third Street. Originally he'd been on good terms with them, but lately not so, and the idea was for me to try persuading them to let us sleep on their floor. It was horrible. I had to call from a morning diner. The old man answered the phone suspiciously. He remembered me from what his son had told him. To our surprise he came down to the lobby and let us in. It was just a sad old brown Frisco hotel. We went upstairs and the old man was kind enough to give us the entire bed. "I have to get up anyway," he said and retired to the little kitchenette to brew coffee. He began telling stories about his railroading days. He reminded me of my father. I stayed up and listened to the stories. Dean, not listening, was washing his teeth and bustling around and saying, "Yes, that's right," to everything he said. Finally we slept; and in the morning Ernest came back from a Western Division run and took the bed as Dean and I got up. Now old Mr. Burke dolled himself up for a date with his middle-aged sweetheart. He put on a green tweed suit, a cloth cap, also green tweed, and stuck a flower in his lapel.

"These romantic old broken-down Frisco brakemen live sad but eager lives of their own," I told Dean in the toilet. "It was very kind of him to let us sleep here."

"Yass, yass," said Dean, not listening. He rushed out to get a travel-bureau car. My job was to hurry to Galatea Dunkel's for our bags. She was sitting on the floor with her fortune-telling cards.

"Well, good-by, Galatea, and I hope everything works out fine."

"When Ed gets back I'm going to take him to Jamson's Nook every night and let him get his fill of madness. Do you think that'll work, Sal? I don't know what to do."

"What do the cards say?"

"The ace of spades is far away from him. The heart cards always surround him—the queen of hearts is never far. See this jack of spades? That's Dean, he's always around."

"Well, we're leaving for New York in an hour."

"Someday Dean's going to go on one of these trips and never come back."

She let me take a shower and shave, and then I said good-by and took the bags downstairs and hailed a Frisco taxi-jitney, which was an ordinary taxi that ran a regular route and you could hail it from any corner and ride to any corner you want for about fifteen cents, cramped in with other passengers like on a bus, but talking and telling jokes like in a private car. Mission Street that last day in Frisco was a great riot of construction work, children playing, whooping Negroes coming home from work, dust, excitement, the great buzzing and vibrating hum of what is really America's most excited city—and overhead the pure blue sky and the joy of the foggy sea that always rolls in at night to make everybody hungry for food and further excitement. I hated to leave; my stay had lasted sixty-odd hours. With frantic Dean I was rushing through the world without a chance to see it. In the afternoon we were buzzing toward Sacramento and eastward again.

CHANDLER BROSSARD

Redemption

> *Life is no longer a jungle. There are*
> *no more predatory beasts; the blood*
> *lust has cooled. Life is a junkyard—a*
> *collection of battered, rusted forms.*
> *Hipster gives place to mobster, and*
> *the struggle between Rebel and So-*
> *ciety, Outsider and Insider, becomes*
> *a sordid dance, a ritual composed of*
> *violence and pain, but with no mean-*
> *ing.* "Redemption" *is an excerpt*
> *from* The Bold Saboteurs.

THE COPS CAUGHT ME only once, and it took
those disgusting hyenas a remarkably long time to do it
too. They caught me through Bobo, who squealed. I knew
I should never have tied up with that guy. True, he was
big and strong but at bottom, he was really quite yellow.

It was the summer when I was sixteen. I had been hanging around Monroe Park with the older drifters and
drunks and thieves. You might say that I was their pro-
tégé. They let me shoot crap and play cards and take a
drink from a pint they chipped in to buy and passed

around until it was killed. And in turn I let them in on some pretty neat tricks. I knew where all kinds of stuff could be stolen and how to go about it. We all got on very well. Bobo was the toughest guy around the park; he was a redheaded Irishman and he had a body like a heavyweight prize fighter. He loved to roll up his dirty sleeves and show off his bulging muscles to anybody who expressed even the slightest interest. These fine muscles were the reward of years of laboring in construction gangs. God only knows how many buildings and roads his Irish sweat had helped juice together.

Everybody was scared of Bobo. When he was drunk he would slug you in the mouth for almost no reason. He was a wee bit off his noodle, you see. I was the only one Bobo did not get hard with, and I guess that was because I was so much smaller than he was, and also because he had a fuddled kind of respect for me. I read books and he thought I was very smart. He never read anything except the comics and the sport pages; that's all his orange cranium could take care of. We pulled a few good jobs together, just the two of us, before this time that I was caught. But all that will come later, in its place.

One night, after we had been sitting around the park all day with nothing to do, just waiting, time smothering us like an evil black smog, Bobo asked me if I wanted to go along with him to visit a nurse he had just met. She was a fat, thick-witted broad and he was sure he could get something out of her, that is, besides a piece of tail. The dumb ones went for him, he was their dream boat. I had nothing better to do that night. None of the other boys were around at the moment to go to the bars with, and there was nothing more thrilling for me at home than my old lady and maybe my big brother Roland. There would probably be just about zero for me to eat at the house, and on top of that I would undoubtedly quarrel with the old lady. So I said all right, I would go with him. I was trying to figure out something I could get from this fat dumb nurse too.

"Tell me if you see any good angles," Bobo said to me on our way to her house.

"Sure," I replied. But actually I was not so sure. I was getting a bit tired of him after an entire summer, and I really did not relish cutting him in any more. If he wasn't smart enough to figure out his own angles, then to hell with him. I had myself to look after.

This new pig of his lived nearly halfway across town, as you would expect, but we had so little dough between us that we could not afford to hop a streetcar, so we hiked it to her place. Neither of us had had dinner, and my stomach was roaring with anguish that I had betrayed it. Just before we got to the nurse's house, we stopped in a diner and had a greasy hamburger and a cup of coffee. That revived me and I felt ready for just about anything.

"She has a terrific ass," Bobo informed me, as we started up the stairs of the brownstone rooming house where our nurse lived. "A piece of art," he went on, and described with his arms what this object looked like. "I like women big, something you can get a grip on. I don't go for this skimpy stuff. You get all cut up on the bones."

Big, little, skinny, plump, I thought I liked them all and I told Bobo that. I had not yet reached the discriminating stage. The mere thought of sex was enough to catapult me into a fantasy of wild action.

I stopped at the door and looked over the front of the huge rooming house, casing it. Looking for entrances and exits, fire escapes, the nearness of the next building. You did this sort of thing automatically when you lived as I did. It had become second nature to me.

Bobo knew where Marie's—the nurse's—rooms were and we went right to them without having to collar anybody for directions. In the downstairs rooms little women clerks were entertaining little men clerks, striving desperately for some bleak pleasure. They giggled at everything that was said. Ugh.

The house was decorated like a Masons' lodge. On the stairs the head of a moose challenged me from the wall, and I barely restrained myself from spitting into its glassy eye. Bobo was flushing and rubbing his hands in anticipation of the pleasure he was going to have with his Queen of the Bedpans. He kept up a running speculation on how many things she would do with him and how great her capacity might be. I was coldly excited about what I could steal. I wondered how much the moose head might bring, but I decided that it would be too awkward to get away with. I could discipline myself about such matters.

"Play it safe now," Bobo cautioned me. "Don't let her suspect anything. I don't want her to know I'm trying to do her."

Shove it, Bobo! I wanted to say. I knew how to handle myself.

I could think rings around that lout. What did he mean by advising me?

Marie was a cow. She greeted us dressed in a loose red housecoat. She could not control her big red face. It kept smiling and smiling and her mouth opened and closed, opened and closed. I looked immediately around her room for her purse and anything else of value. I saw nothing and this depressed me.

"Who's your cute young friend?" she asked Bobo.

"Yogi," he told her, calling me by a nickname that had been slapped on me in the park because I could do somersaults and stand on my hands.

"Are you a Hindu or something?" she said, smiling lewdly at me.

I told her I could be. I never gave my real name if I could help it. I always made one up, it was safer that way. Never let anybody know who you really are; you will live to regret it if you do. I had already learned that. I had hundreds of disguises and tricks to fool the unwary, and at a moment's notice I could become a personality chamber of horrors.

We chewed the fat for a while and then Bobo persuaded Marie to go into an adjoining room with him. He told me to run downstairs and get some cigarettes, making it very plain that I should not rush myself. The itching bastard! When was I going to get my share? I shuffled downstairs and bought the cigarettes at a garish drugstore, whose walls were plastered with suave advice about your bodily functions, and walked leisurely around the block three times, and then returned to Marie's.

In a few minutes she and Bobo came out of the adjoining room, looking as though they had been wrestling on the floors and walls and on the ceiling and under the bed. She was still smiling that uncontrollable stupid cow smile. She seemed deliciously proud of herself. She was whorishly quite desirable, but all my thoughts were on stealing. Bobo flopped on the couch and smoked a cigarette, and I talked to Marie about blood banks and operations; I knew I could have her if I wanted her. She kept smiling at me.

Finally I managed to maneuver jewelry into our conversation, and after a bit I asked her about hers. I said I had heard she had a fine collection, and wouldn't she display it.

"Why do you want to see it?" she asked me, drawing back.

"I'm studying jewelry-making in trade school," I lied. "I like to see new designs."

This creamy explanation relaxed and flattered her. Cellini himself was in her drawing room! She brought out her meager collection. Cheap school rings, graduation presents, signifying advancement to new levels of mediocrity; necklaces, fraternity pins bought with the quick prone position so dear to her ilk. The usual triumph of sordidness, those jewels. I examined each item carefully to determine whether it was worth stealing. The stuff barely made the grade.

Then Marie related to me the stifled, sweaty experiences behind each shiny piece. She must have thought I was compiling a world history of frustration. I felt it was the least I could do to listen to these tales of love and success, but it was hard on me, I'll tell you that.

"Now are you satisfied?" she asked me, putting the stuff away.

"Completely," I replied, watching where she put the stuff.

"He's a real connoisseur," Bobo said from across the room. "He knows more about jewelry than a lot of jewelers."

Marie thought this was funny, but I feared she was unconsciously beginning to sniff a nigger in the woodpile. This would be a good time for me to pull out. I went into the little kitchen and made myself a ham sandwich while Marie and Bobo grappled some more, and coming out, munching, I said I had to go home. They didn't want me there anyway; they could hardly keep themselves from going at it full speed right on the couch in front of me. Marie said to come back and see her sometime. That's just what I had in mind, dearie.

The next morning, shortly after everyone else in the world had committed themselves to their daily death chambers of office work, I returned to Marie's rooming house. The place was deserted except for an old hag of a cleaning woman who was down on her knees polishing the stairway banister. She asked me what my business there was.

"I left a letter in Marie's room last night," I said. "I've come back for it."

She examined me and decided I was passable. That was the big thing in my favor! I did not look in the least like a thief. I looked more like a choirboy. Mothers' bosoms yearned for my curly head.

"The door's open," she said, resuming her life's cleaning. "Make it snappy. Don't you fool around in there."

I told her not to worry. Inside Marie's room I quickly picked out the few solid gold pieces of jewelry and put the jewel box back in its place. Maybe she would not notice the robbery for a few days. On my way out I noticed one of Bobo's dirty socks on the floor, at the foot of the bed. So the big slob had slept with Marie all night. I tried to imagine what she would be like in bed. All that blubber! It was sort of exciting in a stinking way.

Downstairs I thanked the old hag for letting me in, and we threw each other loving grimaces. She smelled of floor wax and sweat and old age and anxiety, an almost overpowering blend. From the way she smiled at me, I knew she ached to get her stained unfulfilled paws on me, on my sweet youth, but I slipped past her too fast, and got outside safe.

I beat it out of that district and to the fringe of the Negro district, to money's pimp, the pawnbroker. In the first shop I explained to the proprietor that I was not interested in selling the jewelry, I only wanted to find out how much it was worth, how much its gold was worth. He weighed the pieces in the palm of his hand, and told me about fifteen dollars. I walked around the block to another pawnbroker's. I knew now how much I should get for the stuff, so I could not be cheated too badly. Pawnbrokers never tell you right when you say you want to sell. Cheating is their business.

The little hunchbacked swine in the second cheatery offered me ten bucks for the lot, after disdainfully pushing it around on the counter as though it were dog offal. I demanded fifteen, shouting that I knew it was worth that much.

"It's junk," he said, almost spitting on the stuff. "I'll give you eleven dollars. I'm too tired this morning to argue."

"Fifteen!" I shouted.

"All right, all right. Twelve. You're hurting my eardrums."

"Fifteen!"

"It's almost not worth melting down. Thirteen."

"Thirteen-fifty!"

"Stop shouting," the man said. "All right, thirteen-fifty. I won't make a cent on it. I'm doing you a favor buying it."

I gave him a fake name and address, for the list he had to turn over to the cops on such deals as this, and left with the cash. It had been a profitable haul. I could live luxuriously for the next two weeks on the money. I could eat three good meals a day and gamble recklessly at the park. I felt now that I was coming up from a deep underground cavern where there was nothing but darkness and moist stone, to the bright wonderful surface of life. Thirteen-fifty! I could even give my old lady a couple of bucks. Bobo? Not a cent to that cretin! He had already got his share of the gravy. To each his own kind of ecstatic shudder. I would make my shudder last two weeks. I would copulate with life for that long.

The money made me anxious, put me in heat, and I could not wait to spend it. So instead of holding on until I was in a white section of town, I went into a Negro lunch counter and amid that rich tabu sensuality of color ordered a beef stew and rolls and coffee from a giant black man behind the counter who smiled at me and said, "That's a man-sized meal, son."

"That's my favorite dish," I said. I felt that he was my brother, and that all the others with their chain-gang color were my immediate family.

"All right," he said. "Don't let me see you leave none of the gravy." Several of the men laughed conspiratorially with him and me. They made me feel like Christ and I loved them all. I used two whole rolls wiping up the exotic juices on my plate, to please my friend the counterman. I felt so good in there that I wanted to tell him about the jewelry haul, but I finally turned thumbs down on that enthusiasm. You had to stop somewhere, even with brotherhood.

I made a lot of noise slurping up the coffee, and my black friend smiled appreciatively at me. I tipped him a dime and said so long.

"You take it easy now, boy," he said. "Don't you work too hard."

"Those are my exact intentions," I said, and waved good-bye to him and the other Negroes.

What a first-rate day it was! I thought I would like to see a movie before heading for the park, where I would confer with the gang. I went into the first double feature movie house I saw—and so to dreamland for three hours, with my stomach happy and full and my pockets loaded with cash. For three hours I was Oedipus in a cowboy suit, Achilles with a .45 Browning automatic in my hand and a scar on my cheek, Napoleon in a dive bomber. I watched my gargantuan dreams of love and conquest and betrayal and revenge and savagery come true, and I felt purged and happy.

This was life, not that Sahara Desert outside. That was for suckers. Bobo was in the park with the gang when I got there later that afternoon. He was showing off as usual, this time by baiting the ancient, half-dead park policeman. "Make believe I'm Capone. Let's see how fast you are on the draw. Go on." He had been pulling this particular stunt ever since he was a nip. The boys had seen it too many times for it to interest them so they started a card game in the summer house. By society's standards, they were all of them failures of one kind or another, but they were the only kind of people I felt comfortable with. Their wounds magnetized my wounds and we were all sick together. A pretty lively bunch of chancres, I must say.

There was Renny, who was a loss both to himself and the world at large. But Renny was so good looking that both men and women paid him money for the pleasure of going to bed with him. One winter he had been kept simultaneously by a banker and the wife of a traveling salesman. Each of them thought he was theirs and theirs alone. Renny actually had sexual interest only in women, but the men were good business, when times were tough, and besides, it amused his warped ego to be what the queers called "rough trade." Renny was to be a great friend to me when all the others failed.

There was Sherry Calder, who had been a tennis champion when he was a boy and was now a disgusting, puking, hopeless drunk, and this particular afternoon he was passed out cold on the croquet field and had pissed his pants. He was a decent sort, but utterly disgusting physically. He sometimes begged on the streets for money. The only person who could stand very much of him was a one-armed bub named Scott. Scott came from rich people and could have been a society playboy, but he preferred the company of thieves and the underworld, a pool table to a cocktail bar, a three-horse parlay to a club cotillion. He always had a copy of the scratch sheet on him. He had once put a man's eye out with the claw on his artificial arm during a brawl over a parking space.

Among the others in the crew at the park was Jimmy, a consumptive who clerked part time in the post office; Piper, who labored fitfully as a river hog and next to Bobo was the hardest man in that part of our divine city; a mechanic named Barton who had served time in jail for handling hot cars; and Ape (honest), a tall, green-toothed specimen who was a numbers runner for a couple of bookies, and who knew where all the good prostitutes lived. There were a few others around us, hangers on, but I did not have much to do with them. They were only voyeurs, and we had little respect for them There are such peepers surrounding all activities, even crime. They have to get their fun somehow.

"How did it go?" I asked Bobo when we were all sitting in the summer house, most of the guys playing showdown. I was not playing; I had told everybody I was broke. I was not going to tell Bobo about my haul, not yet anyway.

"She's a lovely piece," he said, banging me hard on the back. "It's like climbing a small whale."

"What kind of a whale?" somebody asked. "A tiger-whale? A long-nosed blue whale? What kind?"

"Any kind. I don't know what kind."

"Did she give off ambergris?"

"What's that?"

"It's no use. I can see you don't have a scientific mind."

We were always having specialized discussions like that. "Is that all?" I asked Bobo. "Is that all you got? Her?"

"Yes," he said. "But I'm thinking of going back tonight for a couple of medieval swords and a helmet. They're priceless. Come with me."

At times he was quite drunk with stupidity, in the same way, except in reverse, that a fine mind becomes intoxicated by a high flight of intellectuality.

I told him no thanks. Swords and helmets, that was his speed. He would be stealing Roman chariots from the museum next. He was absolutely unregenerate, a mass of uncoordinated muscle. I nonchalantly said Marie's jewelry was a lot of junk, and I was so convincing he agreed with me.

I spent the rest of the afternoon in the summer house watching the card game and sipping from a pint of whiskey being passed about, and I watched the tennis players nearby and the young lovers disappearing into the park arm in arm. And then I watched Sherry stagger drunkenly off the croquet field and down through the woods to the creek to throw himself in it to sober up. He made me think of the old man, both of them being so much alike. What a scum bag of a world it was, what a miserable rat's life. I was getting so depressed I was forgetting the money in my pocket.

In the early evening we all broke up. I told the fellows I might see them later at Sinbad's Bar, and I wished Bobo good luck with his stupid swords. What an idiot. On the way home I bought some meat and vegetables for my dinner. My brother Roland said he would put a roof over my head but he would not feed or clothe me. I had to work for that. My old lady sometimes sneaked me food from their dinner, which they ate together that summer without me. Even in my own house I was a scavenger.

"Did you steal this?" my mother asked me, looking at the food in my arms.

"No," I said. "I helped a friend of mine on his truck today and he gave me three dollars."

"You're lying, aren't you?" She suspected everything I did.

"Stop accusing me!" I yelled. "Goddamn it, can't I bring a little food home for myself without you screaming at me?"

"You will be my death," she said, intoning her mother's catechism.

She let up then. She hated these screaming matches as much as I did. She had had enough of them with my father many years ago; he had worn her out with fighting. While I was washing myself in the tub, she fixed the food for my dinner. It was a good meal, except for the fact that during it my mother told me that Roland had asked her again if I had a job yet, a steady job. He said he would not put up with me very much longer the way I was going on. I told the old lady I did not want to discuss it, and wolfed my food down and went out. The entire world was ganging up on me, I thought, and even now I had lost some of the desire to throw away my money. Everything is ruined sooner or later, and you may as well face that basic fact, my friends.

First I went to a bowling alley where I knew a couple of lugs, and hurled huge balls at helpless, dumfounded pins with them for an hour, standing the boys to cokes afterward, and then I went to an indoor swimming pool in a swanky hotel. I loved this place. I loved slowly to go to pieces under a hot shower, to burst my lungs with daring underwater endurance swims for the benefit and delight of the watching chippies, to paddle near the diving board and stare at their full-breastedness plunging gracefully into the water, to sprawl arrogantly on the racks drying off and nibbling dainty chicken sandwiches on white bread, and letting my mind riot unleashed in fantasies of all sorts. I stayed in the pool until it closed and I had just enough strength left to crawl home and into bed, as deliciously spent as a maharaja after a hard day's work.

The moment I set foot in the park the next day, Barton informed me that the cops were searching for me. Marie had discovered the robbery and howled for the police as though she were the Bank of England and her vaults had been looted of all their gold bullion. They never would have known who to look for if Bobo had not told them who I was, the yellow-bellied son of a bitch. They had picked him up in the park and were holding him until they nabbed me. Maybe he was squealing because I had not cut him in. They had been prowling around the park once today and they would undoubtedly be back.

"Lay low for a few days, Yogi," Barton advised me. "Let it all calm down. The cops aren't going to look for you forever, just for a cheesy haul like that. They've got less important things to do."

Now the chase began: me versus the police department and my ancient rival, organized society. I got the hell out of the park and walked several blocks south to a drugstore where we sometimes hung out, pooling our inertia. I ordered a ham sandwich and some milk, but instead of serving me the counter boy leaned across the counter and whispered that the cops had been there too. He told them he never saw me. He was a good boy. I thanked him and scrammed.

I walked three blocks west to Penn Avenue where I thought I could get lost in the anonymous crowds, but when I got there I felt that everyone around me was a potential captor, needing only the shouts of Stop him! Stop him! to transform them into rabid, bloodthirsty pursuers.

Suddenly I saw a police car cruising slowly toward me. I ducked into the ten-cent store, almost knocking over an old lady with her arms full of ten-cent bargain miracles, and scurried toward the exit facing the other street. My body was a block of iced fear. I was afraid to let myself feel luxuriantly scared because then I knew I would disintegrate into hysteria, which is what I may have wanted to do anyway. I paused by the penny candy counter to look back for my enemies, but they had not seen me after all. Then, like a stalked leopard, I glided unhurriedly through that strange jungle of lurid smells and bright screaming knicknacks and somnolent, pimpled salesgirls, to the other side, and out into the street.

No police around. From there I made it to a poolroom on Potomac Avenue, but instantly the owner came to me and said to clear out because he had heard the cops were on my tail. He didn't want them picking me up there, it would ruin his business. Out I went. The only smart thing for me to do now was to stay clear of that neighborhood for a few days until things cooled off.

There was only one place that I could hide out for any stretch of time, and that was home. Home is where you hide yourself. Well, at least it was good for something. Walking around was too dangerous, so I hopped a trolley and got home that way. They couldn't get me here because nobody knew where I lived. I always kept that a secret too.

At home the old lady nagged me for being such a no-good son, and I agreed with her. "Why aren't you like your brother?" she asked me for the millionth time. "Why don't you do something to make me proud of you?"

"I wish I knew," I said. Comparisons with my brother always depressed me. I was worthless and I knew it, and so why keep yapping about it?

Finally she went out to shop, and I gave her money to buy food for me for a couple of days. Also, I told her to buy me a shirt at the corner haberdashery. I needed a new one desperately, and, besides, I was afraid I would not get a chance to enjoy all of the money I had picked up so easily.

For two days I lay around the house, reading and listening to the radio and going out to the movies and then coming right back. My brother Roland did not molest me; we were not on speaking terms then. After two days I thought I was going stir crazy. I had to get out, I had to get back to the neighborhood of the park and see how things were progressing.

I was aware that I should not do this but I could not help myself. Something drew me back into the area of the chase. This was my obligation to the game I had set in motion.

My behavior had begun to make my mother suspicious, and that too wore me down. To make things look more natural, I took an old tennis racquet along with me as I returned to the park. Maybe I could get up a game, I told myself, a few good rallies to take my mind off my troubles.

The gang at the park were not too conscious of my presence and we said only a few words about the theft and the cops being after me. They were now bored with the whole business, though they did think it sort of funny that I should return so soon. I explained that the cops would never figure me to come back to the park, and for that reason they would be looking elsewhere. I persuaded Sherry, who was only slightly tight so far, to play me a couple of games.

It was a chaotically imaginative few games, Sherry making unbelievable, weird shots and howling like a maniac every time he scored a point. We finally had to call it quits because he had got so very drunk during the game, sipping from a pint in his pocket. He sprawled right out on the tennis court for a snooze. I was hungry and decided to go to the corner delicatessen for a baloney sandwich. At the entrance to the park I passed the old park cop.

"You shouldn't have done it, Yogi," he said, shaking his gnarled head. "They catch up with you every time," and he walked away. To hell with him, too. I didn't ask the old bugger for his senile advice or sympathy. He better save it for himself.

In the delicatessen I ordered a baloney sandwich and a coke, and just as I swallowed the first mustardy bite, the bulls walked in.

"Are you the kid named Yogi?" one of them demanded beefily.

I answered without a moment's hesitation. "Yes sir, that's me." We both knew what he was talking about.

"O.K., you're coming with us," he said. He grabbed me by the back of my pants so that I could not get away.

"You don't have to do that," I said, trying to twist away from his grip. "I'm not going to run."

"Come on, come on," was all he said, tightening his grip on my pants, hurting my crotch, and we got into the squad car outside.

The grocer and his wife came outside to gape, to live for a few filthy seconds on my tough luck, to get their daily transfusion of slime. The neighborhood brats were swarming all around the squad car. They looked at me as though I were Dillinger or Mad Dog Coll. I felt like it. My feelings went far beyond humiliation. Humiliation is a simple feeling for simple situations. I was now in the hands of The Law. That's like being in the hands of God. How can you be humiliated by God? It's impossible. I was Caught. That was my feeling, there is no other feeling like it.

Riding downtown to the police station, imprisoned in the back seat, I did not even think once of jumping out of the car. Escape was out of the question. The cops ignored me and chatted boyishly about baseball. On their short-wave radio the police broadcaster was ominously announcing the score: a robbery at Tenth Street, a shooting on F Street, a screaming lady on a roof, a man beating his wife, a corpse floating in the canal. It was divine, you could not have asked for anything better.

"O.K. Get out," they growled.

We were at the station house, a huge red brick menace with bars on its lower jaw. I stumbled crazily out of the squad car and we resumed our parade, one cop in front, one cop in the rear, me with a huge red Irish hand holding up the back of my pants. The people on the sidewalk stopped and stared at us. The heartless canaille.

There he is, I knew they were saying. The Boy Killer. He looks so sweet and innocent too, but that's the way they all are, murderers behind their baby-blue eyes. Behind that face lies a roomful of shotguns. Little fiends. They should be killed at birth, left out in the snow.

"Well, we finally got the little bastard," one of the cops announced to the sergeant behind the big desk. The cops loafing around the room there looked me over and laughed.

"He ain't going to be using that in here," one cracked, motioning toward my tennis racquet. I had forgotten I even had it. Everybody there thought this crack was a riot. They laughed and laughed. As for me, I would never laugh again as long as I lived.

The feeling I had was that the police house had always been my goal. I had the confused remembrance of a long journey, during which many odd things had occurred, before I arrived here. I had had the feeling, during the journey, that I was going to a particular place, but I could not decide just where it was. But my strong feeling about it had kept me going onward. Now I was quite satisfied that I was finally here.

"You cannot go on walking forever," I said to myself, referring to my journey. "You must arrive some time."

I knew this was a wise understanding of the situation, and I smiled for myself.

There was a great amount of noise in certain parts of the station, and in other parts there was an absolute pure silence. The noise seemed quite separate unto itself and did not seem to enter the quiet areas. Each existed unaware of the other, I realized after a moment of listening to both and thinking about it.

"That is just the way it should be," a small, frail-looking policeman said, as though he had suddenly read my mind.

"I didn't say it wasn't," I replied. "In fact, I like it very much."

Somehow, against my desire, my statement had been turned into a protest, and this disturbed me. I looked startled at the little policeman, wondering what he was thinking.

"Please remember where you are," he admonished me, touching me lightly but authoritatively on the shoulder.

"Thank you, sir, I will," I said meekly. I was so relieved that he had not done something violent to me that I wanted to give him a present—a tennis ball or one of my neckties—but I knew this was not right. Some other time, perhaps; the next time I see him.

In the noisy corner was the ringing of a telephone and also the disembodied voice of the police broadcaster. A moment before, I thought his voice had been harsh and businesslike, but now it was a lovely intimate purr, oh, how lovely. Suddenly I was terrified. The soft purring was all about me, all about secret, disgusting, personal things that I thought nobody would ever find out.

"Don't, please don't!" I shouted in dismay, and rushed into the noisy corner where the voice was. "Tell anything but that! Please!" I was trembling with shame.

Several policemen suddenly materialized around the radio, huddling there like athletes getting special instructions from their head coach. "Keep quiet," one of them yelled at me. "How do you expect us to hear with you shouting like that?"

"I'm terribly sorry," I muttered, and found myself saluting this policeman. "It was very thoughtless of me." The voice kept purring out the secret shameful data on me. I continued to feel very embarrassed, but at the same time I discovered that I was now quite interested in it, as the policemen were. I was huddling there with them, my arms around the shoulders of two policemen, and feeling much, much better, almost palsey.

"Some secrets are not worth keeping," I heard one of the cops say.

"I'm beginning to understand that now," I said. I was quite sure he was talking about me.

In another moment I realized that the soft purring voice on the radio was my own voice. But I was not very surprised, for it was as though I had know this for some time and had preferred not to do anything about it.

All the policemen stood up now and looked at me. "Well, how do you like it?" a burly sergeant asked me, putting his hands arrogantly on his hips.

"You're just pulling my leg," I said sadly, and then moved away from them, quickly. But I was not so quick that I avoided being shoved by a young apprentice policeman, who, I sensed, was very eager to prove himself. Between the two of us, though, there seemed to be a tacit understanding about all this.

"It had to be your turn, sooner or later," I said, without any ill feelings. Why squash roaches, I thought, when there are deer to be bagged?

"Right," he said. "But don't let that make you feel like a martyr."

"Can't you take a joke?" I said, and giggled foolishly, why I did not know.

Passing through the big room, I saw, out of the corner of my eye, all of the prisoners in the cells. They were naked, and they appeared to be quite happy. A fat woman with long hair waved sweetly to me, and I felt obliged to wave back, even though I did not enjoy doing it. Then they all began to sing, and this depressed me very much.

"Stop that!" I shouted. "Wake up to your despair! Wake up!" I tried desperately to make myself heard, but I had suddenly lost my voice for that moment.

One of the prisoners, a starkly naked young man with many pimples on his face, glided softly by me, strumming on an imaginary guitar. His face was very unhappy. I felt so deeply sorry for him that I kissed him gently on the shoulder as he passed. The boy did not even notice me; then, in another moment, he turned and shrilly cried, "You really think you're hot stuff, don't you?"

I struggled. Another misunderstanding. "I did that out of love, not vanity," I explained.

"Oh, sure, sure," the boy sneered. "You would say something like that. Tell me another," and he glided away, strumming on his beloved imaginary instrument.

Now I was in an absolutely quiet corner of the station house. Here

I experienced a strange tidal sensation all around me and inside myself: it was very emotional and a little sexual. Before me was my father, very bloated and dreamy looking and dressed in what resembled a policeman's uniform. He smiled vastly at me but I did not smile back. My father reminded me of some giant fish, a whale or porpoise, that had been stranded on the beach. He was murmuring vast, oceanic nothings to a small man in a black raincoat who was pretending to write it all down in a very official-looking black notebook.

"As if that sort of thing were meant to be recorded," I said aloud.

The man looked up and put his finger to his mouth, sh-shing me. How sinister and weak he looks, I thought. And almost before I knew what I was doing, I had pushed the man away and had climbed into my father's arms. Now I felt happily helpless and I was sobbing and sobbing, and my father was caressing my head.

"I was hoping you would be here," I said, or felt myself say for there was still an absolute, overwhelming silence all around me.

"That makes me feel very proud, son," my father replied in his vast, oceanic voice.

I began to play with his police badge, but under my fingers the badge turned into an ordinary button. I was suddenly stunned by this, and I looked into my father's face for an explanation. But my father now looked old and sick and disgusting, and he stank terribly of whiskey. His uniform had become a shabby suit of clothes.

"You've tricked me! You've tricked me!" I shouted. "Why? Why?"

And I was hitting my father in the face, blow after blow. My father, however, did not react at all to these blows; he just stared helplessly at the floor.

They wrote my true name down in a big black book, lads, and in that second I became a member of the Legion of Dishonor. I now had a police record, and as far as the police were concerned I had just been born. This was only the beginning. From now on, any time you wanted to see how I was growing you could refer to the police blotter.

I was getting tired of standing, so I asked one of the police what I was supposed to do.

"What do you think, you little jerk? Take a stroll around the block?" He turned me around suddenly and viciously kicked me in the ass toward some chairs. I got the idea, and sat down. All the cops laughed at this too. They had a vast, unquenchable sense of humor. I imagine they went into hysterics and rolled on the floor when they saw a cat-o'-nine tails in action.

After three hours of waiting, during which I pictured myself doing a six-month stretch in the reformatory, maybe working in the fields, a small, fat, bottle-shaped detective waddled in, and the cops in blue told him I was the criminal they had been looking for. The detective stood in front of me, his hands plunged arrogantly in his jacket pockets, and surveyed me up and down as though he were the official tailor measuring me for a striped convict suit. "All right," he said, sounding very bored. "What did you do with the stuff?"

I had no will left to resist him, no desire to deny or lie. Once I was caught, I relinquished all rights to ingenuity. I told him where I had sold the jewelry, and how much I had got for it.

He shook his head and grimaced contemptuously. "Thirteen lousy bucks. I could send you up for six months for those thirteen crumby bucks, you know that?"

"Yes sir," I said, expecting him at any moment to slap me right off the chair.

"But you're in luck, son, you're really in luck. The lady you stole the stuff from doesn't want to put your can in jail. She just wants to get the stuff back. Now all you got to do is dig up thirteen bucks to buy it back with. I bet you ain't got a cent of it left, now have you?"

The son of a bitch. I knew he wanted to prolong this for hours. The cops standing by were loving every sordid second of it. This was really living to them, the high life, better than Park Avenue. They were interrupted when a young Negro pansy was brought in crying and looking very roughed up. One of the cops imitated his swishiness much to the loud delight of his colleagues. The Negro boy had a big lump on his head where he had been smacked with a blackjack by the arresting cop, just for fun.

"Ain't he the sweetest, dearest thing you ever saw?" the arresting cop said about this pansy, and violently shoved him to the desk to be booked.

The poor pansy squealed with fear. He had a lot more to look forward to.

I told the detective that I had five dollars of the dough left, and I took it out of my pocket to prove it. He said all I had to do now was get eight-fifty more before the night was over, otherwise he would toss me in the lockup. He said, "Let's get going right now and locate that money, boy."

I did not have the remotest idea where I was going to hustle it up. I didn't know anybody who had eight-fifty, and if they did have it they would certainly never give it to a sorry punk like me. I frantically searched my mind for someone who might possibly come across with the dough, but the heavy oppressive smell of piss and corruption there in the station house had numbed my poor brain, and I felt like a half-awake somnambulist. All I wanted to do was to go back to sleep, for years and years.

We went first to my house, where my mother put on a spectacular show. She screamed and fell on the floor and cried and clawed her face and said she was going to die and it was all my fault. I didn't ask for the show, all I wanted was the eight-fifty and she didn't have it. The fat detective and I were momentarily united by our mutual embarrassment. When I asked Roland for the money, saying I would do anything for him if he gave it to me, he merely turned his back on me. He said it would serve me right if I went to jail for a while, because I was and always would be a moral criminal, and he went back to his reading. I could have killed them both on the spot.

I thought I was a goner. Outside my house the detective and I paused on the steps and he waited for me to tell him where we should go next for the money. But all I could do was stare stupidly into the street and wish I were dead. Everything in the world seemed suddenly to have deserted me, my life stretched out behind me, there was nothing ahead.

"I ain't got all year, boy," he said, nudging me. "And you ain't either."

I wanted to tell him, all right, let's go to jail, I'm licked. But as a final long shot I thought of scouting the section of the park. We drove there quickly in the detective's car and he waited in it while I scuttled in and out of bars and poolrooms and searched street corners for someone I might know. I had just about given up when I saw Renny standing in a dark doorway facing the street. He was dead drunk and he was laughing to himself.

"If it isn't old Yogi," he said, reaching out his hand to me and drawing me in. "Yogi, you look bad. You look like you're running your last lap. You know something, Yogi? All day I've had the feeling that you would come looking for me. No crap. I'm prophetic about these things. And goddamn if you aren't here. And I know just what you want, Yogi, my frazzle-assed friend. You want some money to get back that jewelry, don't you?"

"Listen, Renny," I fairly screamed, grabbing his arm. "I'll pay it back to you in a week, honest to God I will. You've got to lend it to me. I'll go to jail if you don't, Renny. These mother f......rs want to take me out of circulation. Please for God's sake lend it to me. You'll get it back, you know you will."

All this time the fat little inspector was standing near the curb blandly watching us, and from time to time looking wearily at his wrist watch. I didn't have much time left.

Renny swayed drunkenly in the doorway and smiled grotesquely. "Weep no more, Yogi, weep no more today. I'll let you have the lousy money and you can tell that police bug to shove it. But let this be a lesson to you. In the future don't pull any jobs with guys like Bobo. Stay away from the cretins and the cowards. Remember that, Yogi boy, and you will be an unmitigated success in this world."

I grabbed the money from his hand and walked quickly to the curb and shoved it at the inspector. Redemption: price, eight-fifty. It was a bargain that would never repeat itself. The inspector smiled and shook his head. "You guys," he said. He walked to his car, but before he got in it he turned to me and said, "See you later, son."

"No you won't," I promised him.

"Oh yes I will."

"Toodle-oo, Inspector," Renny shouted.

I took Renny by the arm and said, "Let's go somewhere and sit down."

"No. Let's stand here for a minute and watch the people," he said. "Just for laughs. They kill me, Yogi."

"I can't do it," I said, and then I ran to the curb and threw up, threw up on humanity, threw up on my junk-yard past and present and future.

"WILLIAM LEE"

My First Days on Junk

"William Lee" is a pseudonym. By his own description, the author is a drug addict, thief, pusher and pimp. Scion of one of America's most illustrious families, he has not transgressed against established law because of poverty or lack of personal opportunity. Junkie, of which the following is a portion, is no appologia. Rather, it is the description of a human condition—a point of personal descent where the fruits of rebellion are intimately commingled with its penalty: a self-imposed purgatory where the only goal is the next fix.

MY FIRST EXPERIENCE with junk was during the War, about 1944 or 1945. I had made the acquaintance of a man named Norton who was working in a shipyard at the time. Norton, whose real name was Morelli or something like that, had been discharged from the peacetime Army for forging a pay check, and was classified 4-F for reasons of bad character. He looked like George Raft, but was taller. Norton was trying to improve his English and achieve a smooth, affable manner. Affability, however, did not come natural to him. In repose, his expression was sullen and mean, and you knew he always had that mean look when you turned your back.

Norton was a hard-working thief and he did not feel right unless he stole something every day from the shipyard where he worked. A tool, some canned goods, a pair of overalls, anything at all. One day he called me up and said he had stolen a Tommy gun. Could I find someone to buy it? I said, "Maybe. Bring it over."

The housing shortage was getting under way. I paid fifteen dollars a week for a dirty apartment that opened on to a companionway and never got any sunlight. The wallpaper was flaking off because the radiator leaked steam when there was any steam in it to leak. I had the windows sealed shut with a caulking of newspapers against the cold. The place was full of roaches and occasionally I killed a bedbug.

I was sitting by the radiator, a little damp from the steam, when I heard Norton's knock. I opened the door, and there he was standing in the dark hall with a big parcel wrapped in brown paper under his arm. He smiled and said, "Hello."

I said, "Come in, Norton, and take off your coat."

He unwrapped the Tommy gun and we assembled it and snapped the firing pin.

I said I would find someone to buy it.

Norton said, "Oh, here's something else I picked up."

It was a flat yellow box with five one-half grain syrettes of morphine tartrate.

"This is just a sample," he said, indicating the morphine. "I've got fifteen of these boxes at home and I can get more if you get rid of these."

I said, "I'll see what I can do."

At that time I had never used any junk and it did not occur to me to try it. I began looking for someone to buy the two items and that is how I ran into Roy and Herman.

I knew a young hoodlum from upstate New York who was working as a short-order cook in Jarrow's, "cooling off," as he explained. I called him and said I had something to get rid of, and made an appointment to meet him in the Angle Bar on Eighth Avenue near 42nd Street.

This bar was a meeting place for 42nd Street hustlers, a peculiar breed of four-flushing, would-be criminals. They are always looking for a "setup man," someone to plan jobs and tell them exactly what to do. Since no "setup man" would have anything to do with people so obviously inept, unlucky, and unsuccessful, they go on looking, fabricating preposterous lies about their big scores, cooling off as dishwashers, soda jerks, waiters, occasionally rolling a drunk or a timid queer, looking, always looking, for the "setup man" with a big job who will say, "I've been watching you. You're the man I need for this setup. Now listen . . ."

Jack—through whom I met Roy and Herman—was not one of these lost sheep looking for the shepherd with a diamond ring and a gun in the shoulder holster and the hard, confident voice with overtones of connections, fixes, setups that would make a stickup sound easy and sure of success. Jack was very successful from time to time and would turn up in new clothes and even new cars. He was also an inveterate liar who seemed to lie more for himself than for any visible audience. He had a clean-cut, healthy country face, but there was something curiously diseased about him. He was subject to sudden fluctuations in weight, like a diabetic or a sufferer from liver trouble. These changes in weight were often accompanied by an uncontrollable fit of restlessness, so that he would disappear for some days.

The effect was uncanny. You would see him one time a fresh-faced kid. A week or so later he would turn up so thin, sallow and old-looking, you would have to look twice to recognize him. His face was lined with suffering in which his eyes did not participate. It was a suffering of his cells alone. He himself—the conscious ego that looked out of the glazed, alert-calm hoodlum eyes—would have nothing to do with this suffering of his rejected other self, a suffering of the nervous system, of flesh and viscera and cells.

He slid into the booth where I was sitting and ordered a shot of whisky. He tossed it off, put the glass down and looked at me with his head tilted a little to one side and back.

"What's this guy got?" he said.

"A Tommy gun and about thirty-five grains of morphine."

"The morphine I can get rid of right away, but the Tommy gun may take a little time."

Two detectives walked in and leaned on the bar talking to the bartender. Jack jerked his head in their direction. "The law. Let's take a walk."

I followed him out of the bar. He walked through the door sliding sideways. "I'm taking you to someone who will want the morphine," he said. "You want to forget this address."

We went down to the bottom level of the Independent Subway. Jack's voice, talking to his invisible audience, went on and on. He had a knack of throwing his voice directly into your consciousness. No external noise drowned him out. "Give me a thirty-eight every time. Just flick back the hammer and let her go. I'll drop anyone at five hundred feet. Don't care what you say. My brother has two 30-caliber machine guns stashed in Iowa."

We got off the subway and began to walk on snow-covered sidewalks between tenements.

"The guy owed me for a long time, see? I knew he had it but he wouldn't pay, so I waited for him when he finished work. I had a roll of nickels. No one can hang anything on you for carrying U.S. currency. Told me he was broke. I cracked his jaw and took my money off him. Two of his friends standing there, but they kept out of it. I'd've switched a blade on them."

We were walking up tenement stairs. The stairs were made of worn black metal. We stopped in front of a narrow, metal-covered door, and Jack gave an elaborate knock inclining his head to the floor like a safecracker. The door was opened by a large, flabby, middle-aged queer, with tattooing on his forearms and even on the backs of his hands.

"This is Joey," Jack said, and Joey said, "Hello there."

Jack pulled a five-dollar bill from his pocket and gave it to Joey. "Get us a quart of Schenley's, will you, Joey?"

Joey put on an overcoat and went out.

In many tenement apartments the front door opens directly into the kitchen. This was such an apartment and we were in the kitchen.

After Joey went out I noticed another man who was standing there looking at me. Waves of hostility and suspicion flowed out from his large brown eyes like some sort of television broadcast. The effect was almost like a physical impact. The man was small and very thin, his neck loose in the collar of his shirt. His complexion faded from brown to a mottled yellow, and pancake make-up had been heavily applied in an attempt to conceal a skin eruption. His mouth was drawn down at the corners in a grimace of petulant annoyance.

"Who's this?" he said. His name, I learned later, was Herman.

"Friend of mine. He's got some morphine he wants to get rid of."

Herman shrugged and turned out his hands. "I don't think I want to bother, really."

"Okay," Jack said, "we'll sell it to someone else. Come on, Bill."

We went into the front room. There was a small radio, a china Buddha with a votive candle in front of it, pieces of bric-a-brac. A man was lying on a studio couch. He sat up as we entered the room and smiled pleasantly showing discolored, brownish teeth. It was a Southern voice with the accent of east Texas.

Jack said, "Roy, this is a friend of mine. He has some morphine he wants to sell."

The man sat up straighter and swung his legs off the couch. His jaw fell slackly, giving his face a vacant look. The skin of his face was smooth and brown. The cheekbones were high and he looked Oriental. His ears stuck out at right angles from his asymmetrical skull. The eyes were brown and they had a peculiar brilliance, as though points of light were shining behind them. The light in the room glinted on the points of light in his eyes like an opal.

"How much do you have?" he asked me.

"Seventy-five one-half grain syrettes."

"The regular price is two dollars a grain," he said, "but syrettes go for a little less. People want tablets. Those syrettes have too much water and you have to squeeze the stuff out and cook it down." He paused and his face went blank. "I could go about one-fifty a grain," he said finally.

"I guess that will be okay," I said.

He asked how we could make contact and I gave him my phone number.

Joey came back with the whisky and we all had a drink. Herman stuck his head in from the kitchen and said to Jack, "Could I talk to you for a minute?"

I could hear them arguing about something. Then Jack came back and Herman stayed in the kitchen. We all had a few drinks and Jack began telling a story.

"My partner was going through the joint. The guy was sleeping, and I was standing over him with a three-foot length of pipe I found in the bathroom. The pipe had a faucet on the end of it, see? All of a sudden he comes up and jumps straight out of bed, running. I let him have it with the faucet end, and he goes on running right out into the other room, the blood spurting out of his head ten feet every time his heart beat." He made a pumping motion with his hand. "You could see the brain there and the blood coming out of it." Jack began to laugh uncontrollably. "My girl was waiting out in the car. She called me—ha-ha-ha!—she called me—ha-ha-ha!—a cold-blooded killer."

He laughed until his face was purple.

A few nights after meeting Roy and Herman, I used one of the syrettes, which was my first experience with junk. A syrette is like a toothpaste tube with a needle on the end. You push a pin down through the needle; the pin punctures the seal; and the syrette is ready to shoot.

Morphine hits the backs of the legs first, then the back of the neck, a spreading wave of relaxation slackening the muscles away from the bones so that you seem to float without outlines like lying in warm salt water. As this relaxing wave spread through my tissues, I experienced a strong feeling of fear. I had the feeling that some horrible image was just beyond the field of vision, moving, as I turned my head, so that I never quite saw it. I felt nauseous; I lay down and closed my eyes. A series of pictures passed, like watching a movie: A huge, neon-lighted cocktail bar that got larger and larger until streets, traffic, and street repairs were included in it; a waitress carrying a skull on a tray; stars in the clear sky. The physical impact of the fear of death; the shutting off of breath; the stopping of blood.

I dozed off and woke up with a start of fear. Next morning I vomited and felt sick until noon.

Roy called that night.

"About what we were discussing the other night," he said. "I could go about four dollars per box and take five boxes now. Are you busy? I'll come over to your place. We'll come to some kind of agreement."

A few minutes later he knocked at the door. He had on a Glen plaid suit and a dark, coffee-colored shirt. We said hello. He looked around blankly and said, "If you don't mind, I'll take one of those now."

I opened the box. He took out a syrette and injected it into his leg. He pulled up his pants briskly and took out twenty dollars. I put five boxes on the kitchen table.

"I think I'll take them out of the boxes," he said. "Too bulky."

He began putting the syrettes in his coat pockets. "I don't think they'll perforate this way," he said. "Listen, I'll call you again in a day or so after I get rid of these and have some more money." He was adjusting his hat over his asymmetrical skull. "I'll see you."

Next day he was back. He shot another syrette and pulled out forty dollars. I laid out ten boxes and kept two.

"These are for me," I said.

He looked at me, surprised. "You use it?"

"Now and then."

"It's bad stuff," he said, shaking his head. "The worst thing that can happen to a man. We all think we can control it at first. Sometimes we don't want to control it." He laughed. "I'll take all you can get at this price."

Next day he was back. He asked if I didn't want to change my mind about selling the two boxes. I said no. He bought two syrettes for a dollar each, shot them both, and left. He said he had signed on for a two-month trip.

During the next month I used up the eight syrettes I had not sold. The fear I had experienced after using the first syrette was not noticeable after the third; but still, from time to time, after taking a shot I would wake up with a start of fear. After six weeks or so I gave Roy a ring, not expecting him to be back from his trip, but then I heard his voice on the phone.

I said, "Say, do you have any to sell? Of the material I sold you before?"

There was a pause.

"Ye-es," he said, "I can let you have six, but the price will have to be three dollars per. You understand I don't have many."

"Okay," I said. "You know the way. Bring it on over."

It was twelve one-half grain tablets in a thin glass tube. I paid him eighteen dollars and he apologized again for the retail rate.

Next day he bought two grains back.

"It's mighty hard to get now at any price," he said, looking for a vein in his leg. He finally hit a vein and shot the liquid in with an air bubble. "If air bubbles could kill you, there wouldn't be a junkie alive."

Later that day Roy pointed out to me a drugstore where they sold needles without any questions—very few drugstores will sell them without a prescription. He showed me how to make a collar out of paper to fit the needle to an eyedropper. An eyedropper is easier to use than a regular hypo, especially for giving yourself vein shots.

Several days later Roy sent me to see a doctor with a story about kidney stones, to hit him for a morphine prescription. The doctor's wife slammed the door in my face, but Roy finally got past her and made the doctor for a ten-grain script.

The doctor's office was in junk territory on 102nd, off Broadway. He was a doddering old man and could not resist the junkies who filled his office and were, in fact, his only patients. It seemed to give him a feeling of importance to look out and see an office full of people. I guess he had reached a point where he could change the appearance of things to suit his needs and when he looked out there he saw a distinguished and diversified clientele, probably well-dressed in 1910 style, instead of a bunch of ratty-looking junkies come to hit him for a morphine script.

Roy shipped out at two- or three-week intervals. His trips were Army Transport and generally short. When he was in town we generally split a few scripts. The old croaker on 102nd finally lost his mind altogether and no drugstore would fill his scripts, but Roy located an Italian doctor out in the Bronx who would write.

I was taking a shot from time to time, but I was a long way from having a habit. At this time I moved into an apartment on the Lower East Side. It was a tenement apartment with the front door opening into the kitchen.

I began dropping into the Angle Bar every night and saw quite a bit of Herman. I managed to overcome his original bad impression of me, and soon I was buying his drinks and meals, and he was hitting me for "smash" (change) at regular intervals. Herman did not have a habit at this time. In fact, he seldom got a habit unless someone else paid for it. But he was always high on something—weed, benzedrine, or knocked out of his mind on "goof balls." He showed up at the Angle every night with a big slob called Whitey. There were four Whiteys in the Angle set, which made for confusion. This Whitey combined the sensitivity of a neurotic with a psychopath's readiness for violence. He was convinced that nobody liked him, a fact that seemed to cause him a great deal of worry.

One Tuesday night Roy and I were standing at the end of the Angle bar. Subway Mike was there, and Frankie Dolan. Dolan was an Irish boy with a cast in one eye. He specialized in crummy scores, beating up defenseless drunks, and holding out on his confederates. "I got no honor," he would say. "I'm a rat." And he would giggle.

Subway Mike had a large, pale face and long teeth. He looked like some specialized kind of underground animal that preys on the animals of the surface. He was a skillful lush-worker, but he had no front. Any cop would do a double-take at the sight of him, and he was well known to the subway squad. So Mike spent at least half of his time on the Island doing "five-twenty-nine" for jostling.

This night Herman was knocked out on "nembies" and his head kept falling down onto the bar. Whitey was stomping up and down the length of the bar trying to promote some free drinks. The boys at the bar sat rigid and tense, clutching their drinks, quickly pocketing their change. I heard Whitey say to the bartender, "Keep this for me, will you?" and he passed his large clasp knife across the bar. The boys sat there silent and gloomy under the fluorescent lights. They were all afraid of Whitey, all except Roy. Roy sipped his beer grimly. His eyes shone with their peculiar phosphorescence. His long asymmetrical body was draped against the bar. He didn't look at Whitey, but at the opposite wall where the booths were located. Once he said to me, "He's no more drunk than I am. He's just thirsty."

Whitey was standing in the middle of the bar, his fists doubled up, tears streaming down his face. "I'm no good," he said. "I'm no good. Can't anyone understand I don't know what I'm doing?"

The boys tried to get as far away from him as possible without attracting his attention.

Subway Slim, Mike's occasional partner, came in and ordered a beer. He was tall and bony, and his ugly face had a curiously inanimate look, as if made out of wood. Whitey slapped him on the back and I heard Slim say, "For Christ's sake, Whitey." There was more interchange I didn't hear. Somewhere along the line Whitey must have got his knife back from the bartender. He got behind Slim and suddenly pushed his hand against Slim's back. Slim fell forward against the bar, groaning. I saw Whitey walk to the front of the bar and look around. He closed his knife and slipped it into his pocket. Roy said, "Let's go."

Whitey had disappeared and the bar was empty except for Mike who was holding Slim up on one side. Frankie Dolan was on the other.

I heard next day from Frankie that Slim was okay. "The croaker at the hospital said the knife just missed a kidney."

Roy said, "The big slob. I can see a real muscle man, but a guy like that going around picking up dimes and quarters off the bar. I was ready for him. I was going to kick him in the belly first, then get one of those quart beer bottles from the case on the floor and break it over his sconce. With a big villain like that you've got to use strategy."

We were all barred from the Angle, which shortly afterwards changed its name to the Kent Grill.

One night I went to the Henry Street address to look up Jack. A tall, red-haired girl met me at the door.

"I'm Mary," she said. "Come in."

It seemed that Jack was in Washington on business.

"Come on into the front room," she said, pushing aside a red corduroy curtain. "I talk to landlords and bill collectors in the kitchen. We *live* in here."

I looked around. The bric-a-brac had gone. The place looked like a chop suey joint. There were black and red lacquered tables scattered around, black curtains covered the window. A colored wheel had been painted on the ceiling with little squares and triangles of different colors giving a mosaic effect.

"Jack did that," Mary said, pointing to the wheel. "You should have seen him. He stretched a board between two ladders and lay down on it. Paint kept dripping into his face. He gets a kick out of doing things like that. We get some frantic kicks out of that wheel when we're high. We lay on our backs and dig the wheel and pretty soon it begins to spin. The longer you watch it, the faster it spins."

This wheel had the nightmarish vulgarity of Aztec mosaics, the bloody, vulgar nightmare, the heart throbbing in the morning sun, the garish pinks and blues of souvenir ashtrays, postcards and calendars. The walls were painted black and there was a Chinese character in red lacquer on one wall.

"We don't know what it means," she said.

"Shirts thirty-one cents," I suggested.

She turned on me her blank, cold smile. She began talking about Jack. "I'm queer for Jack," she said. "He works at being a thief just like any job. Used to come home nights and hand me his gun. 'Stash that!' He likes to work around the house, painting and making furniture."

As she talked she moved around the room, throwing herself from one chair to another, crossing and uncrossing her legs, adjusting her slip, so as to give me a view of her anatomy in installments.

She went on to tell me how her days were numbered by a rare disease. "Only twenty-six cases on record. In a few years I won't be able to get around at all. You see, my system can't absorb calcium and the bones are slowly dissolving. My legs will have to be amputated eventually, then the arms."

There was something boneless about her, like a deep sea creature. Her eyes were cold fish-eyes that looked at you through a viscous medium she carried about with her. I could see those eyes in a shapeless, protoplasmic mass undulating over the dark sea floor.

"Benzedrine is a good kick," she said. "Three strips of the paper or about ten tablets. Or take two strips of benny and two goof balls. They get down there and have a fight. It's a good drive."

Three young hoodlums from Brooklyn drifted in, wooden-faced, hands-in-pockets, stylized as a ballet. They were looking for Jack. He had given them a short count in some deal. At least, that was the general idea. They conveyed their meaning less by words than by significant jerks of the head and by stalking around the apartment and leaning against the walls. At length, one of them walked to the door and jerked his head. They filed out.

"Would you like to get high?" Mary asked. "There may be a roach around here somewhere." She began rummaging around in drawers and ashtrays. "No, I guess not. Why don't we go uptown? I know several good connections we can probably catch about now."

A young man lurched in with some object wrapped in brown paper under one arm. "Ditch this on your way out," he said, putting it down on the table. He staggered into the bedroom on the other side of the kitchen. When we got outside I let the wrapping paper fall loose revealing the coin box of a pay toilet crudely jimmied open.

In Times Square we got into a taxi and began cruising up and down the side streets, Mary giving directions. Every now and then she would yell "Stop!" and jump out, her red hair streaming, and I would see her overhaul some character and start talking. "The connection was here about ten minutes ago. This character's holding, but he won't turn loose of any." Later: "The regular connection is gone for the night. He lives in the Bronx. But just stop here for a minute. I may find someone in Rich's." Finally: "No one seems to be anywhere. It's a bit late to score. Let's buy some benny tubes and go over to Denny's. They have some gone numbers on the box. We can order coffee and get high on benny."

Denny's was a spot near 52nd and Sixth where musicians came for fried chicken and coffee after one P.M. We sat down in a booth and ordered coffee. Mary cracked a benzedrine tube expertly, extracting the folded paper, and handed me three strips. "Roll it up into a pill and wash it down with coffee."

The paper gave off a sickening odor of menthol. Several people sitting nearby sniffed and smiled. I nearly gagged on the wad of paper, but finally got it down. Mary selected some gone numbers and beat on the table with the expression of a masturbating idiot.

I began talking very fast. My mouth was dry and my spit came out in round white balls—spitting cotton, it's called. We were walking around Times Square. Mary wanted to locate someone with a "piccolo" (victrola). I was full of expansive, benevolent feelings, and suddenly wanted to call on people I hadn't seen in months or even years, people I did not like and who did not like me. We made a number of unsuccessful attempts to locate the ideal piccolo-owning host. Somewhere along the line we picked up Peter and finally decided to go back to the Henry Street apartment where there was at least a radio.

Peter and Mary and I spent the next thirty hours in the apartment. From time to time we would make coffee and swallow more benzedrine. Mary was describing the techniques she used to get money from the "Johns" who formed her principal source of revenue.

"Always build a John up. If he has any sort of body at all, say, 'Oh, don't ever hurt me.' A John is different from a sucker. When you're with a sucker you're on the alert all the time. You give him nothing. A sucker is just to be taken. But a John is different. You give him what he pays for. When you're with him you enjoy yourself and you want him to enjoy himself, too.

"If you want to really bring a man down, light a cigarette in the middle of intercourse. Of course, I really don't like men at all sexually. What I really dig is chicks. I get a kick out of taking a proud chick and breaking her spirit, making her see she is just an animal. A chick is never beautiful after she's been broken. Say, this is sort of a fireside kick," she said, pointing to the radio which was the only light in the room. Her face contorted into an expression of monkey-like rage as she talked about men who accosted her on the street. "Sonofabitch!" she snarled. "They can tell when a woman isn't looking for a pickup. I used to cruise around with brass knuckles on under my gloves just waiting for one of those peasants to crack at me."

One day Herman told me about a kilo of first-class New Orleans' weed I could pick up for seventy dollars. Pushing weed looks good on paper, like fur farming or raising frogs. At seventy-five cents a stick, seventy sticks to the ounce, it sounded like money. I was convinced, and bought the weed.

Herman and I formed a partnership to push the weed. He located a Lesbian named Marian who lived in the Village and said she was a poetess. We kept the weed in Marian's apartment, turned her on for all she could use, and gave her a 50 per cent commission on the sales. She knew a lot of teaheads. Another Lesbian moved in with her, and every time I went to Marian's apartment, there was this huge red-haired Lizzie watching me with her cold fish-eyes full of stupid hate.

One day, the red-haired Lizzie opened the door and stood there, her face dead white and puffy with nembutal sleep. She shoved the package of weed at me. "Take this and get out," she said. She looked at us through heavily lidded eyes. "You bastards!"

I said, "Tell Marian thanks for everything."

She slammed the door. The noise evidently woke her up. She opened the door again and began screaming with hysterical rage. We could still hear her out on the street.

Herman contacted other teaheads. They all gave us static.

In practice, pushing weed is a headache. To begin with, weed is bulky. You need a full suitcase to realize any money. If the cops start kicking your door in, it's like being with a bale of alfalfa.

Teaheads are not like junkies. A junkie hands you the money, takes his junk and cuts. But teaheads don't do things that way. They expect the peddler to light them up and sit around talking for half an hour to sell two dollars' worth of weed. If you come right to the point, they say you are a "bring down." In fact, a peddler should not come right out and say he is a peddler. No, he just scores for a few good "cats" and "chicks" because he is viperish. Everyone knows that he himself is the connection, but it is bad form to say so. God knows why. To me, teaheads are unfathomable.

There are a lot of trade secrets in the tea business, and teaheads guard these supposed secrets with imbecilic slyness. For example, tea must be cured, or it is green and rasps the throat. But ask a teahead how to cure weed and he will give you a sly, stupid look and come-on with some doubletalk. Perhaps weed does affect the brain with constant use, or maybe teaheads are naturally silly.

The tea I had was green so I put it in a double boiler and set the boiler in the oven until the tea got the grennish-brown look it should have. This is the secret of curing tea, or at least one way to do it.

Teaheads are gregarious, they are sensitive, and they are paranoiac. If you get to be known as a "drag" or a "bring down," you can't do business with them. I soon found out I couldn't get along with these characters and I was glad to find someone to take the tea off my hands at cost. I decided right then I would never push any more tea.

CARL SOLOMON

Report from the Asylum

> *Insanity—here is the ultimate retreat,
> more insulating than heroin, weed or
> bop. In a world where the "upward
> and onward" assurance of positivism
> always rings false, madness is the
> most sure way (next to death) of
> breaking the clock, stopping time,
> and splintering life into a stream of
> acutely felt sensations that impose no
> demands and bring no consciousness
> of guilt.*

A BOOK THAT IS ACCEPTED, at the moment, as the definitive work on shock-therapy (Hoch and Kalinowski, *Shock Therapy*) concludes with the astonishing admission that the curative agent in shock-treatment "remains a mystery shrouded within a mystery." This confession of ignorance (and it is extended to both insulin and electric shock-therapies), by two of the men who actually place the electrodes on the heads of mental patients at one of four psychiatric hospitals, certainly opens this field of inquiry to the sensitive layman as well as to the technician. The testimony that follows is that of an eye-witness, one who has undergone insulin-shock treatment and has slept through fifty comas.

One may begin with amusement at the hashish-smokers and their conception of the sublime. They, who at the very most, have been "high," consider themselves (quite properly) to be persons of *eminence* and archimandrates of a *High* Church. A patient emerging from an insulin coma, however, cannot help being a confirmed democrat. There can be no hierarchization of different levels of transcendency when they are induced by an intravenously-injected animal secretion, the very purpose of which is to bombard insulin-space with neutrons of glucose-time until space vanishes like a frightened child and one awakens terrified to find oneself bound fast by a restraining-sheet (wholly supererogatory to the patient, since, in the waking state, spaceless mobility seems inconceivable). The ingenuousness of the hashishins is stupendous.

It is as though the Insulin Man were to call his drug by a pet name and spend days thrashing out the differences between "gone pot" and "nowhere pot."

The difference between hashish and insulin is in many ways similar to a difference between surrealism and magic. The one is affective and is administered by the subject himself; the other is violently resisted by the subject (since this substance offers not even the most perverse form of satisfactions); it is forcibly administered in the dead of night by white-clad, impersonal creatures who tear the subject from his bed, carry him screaming into an elevator, strap him to another bed on another floor, and who, later, recall him from his "revery" (a purely polemical term employed in writing "down" to the hashishin). Thus, insulin comes as a succubus, is effective, suggests grace.

In this respect, the paranoid phantasies released by hashish lack substantiality and are the nature of automatic writing or gratuitous acts. In the case of insulin-shock therapy, one finds oneself presented with a complete symbolism of paranoia, beginning with the rude awakening and the enormous hypodermic-needle, continuing through the dietary restrictions imposed upon patients receiving shock, and ending with the lapses of memory and the temporary physical disfigurement.

Early in the treatment, which consists of fifty hypoglycemic comas,

I reacted in a highly paranoid manner and mocked the doctors by accusing them of "amputating" my brain. Of course, my illness was such that I was perpetually joking (having presented myself to the hospital upon reaching my majority, I had requested immediate electrocution since I was now of age—how serious was this request, I have no way of knowing—and was discharged as cured exactly nine months later, the day before Christmas).

Nevertheless, I noted similar paranoid responses on the part of other patients in shock.

For those of us acquainted with Kafka, an identification with K. became inevitable. Slowly, however, the identification with K. and with similar characters came to imply far more than we Kafkians had ever dreamed. We knew it to be true that we had been abducted for the most absurd of reasons: for spending hours at a time in the family-shower, for plotting to kill a soldier, for hurling refuse at a lecturer. And, in this particular, the text had been followed quite literally. The need for a revision of the Kafkian perspective arose, however, when the bureaucracy suddenly revealed itself as benevolent. We had not been dragged to a vacant lot and murdered, but had been dragged to a Garden of Earthly Delights and had there been fed (there were exceptions and there is a certain small percentage of fatalities resulting from shock, making the parallel to grace even more obvious). This impression arose, somehow, from the very nature of the subjective coma.

Upon being strapped into my insulin-bed, I would at once break off my usual stream of puns and hysterical chatter. I would stare at the bulge I made beneath the canvas restraining-sheet, and my body, insulin-packed, would become to me an enormous concrete pun with infinite levels of association, and thereby, a means of surmounting association with things, much as the verbal puns had surmounted the meaning of words. And beneath this wrathful anticipation of world-destruction lay a vague fear of the consequences.

The coma soon confirms all of the patient's fears. What began as a drugged sleep soon changes organically and becomes one of the millions of psychophysical universes through which he must pass, before being awakened by his dose of glucose. And he cannot become accustomed to these things. Each coma is utterly incomparable to that of the previous day. Lacking a time-sense and inhabiting all of these

universes at one and the same time, my condition was one of omni-
presence, of being everywhere at no time. Hence, of being nowhere.
Hence, of inhabiting that Void of which Antonin Artaud had
screamed (I had been conditioned in illness by classical surrealism).

Invariably, I emerged from the comas bawling like an infant and
flapping my arms crazily (after they had been unfastened), screaming,
"Eat!" or, "Help!"

The nurses and doctors would ignore me, letting me flap about
until my whole aching body and my aching mind (which felt as if
it had been sprained) pulled themselves by their bootstraps out of the
void of terror and, suddenly, attained a perfectly disciplined silence.
This, of course, won the admiration of the dispensers of grace, who
then decided that I was eminently worth saving and promptly brought
me my breakfast tray and a glucose apertif. And in this manner, item
by item, the bureaucracy of the hospital presents the insulin *maudit*
with a world of delightful objects all made of sugar—and gradually
wins his undying allegiance. If we are not deceived by appearances
we will see clearly that it is the entire world of things which imposes
itself upon the would-be *maudit* and eventually becomes the object
of his idolatry.

All told, the atmosphere of the insulin-ward was one in which, to
the sick, miracles appeared to be occurring constantly. And, most
traumatic of all, they were concrete miracles. For example, I am reminded of the day I went into a coma free of crab-lice and emerged
thoroughly infested (the sheets are sterilized daily). I had caught the
lice in somebody else's coma, since these states of unconsciousness are
concrete and are left lying about the universe even after they have
been vacated by the original occupant. And this was so credited by
one of my fellow patients that he refused to submit to the needle the
next day out of fear of venturing into one of my old comas and in-
festing himself. He believed that I had lied and that I'd had crabs
for some time, having caught them in some previous coma.

Meanwhile, on that following day, I was revived from my coma
intravenously by an Egyptian resident psychiatrist, who then, very
brusquely, ordered the nurses to wrap the sheets around me a bit
tighter lest I should free myself prematurely; I shrieked, "Amenhotep!"

And there was the day a young patient who had given the impression of being virtually illiterate, received his intravenous glucose (one is revived from a deep coma in this manner), and then gave ample evidence that he had become thoroughly acquainted with the works of Jacob Boehme in the course of his coma. Simone de Beauvoir, in her book on her travels in America, expresses her consternation upon finding that a member of the editorial board of *Partisan Review* once openly admitted to being ignorant of the writings of Boehme.

Shortly after my mummification and defiance of Amenhotep, I encountered what appeared to be a new patient, to whom I mumbled amicably, "I'm Kirilov." He mumbled, in reply, "I'm Myshkin." The cadence of the superreal was never challenged; not one of us would dare assume responsibility for a breach of the unity which each hallucination required.

These collective phantasies in which we dreamed each others' dreams contributed to the terror created by contact with the flat, unpredictable insulin void, which had not yet been rendered entirely felicitous (as it was to be later) by the persistent benevolence of man and glucose, and from which all sorts of incredible horrors might yet spring.

The concomitants of therapeutic purgation were, for me, a rather thoroughly atomized amnesia (produced by an insulin convulsion of a rare type and occurring in not more than 2% of cases) and a burgeoning obesity caused by the heavy consumption of glucose. Much later in my treatment, when intensive psychotherapy had replaced insulin, both of these phenomena came to assume places of great importance in the pattern of my reorientation. As my illness had often been verbalized, the first effect of the amnesia was to create a verbal and ideational aphasia, from which resulted an unspoken panic. I had quite simply forgotten the name of my universe, though it was also true that this name rested on the tip of my tongue throughout the amnesiac period. All ideas and all sense of the object had been lost temporarily, and what remained was a state of conscious ideational absence which can only be defined in clinical terms—as amnesia. (So great was the sense of tangible loss that I later insisted upon an electroencephalographic examination, to reassure myself that no organic damage had resulted from the convulsion.) I had been handed, by skilled and provident men, the very concrete void I'd sought. During this period, I had gained sixty pounds, and upon consulting a mirror, I was confronted with the dual inability to recognize myself or to remember what I had looked like prior to treatment, prior to reaching my majority.

When I recovered from my amnesia sufficiently to find my way about, I was permitted to leave the hospital on Sundays, in the company of a relative of whom I would take immediate leave. My relatives on these occasions seemed entirely oblivious to any change in my behavior or physique. Generally, still rather hazy, I would be escorted by an old neurotic friend to a homosexual bar where, I would be informed, I had formerly passed much time. However, the most appalling situations would arise at this point, since, in my corpulent forgetfulness, I no longer remotely resembled a "butch" fairy or "rough trade." I had lost all facility with "gay" argot and was incapable of producing any erotic response to the objects proffered me.

Almost imperceptibly, however, the process of object-selection began once more in all realms of activity, and gained momentum.

I amazed my friends in a restaurant one Sunday afternoon by insisting that the waiter remove an entree with which I had been dissatisfied and that he replace it with another. And even greater was their incredulity when they witnessed my abrupt handling of a beggar, this having been the first time that I had ever rejected a request for alms.

> The yearning infinite recoils
> For terrible is earth.
> —Melville, "L'Envoi."

At about this time, I wrote a sort of manifesto, called "Manifest," which is a most pertinent artifact:

> Corsica is an island situated off the coast of Sardinia. Its capital is Ajaccio and it was here that Napoleon Bonaparte was born. Though it is part of the French Empire, Corsica is not part of the mainland. It is an island. As Capri is an island, and Malta. It is not attached to the European mainland. I am in a position to insist upon this point. There is a body of water separating the two, and it is known as the Mediterranean Sea. This is borne out by the maps now in use. I brook

no contradiction. If I am challenged on this point, the world will rush to my assistance in one way or another. What I have just written is a standing challenge to all the forces of evil, of idiocy, of irrelevance, of death, of silence, of vacancy, of transcendency, etc. And I rest secure in the knowledge that my challenge will never be accepted by that *scum* to whom I've addressed it. I've spent considerable time in the clutches of the LOON and I've waited for this opportunity to avenge myself by humiliating the void. Thank you for your kind attention.

—A VEHEMENT ADULT

As the business of selection became increasingly complex, I appeared to develop an unprecedented (for me) suavity in operating within clearly defined limits. Madness had presented itself as an irrelevancy, and I was now busily engaged in assigning values of comparative relevance to all objects within my reach.

My total rejection of psychiatry, which had, after coma, become a fanatical adulation, now passed into a third phase—one of constructive criticism. I became aware of the peripheral obtuseness and the administrative dogmatism of the hospital bureaucracy. My first impulse was to condemn; later, I perfected means of maneuvering freely within the clumsy structure of ward politics. To illustrate, my reading matter had been kept under surveillance for quite some time, and I had at last perfected a means of keeping *au courant* without unnecessarily alarming the nurses and attendants. I had smuggled several issues of *Hound and Horn* into my ward on the pretext that it was a field-and-stream magazine. I had read Hoch and Kalinowski's *Shock Therapy* (a top secret manual of arms at the hospital) quite openly, after I had put it into the dust jacket of Anna Balakian's *Literary Origins of Surrealism*. Oddly enough, I hadn't thought it necessary to take such pains with Trotsky's *Permanent Revolution* and had become rudely aware of the entire body politic I had so long neglected, when, one evening, I was sharply attacked by the Head Nurse of the ward for "communism." He had slipped behind me on little cat feet and had been reading the book over my shoulder.

The psychiatric ineptitude of the official lower echelons became incredible when, one week before Halloween, it was announced to the patients that a masquerade ball would be held on the appropriate date, that attendance was to be mandatory, and that a prize would be given to the patient wearing the "best" costume. Whereupon, the patients, among whom there was a high spirit of competition, threw themselves precipitously into the work of creating what, for each, promised to be the most striking disguise. The work of sewing, tearing, dyeing, etc., was done in Occupational Therapy, where, at the disposal of all, were an infinite variety of paints, gadgets, and fabrics. Supervising all this furious activity was a pedagogic harpy, who had been assigned as Occupational Therapist to see that we didn't destroy any of the implements in the shop (she tried to persuade me to attend the masquerade made up as a dog). Furiously we labored, competing with one another even in regard to speed of accomplishment, fashioning disguised phalluses, swords, spears, scars for our faces, enormous cysts for our heads. When Halloween Night arrived, we were led, dazed and semi-amnesiac, into the small gymnasium that served as a dance floor. Insidious tensions intruded themselves as the time for the awarding of the prize approached. Finally, the Social Therapists seated themselves in the center of the polished floor and ordered us to parade past them in a great circle; one of the nurses sat at the piano and played a march; to the strains of the music, we stepped forward to present our respective embodied idealizations to the judges. There were several Hamlets, a Lear, a grotesque Mr. Hyde, a doctor; there were many cases of transvestism; a young man obsessed with the idea that he was an inanimate object had come as an electric-lamp, brightly-lit, complete with shade; a boy who had filled his head to the point of bursting with baseball lore had come as a "Brooklyn Bum," in derby and tatters. Suddenly, the music stopped; the judges had chosen a winner, rejecting the others; we never learned who the winner had been, so chaotic was the scene that followed. There was a groan of deep torment from the entire group (each feeling that his dream had been condemned). Phantasmal shapes flung themselves about in despair. The nurses and Social Therapists spent the next hour in consoling the losers.

Thus I progressed, after my series of fifty comas had ended, and finally reached my normal weight of 180 pounds and my true sexual

orientation: adult heterosexuality (which became my true sexual orientation only after the basic androgynous death-wish had been re-
directed). It is probably true, however, that my case is atypical and
that the great majority of such transformations are not quite as
thorough-going, and in some cases, fail to materialize at all. There
were those patients who were completely unmoved by the experience
of the coma, and who found that it did nothing more than to stimu-
late their appetites. And there were those Kafkians who remained
confirmed paranoiacs to the bitter end.

I should like to quote a passage from an article by the French poet,
Antonin Artaud, published posthumously in the February, 1949, issue
of *Les Temps Modernes*. Artaud had undergone both electric and
insulin shock-therapies during his period of confinement which lasted
nine years and terminated with his death in March, 1948.

> I died at Rodez under electro-shock. I say dead. Legally and
> medically dead. The coma of electro-shock lasts a quarter of
> an hour. Another half-hour and the invalid is breathing. But,
> one hour after shock I hadn't awakened and had stopped
> breathing. Surprised by my abnormal rigidity, an attendant
> went to look for the chief-doctor, who after auscultation found
> in me no sign of life. I have my own memories of my death
> at that moment, but it is not upon them that I base my
> accusation.
>
> I restrict myself to the particulars which were given to me
> by Dr. Jean Dequeker, young interne of the Rodez asylum,
> who got them from the mouth of Dr. Ferdiere himself.
>
> And the latter had told him that day he believed me dead,
> and that he had summoned two asylum guards to instruct
> them to transport my body to the morgue since I had not
> returned to myself one hour and a half after shock.
>
> And it appeared that at the very moment the attendants
> entered to remove my body it quivered slightly, after which
> I awakened all at once.
>
> I have another recollection of it.
>
> But this memory I had guarded in secret until that day
> when Dr. Jean Dequeker confirmed it for me from without.
>
> And this recollection is that, confirming all Dr. Jean
> Dequeker had told me, I had seen not this side of the world
> but the other. . . .

What he describes above was the experience of us all, but with Artaud and so many others, it stopped short and became the permanent level of existence: the absence of myth represented by the brief "death" was accepted as the culminating, all-embracing myth. Artaud went on to write, in his essay on Van Gogh, that a lunatic "is a man who has preferred to become what is socially understood as mad rather than forfeit a certain superior idea of human honor"; and to write further that "a vicious society has invented psychiatry to defend itself from the investigations of certain superior lucid minds whose intuitive powers were disturbing to it"; and that "every psychiatrist is a low-down son-of-a-bitch." In Paris, quite outrageously, this heart-rendingly skewed essay written by a grievously ill man was honored with a Prix Sainte-Beuve and was underwritten by several of the most distinguished French critics.

I have a small mind and I mean to use it.

The sentence above epitomizes the real lesson of insulin, that of tragedy, and it was neither written nor would it have been understood by Artaud, who remains (he wrote that "the dead continue to revolve around their corpses") a sublime comic figure, one who averted his eyes from the spectre of reality, one who never admitted to having dimensions or sex, and who was incapable of recognizing his own mortality. (In the list of comic figures of our time we can include the homosexual.)

My release from the hospital was followed by a period of headlong and vindictive commitment to substance, a period which continues, which is full of tactical and syntactical retreats and rapid reversals of opinion. It is obvious by this time, though, that the changes of opinion are becoming less frequent, that the truculent drive toward compulsive readjustment, toward the "acting out" of one's adjustment, has been dissipated. My attitude toward the magic I've witnessed is similar to that of the African student I met a month ago, who told me that his uncle had been a witch-doctor. He had seen his uncle turn to a cat before his eyes. He had simply thrown the uncle-cat a scrap of meat, hadn't been particularly impressed by the magic (though conceding its validity), and had come to America to acquire the political and technological skills with which to modernize his country upon his return.

For the ailing intellect, there can be great danger in the poetizing of the coma-void. Only when it is hopelessly distorted and its concrete nature disguised can it serve as material for myth-making. To confront the coma full-face, one must adhere to factual detail and this procedure need not prove deadening. On the contrary, the real coma administers a fillip to one's debilitated thinking processes. Jarry's de-braining-machine was not the surgeon's scalpel but was contained within his own cranium. It was to place the coma thus in context that I undertook this examination of its architectonics.

ALLEN GINSBERG

Howl

FOR CARL SOLOMON

Published originally in Howl and Other Poems by The City Lights Pocket Bookshop, "Howl" received national publicity when San Francisco authorities banned its sale on the grounds that the work was "lewd and obscene." After an intense court battle in which outstanding literary personalities defended the poem as a significant comment on human experience, Judge Clayton W. Horn declared "Howl" to be not obscene. In his decision, he wrote: "Life is not encased in one formula whereby everyone acts the same or conforms to a particular pattern. No two persons think alike. We are all made from the same mould, but in different patterns. Would there be any freedom of press or speech if one must reduce his vocabulary to vapid innocuous euphemism? An author should be real in treating his subject and be allowed to express his thoughts and ideas in his own words."

"Howl" is the extreme protest of the Beat Generation.

I SAW THE BEST MINDS of my generation destroyed
        by madness, starving hysterical naked,
dragging themselves through the negro streets at dawn
        looking for an angry fix,

angelheaded hipsters burning for the ancient heavenly connection to
    the starry dynamo in the machinery of night,
who poverty and tatters and hollow-eyed and high sat up smoking in
    the supernatural darkness of cold-water flats floating across
    the tops of cities contemplating jazz,
who bared their brains to Heaven under the El and saw Mohammedan
    angels staggering on tenement roofs illuminated,
who passed through universities with radiant cool eyes hallucinating
    Arkansas and Blake-light tragedy among the scholars of war,
who were expelled from the academies for crazy & publishing obscene
    odes on the windows of the skull,
who cowered in unshaven rooms in underwear, burning their money
    in wastebaskets and listening to the Terror through the wall,
who got busted in their pubic beards returning through Laredo with
    a belt of marijuana for New York,
who ate fire in paint hotels or drank turpentine in Paradise Alley,
    death, or purgatoried their torsos night after night
with dreams, with drugs, with walking nightmares, alcohol and cock
    and endless balls,
incomparable blind streets of shuddering cloud and lightning in the
    mind leaping toward poles of Canada & Paterson, illuminat-
    ing all the motionless world of Time between,
Peyote solidities of halls, backyard green tree cemetery dawns, wine
    drunkenness over the rooftops, storefront boroughs of tea-
    head joyride neon blinking traffic light, sun and moon and
    tree vibrations in the roaring winter dusks of Brooklyn,
    ashcan rantings and kind king light of mind,
who chained themselves to subways for the endless ride from Battery
    to holy Bronx on benzedrine until the noise of wheels and
    children brought them down shuddering mouth-wracked
    and battered bleak of brain all drained of brilliance in the
    drear light of Zoo,
who sank all night in submarine light of Bickford's floated out and
    sat through the stale beer afternoon in desolate Fugazzi's,
    listening to the crack of doom on the hydrogen jukebox,
who talked continuously seventy hours from park to pad to bar to
    Bellevue to museum to the Brooklyn Bridge,
a lost battalion of platonic conversationalists jumping down the stoops

off fire escapes off windowsills off Empire State out of the
moon,

yacketayakking screaming vomiting whispering facts and memories
and anecdotes and eyeball kicks and shocks of hospitals and
jails and wars,

whole intellects disgorged in total recall for seven days and nights
with brilliant eyes, meat for the Synagogue cast on the
pavement,

who vanished into nowhere Zen New Jersey leaving a trail of
ambiguous picture postcards of Atlantic City Hall,

suffering Eastern sweats and Tangerian bone-grindings and migraines
of China under junk-withdrawal in Newark's bleak furnished room,

who wandered around and around at midnight in the railroad yard
wondering where to go, and went, leaving no broken hearts,

who lit cigarettes in boxcars boxcars boxcars racketing through snow
toward lonesome farms in grandfather night,

who studied Plotinus Poe St. John of the Cross telepathy and bop
kaballa because the cosmos instinctively vibrated at their
feet in Kansas,

who loned it through the streets of Idaho seeking visionary indian
angels who were visionary indian angels,

who thought they were only mad when Baltimore gleamed in super-
natural ecstasy,

who jumped in limousines with the Chinaman of Oklahoma on the
impulse of winter midnight streetlight smalltown rain,

who lounged hungry and lonesome through Houston seeking jazz or
sex or soup, and followed the brilliant Spaniard to converse
about America and Eternity, a hopeless task, and so took
ship to Africa,

who disappeared into the volcanoes of Mexico leaving behind nothing
but the shadow of dungarees and the lava and ash of poetry
scattered in fireplace Chicago,

who reappeared on the West Coast investigating the F.B.I. in beards
and shorts with big pacifist eyes sexy in their dark skin
passing out incomprehensible leaflets,

who burned cigarette holes in their arms protesting the narcotic
tobacco haze of Capitalism,

who distributed Supercommunist pamphlets in Union Square
weeping and undressing while the sirens of Los Alamos
wailed them down, and wailed down Wall, and the Staten
Island ferry also wailed,

who broke down crying in white gymnasiums naked and trembling
before the machinery of other skeletons,

who bit detectives in the neck and shrieked with delight in policecars
for committing no crime but their own wild cooking
pederasty and intoxication,

who howled on their knees in the subway and were dragged off the
roof waving genitals and manuscripts,

who let themselves be . . . . . . in the . . . by saintly motorcyclists,
and screamed with joy,

who blew and were blown by those human seraphim, the sailors,
caresses of Atlantic and Caribbean love,

who balled in the morning in the evenings in rosegardens and the
grass of public parks and cemeteries scattering their semen
freely to whomever come who may,

who hiccupped endlessly trying to giggle but wound up with a sob
behind a partition in a Turkish Bath when the blonde &
naked angel came to pierce them with a sword,

who lost their loveboys to the three old shrews of fate the one eyed
shrew of the heterosexual dollar the one eyed shrew that
winks out of the womb and the one eyed shrew that does
nothing but sit on her ass and snip the intellectual golden
threads of the craftsman's loom,

who copulated ecstatic and insatiate with a bottle of beer a sweetheart
a package of cigarettes a candle and fell off the bed, and
continued along the floor and down the hall and ended
fainting on the wall with a vision of ultimate c . . . and
come eluding the last gyzym of consciousness,

who sweetened the snatches of a million girls trembling in the sunset,
and were red eyed in the morning but prepared to sweeten
the snatch of the sunrise, flashing buttocks under barns and
naked in the lake,

who went out whoring through Colorado in myriad stolen night-cars,
N.C., secret hero of these poems, cocksman and Adonis of
Denver—joy to the memory of his innumerable lays of girls

in empty lots & diner backyards, moviehouses, rickety rows
on mountaintops in caves or with gaunt waitresses in
familiar roadside lonely petticoat upliftings & especially
secret gas-station solipisisms of johns, & hometown alleys too,

who faded out in vast sordid movies, were shifted in dreams, woke
on a sudden Manhattan, and picked themselves up out of
basements hungover with heartless Tokay and horrors of
Third Avenue iron dreams & stumbled to unemployment
offices,

who walked all night with their shoes full of blood on the snowbank
docks waiting for a door in the East River to open to a room
full of steamheat and opium,

who created great suicidal dramas on the apartment cliff-banks of
the Hudson under the wartime blue floodlight of the moon
& their heads shall be crowned with laurel in oblivion,

who ate the lamb stew of the imagination or digested the crab at
the muddy bottom of the rivers of Bowery,

who wept at the romance of the streets with their pushcarts full of
onions and bad music,

who sat in boxes breathing in the darkness under the bridge, and
rose up to build harpsichords in their lofts,

who coughed on the sixth floor of Harlem crowned with flame under
the tubercular sky surrounded by orange crates of theology,

who scribbled all night rocking and rolling over lofty incantations
which in the yellow morning were stanzas of gibberish,

who cooked rotten animals lung heart feet tail borsht & tortillas
dreaming of the pure vegetable kingdom,

who plunged themselves under meat trucks looking for an egg,

who threw their watches off the roof to cast their ballot for Eternity
outside of Time, & alarm clocks fell on their heads every
day for the next decade,

who cut their wrists three times successively unsuccessfully, gave up
and were forced to open antique stores where they thought
they were growing old and cried,

who were burned alive in their innocent flannel suits on Madison
Avenue amid blasts of leaden verse & the tanked-up clatter
of the iron regiments of fashion & the nitroglycerine shrieks
of the fairies of advertising & the mustard gas of sinister

intelligent editors, or were run down by the drunken
taxicabs of Absolute Reality,

who jumped off the Brooklyn Bridge this actually happened and
walked away unknown and forgotten into the ghostly daze
of Chinatown soup alleyways & firetrucks, not even one
free beer,

who sang out of their windows in despair, fell out of the subway
window, jumped in the filthy Passaic, leaped on negroes,
cried all over the street, danced on broken wineglasses
barefoot smashed phonograph records of nostalgic European
1930's German jazz finished the whiskey and threw up
groaning into the bloody toilet, moans in their ears and the
blast of colossal steamwhistles,

who barreled down the highways of the past journeying to each
other's hotrod-Golgotha jail-solitude watch or Birmingham
jazz incarnation,

who drove crosscountry seventytwo hours to find out if I had a
vision or you had a vision or he had a vision to find out
Eternity,

who journeyed to Denver, who died in Denver, who came back to
Denver & waited in vain, who watched over Denver &
brooded & loned in Denver and finally went away to find
out the Time, & now Denver is lonesome for her heroes,

who fell on their knees in hopeless cathedrals praying for each
other's salvation and light and breasts, until the soul
illuminated its hair for a second,

who crashed through their minds in jail waiting for impossible
criminals with golden heads and the charm of reality in
their hearts who sang sweet blues to Alcatraz,

who retired to Mexico to cultivate a habit, or Rocky Mount to tender
Buddha or Tangiers to boys or Southern Pacific to the black
locomotive or Harvard to Narcissus to Woodlawn to the
daisychain or grave,

who demanded sanity trials accusing the radio of hypnotism &
were left with their insanity & their hands & a hung jury,

who threw potato salad at CCNY lecturers on Dadaism and
subsequently presented themselves on the granite steps of

the madhouse with shaven heads and harlequin speech of
suicide, demanding instantaneous lobotomy,
and who were given instead the concrete void of insulin metrasol
electricity hydrotherapy psychotherapy occupational therapy
pingpong & amnesia,
who in humorless protest overturned only one symbolic pingpong
table, resting briefly in catatonia,
returning years later truly bald except for a wig of blood, and tears
and fingers, to the visible madman doom of the wards of the
madtowns of the East,
Pilgrim State's Rockland's and Greystone's foetid halls, bickering with
the echoes of the soul, rocking and rolling in the midnight
solitude-bench dolmen-realms of love, dream of life a
nightmare, bodies turned to stone as heavy as the moon,
with mother finally ******, and the last fantastic book flung out of
the tenement window, and the last door closed at 4 AM and
the last telephone slammed at the wall in reply and the last
furnished room emptied down to the last piece of mental
furniture, a yellow paper rose twisted on a wire hanger in
the closet, and even that imaginary, nothing but a hopeful
little bit of hallucination—
ah, Carl, while you are not safe I am not safe, and now you're really
in the total animal soup of time—
and who therefore ran through the icy streets obsessed with a sudden
flash of the alchemy of the use of the ellipse the catalog the
meter & the vibrating plane,
who dreamt and made incarnate gaps in Time & Space through
images juxtaposed, and trapped the archangel of the soul
between 2 visual images and joined the elemental verbs and
set the noun and dash of consciousness together jumping
with sensation of Pater Omnipotens Aeterna Deus
to recreate the syntax and measure of poor human prose and stand
before you speechless and intelligent and shaking with
shame, rejected yet confessing out the soul to conform to
the rhythm of thought in his naked and endless head,
the madman bum and angel beat in Time, unknown, yet putting
down here what might be left to say in time come after
death,

and rose reincarnate in the ghostly clothes of jazz in the goldhorn
        shadow of the band and blew the suffering of America's
        naked mind for love into an eli eli lamma lamma sabacthani
        saxophone cry that shivered the cities down to the last radio
with the absolute heart of the poem of life butchered out of their
        own bodies good to eat a thousand years.

II

What sphinx of cement and aluminum bashed open their skulls and
        ate up their brains and imagination?
Moloch! Solitude! Filth! Ugliness! Ashcans and unobtainable dollars!
        Children screaming under the stairways! Boys sobbing in
        armies! Old men weeping in the parks!
Moloch! Moloch! Nightmare of Moloch! Moloch the loveless! Mental
        Moloch! Moloch the heavy judger of men!
Moloch the incomprehensible prison! Moloch the crossbone soulless
        jailhouse and Congress of sorrows! Moloch whose buildings
        are judgment! Moloch the vast stone of war! Moloch the
        stunned governments!
Moloch whose mind is pure machinery! Moloch whose blood is
        running money! Moloch whose fingers are ten armies!
        Moloch whose breast is a cannibal dynamo! Moloch whose
        ear is a smoking tomb!
Moloch whose eyes are a thousand blind windows! Moloch whose
        skyscrapers stand in the long streets like endless Jehovahs!
        Moloch whose factories dream and croak in the fog! Moloch
        whose smokestacks and antennae crown the cities!
Moloch whose love is endless oil and stone! Moloch whose soul is
        electricity and banks! Moloch whose poverty is the specter
        of genius! Moloch whose fate is a cloud of sexless hydrogen!
        Moloch whose name is the Mind!
Moloch in whom I sit lonely! Moloch in whom I dream Angels!
        Crazy in Moloch! C . . . sucker in Moloch! Lacklove and
        manless in Moloch!
Moloch who entered my soul early! Moloch in whom I am a
        consciousness without a body! Moloch who frightened me
        out of my natural ecstasy! Moloch whom I abandon! Wake
        up in Moloch! Light streaming out of the sky!

Moloch! Moloch! Robot apartments! invisible suburbs! skeleton
treasuries! blind capitals! demonic industries! spectral
nations! invincible madhouses! granite cocks! monstrous
bombs!

They broke their backs lifting Moloch to Heaven! Pavements, trees,
radios, tons! lifting the city to Heaven which exists and is
everywhere about us!

Visions! omens! hallucinations! miracles! ecstasies! gone down the
American river!

Dreams! adorations! illuminations! religions! the whole boatload of
sensitive bullshit!

Breakthroughs! over the river! flips and crucifixions! gone down the
flood! Highs! Epiphanies! Despairs! Ten years' animal
screams and suicides! Minds! New loves! Mad generation!
down on the rocks of Time!

Real holy laughter in the river! They saw it all! the wild eyes! the
holy yells! They bade farewell! They jumped off the roof!
to solitude! waving! carrying flowers! Down to the river!
into the street!

III

Carl Solomon! I'm with you in Rockland
where you're madder than I am
I'm with you in Rockland
where you must feel very strange
I'm with you in Rockland
where you imitate the shade of my mother
I'm with you in Rockland
where you've murdered your twelve secretaries
I'm with you in Rockland
where you laugh at this invisible humor
I'm with you in Rockland
where we are great writers on the same dreadful typewriter
I'm with you in Rockland
where your condition has become serious and is reported on
the radio

I'm with you in Rockland
> where the faculties of the skull no longer admit the worms
> of the senses

I'm with you in Rockland
> where you drink the tea of the breasts of the spinsters of
> Utica

I'm with you in Rockland
> where you pun on the bodies of your nurses the harpies of
> the Bronx

I'm with you in Rockland
> where you scream in a straightjacket that you're losing the
> game of the actual pingpong of the abyss

I'm with you in Rockland
> where you bang on the catatonic piano the soul is innocent
> and immortal it should never die ungodly in an armed
> madhouse

I'm with you in Rockland
> where fifty more shocks will never return your soul to its
> body again from its pilgrimage to a cross in the void

I'm with you in Rockland
> where you accuse your doctors of insanity and plot the
> Hebrew socialist revolution against the fascist national
> Golgotha

I'm with you in Rockland
> where you will split the heavens of Long Island and resurrect
> your living human Jesus from the superhuman tomb

I'm with you in Rockland
> where there are twentyfive-thousand mad comrades all
> together singing the final stanzas of the Internationale

I'm with you in Rockland
> where we hug and kiss the United States under our
> bedsheets   the United States that coughs all night and
> won't let us sleep

I'm with you in Rockland
> where we wake up electrified out of the coma by our own
> souls' airplanes roaring over the roof they've come to drop
> angelic bombs the hospital illuminates itself   imaginary
> walls collapse   O skinny legions run outside   O starry-

       spangled shock of mercy the eternal war is here   O victory
       forget your underwear we're free
I'm with you in Rockland
       in my dreams you walk dripping from a sea-journey on the
       highway across America in tears to the door of my cottage
       in the Western night

part two

THE ANGRY YOUNG MEN

JOHN WAIN

"I Can't Marry Robert!"

> From birth, a man is fashioned by his
> environment. In helpless childhood
> his parents "guide" his first steps; in
> adolescence he is already in a path he
> cannot remember having chosen.
> Charles Lumley's path has taken him
> to the university, and from there it
> leads broadly and clearly to a middle
> class marriage, material comforts and
> the dull, self-stifling conformity of
> most people's lives. But somewhere a
> man can still turn, can struggle to
> wrest his soul from "the rack of his
> ludicrous predicament."
>
> This selection is from the novel
> Hurry On Down.

CAN'T YOU TELL ME, Mr. Lumley, just what
it is that you don't like about the rooms?"

There was no mistaking the injured truculence in the
landlady's voice, nor her expression of superhuman pa-
tience about to snap at last. Charles very nearly groaned
aloud. Must he explain, point by point, why he hated
living there? Her husband's cough in the morning, the
way the dog barked every time he went in or out, the
greasy mats in the hall? Obviously it was impossible. Why
could she not have the grace to accept the polite lie he had

told her? In any case he was bound to stick to it. He looked into her beady, accusing eyes and said as pleasantly as he could, "Really, Mrs. Smythe, I don't know what's given you the idea that I don't like the rooms. I've always said how comfortable they were. But I told you the other day, I really need something a little nearer my work."

"And where do you work? I've asked you that two or three times, Mr. Lumley, but you've never given me any answer."

"What the hell has it got to do with you where I work?" he would have liked to say. But after all he supposed it was, to some extent, a question she had the right to ask. He had puzzled her from the beginning, he knew that; neither in speech nor dress resembling the dapper young clerks and elementary-school teachers to whom she was accustomed to let rooms. And yet it had been out of the question to say, bluntly: "I have just come down from the University with a mediocre degree in History, I have no job and no prospects, and I am living on fifty pounds I happen to have left in the bank, while I consider my next move." No! he shuddered, as he had often shuddered, at the thought of the demoniac eagerness with which she would have seized on him and his problems; the advertisements of "Situations Vacant" she would have found for him in the paper, the enquiries she would have "felt obliged" to make into the state of his finances. "I shall have to ask you to pay in advance, Mr. Lumley. Your money won't last for ever, you know." He could hear her saying it, her reedy voice full of suspicion.

"I don't understand it. You seem to have some objection to telling me what you do for a living. It's not as if I was an inquisitive person, not at all."

He had been a damned fool not to think up something in readiness for this situation. What could he be? A teacher? But what blasted schools were there in Stotwell? He ought to have made a note of one, somewhere about five miles away so as to support his original untruth. Well, what did he know about Stotwell? There was a greyhound racing track. Could he be employed there? Working the totalisator perhaps. He realized with a start that he had never even seen a totalisator. Besides, he had been at home in the evenings too often. Articled to a solicitor? But she would ask him what solicitor, and where his office was; and it would be useless to invent one, for her suspicions were violently aroused and she would check his story with passionate thoroughness. He must speak. He forced his tongue into action, trusting that it would say something of its own accord, without any help from him.

"Well, it's like this, Mrs. Smythe. You've heard of—of Jehovah's Witnesses?"

Her head swivelled round. She was trying to keep her startled eyes on his.

"You don't mean to say you're one of them?"

"Well, not exactly one of *them*. I mean, not *one* of them."

"Mr. Lumley. *What do you do?*"

"I'm a private detective."

The words jumped out of their own accord. This was it.

"Private detective? Jehovah's Witnesses? Just whatever do you mean? And you'd better tell me, young man, you'd better tell me. I've never had any lodger here but what I've known he was respectable, yes, and in a steady job too, and here you come and won't tell me what it is you do and now you come out with all this, a detective, a man that has to mix with criminals, and bringing them to my house before long I shouldn't wonder, that is IF it's true what you're saying."

Charles dragged out a packet of cheap cigarettes. "Just a minute," he mumbled. "Left matches in bedroom." "Never mind matches now," she shrilled, but he dashed out, slamming the door behind him, and pounded up the stairs to his bedroom. On reaching it his first impulse was to hide under the bed, but he knew it was useless. He must steel himself. Lighting his cigarette, he took a gulp of the acrid smoke and turned to face the landlady as she ran into the room. Then, suddenly, his mind cleared. She had asked for an explanation, and he would give her one. Before she could speak he had launched into a long and circumstantial narrative: how he was employed by the Central Office of the Jehovah's Witnesses to keep his eye on one of the four regional treasurers, a Blackwall man, who was accused of bringing discredit on the movement in various ways which—his voice dropped to a confidential undertone—she would forgive him if he did not specify. He invented a name for the agency in which he was a junior partner. Did she remember the Evans case, the one that got so much space in the *News of the World?* But then, she did not read the *News of the World*, of course, she would not have seen it: anyway, he, Charles, had been responsible for bringing that man to justice. He talked on and on, thoroughly bored but surprisingly calm. And now, to come back to his original point, the suspected man had moved into a small hotel in the town (as she opened her mouth to ask "What hotel?" he forestalled her by asking, gently, if she would mind not forcing him to reveal its name) and he felt it to be his duty to move into the same hotel.

"And so, you see, Mrs. Smythe, when I said that I needed to move so as to be nearer my work, it was," he smiled gravely, "very literally true." And for the first time in fifty-six years Mrs. Smythe was speechless. She had taken in perhaps a third of his involved narrative, and her mind was a swirling chaos. If she had one desire in the world, it was to see the last of Charles Lumley. His point was gained.

Suitcase in hand, Charles stumbled next morning over the greasy hall mat for the last time, and lurched out into the July sunshine. Lying awake in the night, he had dwelt lovingly on the kick he would plant, scientifically and deliberately, in the dog's mouth as it yelped at him; but to-day, for the first time since he had entered the house, the animal was somewhere else, and his exit was silent.

He was aware of Mrs. Smythe's gaze, half suspicious and half impressed, from behind the yellowed lace curtains of the front room, and tried to assume a swagger as he moved away down the street. Yet it was clear to him that his three weeks at Stotwell had been so much wasted time; twenty-one aimless mornings, stupefied afternoons, and desperate evenings, during which his thoughts had obstinately refused to be clarified. How often, in the tumultuous muddle of his last year at the University, he had congratulated himself on having found a way out of the familiar *impasse;* when the insistent question of where, after the few fleeting months were over, he was to find a living wage had intruded itself, he had shrugged it aside, promising himself that he would deal with that and all his other problems in a few weeks of quiet and solitude. "Sorry," he would say in answer to questions about his future, "but I'm not making major decisions just now. One thing at a time, you know. At the moment I'm working for an examination— and," he would add pompously, "trying to live like a normal human being at the same time. When all this comes to an end, I'll turn my attention to the problem of earning a living, without trying to isolate it from all the other big problems." It had all been very comforting.

He had even held a modest ceremony at his lodgings, at which, in the presence of a few friends, he had decided on the town to which he should retire for his all-important spell of concentration. Asking them to write down the names of a dozen or so towns on a sheet of paper, avoiding the big cities where lodgings might be more expensive, he had then, with a fine air of casualness, stuck a pin into the list at random. "I'm quite indifferent," he had said, loftily; "a country village or an industrial town—my gaze will be directed inwards." By a ludicrous coincidence his first jab with the pin had landed on the name of the one town in England that was useless for his purpose, the town where he was born and bred and where his parents lived; it had been written down in all innocence by one of his guests. The second jab had landed on the extreme edge of the paper, and was voted inconclusive, but the third had unequivocally indicated Stotwell. Full of hope, he had scurried across country to this dingy huddle of streets and factories, only to spend his precious weeks in nail-biting indecision. Nothing had been settled, not even the obvious and simple question of a trade, certainly not the deeper and more personal problems which he had shelved for years on the promise of this tranquil interlude.

Why was this? Why had he failed? he asked himself as he dragged the heavy suitcase down the main street towards the station. The answer, like everything else, was fragmentary: partly because the University had, by its three years' random and shapeless cramming, unfitted his mind for serious thinking; partly because of the continued nagging of his circumstances ("Go out this morning or she'll *know* you haven't a job—come to a decision to-day before you waste any more time—look at the papers to see what sort of jobs are offered"), and partly for the blunt, simple reason that his problems did not really admit of any solution. At least, he comforted himself, he had remained stationary; if he had been surrounded by the well-meant fatuity of those who had always sought to "guide" him, there was no telling what disastrous steps might already have been taken. As it was, his position was precisely the same as it had been before his attempt to face the problems that hemmed him about; he had not yet realized, what circumstances were soon to teach him, that his predicament was not one that could be improved by thinking.

It was inevitable, then, that a sense of defeat should bow Charles's shoulders and line his forehead as he paid out his last pound note for a ticket to the town where his parents, relatives, and acquaintances were waiting to ask where he had been. If it were not for Sheila, he thought grimly as he waited for the few shillings' change that now represented his total resources, he'd hold out somehow, sleeping on park benches, selling newspapers for a living. But he had to see her, even though he had nothing to bring her that would make sense of his silence, nothing that would bring their marriage nearer or make it more attractive. What a mess it all was! Charles sighed as he stuffed the ticket into his waistcoat pocket and gathered up the change.

The train drew in, and he clambered indifferently into the compartment that was facing him as it stopped, heaved his suitcase on to the rack and slumped into a corner seat. With the exaggerated reserve implanted in him by his upbringing he studiously averted his eyes from the other two occupants of the compartment, seeing them only as blurred forms, a middle-aged couple without distinctive features. It was only when the train had left the station and the broad fields of a Midland landscape were streaming past the windows that he became aware that they were studying him, timidly, but with an intense interest that was obviously on the point of forcing them to break their silence. He looked up and met their gaze. Yes! Where had he seen them before?

"It's Mr. Lumley, isn't it?" said the man at last.

"That's my name," Charles assented cautiously, mumbling in a rapid undertone, "not sure where had the pleasure remember face of course, let me see."

The woman, who clearly did not share in the embarrassment, leaned forward with an encouraging smile.

"We're George Hutchins's mother and dad," she volunteered kindly. "We met you when we came up to see him at the College."

At once Charles remembered a scene which he would gladly have forgotten. George Hutchins, an unpleasantly dogged and humourless young man, had lived on the same staircase and had indulged a taste for lecturing Charles on the virtues of hard work. "No system," he would say contemptuously, looking round at Charles's bookcase, "just a random collection of texts, no real system. You're just playing at it. Now I can't afford to play at it. I go over each little plot of the subject carefully. Preliminary survey, then a closer reading, and then, three months later, revision. And the whole thing's tied up. That's how these men like Lockwood have got where they are, and I'm going after them." Lockwood was a dreary whey-faced tutor of the college for whom Hutchins had a deep and sincere admiration, and who encouraged him along the road to complacent prigdom. After one of these lectures, Charles would sit staring into the fire, inert and crumpled; the half-fantastic, half-shrewd gleams and pin-points of intuition which served him as a substitute for intellectual method damped and fizzling out in the clammy atmosphere of Hutchins's brutal efficiency.

"I s'pose you've heard all about George's success," said Mr. Hutchins; his voice was bright and confident, but with a curious undertone of bewilderment and pathos. "He's got a Fellowship," he added, using the strange word in inverted commas, grafting it like some strange twig on to the stunted trunk of his artisan's vocabulary.

For the next few minutes the conversation arranged itself on purely mechanical lines; a steady flow of "deserve congratulation worked hard for it now got it" *clichés* from Charles, and an answering dribble of "Well it's what he's always wanted not that it hasn't been a struggle" from the withered couple opposite. Behind the mask Charles was genuinely sorry for them; it was so obvious that they were even more bewildered than on the day, two years ago, when he had walked into Hutchins's room with a request for the loan of a toasting-fork, and found the three sitting dumbly and stiffly together. Hutchins has been so abjectly and obviously ashamed of his parents' working-class appearance and manner that he had tried to avoid introducing them, evidently in the hope that Charles would not realize the relationship. But the family likeness had proclaimed itself, and Charles had lingered, chatting for a few minutes, partly out of a malicious pleasure at Hutchins's discomfiture, and partly out of a genuine desire to comfort these decent and kindly people, to show them that if their son was an ungainly snob there were others who were not, and to try to give them a few pleasant minutes in what was so clearly a disastrous visit. They had never appeared again, and Hutchins had never mentioned them. Charles, with no other intention than to be pleasant, had once asked him if his parents were keeping well, but the scowl he had received in answer had made it clear that Hutchins had regarded the question as a simple insult. The raw cult of success by which he lived could allow of no tolerance of the couple who had spawned him; they were neither prosperous nor celebrated, their Birmingham speech exposed in an instant the unreality of his own diction (an unbelievably exact reproduction of Lockwood's donnish snivelling), and, in short, his resentment of them could go no further. Amid all the problems that beset him, Charles found time to rejoice that he was not as Hutchins was, that his soul, stretched as it was on the rack of his ludicrous predicament, was alive. He was not given to quoting, but a favourite fragment swam into his head, and he muttered, "I am one of those who have created, even if it be but a world of agony." "Beg pardon?" said Mr. Hutchins, surprised, leaning forward. "Just nothing, just nothing," Charles replied; he wished to sound airy and nonchalant, but the words rang out brassily and the effect was one of impertinence. In despair he stood up, dragged his case down from the rack, gabbled "Must get ready getting out next station," and fled down the corridor in search of a fresh compartment. The only one that appeared to have a vacant seat was occupied by four blue-chinned men banging down cards on a suitcase, who looked up at him with such hostility that he retreated again, and, fearing to stand in the corridor lest Mr. or Mrs. Hutchins should come out and see him, spent the forty minutes that remained of his journey cowering in the lavatory.

Despite this discouraging start to the day, by half-past four that afternoon Charles had negotiated a surprising number of obstacles. Arriving at his destination, he had left his suitcase at the station cloak-room, and, determined to put off his official home-coming until it was forced on him, walked rapidly the hundred yards from the station to the long-distance 'bus depot, to wait for a coach to the village five miles away where Sheila and her parents lived. The need to see her, which he had fiercely repressed for months, flared up in his body and brain as the 'bus crawled through the leaf-green lanes; it was so much what he needed—a return, a recognition, a point of rest, which yet involved no recriminations and no immediate practical decision. But this peace was still to be won, and the violence of his inner tension caught and shook him fiercely as he walked up the garden path.

But the situation, once again, was due to collapse into anti-climax. In answer to his unnecessarily firm and prolonged ring at the bell, the front door was opened by a plump, grave man of about thirty-five. It was Robert Tharkles, the husband of Sheila's elder sister Edith. His expression of gravity deepened into positive melancholy, tinged with irritation, at the sight of Charles. This fool again! And the fool had still not smartened himself up! When was he going to smarten himself up?

"Sheila isn't here," he said without waiting for Charles to say anything, and without any greeting.

"Mind if I come in all the same? Come some distance," muttered Charles.

"There's only Edith and me here," said Robert, as if warning Charles that by coming in he was exposing himself to an unpleasant ordeal; which was true.

Without answering, Charles levered himself past Robert and went into the hall. Edith came out of the kitchen and confronted him. "Sheila isn't here," he said. "Know," said Charles, speaking too quickly to be fully intelligible. "Robert told me. Mind if I come in perhaps cup of tea? Or when Sheila be back wanted to see her if I could."

Under their patronising and hostile stares he pulled himself together, walked into the kitchen, and sat down on a chair.

This was typical of all the interviews Charles had ever had with Robert and Edith. It was not because he was unsuccessful that they objected to him; lack of success, in their eyes, was not a punishable offence; one simply left such people alone. What annoyed them was that he did not even seem to be trying. Though they could not have put it into words, their objection to him was that he did not wear a uniform. If he had worn the uniform of a prosperous middle-class tradesman, like Robert, they would have approved of him. If, on the other hand, he had seriously adopted the chic disorder of the Chelsea Bohemian, they would at least have understood what he was at. In their world, it was everyone's first duty to wear a uniform that announced his status, his calling and his ambitions: from the navvy's thick boots and shirtsleeves to the professor's tweeds, the conventions of clothing saw to it that everyone wore his identity card where it could be seen. But Charles seemed not to realize the sacred duty of dressing the part. Even as an undergraduate he had not worn corduroys or coloured shirts. He had not even smoked a pipe. He had appeared instead in non-committal lounge suits which were still not the

lounge suits of a business man, and heavy shoes which were still not
the sophisticated heavy shoes of the fashionable outdoor man. More-
over, all his tentative efforts to ingratiate himself with them had been
ill-judged. He had suggested to Robert, the first time they met, that
they might slip out for a drink before lunch. Robert never slipped out
for drinks, preferring to open half-pint bottles of gassy beer which he
took solemnly from a mahogany cabinet. When he had helped Edith
with the washing up on the maid's day out, she had so fiercely concen-
trated on the probability of his breaking something that in the end he
had dropped and smashed an irreplaceable gravy-boat. When Robert,
playing up to his position as the steady, responsible husband of the
elder sister, had asked this candidate for the hand of the younger
sister, what he intended to Do, and what his prospects were, Charles
had responded in the fashion of the University with evasive and
facetious answers. He did not fit into their world or speak their language, and after a perfunctory attempt to fit him into their prim, grey
jigsaw puzzle they had disliked and rejected him; without, however,
leaving him alone. As they stood and looked at him Charles realized
that he would have to accept, as the price of his cup of tea, another
lump of advice; as hard to swallow, and as useless to the system, as the
cotton wool it so much resembled.

It was Edith who began the offensive, fixing her absurdly small eyes
on him as she stood squarely beside the sink, a Woman on her Own
Ground, in her hideous dress and splashed apron.

"I suppose you wanted to speak to Father." (Thank Heaven at least
she did not refer to the yellowed scarecrow as Daddy.) "Now that
you've taken your degree you'll be wanting to put everything into a
bit better order, I suppose." (An oblique, but not too oblique, reference to his haphazard approach to life.) "He's been wondering when
you'd show up." (Implying that he had been skulking out of the way
of his responsibilities.)

Charles foolishly let himself be hooked. "I don't know that I wanted
to see your father exactly," he said. "I mean, there's nothing immediately—er—"

He realized that he had been trapped. His last half-dozen words
would take so little twisting into a weapon against him (he had "even
gone so far as to say," "seemed unaware of," etc.). Edith's mouth had

opened to yelp out the prepared condemnation, when Robert unexpectedly cut in.

"I met your parents the other day. We had a few minutes' chat about things in general. I must say"—his tone became firm and brisk, the executive with a grasp of essentials—"I think you ought to realize there's a pretty widespread dissatisfaction with the way you're going on. For one thing the way you just disappeared after taking your finals. Your father told me you hadn't even given them your address. They had absolutely no means of getting in touch with you. I must say I think that's pretty shabby."

Charles had indeed made use of the obvious and only method of keeping his parents from surging into his life, shaking it up, wrenching it to pieces, and obscuring with a fog of emotion everything that he was trying to study under his laboriously constructed microscope of detachment. But of course there was no answer to this booby's conviction that a refusal to wallow, at every crisis, in the emotional midden that his parents had spent twenty-two years in digging, was "shabby." A suffocating sense of utter inability to communicate, as in those nightmares in which the dreamer sees himself put away for lunacy, had already begun to drench his mind.

The voices of Robert and Edith splashed on and on. Charles tried to be oblivious of them, but the smug phrases, the pert half-truths, the bland brutalities, ripped down his defences. It was finally a remark of Edith's that brought him to his feet in a sudden rush of anger.

"You never seem to want to repay any of the people who've tried to help you."

In a swirl of resentment Charles saw the faces of those who had "tried to help him": and behind the faces flickered a radiance, the colour of dawn on snow-capped hills, that might (he suddenly knew) have been in his life if he had been left alone to make it without "guidance": if all the people who had cloaked their possessive fumbling under the words "trying to help you" had been, by a miracle, persuaded to leave him in peace. And now she spoke, once again, of repayment!

On his feet, gripping the back of his chair, Charles sought for a quick, devastating reply: a few words so swift and bitter that they would scorch themselves into Edith's mind and live with her, waking and sleeping, till she died.

It was no use, of course. Speech would never work with these people. Indeed, it was inconceivable that anything could be got across to them by means of language, unless one overpowered them and left them gagged and bound in the presence of a gramophone record endlessly repeating a short, concise statement. It would have given him pleasure to begin the composition, there and then, of such a statement; to have outlined in a few simple sentences the nature of the crime against humanity that they and their kind were committing by the mere fact of their existence.

"Your shaft seems to have gone home, Edith," said her husband. "Our friend doesn't quite know how to answer you. It's reduced him to silence."

Charles focused with sudden clarity on Robert. All at once it seemed to him that the stiff brown moustache which he wore to give dignity to his face was curiously non-human. It looked as if it had been clipped from the face of an Airedale.

"I wasn't really thinking about what Edith had said," he replied half apologetically. "I was just wondering why no one's ever found it worth while to cut off that silly moustache of yours and use it for one of those brushes you see hanging out of windows next to the waste pipe."

He spoke quietly and courteously; nevertheless they realized, after a short pause in which their minds groped for the meaning of his words, that he was being definitely insulting. Edith's face seemed to swell up to twice its size, her eyes bulged and she began a loud and unsteady tirade, quavering with hysteria but heavy with menace. Robert, on the other hand, had no difficulty in selecting the basic attitude proper for him to adopt. His mouth tightened, he squared his shoulders, and he moved forward, lightly and yet decisively, like Ronald Colman. When his crisp and well-timed "That's enough of that sort of talk" had failed to penetrate to Charles's consciousness, and Edith's cackle had begun to take on a distinct flavour of tears, Ronald Colman disappeared, and in his place stood Stewart Granger, dangerous, alert, powerful. He grasped Charles by the lapel of his jacket. For an instant surprise gripped Charles and held him motionless. How quickly, how fatally, the situation had developed! So now, finally, he had put himself in the wrong. "Quite abusive. In fact Robert had to put him out. Impossible to have him in the house again."

Robert's pouchy, inane face was thrust aggressively into his. Hell! They could have it if they wanted it. With a sudden twist he broke free, lunged across to the sink and snatched up the washing-up bowl. Edith had just finished washing up when he arrived, and for some reason she had not thrown the water away. Half of the scummy grey flood poured over Charles himself as he dragged the bowl wildly out of the sink, but the other half cascaded gloriously as, with a tremendous sense of release, he swung it round. Almost simultaneously three sounds filled the kitchen—the water's gulping splash, Edith's loud squealing, and the clatter of the empty bowl landing in a corner. It had hardly landed before Charles clawed open the back door and rushed out. A backward glance showed him Edith's face framed in wisps of wet hair, and Robert trying to blink the soap from his eyes.

As the gate clicked shut behind him, and he stumbled forward into the road, Charles suddenly realized the truth about what had happened. It was not Robert and Edith he had quarrelled with: it was Sheila. He had loved her with a passive persistence ever since the burning, spinning evening, when he was seventeen, that had taught him what love was, and she had entered his character and become its core. After a reasonable period of vacillation, she had agreed to marry him when this should be possible, and the prospect had been the foundation of his life in thought and action. Now, in the dusky street, his own footsteps beat into his head the knowledge that it could not happen. Her face rose before his eyes: that air of positive calm, of confident and sweet repose, smashed into his mind—always before it had reassuringly entered as an unexpected guest—and he saw behind her eyes the eyes of her mother, solemn, spectacled, judging him; in the bones of her chin he saw the chin of her father, jutting and scraped clean of its greying stubble below a tight, fussy, mouth. No! He had never been scared of the fact that she would grow older, losing the confident hardness of her limbs in dumpiness or scragginess; but now he saw her not merely growing old, but growing daily more and more of a piece with the prim, hedged gravel from which she flowered. With Robert's complacent whine, with Edith's angry squawk, still in his ears, he knew that he could never face it. It was over. No more Sheila.

At the thought of finality his mind was flooded with images: the ivory bald patches behind her ears, the quivering of her pointed chin as she had raised her face to be kissed for the first time, her delicate wrists . . . his heart lurched over and over in his breast like a cricket ball lobbed along a dry, bumpy pitch; a shudder seized him, so violent that he was flung off his balance and lurched against the stone wall of a prosperous man's garden. The rough solidity of the stone flicked his mind empty again, and a new set of images crowded in: he saw Sheila's face, pale, luminous, resolute, and behind her the meanly precise face of her father, the tame and lumpy face of her mother, Edith's spiteful plucked eyebrows, and presiding over the scene, Robert, with his detestable calf's head and waving plump hands.

"I can't marry Robert!" he said loudly in his agony. A middle-aged woman and a small boy, standing at a 'bus stop, spun round and stared into his face with insane curiosity as he passed. Charles broke into a gallop. He only wanted to get round the next corner and hide his back from their eyes, but as he ran he knew that he was running away from everything that, up to that moment, had been his life.

KINGSLEY AMIS

Merrie England

With Lucky Jim—*one of the most successful novels since the war—The Movement clearly gets under way. The title character is a young history teacher at a provincial British university. Endowed with no particular talents, he really works at playing the academic game; but he can't succeed. The trouble is that he's too honest. He prepares himself to deliver the expected inanities, the mellow dripping phrases which roll from his colleague's tongues without a flicker, and something inside of him always rebels.*

WHAT, FINALLY, IS THE practical application of all this? Can anything be done to halt, or even to hinder, the process I have described? I say to you that something can be done by each one of us here to-night. Each of us can resolve to do something, every day, to resist the application of manufactured standards, to protest against ugly articles of furniture and table-ware, to speak out against sham architecture, to resist the importation into more and more public places of loudspeakers relaying the Light Programme, to say one word against the Yellow Press,

against the best-seller, against the theatre-organ, to say one word for
the instinctive culture of the integrated village-type community. In
that way we shall be saying a word, however small in its individual
effect, for our native tradition, for our common heritage, in short, for
what we once had and may, some day, have again—Merrie England."

With a long, jabbering belch, Dixon got up from the chair where
he'd been writing this and did his ape imitation all round the room.
With one arm bent at the elbow so that the fingers brushed the arm-
pit, the other crooked in the air so that the inside of the forearm lay
across the top of his head, he wove with bent knees and hunched,
rocking shoulders across to the bed, upon which he jumped up and
down a few times, gibbering to himself. A knock at his door was
followed so quickly by the entry of Bertrand that he only had time to
stop gibbering and straighten his body.

Bertrand, who was wearing his blue beret, looked at him. "What are
you doing up there?"

"I like it up here, thanks. Any objection?"

"Come down and stop clowning. I've got a few things to say to you,
and you'd better listen." He seemed in a controlled rage, and was
breathing heavily, though this might well have been the result of
running up two flights of stairs.

Dixon jumped lightly down to the floor; he, too, was panting a
little. "What do you want to say?"

"Just this. The last time I saw you, I told you to stay away from
Christine. I now discover you haven't done so. What have you got
to say about that, to start with?"

"What do you mean, I haven't stayed away from her?"

"Don't try that on with me, Dixon. I know all about your surrepti-
tious little cup of tea with her on the sly yesterday. I'm on to you all
right."

"Oh, she told you about that, did she?"

Bertrand tightened his lips behind the beard, which looked as if it
could do with a comb-out. "No no, of course she didn't," he said violently. "If you knew her at all, you'd know she didn't do things like
that. She's not like you. If you really want to know—and I hope it'll
give you a kick—it was one of your so-called pals in this house who told
my mother about it. You ought to enjoy thinking about that. Every-

body hates you, Dixon, and my God I can see why. Anyway, the point is I want an explanation of your conduct."

"Oh dear," Dixon said with a smile, "I'm afraid that's rather a tall order. Explain my conduct; now that is asking something. I can't think of anybody who'd be quite equal to that task."

"Cut it out," Bertrand said, flushing. "I gave you a straight warning to leave Christine alone. When I say that sort of thing I expect people to have the sense to do as I say. Why haven't you? Eh?"

Bertrand's rage, and the mere fact of his visit here, combined nicely with their superfluousness, in view of Dixon's having already given up his interest in Christine for other reasons. But he'd be a fool not to keep that to himself for a bit and enjoy himself with a spot of sniping. "I didn't want to," he said.

There was a pause, during which Bertrand twice seemed on the point of uttering a long inarticulate bay. His eyes looked like polished glass. Then, in a quieter voice than before, he said: "Look here, Dixon, you don't seem quite to appreciate what you've got yourself into. Allow me to explain." He sat down on the arm of the Pall Mall chair and removed his beret, which went rather oddly with the dark suit, white collar, and vine-patterned tie he wore. Dixon sat down on the bed, which whimpered softly beneath him.

"This business between Christine and myself," Bertrand said, fiddling with his beard, "is a serious business, unquestionably. We've known each other for some considerable period of time. And we're not in it just for a spot of the old slap and tickle, do you follow. I don't want to get married yet awhile, but it's distinctly on the cards that I might marry Christine in a couple of years or so. What I mean is, it's a long-term affair, quite definitely. Now, Christine's very young, younger even than her age. She's not used to having individuals abducting her from dances and inviting her to off-the-record tea-parties in hotels and all the rest of it. In the circumstances, it's only natural she should feel flattered by it, enjoy the excitement of it, and so on, for a time. But only for a time, Dixon. Very soon she's going to start feeling guilty about it and wishing she'd never agreed to meet you at all. And that's where the trouble's going to start; being the sort of girl she is, she's going to feel bad about getting rid of you, and about doing things behind my back—she doesn't know I know about this yet—and about the whole shooting-match. Well, I want to prevent all that, for the very adequate reason that it's not going to help me at all. I've had quite a time straightening her out already; I don't want to have to start all over again. So what I want to say to you is, keep off the grass, that's all. You're causing nothing but trouble by behaving as you are. You won't do yourself any good, and you'll only hurt Christine and inconvenience me. She's got a few days more down here, and it would be silly to spoil them for all concerned. Does that make sense, now?"

Dixon had lit a cigarette to hide the effect on him of this account of Christine's motives; it was more penetrating than he'd have expected from Bertrand. "Yes, it makes sense all right, up to a point," he said in what he hoped was a casual tone. "Except for the part about straightening Christine out, of course, which is mere wishful drooling. Never mind that, though; it all obviously make very good sense to you. None of it does to me, though. You don't seem to realise that it's all only all right if your first assumptions are right."

"I'm only telling you that they're right, my lad," Bertrand said loudly. "That's what I'm telling you."

"Yes, I noticed that. But don't expect me to make your assumptions. It's my turn to tell you something now. The serious, long-term part of this business isn't anything to do with you and Christine. Oh no, it's to do with me and Christine. What's happening isn't me unnecessarily distracting her from you. It's you unnecessarily distracting her from me—just for the moment. It won't go on much longer. How's that for sense, now?"

Bertrand rose to his feet again and faced Dixon with his legs slightly apart. He spoke in a level tone, but his teeth were clenched. "Just get this straight in your so-called mind. When I see something I want, I go for it. I don't allow people of your sort to stand in my way. That's what you're leaving out of account. I'm having Christine because it's my right. Do you understand that? If I'm after something, I don't care what I do to make sure that I get it. That's the only law I abide by; it's the only way to get things in this world. The trouble with you, Dixon, is that you're simply not up to my weight. If you want a fight, pick someone your own size, then you might stand a chance. With me you just haven't a hope in hell."

Dixon moved a pace nearer. "You're getting a bit too old for that to work any more, Welch," he said quickly. "People aren't going to skip out of your path indefinitely. You think that just because you're tall and can put paint on canvas you're a sort of demigod. It wouldn't be so bad if you really were. But you're not: you're a twister and a snob and a bully and a fool. You think you're sensitive, but you're not: your sensitivity only works for things that people do to you. Touchy and vain, yes, but not sensitive." He paused, but Bertrand was only staring at him, making no attempt to interrupt. Dixon went on: "You've got the idea that you're a great lover, but that's wrong too: you're so afraid of me, who's nothing more than a louse according to you, that you have to march in here and tell me to keep off the grass like a heavy husband. And you're so dishonest that you can tell me how important Christine is to you without it entering your head that you're carrying on with some other chap's wife all the time. It's not just that that I object to; it's the way you never seem to reflect how insincere . . ."

"What the bloody hell are you talking about?" Bertrand's breath was whistling through his nose. He clenched his fists.

"Your spot of the old slap and tickle with Carol Goldsmith. That's what I'm talking about."

"I don't know what you're talking . . ."

"Oh, my dear fellow, don't start denying it. Why bother, anyway? Surely it's just one of the things you have because it's your right, isn't it?"

"If you ever tell this tale to Christine, I'll break your neck into so many . . ."

"It's all right, I'm not the sort to do that," Dixon said with a grin. "I'm not like you. I can take Christine away from you without that, you Byronic tail-chaser."

"All right, you've got it coming," Bertrand bayed furiously. "I warned you." He came and stood over Dixon. "Come on, stand up, you dirty little bar-fly, you nasty little jumped-up turd."

"What are we going to do, dance?"

"I'll give you dance, I'll make you dance, don't you worry. Just stand up, if you're not afraid to. If you think I'm going to sit back and take this from you, you're mistaken; I don't happen to be that type, you sam."

"I'm not Sam, you fool," Dixon shrieked; this was the worst taunt of all. He took off his glasses and put them in his top jacket pocket.

They faced each other on the floral rug, feet apart and elbows

crooked in uncertain attitudes, as if about to begin some ritual of
which neither had learnt the cues. "I'll show you," Bertrand chimed,
and jabbed at Dixon's face. Dixon stepped aside, but his feet slipped
and before he could recover Bertrand's fist had landed with some force
high up on his right cheekbone. A little shaken, but undismayed,
Dixon stood still and, while Bertrand was still off his balance after de-
livering his blow, hit him very hard indeed on the larger and more
convoluted of his ears. Bertrand fell down, making a lot of noise in
doing so and dislodging a china figurine from the mantelpiece. It
exploded on the tiles of the hearth, emphasising the silence which fell.
Dixon stepped forward, rubbing his knuckles. The impact had hurt
them rather. After some seconds, Bertrand began moving about on the
floor, but made no attempt to get up. It was clear that Dixon had won
this round, and, it then seemed, the whole Bertrand match. He put his
glasses on again, feeling good; Bertrand caught his eye with a look of
embarrassed recognition. The bloody old towser-faced boot-faced
totem-pole on a crap reservation, Dixon thought. "You bloody old
towser-faced boot-faced totem-pole on a crap reservation," he said.

* * *

Professor Welch uttered the preludial blaring sound, cognate with
his son's bay, with which he was accustomed to call for silence at the
start of a lecture; Dixon had heard students imitating it. A hush
gradually fell. "We are here to-night," he informed the audience, "to
listen to a lecture."

While Welch talked, his body swaying to and fro, its upper half
more strongly illuminated by the reading-lamp above the lectern,
Dixon, so as not to have to listen to what was said, looked furtively
round the Hall. It was certainly very full; a few rows at the back were
thinly inhabited, but those nearer the front were packed, chiefly with
members of Staff and their families and with local people of various
degrees of eminence. The gallery, as far as Dixon could see, was also
packed; some people were standing up by the rear wall. Dropping his
eyes to the nearer seats, Dixon picked out the thinner of the two alder-
men, the local composer and the fashionable clergyman; the titled
physician had presumably come for the sherry only. Before he could
look further, Dixon's vague recurrent feeling of illness identified itself
as a feeling of faintness; a wave of heat spread from the small of his

back and seemed to become established in his scalp. On the point of groaning involuntarily, he tried to will himself into feeling all right; only the nervousness, he told himself. And the drink, of course.

When Welch said ". . . Mr. Dixon" and sat down, Dixon stood up. His knees began shaking violently, as if in caricature of stage-fright. A loud thunder of applause started up, chiefly, it seemed, from the gallery. Dixon could hear heavily-shod feet being stamped. With some difficulty, he took up his stand at the lectern, ran his eye over his first sentence, and raised his head. The applause died away slightly, enough for sounds of laughter to be heard through it; then it gathered force again, soon reaching a higher level than before, especially as regards the feet-stamping. The part of the audience in the gallery had had its first clear view of Dixon's black eye.

Several heads were being turned in the first few rows, and the Principal, Dixon saw, was staring irritably at the area of disturbance. In his own general unease, Dixon, who could never understand afterwards how he came to do it, produced an excellent imitation of Welch's preludial blaring sound. The uproar, passing the point where it could still be regarded as legitimate applause, grew louder. The Principal rose slowly to his feet. The uproar died down, though not to complete silence. After a pause, the Principal nodded to Dixon and sat down again.

Dixon's blood rushed in his ears, as if he were about to sneeze. How could he stand up here in front of them all and try to talk? What further animal noises would come out of his mouth if he did? He smoothed the edge of his script and began.

When he'd spoken about half-a-dozen sentences, Dixon realised that something was still very wrong. The murmuring in the gallery had grown a little louder. Then he realised what it was that was so wrong: he'd gone on using Welch's manner of address. In an effort to make his script sound spontaneous, he'd inserted an "of course" here, a "you see" there, an "as you might call it" somewhere else; nothing so firmly recalled Welch as that sort of thing. Further, in a partly unconscious attempt to make the stuff sound right, *i.e.* acceptable to Welch, he'd brought in a number of favourite Welch tags: "integration of the social consciousness," "identification of work with craft," and so on. And now, as this flashed into his labouring mind, he began to trip up on one or two phrases, to hesitate and to repeat words, even to lose his place once so that a ten-second pause supervened. The mounting murmur from the gallery indicated that these effects were not passing unappreciated. Sweating and flushing, he struggled on a little further, hearing Welch's intonation clinging tightly round his voice, powerless for the moment to strip it away. A surge of drunkenness across his brain informed him of the arrival there of the advanceguard of the whisky—or was it only that last sherry? And how hot it was. He stopped speaking, poised his mouth for a tone as different from Welch's as possible, and started off afresh. Everything seemed all right for the moment.

As he talked, he began glancing round the front rows. He saw Christine's uncle sitting next to Bertrand, who had his mother on his other side. Christine sat on the far side of her uncle, with Carol next to her, then Goldsmith, then Beesley. He noticed that Christine was whispering something to Carol, and seemed slightly agitated. So that this shouldn't put him off, he looked further afield, trying to pick out Bill Atkinson. Yes, there he was, by the central aisle about half-way back. Over the whisky-bottle an hour and a half earlier, Atkinson had insisted, not only on coming to the lecture, but on announcing his intention of pretending to faint should Dixon, finding things getting out of hand in any way, scratch both his ears simultaneously. "It'll be a good faint," Atkinson had said in his arrogant voice. "It'll create a diversion all right. Don't you worry." Recalling this now, Dixon had to fight down a burst of laughter. At the same moment, a disturbance nearer the platform attracted his attention: Christine and Carol were pushing past Cecil and Beesley with the clear intention of leaving the Hall; Bertrand was leaning over and stage-whispering to them. Flustered, Dixon stopped talking again; then, when the two women had gained the aisle and were making for the door, went on, sooner than he should have done, in a blurred, halting mumble that suggested the extremity of drunkenness. Shifting nervously on his feet, he halftripped against the base of the lectern and swayed perilously forward. A hum of voices began again from the gallery. Dixon had a fleeting impression of the thinner alderman and his wife exchanging a glance of disapproving comment. He stopped speaking.

When he recovered himself, he found that he'd once more lost his place in mid-sentence. Biting his lip, he resolved not to run off the rails again. He cleared his throat, found his place, and went on in a clipped tone, emphasising all the consonants and keeping his voice well up at the end of each phrase. At any rate, he thought, they'll hear every word now. As he went on, he was for the second time conscious of something being very wrong. It was some moments before he realised that he was now imitating the Principal.

He looked up; there seemed to be a lot of movement in the gallery. Something heavy crashed to the floor up there. Maconochie, who'd been standing near the doors, went out, presumably to ascend and restore order. Voices were now starting up in the body of the Hall; the fashionable clergyman said something in a rumbling undertone; Dixon saw Beesley twisting about in his seat. "What's the matter with you, Dixon?" Welch hissed.

"Sorry, sir . . . bit nervous . . . all right in a minute . . ."

It was a close evening; Dixon felt intolerably hot. With a shaking hand he poured himself a glass of water from the carafe before him and drank feverishly. A comment, loud but indistinct, was shouted from the gallery. Dixon felt he was going to burst into tears. Should he throw a faint? It would be easy enough. No; everybody would assume he'd succumbed to alcohol. He made a last effort to pull himself together and, the pause now having lasted nearly half a minute, began again, but not in his normal voice. He seemed to have forgotten how to speak ordinarily. This time he chose an exaggerated northern accent as the least likely to give offence or to resemble anybody else's voice. After the first salvo of laughs from the gallery, things quieted down, perhaps under Maconochie's influence, and for a few minutes everything went smoothly. He was now getting on for half-way through.

While he read, things began slowly to go wrong for the third time, but not, as before, with what he was saying or how he was saying it. These things had to do with the inside of his head. A feeling, not so much of drunkenness, but of immense depression and fatigue, was taking almost tangible shape there. While he spoke one sentence, sadness at the thought of Christine seemed to be trying to grip his tongue at the root and reduce him to an elegiac silence; while he spoke the next, anger and fear threatened to twist his mouth, tongue and lips into the right position for a hysterical denunciation of Bertrand, Mrs. Welch, Welch, the Principal, the Registrar, the College Council, the College. He began to lose all consciousness of the audience before

him; the only member of it he cared about had left and was presumably not going to come back. Well, if this was going to be his last
public appearance here, he'd see to it that people didn't forget it in a
hurry. He'd do some good, however small, to some of those present,
however few. No more imitations, they frightened him too much, but
he could suggest by his intonation, very subtly of course, what he
thought of his subject and the worth of the statements he was making.

Gradually, but not as gradually as it seemed to some parts of his
brain, he began to infuse his tones with a sarcastic, wounding bitterness. Nobody outside a madhouse, he tried to imply, could take seriously a single phrase of this conjectural, nugatory, deluded, tedious
rubbish. Within quite a short time he was contriving to sound like
an unusually fanatical Nazi trooper in charge of a book-burning reading out to the crowd excerpts from a pamphlet written by a pacifist,
Jewish, literate Communist. A growing mutter, half-amused, half-
indignant, arose about him, but he closed his ears to it and read on.
Almost unconsciously he began to adopt an unnameable foreign accent and to read faster and faster, his head spinning. As if in a dream
he heard Welch stirring, then whispering, then talking at his side. He
began punctuating his discourse with smothered snorts of derision.
He read on, spitting out the syllables like curses, leaving mispro-
nunciations, omissions, spoonerisms uncorrected, turning over the
pages of his script like a score-reader following a *presto* movement,
raising his voice higher and higher. At last he found his final paragraph confronting him, stopped, and looked at his audience.

Below him, the local worthies were staring at him with frozen astonishment and protest. Of the Staff contingent, the senior members
looked up with similar expressions, the junior wouldn't look up at all.
The only person in the main body of the Hall who was actually producing sounds was Christine's uncle, and the sounds he was producing were of loud skirling laughter. Shouts, whistles and applause
came from the gallery. Dixon raised his hand for silence, but the noise
continued. It was too much; he felt faint again, and put his hands
over his ears. Through all the noise a louder noise became audible,
something between a groan and a bellow. Half-way down the Hall
Bill Atkinson, unable at that distance, or unwilling, to distinguish
between the scratching and the covering of ears, collapsed full length
in the aisle. The Principal rose to his feet, opening and shutting his

mouth, but without any quietening effect. He bent and began urgently whispering with the alderman at his side. The people near Atkinson started trying to lift him up, but in vain. Welch began calling Dixon's name. A stream of students entered and made towards the recumbent Atkinson. There were perhaps twenty or thirty of them. Shouting directions and advice to one another, they picked him up and bore him through the doors. Dixon came round in front of the lectern and the uproar died away. "That'll do, Dixon," the Principal said loudly, signalling to Welch, but too late.

"What, finally, is the practical application of all this?" Dixon said in his normal voice. He felt he was in the grip of some vertigo, hearing himself talking without consciously willing any words. "Listen and I'll tell you. The point about Merrie England is that it was about the most un-Merrie period in our history. It's only the home-made pottery crowd, the organic husbandry crowd, the recorder-playing crowd, the Esperanto . . ." He paused and swayed; the heat, the drink, the nervousness, the guilt at last joined forces in him. His head seemed to be swelling and growing lighter at the same time; his body felt as if it were being ground out into its constituent granules; his ears hummed and the sides, top and bottom of his vision were becoming invaded by a smoky, greasy darkness. Chairs scraped at either side of him; a hand caught at his shoulder and made him stumble. With Welch's arm round his shoulders he sank to his knees, half-hearing the Principal's voice saying above a tumult: ". . . from finishing his lecture through sudden indisposition. I'm sure you'll all . . ."

I've done it now, he managed to think. And without even telling them . . . He drew air into his lungs; if he could push it out again he'd be all right, but he couldn't, and everything faded out in a great roar of wordless voices.

COLIN WILSON

Country of the Blind

The literary bombshell of 1956 was a wild, cranky and frequently brilliant volume by a non-conforming young Englishman named Colin Wilson. Entitled The Outsider, *it set out to explore the theme of the Man Outside, his nature, his problems and his possible destiny.*

Here, in the book's opening chapter, Wilson examines the psychology of the Outsider. Uncertain, self-divided—conscious of his nothingness in a world that means nothing, the Outsider still demands . . . what? Wilson carries us to the center of the existentialist problem.

AT FIRST SIGHT, the Outsider is a social problem. He is the hole-in-corner man.

In the air, on top of a tram, a girl is sitting. Her dress lifted a little, blows out. But a block in the traffic separates us. The tramcar glides away, fading like a nightmare.

Moving in both directions, the street is full of dresses which sway, offering themselves airily, the skirts lifting; dresses that lift and yet do not lift.

In the tall and narrow shop mirror I see myself

approaching, rather pale and heavy-eyed. It is not a woman I want—it is *all* women, and I seek for them in those around me, one by one . . .

This passage, from Henri Barbusse's novel *L' Enfer*, pinpoints certain aspects of the Outsider. His hero walks down a Paris street, and the desires that stir in him separate him sharply from other people. And the need he feels for a woman is not entirely animal either, for he goes on:

> Defeated, I followed my impulse casually. I followed a woman who had been watching me from her corner. Then we walked side by side. We said a few words; she took me home with her. . . . Then I went through the banal scene. It passed like a sudden hurtling-down.
>
> Again, I am on the pavement, and I am not at peace as I had hoped. An immense confusion bewilders me. It is as if I could not see things as they were. *I see too deep and too much.*

Throughout the book, this hero remains unnamed. He is the anonymous Man Outside.

He comes to Paris from the country; he finds a position in a bank; he takes a room in a "family hotel." Left alone in his room, he meditates: He has "no genius, no mission to fulfil, no remarkable feelings to bestow. I have nothing and I deserve nothing. Yet in spite of it, I desire some sort of recompense." Religion . . . he doesn't care for it. "As to philosophic discussions, they seem to me altogether meaningless. *Nothing can be tested, nothing verified.* Truth—what do they mean by it?" His thoughts range vaguely from a past love affair and its physical pleasures, to death: "Death, that is the most important of all ideas." Then back to his living problems: "I must make money." He notices a light high up on his wall; it is coming from the next room. He stands on the bed and looks through the spy-hole:

> I look, I see. . . . The next room offers itself to me in its nakedness.

The action of the novel begins. Daily, he stands on the bed and stares at the life that comes and goes in the next room. For the space of a month he watches it, standing apart and, symbolically, above.

His first vicarious adventure is to watch a woman who has taken the room for the night; he excites himself to hysteria watching her undress. These pages of the book have the kind of deliberate sensationalism that its descendants in post-war France were so consistently to be accused of (so that Guido Ruggiero could write: "Existentialism treats life in the manner of a thriller").

But the point is to come. The next day he tries to recreate the scene in imagination, but it evades him, just as his attempt to recreate the sexual pleasures with his mistress had evaded him:

> I let myself be drawn into inventing details to recapture the intensity of the experience. "She put herself into the most inviting positions."
> No, no, that is not true.
> These words are all dead. They leave untouched, *powerless to affect it, the intensity of what was.*

At the end of *L' Enfer*, its nameless hero is introduced to a novelist who is entertaining the company with an account of a novel he is writing. A coincidence . . . it is about a man who pierces a hole in his wall and spies on all that happens in the next room. The writer recounts all of the book he has written; his listeners admire it: Bravo! Tremendous success! But the Outsider listens gloomily. "I, who had penetrated into the very heart of mankind and returned, could see nothing human in this pantomimic caricature. It was so superficial that it was false." The novelist expounds: "Man stripped of his externals . . . that is what I wish to show. Others stand for imagination . . . I stand for truth." The Outsider feels that what he has seen *is* truth.

Admittedly, for us, reading the novel half a century after it was written, there is not so much to choose between the novelist's truth and the hero's. The "dramas" enacted in the next room remind us sometimes of Sardou, sometimes of Dostoevsky when he is more concerned to expound an idea than to give it body in people and events. Yet Barbusse is sincere, and this ideal, to "stand for truth," is the one discernible current that flows through all twentieth-century literature.

Barbusse's Outsider has all of the characteristics of the type. Is he an Outsider because he's frustrated and neurotic? Or is he neurotic because of some deeper instinct that pushes him into solitude? He is preoccupied with sex, with crime, with disease. Early in the novel he recounts the after-dinner conversation of a barrister; he is speaking of the trial of a man who has raped and strangled a little girl. All other conversation stops, and the Outsider observes his neighbours closely as they listen to the revolting details:

> A young mother, with her daughter at her side, has half got up to leave, but cannot drag herself away. . . .
> And the men; one of them, simple, placid, I heard distinctly panting. Another, with the neutral appearance of a bourgeois, talks common-places with difficulty to his young neighbour. But he looks at her as if he would pierce deeply into her, and deeper yet. His piercing glance is stronger than himself, and he is ashamed of it. . . .

The Outsider's case against society is very clear. All men and women have these dangerous, unnameable impulses, yet they keep up a pretence, to themselves, to others; their respectability, their philosophy, their religion, are all attempts to gloss over, to make look civilized and rational something that is savage, unorganized, irrational. He is an Outsider because he stands for Truth.

That is his case. But it is weakened by his obvious abnormality, his introversion. It looks, in fact, like an attempt at self-justification by a man who knows himself to be degenerate, diseased, self-divided. There is certainly self-diversion. The man who watches a woman undressing has the red eyes of an ape; yet the man who sees two young lovers, really alone for the first time, who brings out all the pathos, the tenderness and uncertainty when he tells about it, is no brute; he is very much human. And the ape and the man exist in one body; and when the ape's desires are about to be fulfilled, he disappears and is succeeded by the man, who is disgusted with the ape's appetites.

This is the problem of the Outsider. . . .

Barbusse has suggested that it is the fact that his hero *sees deeper* that makes him an Outsider; at the same time, he states that he has "no special genius, no message to bestow," etc., and from his history during the remainder of the book, we have no reason to doubt his word. Indubitably, the hero *is* mediocre; he can't write for toffee, and the whole book is full of clichés. It is necessary to emphasize this in order to rid ourselves of the temptation to identify the Outsider with the artist, and so to oversimply the question: disease or insight? Many great artists have none of the characteristics of the Outsider. Shakespeare, Dante, Keats were all apparently normal and socially well-adjusted, lacking anything that could be pitched on as disease or nervous disability. Keats, who always makes a very clear and romantic distinction between the poet and the ordinary man, seems to have no shades of inferiority complexes or sexual neuroses lurking in the background of his mind; no D. H. Lawrence-ish sense of social-level, no James Joycian need to assert his intellectual superiority; above all, no sympathy whatever with the attitude of Villiers De Lisle Adam's Axel (so much admired by Yeats): "As for living, our servants can do that for us." If any man intended to do his own living for himself, it was Keats. And he is undoubtedly the rule rather than the exception among great poets. The Outsider may be an artist, but the artist is not necessarily an Outsider.

What can be said to characterize the Outsider is a sense of strangeness, of unreality. Even Keats could write, in a letter to Browne just before he died: "I feel as if I had died already and am now living a posthumous existence." This is the sense of unreality, that can strike out of a perfectly clear sky. Good health and strong nerves can make it unlikely; but that may be only because the man in good health is thinking about other things and doesn't look in the direction where the uncertainty lies. And once a man has seen it, the world can never afterwards be quite the same straightforward place. Barbusse has shown us that the Outsider is a man who cannot live in the comfortable, insulated world of the bourgeois, accepting what he sees and touches as reality. "He sees too deep and too much," and what he sees is essentially *chaos*. For the bourgeois, the world is fundamentally an orderly place, with a disturbing element of the irrational, the terrifying, which his preoccupation with the present usually permits him to ignore. For the Outsider, the world is not rational, not orderly. When he asserts his sense of anarchy in the face of the bourgeois' complacent acceptance, it is not simply the need to cock a snook at respectability that provokes him; it is a distressing sense *that truth must be told at all costs*, otherwise there can be no hope for an ultimate restoration of order. Even if there seems no room for hope, truth must be told. (The example we are turning to now is a curious instance of this.) The

Outsider is a man who has awakened to chaos. He may have no reason to believe that chaos is positive, the germ of life (in the Kabbala, chaos —*tohu bohu*—is simply a state in which order is latent; the egg is the "chaos" of the bird); in spite of this, truth must be told, chaos must be faced.

The last published work of H. G. Wells gives us an insight into such an awakening. *Mind at the End of Its Tether* seems to have been written to record some revelation:

> The writer finds very considerable reason for believing that within a period to be estimated by weeks and months rather than by aeons, there has been a fundamental change in the conditions under which life—and not simply human life but all self-conscious existence—has been going on since its beginning. If his thinking has been sound . . . the end of everything we call life is close at hand and cannot be evaded. He is telling you the conclusions to which reality has driven his own mind, and he thinks you may be interested enough to consider them, but he is not attempting to impose them on you.

This last sentence is noteworthy for its curious logic. Wells's conviction that life is at an end is, as he says, a "stupendous proposition." If it is true, then it negates the whole pamphlet; obviously, since it negates all life and its phenomena. Vaguely aware of the contradiction, Wells explains that he is writing "under the urgency of a scientific training that obliged him to clarify the world and his ideas to the limits of his capacity."

> His renascent intelligence finds itself confronted with strange, convincing realities so overwhelming that, were we indeed one of those logical, consistent people we incline to claim we are, we would think day and night in a passion of concentration, dismay and mental struggle upon the ultimate disaster that confronts our species. We are nothing of the sort. We live with reference to past experience, not to future events, however inevitable.

In commenting on an earlier book called *The Conquest of Time,* Wells declares: "Such conquest as that book admits is done by time rather than man."

Time like an ever rolling stream bears all its sons away
They fly forgotten as a dream dies at the opening day.

This is the authentic Shakespearian pessimism, straight out of
Macbeth or *Timon*. It is a surprising note from the man who had
spent his life preaching the credo: If you don't like your life you can
change it: the optimist of *Men Like Gods* and *A Modern Utopia*.
Wells declares that, if the reader will follow him closely, he will give
the reason for this change of outlook:

> The reality glares coldly and harshly upon any of those who
> can wrench their minds free . . . to face the unsparing ques-
> tion that has overwhelmed the writer. They discover that a
> frightful queerness has come into life. . . . The habitual
> interest of the writer is his critical anticipation. Of everything
> he asks: To what will this lead? And it was natural for him
> to assume that there was a limit set to change, that new things
> and events would appear, but that they would appear con-
> sistently, preserving the natural sequence of life. So that in
> the present vast confusion of our world, there was always the
> assumption of an ultimate restoration of rationality. . . . It
> was merely the fascinating question of what forms the new
> rational phase would assume, what over-man, Erewhon or
> what not would break through the transitory clouds and tur-
> moil. To this the writer set his mind.
>
> He did his utmost to pursue that upward spiral . . . towards
> their convergence in a new phase in the story of life, and the
> more he weighed the realities before him, the less he was able
> to detect any convergence whatever. Changes had ceased to be
> systematic, and the further he estimated the course they
> seemed to be taking, the greater the divergence. Hitherto,
> events had been held together by a certain logical consistency,
> as the heavenly bodies have been held together by gravitation.
> Now it is as if that cord had vanished, and everything was
> driving anyhow to anywhere at a steadily increasing velocity.
> . . . The pattern of things to come faded away.

In the pages that follow, these ideas are enlarged on and repeated,
without showing us how they were arrived at. "A harsh queerness is
coming into things," and a paragraph later: "We pass into the harsh
glare of hitherto incredible novelty. . . . The more strenuous the

analysis, the more inescapable the sense of mental defeat." "The cinema sheet stares us in the face. That sheet is the actual fabric of our being. Our loves, our hates, our wars and battles, are no more than phantasmagoria dancing on that fabric, themselves as insubstantial as a dream."

There are obviously immense differences between the attitudes of Wells and Barbusse's hero, but they have in common the Outsider's fundamental attitude: non-acceptance of life, of human life lived by human beings in a human society. Both would say: Such a life is a dream; it is not real. Wells goes further than Barbusse in the direction of complete negation. He ends his first chapter with the words: "There is no way out or round or through." There can be no doubt that as far as Wells is concerned, he certainly sees "too deep and too much." Such knowledge is an impasse, the dead end of Eliot's Gerontion: "After such knowledge, what forgiveness?"

Wells had promised to give his reasons for arriving at such a stupendous proposition. In the remainder of the pamphlet (nineteen pages) he does nothing of the sort; he repeats his assertion. "Our doomed formicary," "harsh implacable hostility to our universe," "no pattern of any kind." He talks vaguely of Einstein's paradox of the speed of light, of the "radium clock" (a method geologists use to date the earth). He even contradicts his original statement that *all* life is at an end; it is only the species *Homo sapiens* that is played out. "The stars in their courses have turned against him and he has to give place to some other animal better adapted to face the fate that closes in on mankind." In the final pages of the pamphlet, his trump of last judgement has changed into the question: Can civilization be saved?

"But my own temperament makes it unavoidable for me to doubt that there will not be that small minority who will see life out to its inevitable end."

All the same, the pamphlet must be considered the most pessimistic single utterance in modern literature, together with T. S. Eliot's "Hollow Men." And Eliot's despair was essentially religious; we should be tempted to assume that Wells's despair is religious too, if it were not for his insistence that he is speaking of a scientific fact, an objective reality.

It is not surprising that the work received scant attention from Wells's contemporaries: to make its conclusions credible it would need the formidable dialectical apparatus of Schopenhauer's *Welt als Wille und Vorstellung* or Spengler's *Decline of the West*. I have heard it described by a writer-contemporary of Wells as "an outburst of peevishness at a world that refused to accept him as its Messiah." Certainly, if we accept it on the level on which he wrote it—acquiescing to every sentence—we feel the stirring of problems that seem to return into themselves. Why did he write it if he can hold out no hope of salvation? If the conclusions he has reached negate his own past life, and the possible futures of all the human race, where do we go from there? Wells's thesis is that we have never been going anywhere—we have been carried along by our delusions, believing that any movement is better than none. Whereas the truth is that the reverse, *no movement*, is the final answer, the answer to the question: What will men *do* when they see things as they are?

It is a long way from Mr. Polly's discovery (If you don't like your life you can change it) to: There is no way out or round or through. Barbusse has gone half-way, with his, Truth, what do they mean by it?, which has as a corollary, Change, what difference does it make? Wells has gone the whole distance, and landed us on the doorstep of the Existentialist problem: Must thought negate life?

Before we pass on to this new aspect of the Outsider's problem, there is a further point of comparison between Barbusse and Wells that deserves comment. Barbusse's hero is an Outsider when we meet him; probably he was always an Outsider. Wells was very definitely an Insider most of his life. Tirelessly he performed his duty to society, gave it good advice upon how to better itself. He was the scientific spirit incarnate: reviewing the history of the life and drawing conclusions, reviewing economics and social history, political and religious history; a descendant of the French Encyclopedists who never ceased to compile and summarize. From him: Truth, what do they mean by it? would have elicited a compendious review of all the ideas of truth in the history of the seven civilizations. There is something so shocking in such a man's becoming an Outsider that we feel inclined to look for physical causes for the change: Wells was a sick, a tired man, when he wrote *Mind at the End of Its Tether*. May we not accept this as the whole cause and moving force behind the pamphlet?

Unfortunately, no. Wells declared his conclusions to be objective;

if that is so, then to say he was sick when he wrote them down means no more than to say he was wearing a dressing-gown and slippers. It is our business to judge whether the world *can* be seen in such a way that Wells's conclusions are inevitable; if so, to decide whether such a way of looking at things is truer, more valid, more objective, than our usual way of seeing. Even if we decide in advance that the answer is No, there may be much to learn from the exercise of changing our viewpoint.

*   *   *

The Outsider's claim amounts to the same thing as Wells's hero's in *The Country of the Blind:* that he is the one man able to see. To the objection that he is unhealthy and neurotic, he replies: "In the country of the blind, the one-eyed man is king." His case, in fact, is that he is the one man who knows he is sick in a civilization that doesn't know it is sick. Certain Outsiders would go even further and declare that it is human nature that is sick, and the Outsider is the man who faces that unpleasant fact. These need not concern us yet; for the moment we have a *negative position* which the Outsider declares to be the essence of the world as he sees it. "Truth, what do they mean by it?" "There is no way out or round or through." And it is to this we must turn our attention.

When Barbusse made his hero ask the first question, he was almost certainly unaware that he was paraphrasing the central problem of a Danish philosopher who had died in 1855 in Copenhagen. Søren Kierkegaard had also decided that philosophic discussion was altogether meaningless, and his reason was Wells's reason: Reality negates it. Or, as Kierkegaard put it, existence negates it. Kierkegaard's attack was directed in particular against the German metaphysician Hegel, who had (rather like Wells) been trying to "justify the ways of God to man" by talking about the goal of history and man's place in space and time. Kierkegaard was a deeply religious soul for whom all this was unutterably shallow. He declared: Put me in a System and you negate me—I am not just a mathematical symbol—I *am*.

Now obviously, such a denial that logic and scientific analysis can lead to truth has curious consequences. Our science is built on the assumption that a statement like "All bodies fall at thirty-two feet per second in the earth's gravitational field" has a definite meaning. But if you deny the ultimate logic, it becomes nonsensical. And if you don't deny logic, it is difficult, thinking along these lines, to pull up short of Wells and John Stuart Mill. That is why Kierkegaard phrases it: Is an Existentialist System possible; or, to put it in another way, Can one live a philosophy without negating either the life or the philosophy? Kierkegaard's conclusion was No, but one can live a religion without negating life or religion. We need not pause here over the reasoning that led him to this conclusion (readers interested enough can consult the *Unscientific Postscript*). What is worth noticing at this point is that his affirmation of Christian values did not prevent him from violently attacking the Christian Church on the grounds that it had solved the problem of living its religion by cutting off its arms and legs to make it fit life. It is also an amusing point that the other great Existentialist philosopher of the nineteenth century, Frederick Nietzsche, attacked the Christian church on the opposite grounds of its having solved the problem by chopping down life to fit the Christian religion. Now, both Kierkegaard and Nietzsche were trained thinkers, and both took a certain pride in stating that they were Outsiders. It follows that we should find in their works a skilled defence of the Outsider and his position. And this in fact is what we do find.

Nietzsche and Kierkegaard evolved a philosophy that started from the Outsider; nowadays, we use Kierkegaard's phrase in speaking of it, and call it Existentialism. When, in the nineteen-twenties, Kierkegaard was re-published in German, he was taken up by the professors, who discarded his religious conclusions, and used his methods of analysis to construct the so-called *Existenzphilosophie*. In doing so, they removed the emphasis from the Outsider and threw it back again on to Hegelian metaphysics. Later, in France, Existentialism was popularized by the work of Jean-Paul Sartre and Albert Camus, who once more restored emphasis to the Outsider, and finally arrived at their own conclusions upon the question of how to live a philosophy. . . .

*   *   *

In his early novel, *La Nausée*, Sartre skillfully synthesizes all the points we have already considered in connection with Wells and Barbusse: the unreality, the rejection of people and civilized standards, and, finally, the "cinema sheet" of naked existence, with "no way out or round or through."

La Nausée purports to be the journal of an historian named Roquentin: not a full-fledged scientific historian like Wells, but a literary historian who is engaged in unearthing the life of a shifty diplomat-politician named Rollebon. Roquentin lives alone in a Hotel in Le Havre. His life would be a quiet record of research, conversations in the library, sexual intercourse with the café *patronne*: "I live alone, entirely alone; I never speak to anyone, never; I receive nothing, I give nothing. . . ."

But a series of revelations disturb him. He stands on the beach and picks up a flat stone to skim on the sea, and suddenly . . . "I saw something which disgusted me; I no longer know whether it was the stone or the sea." He drops the stone and walks off.

Roquentin's journal is an attempt to objectify what is happening to him. He searches his memory, examines his past. There was something that happened in Indo-China; a colleague had asked him to join an archaeological mission to Bengal; he was about to accept—

> . . . when suddenly I woke up from a six year slumber. . . . I couldn't understand why I was in Indo-China. What was I doing there? Why was I talking to these people? Why was I dressed so oddly? . . . Before me, posed with a sort of indolence, was a voluminous, insipid idea. I did not see clearly what it was, but it sickened me so much I couldn't look at it.

Certainly something is happening. There is his ordinary life, with its assumptions of meaning, purpose, usefulness. And there are these revelations, or, rather, these attacks of nausea, that knock the bottom out of his ordinary life. The reason is not far to seek. He is too acute and honest an observer. Like Wells, he asks of everything: to what will this lead? He never ceases to notice things. Of the café *patron*, he comments: "When his place empties, his head empties too." The lives of these people are contingent on events. If things stopped happening to them, they would stop being. Worse still are the *salauds* whose pictures he can look at in the town's art gallery, these eminent public men, so sure of themselves, so sure that life is theirs and their existence is necessary to it. And Roquentin's criticism is turning back on himself; he too has accepted meanings where he now recognizes there were none. He too is dependent on events.

In a crowded café, he is afraid to look at a glass of beer. "But I can't explain what I see. To anyone. There: I am quietly slipping into the water's depths, towards fear."

A few days later, again, he describes in detail the circumstances of an attack of the nausea. This time it is the braces of the café *patron* that become the focus of the sickness. Now we observe that the nausea seems to emphasize the sordidness of Roquentin's surroundings. (Sartre has gone further than any previous writer in emphasizing "darkness and dirt"; neither Joyce nor Dostoevsky give the same sensation of the mind being trapped in physical filth.) Roquentin is overwhelmed by it, a spiritual counterpart of violent physical retching.

> . . . the nausea is not *inside* me; I feel it *out there*, in the wall, in the suspenders; everywhere around me. It makes itself one with the cafe; I am the one who is within it.

Like Wells, Roquentin insists on the objective nature of the revelation.

Somebody puts on a record; it is the voice of a Negro woman singing "Some of These Days." The nausea disappears as he listens:

> When the voice was heard in the silence I felt my body harden and the nausea vanish; suddenly it was almost unbearable to become so hard, so brilliant. . . . I am *in* the music. Globes of fire turn in the mirrors, encircled by rings of smoke.

There is no need to analyze this experience; it is the old, familiar aesthetic experience; art giving order and logic to chaos.

> I am touched; I feel my body at rest like a precision machine. I have had real adventures. I can recapture no detail, but I perceive the rigorous succession of events. I have crossed seas, left cities behind me, followed the course of rivers or plunged into forests, always making my way towards other cities. I have had women; I have fought with men, and never was I able to turn back any more than a record can be reversed.

Works of art cannot affect him. Art is thought, and thought only gives the world an appearance of order to anyone weak enough to be convinced by its show. Only something as instinctively rhythmic as the blues can give him a sense of order that doesn't seem false. But even that may be only a temporary refuge; deeper nervous exhaustion would cause the collapse of the sense of order, even in "Some of These Days."

In the Journal, we watch the breaking-down of all Roquentin's values. Exhaustion limits him more and more to the present, the here-now. The work of memory, which gives events sequence and co-herence, is failing, leaving him more and more dependent for mean-ing on what he can see and touch. It is Hume's scepticism becoming instinctive, all-destroying. All he can see and touch is unrecognizable, unaided by memory; like a photograph of a familiar object taken from an unfamiliar angle. He looks at a seat, and fails to recognize it: "I murmur: It's a seat, but the word stays on my lips. It refuses to go and put itself on the thing. . . . Things are divorced from their names. They are there, grotesque, stubborn, huge, and it seems ridiculous to call them seats, or to say anything at all about them. I am in the midst of things—nameless things."

In the park, the full nature of the revelation comes to him as he stares at the roots of a chestnut tree:

> I couldn't remember it was a root any more. The words had vanished, and with them, the significance of things, their methods of use, and the feeble points of reference men have traced on their surface. I was sitting . . . before this knotty mass, entirely beastly, which frightened me. . . . It left me breathless. Never, until these last few days, had I understood the meaning of *existence*. I was like the others. . . . I said with them: The ocean *is* green, that white speck up there *is* a sea-gull, but I didn't feel that it existed. . . . And then suddenly existence had unveiled itself. It had lost the look of an abstract category; it was the very paste of things; this root was kneaded into existence. . . . These objects, they inconvenienced me; I would have liked them to exist less imposingly, more dryly, in a more abstract way. . . .

He has reached the rock bottom of self contempt; even things negate him. We are familiar enough with his experience in the face of other human beings; a personality or a conviction can impose itself in spite of resistance; even the city itself, the confusion of traffic and human beings in Regent Street, can overwhelm a weak personality and make it feel insignificant. Roquentin feels insignificant before things. Without the meaning his Will would normally impose on it, his existence is absurd. Causality—Hume's bugbear—has collapsed; consequently *there are no adventures.* The biography of Rollebon would have been another venture of "bad faith," for it would have imposed a *necessity* on Rollebon's life that was not really there; the events didn't really cohere and follow one another like a story; only blindness to the fact of raw, naked existence could ever produce the illusion that they did.

What then? Is there no causality, no possible meaning? Sartre summarizes life: "*L'homme est un passion inutile.*" There is no choice, in Roquentin's reckoning; there is only being useless and knowing it and being useless and not knowing it.

Yet Roquentin had had his glimpse of meaning and order; in "Some of These Days." There was meaning, causation, one note following inevitably on another. Roquentin wonders: why shouldn't he create something like that; something rhythmic, purposive—a novel, perhaps, that men could read later and feel: There was an attempt to bring order into chaos? He will leave Havre and the life of Rollebon; there *must* be another way of living that is not futile. The Journal comes to an end on this note.

*   *   *

Roquentin lives like Barbusse's hero; his room is almost the limit of his consciousness. But he has gone further and deeper than the hole-in-the-wall man. His attitude has reached the dead-end of Wells; "Man is a useless passion": that could be taken as a summary of *Mind at the End of Its Tether.* Complete denial, as in Eliot's "Hollow Men": We are the hollow men, we are the *salauds.* Roquentin is in the position of the hero of *The Country of the Blind.* He alone is aware of the truth, and if all men were aware of it, there would be an end of life. In the country of the blind, the one-eyed man is king. But his kingship is kingship over nothing. It brings no powers and privileges, only loss of faith and exhaustion of the power to act. Its World is a world without values.

This is the position that Barbusse's Outsider has brought us to. It was already explicit in that desire that stirred as he saw the swaying dresses of the women; for what he wanted was not sexual intercourse, but some indefinable freedom, of which the women, with their veiled and hidden nakedness, are a symbol. Sexual desire was there, but not alone; aggravated, blown up like a balloon, by a resentment that stirred in revolt against the bewilderment of hurrying Paris with its well-dressed women. "Yet in spite of this I desire some compensation." In spite of the civilization that has impressed his insignificance on him until he is certain that "he has nothing and he deserves nothing," in spite of this he feels a right to . . . to what? Freedom? It is a misused word. We examine *L'Enfer* in vain for a definition of it. Sartre and Wells have decided that man is never free; he is simply too stupid to recognize this. Then to what precisely is it that the Outsider has an inalienable right?

JOHN BRAINE

The Choice

A man may desire only what the world thinks he should desire, and he may desire what he truly loves. For Joe Lampton, protagonist of Room at the Top, the one is Susan Brown, young, rich and beautiful; the other Alice, not so young nor so beautiful, entangled in the skein of a hopeless marriage. Lampton's choice seems inevitable. And because it does, it illuminates the tragic gulf between the individual and his social image.

THE LEDDERSFORD Conservative Club was a large Italianate building in the centre of the city. The stone had been a light biscuit colour originally—sometimes I wonder if all nineteenth-century architects weren't a bit wrong in the head—and a hundred years of smoke had given it an unhealthy mottled appearance. The carpet inside the foyer was plum-coloured and ankle-deep, the furniture was heavy and dark Victorian, and everything that could be polished, right down to the stair rods, gave off a bright glow. It smelled of cigars and whisky and sirloin, and over it hung a brutally heavy quiet. There were a great many pictures of Conservative notabilities: they shared a sort of mean sagacity of expression, with watchful eyes and mouths like spring traps, clamped hard on the thick juicy steak of success.

I felt a cold excitement. This was the place where the money grew. A lot of rich people patronised expensive hotels and roadhouses and restaurants too; but you could never be really sure of their grade, because you needed only the price of a drink or a meal and a collar and tie to be admitted. The Leddersford Conservative Club, with its ten-guinea annual subscription plus incidentals (Put me down for a hundred, Tom, if the Party doesn't get it the Inland Revenue will), was for rich men only. Here was the place where decisions were taken, deals made between soup and sweet; here was the place where the right word or smile or gesture could transport one into a higher grade overnight. Here was the centre of the country I'd so long tried to conquer; here magic worked, here the smelly swineherd became the prince who wore a clean shirt every day.

I gave my name to the commissionaire. "Mr. Lampton? Yes, sir, Mr. Brown has a luncheon appointment with you. He's been unavoidably delayed, but he asked you to wait in the bar." He looked at me a trifle doubtfully; not having had time to change, I was wearing my light grey suit and brown shoes, my former Sunday best. The shoes were still good but much too heavy for the suit, and the suit was too tight and too short in the jacket. Third-rate tailors always make clothes too small. I saw or fancied that I saw, a look of contempt in the commissionaire's eye, so I put back the shilling I was going to give him into my pocket. (It was fortunate that I did; afterwards I found out that you never tip club servants.)

The bar was crowded with businessmen slaving to help the export drive. An attempt had been made to modernise it; the carpet was a glaring zigzag of blue and green and yellow and the bar was topped with some kind of plastic and faced with what appeared to be black glass. There wasn't any sign that it was the stamping ground reserved for the higher grades, unless you counted the picture of Churchill above the bar—a picture which you could find in most pubs anyway. And by no means all of them spoke Standard English. Leddersford's main manufacture is textiles, and most of its ruling class receive their higher education at the Technical College, where to some extent they're forced to rub shoulders with the common people and consequently pick up some traces of a Northern accent. What marked the users of the bar as being rich was their size. In Dufton or even Warley, I was thought of as being a big man; but here there were at least two dozen men as big as I, and two dozen more who were both taller and broader. And one of them, standing near me, was at least six foot four and as broad-shouldered as a gorilla—it would be genuine bone and muscle too, there'd be no padding in *that* suit. He could have broken my back across his knee without putting himself out of breath and doubtless would have done if he'd been given half a chance, to judge from the way he was scowling at me. Then the scowl changed into a social smile, and I saw that it was Jack Wales.

"How are you, old man?"

"Very fit," I said. "Had a good holiday in Dorset. *You* seem to be bursting with health, I must say."

"Been to Majorca. Cambridge seems a bit damp and chill after it. I'm just returning there—I made a flying visit to Warley. Papa's rather off-colour. Works too hard."

"I'm sorry to hear that," I said, wondering maliciously whether it was gout, prostate trouble, or high blood pressure that was making Wales Senior ill.

"He's all right now," he said. He smiled at me. "My father puts in a sixteen-hour day, you know. Drink, old man?"

"Whisky."

"Have a double. Then you don't have to catch the waiter's eye twice."

"You shouldn't have any trouble that way."

"Whatsay? Oh, see what you mean. My height's a curse, actually. Can't get away with anything . . . What brings you here anyway? Thought you were a red-hot Labour man. Seen the light, eh?" He gave one of his hearty false laughs.

"I'm meeting Mr. Brown."

"Susan's father?"

"Uh-uh."

"Nice chap. Don't let him overpower you, though. Stick out for the highest figure the traffic will bear—I suppose it's a job you're discussing?"

"Could be," I said. There wasn't anything else that I could say.

"You're cagey," he said. "Wise man." He looked at the gold watch that seemed effeminately small on his huge hairy wrist. "Well, I must push off." He finished his whisky.

"Another?"

"No thanks, old man. In any case, you can't buy one; club rule." He clicked his finger at the waiter. "Double whisky for Mr. Lampton, Henry." He gave the waiter a note, and shovelled the change into his pocket without bothering to count it. "Goodbye for now, Joe."

"Goodbye, Jack."

I saw Brown enter the room. He came straight over to me.

"Seem to have made yourself at home, young man. Think I'll have one of those whiskies while there's still some left." He crooked his finger and the waiter glided over to him.

"I'm very annoyed with you, young man," he said. He had very heavy black eyebrows and in conjunction with his grey hair and red face they were a little alarming; compressed over his deep-set eyes the effect was that of a hanging judge, a jolly old *bon viveur* sentencing some poor devil of a labourer or a clerk to death by dislocation of the neck as an aperitif to a good dinnah with a bottle of the best—the *very* best, waitah—port.

He took out a gold cigarette-case and offered me one.

"No, thanks."

"You're sensible. Bad habit before meals. It's the only thing you are sensible about; in all other respects you've been a bloody fool."

I felt myself going red in the face. "If that's all you wanted to see me about, there's no point in me staying."

"Don't be any dafter than you can help. I've a proposition for you. Anyway—" he gave me one of his unexpectedly charming smiles, the hanging judge becoming a Santa Claus who would send absolutely every item on the list—"you might as well have lunch first. Not that you'll have a very good one; this place has gone down the hill since rationing started."

"No one here seems to be starving."

"Never said they were. Just that you couldn't get a decent meal here any more. This the first time you've been to this club?"

"This or any Conservative club," I said. "My father'd turn in his grave if he could see me."

"So would mine," he said, and winked. "So would mine, lad. But we're not bound by our fathers."

I looked at him coldly. The bluff friendliness approach no doubt came automatically; the fustian glove on the steel fist which, any moment now, I was going to be given a mouthful of. Why didn't he get it over with?

A waiter approached us and, with much bowing and scraping, led us to a table in the dining room. This was in the same style as the foyer; the linen was blindingly white and sailcloth-stiff and the cutlery heavy enough to be silver. It wasn't a room that any moderately good hotel couldn't duplicate; but there wasn't one chip, one scratch, one speck of dust anywhere, and you had the feeling that the waiters would without flicking an eyelash, bring you anything that you wanted the way you wanted it, even, if you really insisted, their own ears and eyes, braised in sherry.

I was taking the first spoonful of game soup when Brown said casually: "I'm thinking of setting you up in business."

I nearly choked. "Are you serious?"

He scowled. "I didn't bring you here to play jokes. You heard what I said. You can name your figure." He leaned forward, his hands gripping the table. His nails were white at the top with pressure. "You're a clever young man. You don't want to stay at the Town Hall all your life, do you? Now's the time when accountants can do well for themselves. Supposing I lend you what's necessary to buy a partnership somewhere? I won't sell you a pup; and I'll even send business your way."

"There's a catch somewhere," I said.

"There is. I'll make you a rich man—a damned sight better off than you'll ever be in local government—on one condition." He paused; suddenly he looked old and sick. "Just one condition: you never see Susan again or communicate with her in any way."

"I'm to leave Warley too, I take it?"

"Yes, you're to leave Warley too." He wiped his forehead with a white silk handkerchief. "There's no need for you to think twice about it, is there? There's nothing for you if you don't take the offer. In fact, I'll go out of my way to make things unpleasant for you."

There was a roaring in my ears; I wanted to knock over the table and hit him until my arm had no more strength in it, then give him the boot give him the boot give him the boot—I drew a deep breath. "No. Definitely no. If you were a younger man, I'd knock you down, by God I would!" To my horror, I found my accent growing broader. "Ah reckon nowt to your bloody rotten offer. Ah'll dig ditches afore Ah'll be bought—" My voice stopped shaking as I regained my self-control. "Listen. You wouldn't understand, but I love Susan."

"I wouldn't understand," he said, dragging out the words. "I wouldn't understand about love."

"I'm not in love with her," I said. "I *love* her. She's absolutely the best girl I've ever met. I wanted to marry her the first moment I saw her; I didn't know who she was then, and I didn't care. Damn it, I'll bring it before the magistrates. She can stay at my home if you throw her out. The magistrates won't refuse us permission to marry, and even if they do, I'll kick up the hell of a row—"

"You'll do no such thing, Joe," he said quietly.

"Why won't I?"

"Because you're marrying her. With my consent. Right quick."

I looked at him with my mouth open.

He'd regained his normal floridity now, and was actually smiling. I could only gape at him.

"Finish your soup," he said. "There's many folk 'ud be glad of that and you're letting it grow cold."

I spooned it up obediently as a child. He looked at me with a bristling kindliness.

"Why did you make me that offer?" I asked.

"I wanted to be sure you were right for her. Mind you, it would have been a good investment anyway. You're a bright lad."

"She was only sixteen," he said, almost apologetically. "He was a clerk at the works. Fancied himself as a writer. And a fortune hunter. I got him a job with an advertising firm. It wasn't anything—just calf love. He caved in straightaway. If you just spoke rough to that chap, he was licking your boots the next moment. But that's of no importance. The first thing is to fix the wedding date."

"You've been against us marrying right from the start," I said, "and you want us to get married quickly . . . I still can't see why."

"The reason's very simple. Yes, I'm glad you've the grace to blush."

"But why didn't she tell me?"

Brown looked at the chicken the waiter had just brought him.

"Chicken again," he grumbled. "I'll be turning into one soon. Well, Joe, she didn't tell you because she didn't want you to wed her just out of a sense of duty. And I didn't tell you because I didn't want you to wed her as a financial proposition. And why the hell should I present you with a gun to hold at my head?"

My respect for him increased. And then I was seized with the fact of sharing life, all life, of being in the main current—everyone talks about the joys of motherhood, but they say very little about the joys of fatherhood, when you feel an immense animal tenderness towards a woman; the Bible puts it exactly right when it talks of your bowels yearning towards someone.

"You mean that you'd let her have the baby and say nothing to me?"

"I'd sooner have that happen than have her miserable for the rest of her life."

"Susan with my son," I said, and smiled. I was dizzy with happiness. It was a happiness as wholesome as honey on the comb, I was a man at last. Instead of having the book snatched from me halfway I was reading in to the next chapter.

"You've nothing to grin about," Brown said roughly. "This isn't the way I'd planned to have my daughter wed." His eyes turned opaque as mercury and his voice had a knuckleduster menace. "Some fathers have sent their daughters away to—nursing homes. It's not too late for that."

"She wouldn't consent," I said in agony. "You couldn't do it either, you couldn't murder your grandchild. I can't believe that anyone would be so rotten. I'll take her away with me tonight, I swear I will."

"You don't know what I can do," he said. "I can get my story in first, and I can handle her better than you can."

"You try it. You try it. I'll take the matter to the police before I let you do it."

"I believe you would." He seemed pleased about it. "I really believe you would. You're an awkward customer, aren't you?"

"Being decent isn't the same thing as being awkward."

"True enough. I've no intentions of sending Susan away, in any case."

"Then what did you give me such a fright for?"

"Wanted to see what you were made of," he said with his mouth full.

"I suppose that's why you warned me off Susan, too?"

"I never warned you off Susan," he said, helping himself to roast potatoes. "My wife had a word with Hoylake at a church social and he took it upon himself to tell you to keep away from her. That is, as much as he ever tells anyone anything. Proper Town Hall type, that chap."

"Why didn't you say something to me?"

"Why should I? If you had owt about you, I knew you'd damn my eyes and go ahead. If you were gutless, you'd let yourself be frightened off by a few vague threats, and everyone'd be saved a lot of bother. The point is, lad, that a man in my position can't get to know a man in your position very well. So I let you sweat it out."

"Jack Wales didn't have to sweat it out," I said sulkily.

Brown chuckled. "You should have seen to it that your parents had more brass. I didn't make the world."

There was now the luxury of confirming the details of my good fortune, of admiring the pretty colours of the check. "There's one thing I don't understand," I said. "I thought that you had it all fixed between him and Susan. There was talk of a merger . . ."

"There was nothing fixed and the merger had nowt to do with it. I'm not a sort of king, I don't give my daughter away to seal a bargain."

"Will this mess up the merger?"

"You've some peculiar notions about business, young man. I never for one moment thought seriously about joining forces with Wales. For one thing, I've been boss of my own works too long to relish being just another co-director; and for another, I don't like the way they're going. They're making money hand over fist, but anyone capable of counting up to ten can do that nowadays . . . However, I didn't bring you here to talk about the Wales family. I want you to leave the Town Hall as soon as you can."

"I've not qualified as a cost accountant yet, you know. I've only got the C.S.—"

He silenced me with a wave of his hand. "I judge people by what they do, not by little bits of paper. I've no time to go into much detail now, but what I need, and need damned quick, is someone to reorganise the office. There's the hell of a lot too much paper; it started during the war, when we took everyone we could get hold of, thinking we could always find use for them. I'm an engineer, I'm not interested in the administrative side. But I know what we can and what we can't afford."

"So I'm to be an efficiency expert?"

"Not quite. Don't like those chaps anyway; there's bad blood wherever they are. Alterations have to be made which are best made by a new man. That's all."

"I've a wife and family to support," I said. "How much salary?"

"Thousand to begin with. Nowt at all if you don't make a success of it. You can have one of the firm's cars; there's depots at Leeds and Wakefield you'll be visiting a good deal."

"It's too good to be true," I said, trying to look keen and modest and boyish. "I can't thank you enough."

"There's just one matter to be cleared up," he said. "And if you don't, then it's all off. You've been too bloody long about it already." He scowled. "God, you have a nerve. Whenever I think about it, I could break your neck."

He fell silent again; after a minute I couldn't take it any longer. "If you tell me what's wrong, I can do something about it," I said. "I can't read your mind."

"Leave off Alice Aisgill. Now. I'm not having my daughter hurt any more. And I'm not having my son-in-law in the divorce courts either. Not on account of an old whore like her."

"I've finished with her. There's no need for you to use that word."

He watched me through narrowed eyes. "I use words that fit, Joe. You weren't the first young man she's slept with. She's notorious for it—" I suddenly remembered, down to the last intonation, Eva's crack—"there's not many likely lads haven't had a bit there. She has a pal, some old tottie that lends her a flat . . . Jack Wales . . ."

On a trip over Cologne the bomb aimer got a faceful of flak. I say a faceful because that takes the curse off it somehow; it was actually a bit of metal about two inches square that scooped out his eyes and most of his nose. He grunted when it happened, then he said: "Oh no. Oh no."

That is what I said when Brown spoke Jack Wales's name and, pressing his advantage home, went on to give chapter and verse.

There was a handshake, there was talk of a contract, there was tolerance—*I've been young and daft myself*—there was praise—*You're the sort of young man we want. There's always room at the top*—there was sternness—*See her tomorrow and get it done with, I'll not have it put off any more*—there was brandy and a cigar, there was a lift back to Warley in the Bentley; and I said yes to everything quite convincingly, to judge from Brown's satisfied expression; but inside, like that sergeant until the morphine silenced him, all that I could say, again and again and again, was the equivalent of those two syllables of shocked incredulity.

*   *   *

The month was September, the time was eight o'clock, the weather was unsettled, with a sky mottled with indigo, copper, and tinges of oxblood red. The place was Elspeth's flat, the exact point of space from where I told her it was all over was the brown stain on the carpet in the lounge, just by the door into the corridor. I knew that stain well; I'd spilled some cherry brandy there one night before Christmas. By the time I'd finished telling Alice that I didn't love her, I could have drawn a coloured map of it and its surroundings, correct down to the last scroll of the silly little gilt chair next it.

I couldn't bring myself to look at her and I didn't want to come close to her. I did look at her, of course; she was wearing a black silk dress and a pearl necklace and a sapphire on her right hand which I'd not seen before. Her hands were clenched by her side, and the rouge which she had so carefully applied stood out in two patches on her cheeks. She wasn't wearing her usual lavender but something strong and musky with an animal smell in the background like a newly bathed tiger if anyone were ever to bathe a tiger.

"So you've finished with me, Joe?" Her lips scarcely moved and she was breathing very quickly.

"I love Susan."

"That's very sensible of you."

"There's no need to be bitter."

"I'm not bitter. Only surprised. How quickly you've changed. How long is it since you—?"

She described everything we'd done together in Dorset, using the simplest Anglo-Saxon words and talking with a cool, dry detachment.

"It hasn't left any mark on you, has it? It was only our bodies that did these things—your young one and my—my *old* one that's well past its best. Why don't you say it, Joe? I'm thirty-four and she's nineteen—

you want someone young and strong and healthy. I don't mind, I should have expected it anyway, but why in God's name can't you be honest?"

"It isn't like that," I said wearily. "I did love you, but I can't now. Let's leave it at that."

I couldn't tell her about Jack Wales; it didn't seem important any longer. The knowledge that once she'd made love with him, him of all the people in the world, here on the very bed where I'd lain with her, had come between me and sleep all night; but now that I was with her it didn't matter, it was as dead as yesterday's newspaper. That she had let him make love to her had proved only her contempt for him; she'd used him in an idle hour—as a man might take a quick whisky when tired and depressed—and forgotten him. He was a trivial detail of a past era, dead millions of seconds Before Joe, just as my own dreary copulations in Dufton and Lincolnshire and Germany had been Before Alice.

"It wasn't wise for us to go on," I said. "It would have blown up in our faces anyway. Eva's found out about us, and it's only a matter of time before George does. He's too crafty to be found out himself—I'm going in no mucky divorce courts, and that's flat. And I'm not going to be thrown out of Warley either. What would we live on?"

Her mouth twisted. "You're a timid soul, aren't you?"

"I know which side my bread is buttered on," I said.

She slumped ungracefully into the nearest chair, shading her eyes as if against some arc lamp of interrogation.

"There's something else," she said. "Why are you holding it back? Scared of hurting me?"

"I hate hurting you." My head began to throb; it wasn't aching but it felt as if a big hammer inside it were stopping just short of the threshold of pain. I wanted to escape from the stuffy little room with its smell of scent and ill-health, I wanted to be in Warley. Alice didn't belong to Warley. I couldn't have both her and Warley: that was what it all boiled down to. I knew that I couldn't explain this to her, but I was forced to try.

"I'm engaged to Susan," I said. "I'm going to work for her father. But that isn't the reason that we've got to call it a day. It's impossible for us to love each other in Warley, and I can't love anyone anywhere else—can't you see?"

"No," she said. "I wish you wouldn't lie to me. It's perfectly simple and understandable and I wish you luck. You needn't dress it up with all this nonsense. Places don't matter." She rose and came over to me. I put my arms around her waist automatically. The hammer inside my head broke into the threshold of pain; it was a crackling neuralgic ache but it had no effect upon the tenderness and happiness that visited me when I touched her.

"There *is* something else," she said. "Please tell me, Joe. That's all I ask." She looked at me as pleadingly as a German child. Belsen or no Belsen, you gave those skinny little brats your chocolate ration; truth or no truth, I had to give Alice her self-respect. Susan wasn't the real reason for me ending our affair; but to have made it clear to her that I was leaving her for Warley would have damaged her pride past endurance. So I told her what was, with her body touching mine, a lie; though it wouldn't have been a lie the day before.

"I heard that Jack Wales was your lover once," I said. She stiffened in my arms. "I couldn't bear that. Not him. Anyone else, but not him. Is it true?"

If she'd denied it, I think that I would have taken her back. Honour, like freedom, is a luxury for those with independent incomes, but there is a limit to dishonour, a sort of soft-shoe line of decency which marks the difference between manhood and swinishness.

"You hate Jack," she said. "I'm sorry about that. You needn't, because he doesn't hate you."

"He doesn't know I'm alive."

"He didn't when we first met. You hadn't come to Warley then. But he likes you."

"You've been with him—lately?"

She unloosened herself from me and went over to the sideboard. "I think we both need a gin." Her voice was calm. "I went with him twice. Once in his car, if you really want to torture yourself, and once here. He took me home from the Thespian Ball the first time." She handed me a drink. "There's only lime juice."

"I don't want anything." I took it at a gulp, and coughed. "What about the second time?"

"That was after we quarreled. The night after. I ran across him in a hotel bar."

"Why didn't you tell me?"

"It didn't seem important. I never asked you about your past—or your present, for that matter. We had an agreement about it, in case you've forgotten."

There was a heavy silence in the room, as if some had seeped in from the long grey corridors outside. There suddenly was nothing left to say. She was standing with her back to me at the sideboard; the sun had gone down and I couldn't see her very well, but I think that she had begun to cry.

"Goodbye, Alice," I said. "Thank you for everything."

She didn't answer, and I went out very quietly, as from a sickroom.

*   *   *

The Town Hall atmosphere seemed all the more pleasant to me next morning because I was going to leave it. I could see the machinery of local government as it really is, appreciate its blend of efficiency and cosiness; I hear a lot of nasty things said about municipal bureaucrats nowadays, but if every business was run as smoothly as even the most slatternly little urban district, then Americans would come over here to learn the technique of greater productivity instead of it being the other way about. I reflected on this, making a neat little speech for the NALGO conference, and when the delegates had finished applauding me—only through sheer exhaustion did they stop—I took out my good news of yesterday, adding to it the fact that I'd parted from Alice with at least a sufficiency of dignity and a minimum of pain, and unfolded it slowly, admiring its glittering colour and intricate pattern an item at a time.

I'd just finished furnishing a house in St. Clair Road, and was driving to the Civic Ball in a new Riley, Susan by my side in a scarlet dress that would make all the other men sick with lust for her and murderous with envy of me, when Teddy Soames entered.

"Heard that you had lunch with Brown on Wednesday," he said. "Leaving us for the lush pastures of private enterprise?"

"Eventually."

"Mention me, will you? I can fiddle an expense account as well as the next man."

"All that I know about fiddling I learned from Mr. Edward Soames, Chief Audit Clerk, Warley UDC—will that do?"

"Just the job. Well, Lampton, we'll get our money's worth out of you before you go—glance through these accounts, will you?"

The tone was supposed to be one of mock severity, but it came out vicious. I grinned and tugged my forelock.

"Yes, Master. Right away."

He gave me the folder of accounts and a cigarette. "I'll expect a box of Havanas in return." He frowned at me. "You don't seem bothered about Alice Aisgill," he said. "Or hadn't you heard?"

"What about her?"

"She's dead."

Oh merciful God, I thought, she's committed suicide and left a note blaming me. That's finished it. That's finished me in every possible way. Teddy's eyes were a pale blue, as if all the colour had been drained from them; they were probing my face now.

"She was a friend of yours, wasn't she?"

"A very good friend," I said. "How did she die?"

"Ran her car into a wall on Warley Moor. She'd been drinking all night at the Clarendon and the St. Clair. They wouldn't serve her any more at the St. Clair."

"He let her drive home, though," I said. "And he took her money for booze so that she could kill herself." It was hardly fair to blame poor old Bert; but I had to say something.

"She must have been going at the hell of a pace," Teddy said. "They say that the car's bent like that"—he cupped his hand— "and there's blood all over the road. It wasn't till this morning that they found her."

"Where exactly was it?"

"Corby Lane. You know, right up in the north, above Sparrow Hill. It's the last place that God made. What she was doing there at that time I can't imagine."

"Me neither," I said; but I could. I could imagine everything that had happened to Alice after I'd left her. She'd stayed in the flat the duration of two more double gins. Then everything in the room—the little gilt clock, the Dresden shepherdesses and Italian goat boys, the photos of dead names of yesterday, the flounces and the gilt, the bright chintz curtains, the glass I'd drunk from—had gathered together and attacked her, trivial individually but as deadly collectively as those little South American fish which gnaw swimmers to the bone in five minutes. So she'd run out of the flat and into the Fiat; but once in

Warley (she didn't know she reached there, there was a blank until
she found herself waiting at the lights in Market Street repeating my
name under her breath) she didn't know what to do with herself. She
turned up St. Clair Road with the idea of going home. Home would
be an abstract notion—Father, Mother, safety, hugs, and hot milk and
a roaring fire and all the trouble and grief forgotten in the morning.
But as she'd gone past Eagle Road (Joe lives there) she'd recovered
her bearings. Home was the house where she lived with a husband
she didn't love; she was fleeing towards an electric radiator and
George's cold tolerance, she was too old for hot milk, there were no
hugs going, even if she wanted any from him, and it would all be
even more unbearable tomorrow. She'd reversed at Calder Crescent
or Wyndham Terrace and gone to the Clarendon. Probably she'd used
the Snug, where she was less likely to see anyone she knew—the Thes-
pians always used the Lounge. If she needed company, if she were
able to persuade herself that she didn't care about me ditching her,
she could move out of the Snug and return to the main stream, return
to, perhaps not happiness, but a sort of emotional limbo. When she
heard their voices from the Lounge at about nine-fifteen, she discovered that she didn't want to see anyone whom she knew or who
knew me. She slipped out of the back door. To the double gins which
she'd had at the flat would have been added three or four more. She
still wouldn't want to go home. There was only the St. Clair. The gins
rolled their sleeves up and got to work on her: you must eliminate
him from your system, they said. Eliminate, obliterate, expunge.
You've been to the St. Clair often with him? Very well, then, walk
straight in and sit where you used to sit with him. Spit in his eye—

Or had she gone there in an attempt to recapture the decent and
wholesome happiness we shared once when I was nearly a year
younger and fully ten years more innocent? More gins had been called
upon to assist her nearer towards whichever stage of illusion she
wished for, and then she'd started to sing or to swear or to fall flat upon
her face or all three, and Bert, who kept a respectable house, had persuaded her to leave. She drove up St. Clair Road again, then along
the narrow switchback of Sparrow Hill Road; but she couldn't exor-
cise my presence by stopping at the old brick works. And she still
couldn't go home. If she pressed the accelerator down still harder, she
could travel out of herself—I was beside her in the car now, she was

approaching that double bend which only a racing car could take at over twenty—

"What a damned awful way to die," Teddy said.

"I expected it," Joe Lampton said soberly. "She drove like a maniac. It doesn't make it any the less tragic, though." I didn't like Joe Lampton. He was a sensible young accountant with a neatly pressed blue suit and a stiff white collar. He always said and did the correct thing and never embarrassed anyone with an unseemly display of emotion. Why, he even made a roll in the hay with a pretty little teen-ager pay dividends. I hated Joe Lampton, but he looked and sounded very sure of himself sitting at my desk in my skin; he'd come to stay, this was no flying visit.

"Alice wasn't perfect," Joe Lampton said. "But who is? She was a jolly good sort, and I'm going to miss her very much." He shook his handsome dignified head slowly. That meant that a moral exordium was on the way. "I enjoy a drink myself, but no one in charge of a car should be allowed into a pub. It's lucky she killed only herself. My God, only yesterday she was alive and cheerful, and then, all in a second—"

"A second?" Teddy said. "She was still alive when the ambulance came. She didn't die until eight o'clock."

"Jesus Christ," I said. "Jesus Christ." I turned on Teddy fiercely. "Who told you? Who told you?"

"My cousin works at Warley Hospital," he said. "Turned me up a bit when I heard about it. She was crawling round the road when a farm labourer found her. She was scalped and the steering-column—"

I half ran out of the office and went into the lavatory. But the w.c. door was locked, and it was nearly ten minutes before it opened and one of the Health Department juniors came out looking sheepish and leaving the compartment full of tobacco smoke. I locked the door and sat on the w.c. seat with my head between my hands, those gentle loving hands that had so often caressed what was, because of the treachery in the brain in the head between the hands, a lump of raw meat with the bones sticking through.

At twelve o'clock I told Teddy that I was sick. I don't know what I did till then; I hope that I had at least the decency to make a lot of mistakes checking the accounts. I stood about at the station end of Market Street for about ten minutes, then caught a bus to Leddersford. I couldn't eat any lunch, and I couldn't stay in Warley, and I couldn't face the Thompsons. They were sure to talk about her, and then Joe Lampton would take possession of me again. Joe Lampton Export Model Mark IA warranted free of rust, flaws, cracks, dust or pity; as long as I was in the bus I was safe. I tried to make my mind a blank as it speeded up on the main road; a stationer's, a draper's, a tobacconist's, a cricket field, a little girl pulled along by an Alsatian, an old woman wincing away from the Alsatian, who only wanted to lick her face anyway. Then there were fields and cows and narrow roads wriggling like tapeworms into the new Council estate. But Alice had been killed, and what I saw was the components of a huge machine that now only functioned out of bravado: it had been designed and manufactured for one purpose, to kill Alice. That purpose was accomplished; it should have been allowed to run down and then stop, the driver asleep at the wheel, the passengers sitting docilely with their mouths wide open, waiting for the bus to fly away, the estate left unfinished, the shops shuttered and overrun with rats, the unmilked cows lowing in agony with swollen udders, the dogs and cats running wild and bloody-mouthed, and then a great storm to scour the whole dirty earth down to clean rock and flame. I licked my dry lips, looking round the bus at the other passengers, sleek, rosy, whole, stinking of food and tobacco and sleep; I closed my eyes as a big sickness came over me. I was cold and trembling and on the point of vomiting, but it was more than that. It was an attack of the truth: I saw quite clearly that there were no dreams and no mercy left in the world, nothing but a storm of violence.

I sat with my hands clasped tightly, waiting for the next blow. It didn't come; so when the bus reached Leddersford I went into the first pub that I saw.

It was an old building with an atmosphere of damp plaster and dusty plush; the front door opened directly into the saloon bar. As I opened it, the noise and light from the street outside was cut off. There were a lot of people at the bar, talking in subdued voices. I ordered a rum and a half of bitter, and stood at the bar staring at the pictures which were hung round the walls and on the staircase leading to the Ladies'; they were all battle scenes, rather pleasant coloured prints with energetic marionettes waving swords with red paint on the tips, firing muskets which each discharged one round puff of white smoke, planting their standards on little cone-shaped hills above the perfectly flat battlefield, advancing relentlessly in perfect parade-ground formation and, occasionally, dying very stiffly with their left hand clutching their bosoms and their right hand beckoning their comrades on to victory. The beer tasted like water after the rum, and for a moment I was nauseated, and couldn't face the idea of having another drink. Then I felt the first tiny glow of warmth in my belly and ordered another; the glow increased until, at the fourth or the fifth, a slatternly happiness sidled up to me: I had eight hundred in the bank, I was going to be an executive with an expense account, I was going to marry the boss's daughter, I was clever and virile and handsome, a Prince Charming from Dufton, every obstacle had been magically cleared from my path—

Every obstacle? That meant Alice. That wasn't magic. How long must she have crawled round in her own blood in the dark? Where was I now? There was Dufton, there was Cardington, there was Compton Bassett, there was Cologne and Hamburg and Essen from the air, there was the wine-growing country of Bavaria, there was Berlin and the pale schoolgirls and their mothers. Five Woodbines for the mother, ten for the daughter. And Dufton again, then Warley, only a year ago. I should have stayed in the place where I was born, and then Alice would be walking round Warley now with her hair shining in the sun or lying on the divan at home reading a play for the Selection Committee or eating chicken and salad if it were the season for salad. I put my hand to my head.

"You ill?" the landlord asked. He had a doughy, expressionless face and a gratingly heavy voice. Up to that moment he'd been talking about football to a knot of his cronies. Now, the wheels of whatever passed for his intelligence creaking, he turned his attention to me. I took my hand away from my head and ordered a brandy. He didn't move to serve me.

"I said, Are—you—ill?"

"Uh?"

"Are you ill?"

"Of course not. I asked for a brandy."

Everybody had stopped talking and were devouring me with glittering eyes, hoping that there'd be a fight and that I'd get my face bashed in; there was nothing personal about it, it's simply that, at any given moment, the majority of people are bored stiff. I glanced round the room and saw that it wasn't a pub for casuals; it was a betting-slip and pansy pub (there were three of them next to me now, standing out like sore teeth among the surrounding roughs).

"You've had enough," the landlord repeated. I scowled at him. There was no reason why I shouldn't have walked out; but my feet seemed bolted to the floor.

"I'll buy you one, dear," one of the pansies said. He had dyed hair of a metallic yellow and smelled of geraniums. "I think you're awfully mean, Ronnie." He smiled at me, showing a mouthful of blindingly white false teeth. "You're not doing anything wrong, are you, dear?"

"You'll get yourself into trouble," the landlord said.

"Yes, *please*," the pansy said, and they all giggled in unison. I let him buy me a double-brandy, and then asked him what he'd have. It was tonic-and-lemon; pansies only use pubs for picking up boy friends. They don't booze themselves, any more than you or I would if surrounded by bedworthy women who might be had for the price of a few drinks.

"My name's George," he said. "What's yours, handsome?"

I gave him the name of the Superintendent Methodist Minister of Warley, who'd Struck Out Fearlessly Against Immorality (meaning sex) in last week's *Clarion*.

"Lancelot," he said. "I shall call you Lance. It suits you. Isn't it a funny thing, how you can tell just what a boy's like from his first name? Will you have another brandy, Lance?"

I went on drinking at his expense until five minutes to three, then slipped out on the pretence of a visit to the Gents'. Then I bought some peppermints at a chemist's and sat in a news theatre until half past five. Joseph Lampton was doing the sensible thing, keeping out of harm's way until the rum and the beer and the brandy settled down; and Joseph Lampton was keeping a barrier of warmth and darkness and coloured shadows between himself and pain. I came out into the acid daylight with that headachy feeling that matinees always induce; but I'd stopped thinking about Alice and I was walking steadily.

I went into a café and ate a plateful of fish-and-chips, bread and butter, two queer-tasting cream cakes (that was the time that confectioners were using blood plasma and liquid paraffin), and a strawberry ice. Then I drank a pot of mahogany-coloured Indian tea. When

I'd finished my third cigarette and there wasn't a drop of tea left in the pot I looked at my watch and saw that it was half past six. So I paid the bill and strolled out into the street; I was pretty well in control of myself by then, and it occurred to me that my becoming hopelessly drunk wasn't going to help anyone, least of all Alice. I'd go home—for Warley, after all, *was* my home, I'd chosen it myself—and go to bed with a hot-water bottle and a couple of aspirins. I wasn't Alice's keeper; let George take over whatever guilt there was to bear. Then I saw Elspeth.

She stood in my path, a henna-haired, tightly corseted old woman swaying slightly on her three-inch heels. I had never seen her look such a wreck; her face was so bedizened with powder, rouge, and lipstick, all in shades meant for the stage, that only her red-rimmed eyes were human.

"You pig," she said. "You low rotten pimp. You murdering little—" she glared up at me— "ponce. Are you happy now, you bastard? Got rid of her nicely, didn't you?"

"Let me go," I said. "I didn't want her to die."

She spat in my face.

"You can't punish me anymore," I said. "I'll punish myself. Now for Christ's sake leave me alone. Leave us both alone." Her face changed; tears began to furrow the makeup. She put her skinny hand on mine; it was dry and hot. "I phoned this morning and they told me," she said. "I knew what had happened. Oh Joe, how could you do it? She loved you so much, Joe, how could you do it?"

I shook off her hand and walked off quickly. She made no attempt to follow me, but stood looking sadly at me, like a young wife watching a troopship leave harbour. I half ran through the maze of side-streets off the city centre, making my way to the working-class quarter round Birmingham Road. Birmingham Road, if you keep on for about a hundred and fifty miles, does eventually take you to Birmingham; that was another reason for my wanting to become really drunk. All the voyages of the heart ended in a strange city with all the pubs and the shops shut and not a penny in your pocket and the train home cancelled without notice, cancelled for a million years—*Leave us alone*, I'd said to Elspeth; but who was *us*? Myself and a corpse, a corpse that would soon be in the hands of the undertaker—a little rouge, a little wax, careful needlework, white silk bandages over the

places past repair, and we wouldn't be ashamed to face anyone. I was
the better-looking corpse; they wouldn't need to bury me for a long
time yet.

It was the trams and the warehouses which forced the drill against
the decay inside me. Each time a tram ground and swayed past me,
missing unconcerned pedestrians by inches, I saw Alice under the
wheels, bloody and screaming; and I wanted to be there with her, to
have the guilt slashed away, to stop the traffic, to make all the bovine
pay-night faces sick with horror. I didn't mind the other traffic, I don't
know why; and I don't know why I thought of such an irrelevant kind
of death. Nor why I didn't dare look at the warehouses. There was
one with a new sign—Umpelby and Dickinson, Tops and Noils, Est.
1855—that still gives me bad dreams. It had sixty-three dirty windows
and four of the raised letters on those adjacent the main office were
missing. Umpelb and D kinso are the three most terrible words that
I have ever seen. I think now that I was frightened because the warehouses didn't care about what had happened to Alice; but why did I
hate the innocent friendly trams?

I went on for about a mile, going farther and farther from the main
road, but still with the sound of the trams grinding in my ears. It
was a fine evening for the time of the year, with an unseasonable soapy
warmth trickling along the mean little streets; most of the house doors
were open and the people were standing inside them, just standing,
saying nothing, looking at the black millstone grit and the chimneys
and the dejected little shops. It was Friday and soon they'd go out and
get drunk. At this moment they were pretending that it was Monday
or even Thursday and they hadn't any money and they'd be forced
to sit in the living room among the drying nappies looking at their
wife's pasty face and varicose legs and hating the guts of the bastard
in the next street who'd won a cool hundred on a five-shilling ac-
cumulator; then they'd stop pretending and gloat over their spending-
money, at least three quid—

I stopped and leaned against a lamppost because I couldn't go on
any longer. I should have gone into the country. You can walk in the
country without wanting to vomit, and you're not hurt because the
trees and the grass and the water don't care because you can't expect
them to, they were never concerned with love; but the city should be
full of love, and never is.

A policeman walked past, and gave me a hard inquiring look. Five minutes later he walked past again; so there was nothing else to do but go into the nearest pub. I went into the Bar first, where the customers mostly seemed to be Irish navvies; even when they weren't talking, they gave an impression of animated violence. I was out of place there, as they would have been out of place at the Clarendon, and they knew it. I sensed their resentment with a deep enjoyment. It was what I needed, as satisfyingly acrid as cheap shag; I took half my pint of bitter at one gulp, looking with a derisive pity at the stupid faces around me—the faces of, if they were lucky, my future lorry drivers and labourers and warehousemen.

I drank another pint. It changed taste several times: bitter, scented, sour, watery, sweet, brackish. My head was full of an oily fog that forced its way up through my throat, the pressure increasing until it seeped into my eyes, and the chairs and the mirrors and the faces and the rows of bottles behind the bar blurred together into a kind of pavane on the slowly heaving floor. The bar had a brass rail, and I clung to it tightly, taking deep breath after deep breath until the floor, under protest like a whipped animal, stayed quiet.

After two rums I moved into the Lounge next door. There were no vacant seats in the Bar and my legs were aching, but that wasn't the reason for my going there. The true reason was sitting alone near the entrance; as soon as I saw her I discovered that she was the one thing necessary to round the evening off, the one drug that I hadn't tried.

She was about twenty, with frizzy blonde hair and small bones; she wasn't bad-looking, but her face had a quality of inadequacy, as if there hadn't been enough flesh available to make a good job of her femininity. When she saw me looking at her, she smiled. I didn't like it very much when she smiled; the pale flesh seemed as though it were going to split. But one hasn't to be too choosy about pick-ups; they're not so easy to come by in peacetime as the respectable would suppose. And there was something about her that suddenly prodded to life a side of me that I thought had been dead for years, a lust that was more than half curiosity, a sly, sniggering desire to see what she was like under her clothes.

I sat down beside her. "I'm not squeezing you, am I?"

She giggled. "There's plenty of room."

I offered her a cigarette.

"Thank you very much," she said. "Oh, what a lovely case." She stroked the silver, her long thin fingers with their too curved red nails brushing mine. "You don't come from round here, do you?"

"Dufton. I'm a traveller."

"What in?"

"Ladies' underwear," I said. When she laughed I noticed that her upper teeth were scored horizontally with a brown line of decay.

"You're a devil," she said. "Will you give me a free sample?"

"If you're a good girl," I said. "Will you have a drink with me?"

"IPA, please."

"You don't want beer," I said. "How about something short? I've sold thousands of pairs of knickers this week."

"You're cheeky," she said; but she had a gin-and-it and another and another and then a brandy, and soon we were touching each other lightly all the time, coming closer and closer together and yet farther and farther apart; we were, I saw in a moment of clarity before brandy and lust closed over my head, only touching ourselves. But at least I wasn't thinking of Alice. She wasn't crawling round Corby Lane now with her scalp in tatters over her face. She hadn't been born, there had never been any such person; and there was no Joe Lampton, only a commercial traveller from Dufton having a jolly evening with a hot piece of stuff.

I think that it was about half past eight when I was aware of a nasty silence over the room. I looked up; a young man was standing scowling over us. He had the sort of face that one's always seeing in the yellow press—staring-eyed, mousy, the features cramped and shapeless and the mouth loose. He was wearing a light blue double-breasted suit that was so dashingly draped as to look décolleté and he had a blue rayon tie of an oddly slimy-looking texture. At that moment he was enjoying what a thousand films and magazines had assured him to be righteous anger: His Girl had been Untrue.

"Come along," he said to her. "Come along, Mavis."

"Oh go away," she said. "We were all right until you came."

She took out her compact and began to powder her nose. He grabbed her hands. "Bloody well stop that," he said. "I couldn't help being late, see? I was working over."

I'd been measuring him up, wondering whether or not to leave her

to him. I wasn't so drunk that I wanted to be beaten up in a Birmingham Road pub. But he was no Garth: he was as tall as me, but his
shoulders were all padding and he had a look of softness about him;
he was the type whose bones never seem to harden.

"Leave her alone," I said.

"Who the hell are you?"

"Jack Wales."

"Never heard of you."

"I don't expect that you have." I stood up. "You heard what I said."
My hand groped about on the table independently of me until it
found an empty beer glass. There wasn't a sound in the room. There
was a decently dowdy-looking middle-aged couple at the next table
who looked frightened. The man was small and skinny and the
woman had pale horn-rimmed spectacles and a little button of a
mouth. I remember feeling rather sorry for them, and an anger as
smooth and cold and potentially as jagged and murderous as the beer
glass started to grow inside me.

"Take your hands off her." I lifted the beer glass as if to strike it
against the table. His hand loosened and she pulled her wrist away.
The compact dropped, and a little cloud of powder floated up from it.
He turned and went out without a word. The ordinary noises of the
pub began again, the incident obliterated as quickly as it had begun.

"He's not my boy friend really, Jack," she said. "I'm sick of him.
Thinks he owns me just because I've been out with him a time or
two."

"He's introduced us, anyway," I said. "Mavis. It suits you, darling."
She stroked my hand. "You say that nicely," she said.

"It's easy to say things nicely to you."

"You're the best-looking boy I've ever met. And you have lovely
clothes." She felt the texture of my suit. It was new, a mid-grey hop-
sack made from a roll of cloth that Alice had given me five months
ago. "I work in a mill, I know good cloth."

"If you like it, Mavis, I'll never wear anything else," I said. My
words were beginning to slur. "I feel so happy with you, you're so
gentle and bright and beautiful—" I went into the old routine, mixing
scraps of poetry, names of songs, bits of autobiography, binding it all
with the golden syrup of flattery. It wasn't necessary, I well knew; a
skinful of shorts, a thousand lungfuls of nicotine, and ordinary good

manners, were enough to get me what I wanted; but I had to have my
sex dressed up now, I was forced to tone down the raw rhythms of
copulation, to make the inevitable five or ten minutes of shuddering
lunacy a little more civilised, to give sex a nodding acquaintance with
kindness and tenderness.

"Let me buy the drinks," she said after we'd had two more.

"That's all right," I said.

"You've spent pounds, I know you have. I'm not one of those girls
who's just out for what she can get, Jack. If I like a boy, I don't care
if he can only afford tea. I earn good money. I took home six pounds
last week."

I felt the tears coming to my eyes. "Six pounds," I said. "That's
very good money, Mavis. You'll be able to save for your bottom
drawer."

"You've got to find the chap first," she said. She fumbled in her
handbag. It was a large one of black patent leather, with diamanté
initials. There was the usual litter of powder and lipstick and cotton
and handkerchiefs and cigarettes and matches and photos inside it.
She slid a ten-shilling note into my hand. "This is on me, love," she
said. The warm Northern voice and the sight of the open handbag
gave me an intolerable feeling of loneliness. I wanted to put my head
between the sharp little breasts and shut out the cruel world in which
every action had consequences.

I ordered a bottle of IPA and a gin-and-it. Time was beginning to
move too quickly, to slither helplessly away; each minute I looked at
my watch it was ten minutes later; I knew that I'd only that minute
met Mavis, but that minute was anything up to a year ago; as I drank
the sharp summer-smelling beer the floor started to move again. Then
every impression possible for one man to undergo all gathered together from nowhere like a crowd at the scene of an accident and
yelled to be let in: time dancing, time with clay on its hobnailed boots,
the new taste of the beer and the old taste of brandy and rum and fish
and cornflour and tobacco and soot and wool scourings and Mavis's
sweat that had something not quite healthy about it and her powder
and lipstick—chalk, orris root, pear drops—and the hot hand of brandy
steadying me again and just as it seemed that there wasn't to be any
other place in the world but the long room with the green *art moderne*
chairs and glass-topped tables, we were out in the street with our arms

around each other's waists and turning in and out of narrow streets and alleys and courts and patches of waste ground and over a foot-bridge with engines clanging together aimlessly in the cold below as if slapping themselves to keep warm and then were in a corner of a woodyard in a little cave of piled timber; I took myself away from my body, which performed all the actions she expected from it. She clung to it after the scalding trembling moment of fusion as if it were human, kissing its drunken face and putting its hands against her breasts.

There were houses very near on the dirt road at the top of the wood-yard; I could hear voices and music and smell cooking. All around were the lights of the city; Birmingham Road rises from the centre of Leddersford and we were on a little plateau about halfway up; there was no open country to be seen, not one acre where there wasn't a human being, two hundred thousand separate lonelinesses, two hundred thousand different deaths. And all the darkness the lights had done away with, all the emptiness of fields and woods long since built over, suddenly swept over me, leaving no pain, no happiness, no despair, no hope, but simply nothingness, the ghost in the peepshow vanishing into the blank wall and no pennies left to bring him out again.

"You've lovely soft hands," Mavis said. "Like a woman's."

"They're not—not lovely," I said with difficulty. "Cruel. Cruel hands."

"You're drunk, love."

"Never feltfeltbetter." I'd returned to my body, I realised with horror, and didn't know what to do with it.

"You're a funny boy," she said.

I fumbled for my cigarette case. It was empty. She brought out a packet of Players and lit two. "Keep these," she said. We smoked in silence for awhile. I was trying to will myself into sobriety, but it was useless. I honestly couldn't even remember where I lived, and I literally truly Fowler's English Usage didn't know whether I was awake or dreaming.

"Jack, do you like me?"

"From the veryfirstmomentthat—that I saw you." I made another effort. "You'reverysweet. Like you verymuchveryverymuch."

The lights started to wheel around and there was a clanging sound in my ears. "Those bloody engines," I said. "Those bloody engines. Why can't they stop?"

She must have half carried me away; I don't know how she managed it. We stopped outside a terrace house eventually; I was trying to keep myself upright, and not succeeding very well. Finally I propped myself against the garden railings.

"Are you all right now, Jack?"

"Fine," I said. "Fine."

"You turn left and keep straight on—have you enough for a taxi?"

I pulled out a fistful of notes.

"You be careful," she said. A light came on above us, and I heard a man's voice growling her name. "Oh God," she said, "they've woken up." She kissed me. "Goodbye, Jack. It's been lovely, really it has." She ran into the house.

I walked away, weaving my body from side to side in a pattern of movement which I felt to be not only graceful and harmonious but so exquisitely funny that I had to laugh.

A hand on my shoulder broke the laugh in half and started the Unarmed Combat reflexes working. The gears were stiff, but any second now, I thought with joy, pain and humiliation would move forward to crush the stupid bodies of the two men who faced me.

One of them was Mavis's ex-lover. I didn't know the other, but he was the one who had me worried the most. He seemed quite sober and his shoulders were broader than mine.

"This is the—" Mavis's ex-lover said. "Full of brandy and conceit, the bloody bastard—" He swore at me monotonously; the words depressed me more than they annoyed me. "She's *my* woman, see? We don't like strangers muscling in, see?" His hand tightened on my shoulder. "You're going to be bloody sorry you came round these parts, chum."

"Shove off," I said.

"*You're* shoving off. But not before—" He struck out with his fist; I sidestepped, but not quickly enough, and he hit my cheekbone, cutting it with something (a ring, I realised afterwards). But I thought it was a razor, so I hit him in the Adam's apple. He gave a sound halfway between a baby's gurgle and a death rattle and staggered away from me, his hands to his throat.

"You dirty bastard," his friend said, and tried to kick me in the groin. More by good luck than good management I turned sideways; but not properly as the PT Sergeant had taught me; his foot landed home on my thigh and I lost my balance and went down with him on top of me. We rolled about on the pavement like quarreling children; I was trying to keep him off and he, I think, had no idea in his head that wasn't based upon making me suffer as much as his friend (whom I could still hear choking with agony) had been made to suffer by me. He got both hands around my throat and began to squeeze; a black and red stream of pain spread like lava behind my eyes. My hands had lost their strength and I couldn't move my legs and I could taste blood from my cut cheek and smell his hair oil and the laundered stiffness of his shirt and orange and fish and dog from the gutter; the lampposts shot up suddenly to a hundred times their height like bean flowers in educational films, taking the buildings with them in elongated smudges of yellow light; and then I remembered another of the PT Sergeant's maxims, and I spat in his face. He recoiled instinctively, his hold relaxing for a second; then I remembered a lot more things and within thirty seconds he was in an untidy heap on the pavement and I was running as fast as I could down the street.

My luck was in that night; I didn't see one policeman, and I heard no pursuing footsteps. After I'd been running for about ten minutes I came to the main road and caught a tram to the city centre. My hands and face were bleeding when I mounted it, and I saw from my reflection in the lighted window that my suit had big splotches of dirt and blood on the jacket, and that not one button on my fly was fastened. Fortunately there were a lot of other drunks on board, so I was not as conspicuous as I might have been. I was squeezed up against a woman who seemed the only sober person on the tram, white-haired, with an old-fashioned thick wedding ring, who kept looking at me with a disgusted expression. The words of a Salvation Army hymn erupted to the surface of my mind and, without knowing it, I started to sing under my breath—*The old rugged cross the old rugged cross I will CLING to the old rugged cross*—The disgust on her face deepened to contempt. She looked so clean and motherly, her blue boxcloth coat showing a vee of crisply starched white blouse, that I found tears coming to my eyes. I was grateful to her for noticing me, for caring enough to be disgusted.

The lights and the noise and the cars and the buses and the trams

and the people in the centre of the city were too much for me. I was
nearly run over twice, and I was just as frightened of the people as
I was of the traffic. It seemed to me as if they too were made of metal
and rubber, as if they too were capable of mangling me in a second
and speeding away not knowing and not caring that they'd killed me.

The Warley bus station was away from the city centre. I couldn't
remember the way, and I couldn't remember the time of the last bus.
I lit a cigarette which tasted of Mavis's powder and stood, or rather
swayed, outside a milk bar near the railway station. I wondered if the
police had picked up the two yobs; I'd probably hurt them badly. I
thought of the first one's hands, red and scarred, with black ridged
nails, clutching his throat, and the limp body of the other with his
nice clean collar and new rayon tie spoiled, and I felt a deep shame, as
if I'd hit a child.

I walked around until I found a taxi rank. It took a great deal of
finding; having visited Leddersford a few times, I kept a mental street
map of the place, which normally I could unfold in a second. That
night it had been turned upside down and all the streets had changed
their names; I went up one street and found myself in Birmingham
Road again, and twice I repassed the milk bar from where I'd set off.
When I saw the row of taxis at the other side of the road, I paused for
a second to see if it was safe to cross.

Then I found myself falling. There was a kind of exhilaration about
it; I imagined a mattress below me to break my fall, to bounce away
from, higher and higher into the sky. . . . There was only the pavement, the cold stone that I wanted to lie upon, to kiss, to sleep with
my face against. I struggled up to my feet when I heard a car stop
beside me, holding on to a lamp standard. If it was the police, there
was nothing left but to face them; I was too tired and confused to run
away, and I knew that if I tried to cross the road by myself I should be
killed. I braced myself for the official questions, staring at the dark
green standard.

"Time for you to come home, Joe." I turned. It was Bob Storr.

"I have no home."

"Yes, you have. We've all been worrying about you." He took my
arm. Eva came out of the car and took my other arm; as soon as she
came, I let myself be taken quietly, but I still insisted that I had no

home. I sat in the back with her; I was trembling with cold, and she put a rug over my knees.

"My God," she said, "what have you been up to? There've been search parties out all over Yorkshire for you . . ."

"Susan," I said. "What about Susan?"

"You *are* pie-eyed, aren't you?" Eva said. "She went to London for a wedding dress this morning. Had you forgotten?"

"Leave him alone," Bob said. "He's had enough for one day."

"I murdered Alice," I said, and began to cry.

"Don't talk rubbish," Bob said.

"Everyone knows that I killed her."

The car was climbing the eastern heights of the city now, away from the smoke and the dirt and the black fingernails scrabbling the pavement and the sad, lost faces that had tried to keep up with me; the engine purred smoothly, as it would have done if Alice had been beside me instead of Eva, as it would have done if Bob had suddenly grown talons and horns, as it would have done if the world were due to end in five minutes.

I went on crying, as if the tears would blur the image of Alice crawling round Corby Road on her hands and knees, as if they would drown her first shrill screams and her last delirious moans. "Oh God," I said, "I did kill her. I wasn't there, but I killed her."

Eva drew my head on to her breast. "Poor darling, you mustn't take on so. You don't see it now, but it was all for the best. She'd have ruined your whole life. Nobody blames you, love. Nobody blames you."

I pulled myself away from her abruptly. "Oh my God," I said, "that's the trouble."

J. P. DONLEAVY

The Interview

If there is a physical link between the Beat Generation and the Angry Young Men, J. P. Donleavy is it. An expatriate New Yorker living in London, Donleavy combines the skepticism and self-mockery of the British writers with the Americans' brand of subterranean optimism. In his first novel The Ginger Man he launched a frontal attack on the emotional fatuity of our times. Here, in a scene adapted by the author from his second novel Helen, soon to be published, he takes up the theme again. A young man presents himself to the president of a spark plug firm with the declaration, "Mr. Mott, I'd like to make money." What follows is the kind of confusion which can only exist where human relations have lost all meaning.

(*Close-up: A hand hanging at side of dark suit, the thumb gliding back and forth along tips of fingers*)

Sᴇᴄʀᴇᴛᴀʀʏ (*Off*): Mr. Mott will see you now, Mr. Frost.

(*Hand opening and reaching, taking a younger hand, grip tightening slowly*)

ꜱᴛᴇᴘʜᴇɴ ᴍᴏᴛᴛ (*Off*): Well if it isn't my boy Frost, isn't it?

(*Hands shaking*)

(*Cut to: Whole luxurious office, Mott a man of fifty-five, Frost thirty*)

ELMER FROST: Yes, Mr. Mott, it is.

MOTT: Well sit down, delighted to see you, son. Have a smoke, my boy.

FROST: No thanks.

MOTT: Well what can I do for you?

FROST: Mr. Mott, I'd like to make money.

MOTT: Ha ha. Well that's pretty straightforward, you might say that it's a universal incentive. A word we use a lot around here, I mean incentive. Like that type of word, connotes purpose. Well now. How do you feel we can help? Got something to offer us?

FROST: Myself.

MOTT: Well now, another pretty straight-forward answer. I like that. It's Elmer Frost, isn't it?

FROST: Yes.

MOTT: Well now, I'll call you Elmer. Well, Elmer, so you'd like to make money? Come over here. (*over to window*) Down there's the harbour of New York. Just look down there. What put us way up here?

FROST: The elevator.

MOTT: Boy, I'm talking on a different level.

FROST: Oh.

MOTT: Ingenuity. It's a word we use around here. Say it.

FROST: Well—ingenuity.

MOTT: Come on, let's have some lung.

FROST: Ingenuity.

MOTT: That's better, boy. I remember you. A party of my son's, wasn't it? Few months back. Just back from Europe, weren't you? Yeah. Remember couple comments you made caught my ear. Look, tell you what. Bit rushed just now, excuse me a second. (*Back to and leans over desk, flicks switch*) Miss Peep, get me personnel, Mr. How. Hello Howard. Got a young man here, friend of my boy's. He wants to make money. Want you to talk to him and show him around. Thinks we can use him. Yes. Yes. (*Turning to Frost*) Elmer, you free a few hours?

FROST: Certainly, yes.

MOTT: All right Howard, you take care of that. Kids, Howard, O.K.? Fine. Well, life will get less noisier as you get older, Howard. Great. Fine. Great. That's great. O.K. Howard. Bye (*Turning to Frost*) Well Elmer, our Mr. How will show you around. See what we can do. And he'll talk it over with you. Maybe we can have a chat again. I like to talk to the young kids coming along. Now what's that word?

FROST: Ingenuity.

MOTT: 'At a boy, Frost.

FROST: Thanks very much, Mr. Mott.

MOTT: Anytime, Frost.

FROST: And hope that spot's a little better. (*Mott surprised*) You know, the spot you had in front of your eye, said you could follow it out the window like it was a bumble bee only it would always come back again.

MOTT: (*The narrow eyes*) You got some memory, boy. Memory makes money. Remember that utterance. Words are wonderful. Remember that too.

FROST: It's been extremely good of you, Mr. Mott.

MOTT: Anything anytime for the young people. Keep in touch. Find Mr. How five floors down.

FROST: Thanks again, Mr. Mott. (*Mott's smile*)
    (*Cut to: Frost's entry to the office of Howard How. How forty, friendly with his teeth which he lets out at each sentence*)

HOWARD HOW: Mr. Frost?

FROST: Yes.

HOW: I'm Howard How.

FROST: Hello. I'm thinking of moving to the Bronx. (*Frost, his hand to lip*)

HOW: You're what?

FROST: O sorry, Mr. How. Guess I'm nervous. I've just strangely just had something on my mind about the Bronx. Once it was meadow land, I've been reading in an old guide book.

HOW: Oh?

FROST: Yes, ha ha. Was thinking maybe some parts might still be meadow land.

HOW: We manufacture spark plugs, Mr. Frost.

FROST: Of course, of course. I don't dispute that for a minute.

HOW: And there are no meadows left in the Bronx.

FROST: I would never dispute that either.

HOW: What do you dispute?

FROST: I don't dispute anything. Nothing at all. Oh there are some things I don't like all right. But I don't dispute anything. It was just that when I was looking out of the train (*Frost holds up a left supplicant palm and looks upon it*) I just thought once there were real Indians running around here.

HOW: Well, let's get back to the Twentieth Century now. (*Close-up: How's naked teeth*)

FROST: Sure.

HOW: And you're interested in our using you.

FROST: I'd like it if you could.

HOW: Point is, Mr. Frost, just what can we use you for? I note you have a rather English tone to your voice. Didn't by any chance pick that up in the Bronx?

FROST: As a matter of fact I learned it out of a book.

HOW: Oh. Now look, I'm not trying to hurt your feelings. For what it's worth, you might as well know Mr. Mott likes to have an English quality about the place. You've noticed the rural scenes of England on the walls.

FROST: Yes, nice and green, I mean, you know, rustic.

HOW: Nice contrast to the product. Now what, Mr. Frost, are you exactly interested in doing? What are your qualifications, your degrees?

FROST: Well as a matter of fact, Mr. How—

HOW: (*Leaning way back*) That's what we want Frost, the facts.

FROST: (*Blows nose*) I just missed, by only a few subjects of course, getting my degree. At that time I had a lot of things on my mind, you see, I've always been deeply interested in human nature and I guess I got distracted—

HOW: (*Leaning forth to desk*) Sorry Mr. Frost, but I understand you don't have a degree.

FROST: Except of misery I guess. (*Leaning forward in anxiety*) But I almost made it.

HOW: Don't be alarmed Frost, these notes I'm making are just a few facts. Note you got alacrity with words.

FROST: But I almost made it, I really did.

HOW: Easy boy. Easy. We make spark plugs. You want to make money? (*Close-up: Frost's face in fervor*) (*Close-up: How's face impressed with Frost's sincerity*) I can see you really do, don't you.

FROST: I do.

HOW: I'm glad your desire is sincere.

FROST: Thanks.

HOW: You're a friend of Mr. Mott's son I presume. Mr. Mott's a friendly but very busy man and this affair more or less, you understand me, rests in my hands if we're going to find something for you. Do you have any preference as regards production or management?

FROST: Well, I'd like to manage if that can be arranged.

HOW: Just give that pitcher of water a push in my direction, will you. Want some water?

FROST: Thanks a lot.

HOW: Don't mention it. (*The drinking of water*) We want men with ideas. Ideas more than anything. Can you type?

FROST: Well, my parents gave me one of those little typewriters when I was a kid but I don't expect that would qualify me as a typist at the moment, but it's something I could pick up. I pick most things up rather easily—

HOW: Like your degree.

FROST: Look Mr. How, I'm after a job. I don't want to misrepresent myself or give a false impression, but as I said I'm interested in human nature.

HOW: You said that.

FROST: I don't have a degree. O.K. Maybe I was too distracted by human nature in college, but I wasn't stupid, you know.

HOW: Look, Mr. Frost, you don't mind if we don't bother seeing things today. I mean you'll understand that until we know what you can do, there isn't really much point in my showing you our setup at the moment. I know Mr. Mott's one of the friendliest men you could ever want to meet and I know he wants to help you but it is rather a question, in the end, can you help us?

FROST: Yes, I understand.

HOW: You're a very presentable person and of course well spoken and by the way, I like the way you tie your knots, that's a nice tie, always be sure of a man in this business if he wears a knitted tie. Just want us to both face the facts, Frost. Just the facts.

FROST: O.K.

HOW: Got an opening for a courier representative. Dispatch and deliver various important papers. Expenses, taxi and all the rest.

FROST: I'm almost thirty years old. You mean I deliver papers? Like a messenger boy?

HOW: Not in so many words, Mr. Frost. Not in so many words. It's of the nature of a confidential dispatch agent and you would, of course, hold the title of executive courier.

FROST: What are the friends I've known all my life going to say? I went to college, you know.

HOW: A lot, an awful lot of people go to college, Mr. Frost. Mr. Mott never went to college and he controls a business extending to twenty-nine states. We just added Texas yesterday.

FROST: Well, I've had a job before.

HOW: Well, I'm perfectly reasonable, Mr. Frost. What sort of work did you do? I'm not here to bring about a stalemate, as you might say, with applicants. I'm here to hire the right man for the right job. What exactly are you experienced in?

FROST: Does it matter?

HOW: That's up to you. I'm only trying to help. Just testing your qualifications. Want to know the sort of work you're best suited for. Where your interests lie. We're an outfit you know, where, when it's expedient we take off our jackets, you understand me.

FROST: To be frank I've been, well, I'm experienced. (*Frost's feet, shifting the weight, polishing tips of shoes on pants*)

HOW: Frank with the facts, Frost. How were you used?

FROST: They used me, I guess as a sort of representative, as you might say. A specialist in human relations. As I've said, I could count myself as a student of human nature.

HOW: Yes, I know, you've said that three times now. You were in public relations then.

FROST: Well, yes, sort of, I guess. I wasn't too clear at the time because I had a lot of things on my mind.

HOW: What firm was this?

FROST: As a matter of fact—

HOW: That's right, the facts, Frost—

FROST: It was called the Stars of the Forest, I guess Inc.

HOW: How's that, boy?

FROST: Stars of the Forest.

HOW: Don't mind telling me their product. Briefly.

FROST: Death.

HOW: How's that boy?

FROST: Death.

HOW: What?

FROST: What I'm telling you, death. One word.

HOW: You mean an undertaker?

FROST: Since we're down to one word, yes, an undertaker. A Mr. Vine said I excelled in that professional capacity.

HOW: Well, you know, (*How's hand on brow*) God help me, Mr. Frost, I honestly don't know what to make of you. Get that chair over there and sit down. It's not been in my experience previous to this to consider anybody in the light, or forgive me, darkness of these circumstances. How long did you undertake?

FROST: I undertook for, well, not long. I'm begging for a chance to prove myself, Mr. How. Just one chance.

HOW: Easy. Take it easy. Just got to think. What an interview! Just let me ask you a question, will you. Wait, excuse me a second. (*Speaking into desk microphone*) Miss Kelly, would you please play over to me the background music we've chosen for Friday's conference for our Chicago representatives.

MISS KELLY: (*Off*): It's on now, Mr. How.

HOW: Thanks. (*Andante Catabile for Strings*) Boy oh boy, Elmer. Now look, tell me, why were you looking for this job? Don't have to answer that if you don't want.

FROST: Someone close to me died.

HOW: Sorry to hear that. By the way, you like this music?

FROST: It's nice.

HOW: Soothes, doesn't it. Guess it's been one of the most successful innovations Mr. Mott introduced into business practice, almost like the invention of the wheel. (*Frost slumping in chair, glum*) Come on Elmer, cheer up. Only thing is we got a problem here. Your job in the funeral parlour business is not going to cut much ice with Mr. Mott; in fact, the mere mention of it will throw a distinct chill

into him. But I'll tell you something before we go any further. You
know, I like you, I think you're O.K.

FROST: Thanks.

HOW: You know, most of the people sent along to me with pull with
Mr. Mott aren't worth their weight in paper, strictly between us,
you understand. You strike me as a guy with imagination. I'm
going to give you a chance. If I assign you to our idea department,
do you suppose you could get some ideas? It'd be a trial, you understand.

FROST: Ideas about what?

HOW: Come on, Elmer, what am I letting myself in for? Quick. Ideas.
We make spark plugs and Mr. Mott loves the use of words. Think
of something. Quick.

FROST: (*Hand to brow*) My mind's a blank at the moment.

HOW: (*Leaning into microphone*) Miss Kelly give us something faster,
for a fast idea session of approximately forty-five seconds starting
ten seconds from now.

MISS KELLY (*Off*): Coming ten seconds from now.

FROST: Gee, I'm worried. My whole life depends upon what I might
say.

HOW: Wouldn't put it like that. Think. One sentence. One idea, a
rhyme, anything, don't care what it is, so long as it underlines an
inescapable fact.

FROST: But all my facts have escaped.

HOW (*Liszt's Hungarian Rhapsody*): Go, go, boy.

FROST: I can't go anywhere, Mr. How, I swear it. The facts have
escaped.

HOW (*Throwing out a fist*): Go after them, boy. I know you can do
it. Think of something to do with a sparkplug. Think of the money.
Money, boy. Think of the money.

FROST: I am. Wait. If you've got a heart, you've got a spark that could
be a heart by Mott. (*Close-up of How's delighted smile; Frost's sigh
of relief and relaxing back in chair*) When you said money, those
words just came pouring into my mind.

HOW: Don't be ashamed of that boy. (*Leaning to microphone*) Miss
Kelly, good, it did the trick, neat selection, make a note of it.

MISS KELLY (*Off*): Glad it worked, Mr. How.

HOW: It was swell, and make a note, we've got a new man for our idea department starting right away.

MISS KELLY (*Off*): Yes indeed, Mr. How.

HOW (*Standing, holding out a hand to Frost. Frost dazed, makes no move*): Hey, boy. Hey, there.

FROST (*Comes to, jumps up to take the hand*): Oh.

HOW: You're in.

FROST: Mean I'm hired?

HOW: Of course.

FROST: Just like that?

HOW: Of course, just like that.

FROST: Well, isn't it too quick? Isn't there something more? I just don't feel it's me.

HOW: Elmer, you've got what it takes. Wow! If you've got a heart, you've got a spark that could be a heart by Mott. Here, gee, have a drink of water. Yes. Ingenuity—

FROST (*Mouth coming out of the glass of water*): Makes industry.

HOW (*Leaning over switch*): Miss Kelly, can you hear what's happening in here?

MISS KELLY (*Off*): Yes I can, Mr. How. It's wonderful.

HOW: Well, get it down.

MISS KELLY (*Off*): Got it, Mr. How.

HOW: Flash those two things to Mr. Mott. He's got to hear about this right away. Ingenuity makes industry. A follow up to Mr. Mott's favorite word.

FROST: But this is awful, I mean I feel overrated, just for a few words.

HOW (*Looking down an index finger at the level of his eye*): We find a guy, Elmer, with words like that coming out of his head, we buy that head.

FROST: Mr. How, I'm—I think I'd rather be a messenger boy.

HOW (*Leaning into desk microphone*): Miss Kelly, I want you to shout back just what you think of Frost's word formations.

MISS KELLY (*Off*): They're really impressive.

HOW (*The smile of the teeth*): Now, boy, hear that?

FROST: But I'll tell you the truth—(*How's face calmly waits with interest for truth*) no, maybe I better not. (*How smiles warmly*) But I don't know a thing about sparkplugs or industry.

HOW (*Into desk microphone*): Miss Kelly, come in please. (*Miss*

Kelly, trace of smile and warm eyes for Frost, stands hands held across belly) Look. Just look at Mr. Frost. Now tell him. *(Kelly coy)* Don't be shy. Tell him.

KELLY: Well.

HOW: Exactly what you think.

KELLY: *(Frost slight wringing of hands)*: Well. I think you're really spontaneous.

HOW *(Triumphant)*: There you are, boy!

FROST: I'm only just a reasonably normal person.

HOW: So are we all. *(Frost glum)* Oh come on now, Elmer. Look Miss Kelly, would you leave Elmer and myself together here for a few minutes and stop all calls? We just need a little talk.

MISS KELLY: Certainly, Mr. How. Anything for background music?

HOW: Not for the moment, thanks. *(Kelly goes)* Now look, Elmer, let's sit over here. *(Side by side on leather sofa)* I'll give it to you straight. When Mr. Mott gets these messages he's going to want to see you right away. Now I'm going to risk my life. You know why? Because I like you. When you first came in here I just thought you were another snooty sophisticate come out of the ivy leagues. But you know, you've got a real quality in you.

FROST: I guess it was my job in the funeral parlor. But it was the only thing I could get when I first got back from Europe.

HOW: That's what I want to talk about. Yeah. It's Europe. That's the thing's given you this quality too. A sort of thing that's real. But look. I've got absolute faith in you. You could dazzle this industry.

FROST: Thanks, Mr. How. But you're making a mistake. I'm not like that at all. That's just the way I appear. Some of the things I really think would shock you. I'm almost a criminal type.

HOW: What a remark. You're just full of ideas, boy. Why you're not more of a criminal than I am—I mean, I just mean we're alike. But look. I'm maybe ten years older than you. Got wife, kids, nice home out Long Island. The real things. But I'll tell you something. See those binoculars. Want you to look out the window with them. Go ahead. *(Frost to window with binoculars)* Towards the Statue of Liberty. Got it? Now a little to the left.

FROST: Yes.

HOW: See those barges?

FROST: I think I do.

HOW: That's refuse. I watch those barges every day. Come down the Hudson and East River filled with stuff that's no more use. They dump it. Frost, it's made an awful impression on me. See, got to be of use in this world, or to put it pretty bluntly, we get dumped, maybe not in a river, but you know what I mean.

FROST: It's got me more worried than ever, now Mr. Mott's involved. I wouldn't mind being on one of those barges right now being dumped.

HOW: Boy, don't ever say a thing like that.

FROST: But I mean it, Mr. How.

HOW: Call me Howard. Elmer, as a personal favor I'm asking you right now to take this job. I know everything's going to click. Do it for me. You know, I've got to laugh; here I am begging you to work for us and ten minutes ago I was wondering how I was politely going to discourage you.

FROST: Dump.

HOW: Well, yeah, but—no, no—

KELLY (*At door*): Excuse me for interrupting, Mr. How, but Mr. Mott wants you to come up to his private reception room right away.

HOW (*Turning to Frost*): There, boy. Thanks, Miss Kelly. Right. Now Elmer. I'm asking you now, please. I've got to go through with this now. Just be yourself. Only just don't give any hint of your past employment. Mr. Mott's toleration for the suppression of facts is nil, but to me it's worth the risk. Just go in with the trace of a smile, that's all I'm asking you. (*Frost's gloom*) But don't look like that.

FROST: I'm O.K., Mr. How.

HOW (*Motioning*): Just say that thing once more.

FROST: You mean about industry?

HOW: Please. With conviction. Ingenuity makes—

FROST: I think I've got something better. Ingenuity made Mott, Mott makes industry.

HOW (*Whispering*): Miss Kelly, get something for my heart, quick, it's missing beats and get this down, it's Frost again. Ingenuity made Mott, Mott makes industry.

KELLY (*Off*): Shall I flash that to Mr. Mott?

HOW: No, no, no. He's got a weak heart too.

> (*Cut to: Frost and How standing at large door which slides open. They step into cathedral-like room. Mott sitting legs*

crossed. *He holds up his hand for Frost to shake. Frost walks across and takes it. All voices echo. How is wringing his hands*)

MOTT (*Shaking Frost's hand*): Howard, you saw what I didn't see, at first sight, that is.

HOW: It was nothing, Steve. Miss Kelly selected the background music.

MOTT: Well, let's hear all these nice things.

HOW: Steve, he's got something even better, didn't want to flash it.

MOTT: Give us a flash now, Frost.

FROST: Ingenuity made Mott, Mott makes industry.

MOTT: Very happy. Very happy indeed. Let's have that once more with lung. Lots of lung.

FROST: Ingenuity made Mott, Mott makes industry.

MOTT: Not bad. It's good. Youth refreshes. Of course you expect to improve on it.

FROST: But I think it's good.

MOTT: Oh it's good. Youth refreshes. Well, you're not kidding us son, I can see that.

HOW: He's not, Steve.

MOTT (*Close-up*): No. At the risk of sounding too full of myself, which I do not want to sound. On the other hand, I'd like to sketch in my general attitude towards the way I personally tackle things. Don't get the idea that I think of myself as a king or anything. But I like to acquire the evidences of man's creative impulse from outside my own orbit. But sadly, not many are blessed with the creative impulse, but of course, there's the repulsive creative impulse too. But if there are bright brains, I don't care what kind of a head you got the brains in. (*Frost feeling his face*) Your head's all right, Frost, don't get nervous. But a head, square, ten feet high or like a pingpong ball is all right so long as it works. But don't let me sound like a king. So. I think you have a future, Frost. Now what about the past?

HOW: Steve, I've been through his past with him.

MOTT: Once more fast won't hurt.

HOW: Thought we could get around to it later. Past's fine.

MOTT: I'm interested. At that party back there, that night Frost, you had a lot of pretty pertinent things to say with maybe a few impertinent. What have you been working at?

HOW: Steve.

MOTT: Howard, will you give the boy a chance?

HOW: Steve, do you think we should discuss this now?

MOTT: It has always been my habit to discuss things now. Because after now might be the hereafter, you get me? Frost's been out of college awhile.

HOW: But Frost here is a peculiar case.

MOTT: Why?

HOW: I think his creative qualities are rare.

MOTT: That so?

HOW: Well (*A hand towards Frost*) you've heard him yourself, Steve, a natural alacrity with words.

MOTT: Howard, press the button there for the curtains. (*Curtains on high window open, a pair of binoculars hang in corner*) I don't usually show people this. But I want you to look out there, Howard. See the barges out there, going past the Statue of Liberty? Know what they are?

HOW: I think so, Steve.

MOTT: Well, it's a private little object lesson of mine.

HOW: I understand completely, Steve.

MOTT (*Smiling*): Here today, gone tomorrow.

HOW: I completely understand.

MOTT: So now that nobody misunderstands let's hear about your past career. Not that I'm buying your past, just your future. Nevertheless past gives indication of future.

FROST: Mr. Mott, I was employed as the star receptionist for Stars of the Forest Inc. A funeral parlour.

MOTT (*Turning from Frost to How*): Howard.

HOW: Yes, Steve.

MOTT: Howard.

HOW: Yes, Steve.

MOTT: Howard, I'm talking to you.

HOW: I know, Steve.

MOTT: What about this?

FROST (*Raised voice*): I was expelled from school for lying and cheating. Didn't get my degree from college. And since then I've been working at a job in which I conducted the arrangements for those finding their final resting place. And nothing unseemly ever marred proceedings.

HOW: In the nature of human relations, Steve.

MOTT: I've got my own eyes and ears, Howard. Let me utter three things. Life is for the living. A dime is a dime and lastly and the most, a dollar is a dollar. I put my throat in a collar three times a day. I also, yesterday, was on a plane from Washington when the steward asks me was I any relations to the Motts who had a mausoleum at Throggs Neck. When I said yes he tells me his father takes care of it. Now young Frost here tells me he's a liar and a cheat, degreeless and can smoothly conduct people to their final resting place. Run the Mott empire like a morgue. Now just what exactly do you take me for? Why weren't the facts laid bare in the first instance?

HOW: Don't let facts fool you, Steve.

MOTT: Don't you be too hasty, Howard.

HOW: I feel most recent facts take precedence over previous.

MOTT: I am of the opinion, not wanting to be a king about it, that past facts forecast future facts.

HOW: You're wrong.

MOTT: Come again, Howard?

HOW: You're not exactly right in judging personalities.

FROST (*Standing up slowly*): I think I better go.

MOTT: Stay Frost, we'll have this out.

FROST: But I didn't think I'd be coming between two people. Breaking up a friendship. (*How and Mott look at each other*)

MOTT (*Close-up, small chuckle*)

HOW (*Close-up, teeth just showing in a smile*)

FROST: I know this is a business empire, but aren't you two people friends?

MOTT: You have the habit of asking a lot of direct questions.

FROST: In this fact finding maybe I ought to find some, that's all.

MOTT: Those don't sound like the words of a liar and a cheat. I just would like to know what the score is on you, don't want to be rude or hurt your feelings. But, you know, underneath this gentle innocent exterior of yours, you seem to throw your weight about. In fact, I distinctly feel I'm being pushed. That little remark about friendship and coming between two people. And the night at that party.

You remember my spot. And I remember overhearing a few remarks about my house as well—(*Frost quizzical innocence*) don't look innocent—about the new rich vulgarity. And don't think I planned this, either, getting you up here with Mr. How to give you a working-over. I was impressed but don't think that you can just push us all over.

FROST: What makes you think this—

HOW: Steve, I've never met such a candid fellow as Frost.

MOTT: Oh, you think a fellow is candid because he tells you to your face that he is a liar and a cheat and sweated away in a funeral parlour guiding people to their final resting places. And with a little background music he starts to spout beautiful utterances. Howard, don't be so naive. Frost here could dazzle you all night with slogans, each one better than the last.

HOW: Wouldn't it be sad then, Steve, to ignore this talent?

MOTT: It just so happens I know Frost's background.

HOW: Steve, please let me in on all of this.

MOTT: You're not surprised, Frost.

FROST: Whatever you say, Mr. Mott. But I think I really ought to be going.

MOTT: Aren't you going to abuse us a little before you leave, Frost. Call us vulgar stuffed shirts.

FROST: What makes you think you're in a position to say that, Mr. Mott? Because you think there's nothing I can do about it?

MOTT: Don't threaten me.

FROST: I'm not threatening you.

HOW: Please, please, let me in on this.

MOTT: And I suppose you thought that if you used a frontal assault I'd be afraid to go into this little background. What happened between yourself and your wife is your own business—

FROST: Thanks.

MOTT: But what you do where I'm personally—

HOW: Steve, isn't there a sunny side to this situation. Frost didn't tell me he was married.

MOTT: He's not.

HOW: How does a wife come into it?

MOTT: She's out of it for keeps.

HOW: You mean she threw a seven?

MOTT: That's how Mr. Frost here got into the undertaking trade.

HOW: Hope I'm not disrespectful. This is way over my head.

FROST: Mr. Mott wants to avoid unnecessary contacts with ghouls and charlatans.

MOTT: That's enough.

FROST: I came here genuinely looking for a job to make money.

MOTT: And you thought I didn't have the guts to tell you to your face that I know the whole score on you and that I'd let you just drift into my organization and blackmail my emotional life.

FROST: Preposterous rot.

MOTT: Don't go all British with me.

HOW: Can't we galvanize this into a new situation from which it might be possible to evolve a solution. I think, despite the terrible things that have been said here, that underneath it all, we're good-hearted people. That there is still something that could be considered constructive determined from—

MOTT: Determined to be a solve-it-all, are you, How, with your hired honey.

HOW: Nobody has ever talked to me like that before, not in the three years I've been working here.

MOTT: All right, Howard, all right, this is an emotional moment.

FROST: Meanwhile I've been insulted but, Mr. Mott, thank you for speaking the truth, as you see it.

HOW: Now there's something we can start with. If the truth were spoken, well, don't we feel better for it? Maybe? (*Close-up, How looking from Frost to Mott*) Hasn't the air been cleared? Maybe? Isn't it just a case where personal history has intruded needlessly, personal lives dragged in and personalities giving vent to feelings that have just become too emotional for words—

FROST: I never laid a hand on my wife, Mr. Mott.

MOTT: Stop being candid and embarrassing.

FROST: It's only right that you should know. My wife's death was a blow and I said a lot of peculiar things immediately following it—

HOW: I was really proud of the impression Elmer made on me, Steve, and I know the things you've said were tempered by some fact that could just as easily be fiction.

MOTT: Why weren't the facts laid bare, that's all, Howard? Naturally what can you expect if you attempt to obscure the facts—

HOW: I'm sorry, Steve.

MOTT: Maybe I was a little sudden myself, sorry to drag in your personal background like that, Frost.

FROST: Maybe I said some things I shouldn't have said.

MOTT: Well, I guess I know I did—

HOW (*Smile warming on face, teeth coming out again*) We all did.

FROST (*Rising*): Well I better be going.

MOTT (*Putting out hand*): There's a place for you here, Elmer.

HOW (*Smiling all teeth*): Construction from confusion.

FROST (*Off*) (*Close-up, hands in handshake*): I'm glad you said that, Mr. Mott.

MOTT (*Off*): I'm glad I was king enough to say it.

THOMAS HINDE

Pity Not the Sheep

> *To be oneself is also to be vulnerable. For man is a thing of infinite possibilities, divine and ridiculous, and it is often the moment that decides for him. The very formulas which bind the Mr. Prices of this world give them a seeming strength. They know what they must do. And so the dead vanquish the living.*
>
> *This selection is from the novel* Happy as Larry.

*L*A RECHERCHE stood alone at the end of a new concrete road, the furthest advance of the town into the country. Even at night he could tell it was made of concrete. It had two concrete towers. It was like a lot of shoe boxes put together. The hills which rose from its back garden showed above it, round and massive. Larry stopped at the front gate. He must form at least one sentence before he went in. It wasn't easy.

His head ached and throbbed. He put his hand to it and found a large unexpected knob behind one ear. It was covered with short hair. It felt soft at the surface but firm. He was astonished that such a large addition to his head could have arrived unknown to him. When he pressed it there was a violent shooting pain which came and went for half a minute.

He must not stand here, like a burglar contemplating entry, for any policeman to see. He opened the gate. He needed time. From here he could look down on the grey town, its streets empty and silent in the night. Presently he could feel the wet grass though his trousers.

"Good evening," Mr. Price said.

"Oh, good evening." He got up quickly and came forward, tripping on the concrete path. He stopped in front of the door.

Mr. Price stood in the doorway, staring and stern. He wore a dark silk dressing gown.

"I hope you got my wire."

"It was telephoned at eleven-fifteen p.m." Mr. Price said, quietly, as if the shocking fact needed no emphasis.

"Terrible service."

"I don't know about the service."

"Oh, yes, I've noticed it a lot lately. Particularly at the beginning of the month. The gas meters," he began, "they're emptied . . ." but he had forgotten the connection. He was sure there had been a connection.

"You'd better come in." It was said between narrowed teeth, with a real sound of anger. Larry wondered why he wasn't as frightened of Mr. Price as he should have been. Perhaps because he did not feel that there was any real danger of Mr. Price attacking him. His anger gave no sense of animal violence which could only just be troubled with words.

"How angry do you get?" Larry said. "I mean do you see red?"

Mr. Price had stood aside and Larry went past him into the white passage.

"I don't know what you're talking about."

"Oh, please don't be dignified; it's important."

"Might I remind you that there are people asleep in this house?" He went upstairs and Larry followed. The upper landing was a cream box. There was no furniture except the jardinière of potted plants, stretching away from the stair head. It was like a wire pig trough. He wondered if Mr. Price still dusted the leaves.

Looking up he saw movement on the landing above. Someone was there in a pale nightdress. Mr. Price saw too. "Go to bed, dear," he said in a loud whisper. Larry was astonished by its warmth and tenderness.

The nightdress moved and was gone. It was Betty. He knew by the way she did what she was told, saying nothing.

"This is your room." Mr. Price opened a door and Larry went in. "Breakfast at eight o'clock." He looked at his watch. "That's in three and a half hours." He looked at Larry and gave a small grin. That was the difficulty with Mr. Price. Despite everything, he did not seem able to avoid sometimes accidentally being friendly. He shut the door.

There was no chair in the room. There was no mat, dressing table, chest of drawers or basin. The light came from an opaque glass square in the ceiling. Larry sat on the bed. The bed was an iron divan with no head or foot.

He began to notice the papered doors flush with the walls which concealed hanging cupboards. He noticed the metal-framed window. The door handle was a metal half circle which fell back into a recess to leave no projection. He looked at his feet.

He wished they weren't so large. He had an idea that many of his troubles could be traced to the largeness of his feet. It was difficult to think of an example but he was sure he was right. Quite soon he knew he could not stay in this room.

He lit a cigarette. There was nowhere to throw the match. He switched off the opaque glass panel and quietly opened the door. The house was black and silent. He closed the door behind him and went slowly forward. His feet moved on soft carpet. He was surprised at how friendly to Mrs. Price the soft carpet on her first floor landing made him feel. He remembered his cigarette, but he could not drop it yet. It might be useful—something about holding it sideways at arm's length—or was that when the shooting started?

After several minutes the landing became a little less black and he could see the outline of a window, but the night outside was so dark that it remained a faint grey rectangle. A long, low gust of wind howled somewhere above him on the second floor. When it had passed the house was silent. He found the stairs and went down.

At the door of the sitting-room he struck a match. He saw the room he remembered. It was curiously different from the rest of the house, as if the architect had suddenly noticed that something was missing from his design and worked hard to compensate. It was long and low, with patches of panelling and squares of tasteful unplastered brick. The floor was parquet and the ceiling between neat black beams was papered with faint silver stripes. The fireplace was open with a wide hearth and imitation ingle nooks. Larry went quickly across between comfortable armchairs and low tables to the dining recess. He pushed at the glass-fronted sideboard, afraid for the moment that it was locked. Then it slid. He struck a match to find the right bottle.

What did they want, that was what puzzled him. They were on some track but he could not guess it. Mr. Price could not still have hopes of the cabinet. He took a big warm mouthful. Its warmth made him shudder. He felt it spreading down inside him to his stomach. Mrs. Price was easier. There was no reason to think that she looked further than the power over people she enjoyed each day. One more mouthful. No time to add warm water to the bottle to make it level. Suddenly he was hearing noises. He crouched close to the floor. There was a singing in his ears which interrupted his listening. He was sure he had heard a noise but could not remember what, or be sure that it had been a noise so much as a sensation of just having heard one. After a minute he slowly relaxed. Accidentally he put the bottle to his mouth and took a large mouthful. When he had swallowed he was worried. The level must not be noticeably low. He did not dare strike a match to see. He put it in the cupboard with great care and closed the glass front. As he did so he heard quite distinctly a small ringing noise like the tapping of a wine glass.

It came from the kitchen. He remembered now a hatch which led from the kitchen to this part of the sitting-room. He was surprised that there were no cracks of light. The only conclusion was that someone else was in there also drinking in the dark. Treading softly, he went across the sitting-room and upstairs. The darkness made it curiously difficult to balance and several times he had to move a foot quickly to stop himself falling.

On the first landing he heard crying. At first it seemed a long way away, just a noise which he could not identify. Then it was terrible, miserable crying. He thought he had never heard such unhappiness. In the silent house it was clear but distant, as if it came from behind a heavy closed door. He could imagine that it would be loud if the door was opened.

He went forward quickly through the darkness, feeling for the stairs, then up the second landing. It had stopped. The passage led right and left to the two towers. He could not decide which way to go. A long gust of wind blew past the house and away over the town and the moors and hills beyond. He was near the window where it was howling. He opened it softly and leant out into the damp mild darkness.

The hills rose steeply into the night. He wished he was out there, with the gusts of wind filling his clothes and hair, blowing into his lungs, making him feel young and healthy, instead of half whiskey drunk, with a taste of decay in his mouth and the smell of a year's petrol fumes in his nose. If only he felt healthy once more he might again have great hopes and want to do great things. He wondered if there were still sheep on the hill. He remembered them, small and grey, their lonely bleating in the summer evenings. They at least had the courage to regret their pointless days and small stupid brains. When he looked back into the passage there was a line of light under a door at one end.

He went forward, up the three steps and quietly opened the door. Inside the light was low and pink. On a bed, his mouth open and snoring a little, was a small, old Indian. He had a wrinkled khaki face and little white beard. There was a distinct scent in the room, not like English scents. He was wearing a hair net. Probably a patient— or a medium. Larry closed the door. Immediately the crying began again. It was in the other tower and he ran, stumbling and feeling, across the landing, up the steps.

At the first noise of the door handle it stopped. The room was black. "Betty," he said. There was no answer. He went in and softly closed the door.

Suddenly she began again, and loud so that he jumped and sweat came on his face. "Betty." He tried to speak calmly to quiet her but her crying drowned the word. He felt for the bed.

She was sitting upright, like a child who has woken from a nightmare and does not know where she is. He put his arm round her shoulders. He sat on the bed and held her close to him, crying and shuddering against him, feeling her warm tears running into his shirt.

"Poor Betty," he said. "Poor dear Betty."

Presently she was quieter. He sat in the darkness, holding her closely with both arms, rocking her a little.

"I get such silly ideas." Her voice and nose were full of tears.

"Poor Betty. What ideas?"

"Silly ideas. It doesn't matter."

He felt for the bedside lamp. It lit the room with a low, yellow light. Her hair had been cut short.

"Why have you come?" she said.

"To see you."

"It's no good."

"Why not?"

"Oh dear." She turned away, as if looking for somewhere to hide. "You'll hate it."

"What?"

"You weren't meant to see." He thought she was going to cry again.

"But I like it." He felt sure he would like it soon. It had been made into short black curls. He supposed there had been no alternative, after half had been shaved.

"Do you really?" He was sad at the way she believed him.

He lifted her small red hands and kissed them. "Dear Betty." She smiled but at once put them under the bed clothes.

"It's no good," she said.

"It's not meant to do good. It's because I want to see you."

"I've been very pulled down." He was miserable at how she repeated her mother's phrases.

Somewhere below a door shut. She was badly frightened now. She sat upright, staring at him, her eyes wide with alarm. He put an arm round her to hold her again but she pushed it away. He was surprised and hurt by the force she used.

"They can't stop me seeing you."

"Sh," she said in a frightened whisper.

"Why. . . ?"

He saw the terrible fright in her eyes. After a moment he could not bear to make her so unhappy. It was to her parents he must say these things. "I'll be back," he said, but she wouldn't answer. He went out quickly.

As he came down the stairs he heard soft steps in slippers coming up from the ground floor. He reached the landing and moved quickly towards the room. His legs met something. He tried to stop himself but was going too fast. He pitched forward on to the landing. He felt it move with him, tip and crash, then squash under his weight. It was the wire jardinière. He heard several of the pots smash. One rolled off the carpet on to the boards, reached the stairs and fell a few steps, smashing as it went. He stumbled forward. By good luck he found the darkness of his room and went in. He stood still in the darkness, panting, then rubbing his shin. Outside he heard low conversation. Doors opened and shut. Then there was silence. He switched on the light. It was the wrong room. It was identical but a different colour. His shoes and socks weren't there.

It was light when he woke and he got quickly off the bed. If only he could have his feet under the breakfast table before anyone else came down. The landing was bad. There were several broken pots, spilling earth on to the Wilton carpet. The plants, lying on their sides, had drooped. The wire jardinière was squashed at one end where he had knelt on it. He tried to stretch it. A shower of white paint flakes fell from it and several wires snapped. He stood it up gently and went downstairs.

Mr. and Mrs. Price were at the breakfast table. From where they sat in the dining recess they could see him for the whole length of the sitting-room as he approached. He wished he had washed his feet more recently. He remembered their black stains but he wasn't going to look down. If only they weren't so big. He must pretend that it was his habit to breakfast with bare feet. Their eyes were on him as he came forward.

"Good morning," he said, and sat down quickly without being asked.

They went on eating, saying nothing. They were too angry to speak. He was sad when he remembered the interview he had planned. "You are keeping Betty here against her will. Apart from the legal aspect . . ." His measured anger.

"After breakfast we'll find you the vacuum cleaner," Mrs. Price said.

"Oh, of course."

She was plump and round faced. She looked thirty-five but he knew she was fifty. In the early morning her face seemed a little puffy. She was deceptively unformidable. This was her strength. This and her small mind which allowed her to concentrate with so much energy and skill on what she wanted.

"And then you can get out," Mr. Price said. He said it viciously, spitting out a crumb of toast. He gave an impression of terrible cold anger. His wife inspired him to an exceptional performance. The crumb of toast was a perfect touch.

Larry did not contradict. He felt that he must allow him to show his anger, so that later he would be glad to show his reasonableness.

"Does Betty know that breakfast's ready?"

"It may have escaped your notice but your wife is an invalid."

He wondered what they meant and was frightened to ask.

"The shock of her accident has left her mind . . ."

"I know that."

"You know it?"

"I wonder, could I speak to you?" he said to Mr. Price. Somehow he must put off this interview till he had found his shoes.

"We're listening," Mr. Price said.

"But are you really? Aren't you just waiting to be angry?"

"The idea may be strange to you but we feel some responsibility for our daughter."

"Oh, but are these things you really think?"

"Think," Mr. Price shouted. "What else can we think?" This was the moment to shout, to become incoherent with rightful anger. But he should have been able to invent a few more phrases. He closed his mouth and was silent for several seconds, giving an impression of controlling himself with difficulty, but as he sat completely still it seemed possible that he was wondering what to say next. "For your information," he said slowly and distinctly as if now beyond anger in a state of terrible cold passion, "we are not disposed to return our daughter to a husband who has nowhere for her to live and is heavily in debt."

"How do you know?"

"We have made inquiries."

"Even if it's true it won't be always."

"What guarantee can you give us that it isn't just a pious hope?"

"No guarantee. But it isn't just hope. I'd rather not be specific."

"I can imagine."

"No, no, you must believe me. It's true. It's just that for certain reasons . . ."

"You leave us no alternative but to presume . . ."

"Well, I'll tell you some of it. As soon as I recover this photograph—you see it's to do with a photograph . . ."

"And how will a photograph make you suddenly rich?"

He was sorry he had mentioned it.

"What sort of a photograph?"

"A bad photograph."

"What's that?" Mr. Price said.

"Indecent?" Mrs. Price said.

"Indecent photography?" Mr. Price said.

Larry didn't answer.

"Is that what you mean but daren't say? Is that what you offer as a safeguard for our daughter's well being? The hope that you'll keep her by dealing in indecent photographs? It's astounding. It's incredible . . ."

"I didn't say that," Larry said in a low voice. But he knew that it was too late to contradict. He would never make them believe.

"It's preposterous." Mr. Price stood up, as if to let himself breathe freely. "Never have I heard . . ."

"Surely what matters is what Betty wants?" Larry said.

"We'll soon settle that," Mrs. Price said. She went out, waddling in her house coat.

He wished he hadn't suggested it. He sat opposite Mr. Price, waiting and listening. Surely Mr. Price could not be so foolish as to believe what he was pretending to believe, but there seemed no way to persuade him even to consider what he really believed. Perhaps his opinion of Larry made it seem entirely probable. Outside the morning was grey and heavy with a wet wind. The hill rose steeply so that he could see no sky but only the brown slope and the small white animals he knew were sheep. He could hear them now, bleating for the rain that was coming. He could bear it no longer.

"Where are you going?" Mr. Price came after him.

On the first landing he could hear her sobbing. He ran quickly up the second flight. From the top he could see them, but the effort, or the whiskey, or the blow on his head suddenly caught him and he could only stand at the top, gripping the banisters, trying not to faint. Quite slowly everything became indistinct, then began to spin in fast circles. A curious whiteness came in front of his eyes and he could see nothing. He only knew that he must go on gripping the banisters as hard as he could. Slowly, with a pain in his eyes, he began to see again. They were still there, at the end of the passage up three steps in the doorway, sobbing on to each other.

Betty sat on the edge of the bed, her arms around her mother's big chest, her head against her heavy bosom, sobbing on it. Her mother stood over her crying in her hair.

Larry ran towards them. "What have you told her?" he shouted.

Mrs. Price did not let go but turned her face. It was red and blubbery from crying. "Go away," she said.

From behind Mr. Price seized his collar. Faintness came over him again and he found himself moved away downstairs. Trying to look back he turned his head in the wrong direction and saw that the opposite door was ajar. Inside, the Indian was doing physical exercises. He wore only a pair of cotton pants. His body was grey and wrinkled and very thin. He bent on his haunches, stretched, and rose on his toes.

Larry broke away and went quickly down the stairs, across the hall, out into the garden. He stood there, shivering a little, breathing the mild damp air.

Presently a window opened. First one, then the other shoe flew over his head and landed in the road.

GEORGE SCOTT

Time and Place

*What are the factors which have
shaped the Angry Young Man—
which have eroded his idealism and
left him incapable of "commitment"?
In his unique autobiography* Time
and Place, *thirty-one-year-old George
Scott reflects on the experiences
which he has shared in common with
the youth of his generation. Having
no panaceas—typically suspicious of
all panaceas—Scott yet feels that the
writers of the Thirties no longer have
anything valuable to say. Although
hardly less critical of his own contemporaries, he sees in their very con-
temporaneity a force which is dis-
persing the illusions of the immediate
past.*

LIFE BEFORE THE WAR, meaning that part of
life concerning wars, political movements, international
affairs and social conditions, is for me something in books
or something about which older men tell stories I can
illustrate with a few mental pictures and one or two dramatic headlines. The man with adult memories of the
Twenties and Thirties seems just as remote to me as the
man who can say that he was a Tommy in that strangely
idealistic, chivalric and ultimately futile and filthy war of
the Trenches. Some men of my age who grew up in

families where politics and international affairs were common ground for conversation will feel more intimate with those days than I, although even their intimacy must be that of the child eavesdropping on adult talk.

But my first-hand knowledge of that era is limited to the memory of *Daily Mirror* kind of talk. Mussolini and Hitler were figures of fun and contempt, lunatics ruling lunatic foreign lands. Black Shirts, cardboard tanks; and of course The Bolshies. Politically my family was invulnerably Tory. It was useless for the Labour Party to talk of inequalities of wealth as of an evil; to my father and thus to his children inequality of wealth was of the natural order of things. It represented stability—but also opportunity. The man at the top with the money had earned it, and there was always the chance for other men to get to the top if they worked hard enough and were clever enough.

Oxford, however, was a place for The Nobs and I remember the derision with which my father greeted the first mention of my young ambition to have a flat of my own in London. The cause of this derision was that he associated the term "London flat" with a quite unreal splendour—though no more unreal than my adolescent conceptions. Neither of us thought of a London flat in terms of one room in a Bloomsbury block, or a squalid semi-basement in Bayswater. He had taken his picture from Edwardian London when, so far as I can make out, he had been, among other things in his wandering career, a waiter and a chef. He knew a "real gent" when he saw one and had the highest contempt for the jumped-up little provincial business men and their wives who bought tinny, spluttering cars and put on the airs of ladies and gentlemen. My picture of a London flat came probably from romantic fiction such as that of P. G. Wodehouse or, later, the plays of Noel Coward.

Social reform was construed by my father as trying to help those who would not help themselves. I remember the anger with which, in the first flush of my evangelical, socialistic fervour, I encountered his stubborn taunts about people who used their baths to store the coal. "You can't change them," he said. "I know. You haven't seen them, but I have. If you put them in a mansion they'd still make a slum of it." He granted that a minority might be educable, but only a minority. Only one Labour politician was held in anything like respect in our house. Both my mother and father agreed that George Lansbury was a "good man," whatever errors there might be in his political thinking.

I have tried to catch up with the facts and emotions of the pre-war world. I have read many books and shall go on reading books about the period. It is a historical period about which I cannot learn too much. Naturally its contacts with the present day as well as with my own life and thought make it infinitely more interesting than any other period in history. But I must emphasize its remoteness. I was one year old at the time of the General Strike. I was eleven when the Spanish War started. This was the war which engaged the hot, courageous idealisms of some of our finest young writers, the war which demanded the physical demonstration of intellectual and emotional convictions and also started them on the long, tortuous, agonizing road towards disillusion. But this war I can remember only through a newsreel picture of antiquated biplanes bombing a hazy Madrid. As far as I can recall it made no impression whatever upon my family beyond provoking the normally sorrowful exclamation of "terrible," a word they would use for any war, anywhere, which could maim and kill men.

I have since read one account after another by men who took part in the Spanish war. But I have been denied the final pleasure of discovery, for the end of the story has been known to me; any partial enthusiasms I might conceive have been tainted and poisoned in advance by having inherited their disillusion.

In some ways the men of my age must count themselves fortunate in having to "read up" the Spanish war instead of having lived through it, fought in it, and lost our souls in it. Too many of our unfortunate and brilliant elders seem to have been fixated by their experiences in that war. Time has gone on, but though they may try to write of present experiences their hearts and minds seem to have stopped in the Spain of the Civil War; they are like old, embittered men who return to their images of first love seeking to recapture beauty in their lives, that beauty of faith and hope and trust which they have lost for ever. They have shown themselves incapable of making the transition to the modern world. They cannot *attach* themselves to the present day, but are doomed to wander in the paradise of their memories like men who dream of inhabiting the world which existed before Adam fell. Or else they turn upon their old love in the spirit of vicious revenge; they seek to banish the bad memory by digging out its decay in their minds, but they can never drill deep enough: the pain always comes back and they have to return for another assault upon it. Or else they seek a new love, a new commitment for their passion, which will absorb them, which will exhaust their powers and obliterate their pains. They are seeking a substitute for that ecstatic first love, but even as they search they remember the betrayal of that love and they are consumed with doubt and distrust demanding the new love shall give such avowals and proofs of requited passion that they must always search in vain. They are too distrustful to give all of themselves again until all has been given them. And they can find no God, no political faith that can answer their exorbitant demands.

There are some who have found comfort by burying their heads in the deep bosom of the Roman Church, receiving absolution for their sins and balm for their agonies; they are concerned only with finding peace for their own souls and are content to let the world soul writhe in torment. Finally, there are those who have escaped into consoling clouds of mysticism and metaphysics in which they can hide safely away from the trivial realities of fleshy existence. But whether they have chosen to dwell for ever in the Garden of Eden or the Gardens of Bloomsbury or whether they resemble the over-fastidious, over-cautious bachelor who will spend his life searching in vain for the Ideal Woman, they have abstracted themselves from the modern world. They may provoke our compassion; we may grant them a sort of spiritual public assistance, but we must now write off their unfulfilled promises of achievement as bad debts. They will never be able to redeem the talents they pledged to the Marxist pawnbroker.

And have the writers and thinkers of my own generation been so noticeably successful so far in facing modern problems and horrors and in combating them? Of that I shall write later. Meanwhile I should be stupid to deny that in depreciating the present work of the previous generation I am to some extent impelled by a natural and entirely conscious desire to tip them out of their seats of power and dignity to make room for us. On the other hand this is far from being my only reason. There is the perfectly valid one I have already made: that the previous generation, with few exceptions, seem incapable of giving us the kind of leadership we require.

Their advice and wisdom is mostly of a negative, admonitory sort.

They can tell us so many things we should not do, and this is valuable up to a point. But there comes a time when a young man tires of dont's and looks for more positive and illuminating and inspiring words. He is ready enough to be led by his elders, but only if his elders can show themselves possessed of greater prescience than he.

There was a time long, long ago, we understand, when age and experience brought the kind of wisdom which younger men could admire and respect and envy and seek to emulate. The old men held their position of power because they could show that age had brought them breadth of understanding and an enriched vision of the way ahead. It is just one of the curiosities of the modern world that age and experience have brought to so many only the sickness of self-despair and the desire to escape from the realities of existence if not through suicide then by bolting down a variety of intellectual and emotional hidey-holes.

It is the claim of my generation that we can understand the causes which have driven our elders to this situation and can pity them. We can sympathize with their torments and admire the original courage and enthusiasm which brought them into peril. We do not condemn them for their inability to make the transition to the present day. Yet strangely these same men who have lost their own way and are so publicly conscious and even proud of their stigmata are quick to castigate us for our apparent lack of violent enthusiasms, for failing to "commit" ourselves, for not wanting to turn the world upside down. Surely we are not to be blamed for learning by their mistakes? Must violence of beliefs and actions be accounted the only virtue? Are we then to admire a volcano for its spectacular show of power and ignore the damage it does? Is it so very timid, or could it possibly be wise, to suggest that enthusiasm *can* be dangerous and even stupid?

Since science in the name of progress has brought us passionately, enthusiastically and blindly to a condition somewhat less desirable than the optimistic prophets foretold, we may be excused for questioning for a moment whether passion and enthusiasm are always the qualities we should cultivate. It might even be that the world was better the way it was before the passionate enthusiasts turned it upside down, although it is futile to imagine that we could make it look again just the way it used to be or should even wish to do so.

*   *   *

I wonder if the present spasm of tough, "anti-wet" writing can be attributed to the influences of the war. It seems to me that life in the Services had one permanent effect on the majority of us and that was a deliberate hardening of oneself against the pain of any deeply-felt emotion. The longer a man served the more conscious this process became. I cannot say how many enjoyable relationships I formed with men and women during my short time in the Navy. Even the shortest stay in a place was sure to bring me into new friendships. I gave much of myself to these relationships as might be expected from a man between the years of eighteen and twenty-one. But as experience taught me the soon familiar lesson I began to hold back part of myself in self-protection. Sooner or later, one knew—and it was usually sooner—either one or the other would get a draft chit and would leave. So the relationship, no matter how urgently precious, would be broken and it was extremely rare for letters to preserve it. So it was that farewells were sincere but deliberately casual; at the moment of the handshake or the kiss the process of cutting free would begin, the joke or the piece of mockery hastily produced to dam any dangerous spurt of emotion. The moment the word came yet again for the packing of kitbags, the doors would begin to close on emotion so that, despite the irrepressible feeling of sickness as the bag was lugged on to the shoulder, it would be possible to arrive uninjured at the next place. When one relaxed these precautions the results might be regrettable.

I knew one friend particularly well. His name was Gair Buchan. We were together in England, America and again in England for something like eighteen months on and off. The fact that we were on the same course, training as pilots, gave a certain sense of permanency to our relationship. In England and America we lived in the same barrack-rooms, drank together, went dancing and "picked up" girls together. He was a couple of years older than I, an ex-biology student of London University. Before coming into the Fleet Air Arm he had served with the Merchant Navy and had been injured by a depth-charge explosion. Injured not physically, to any permanent extent of course, otherwise he would never have got into the Fleet Air Arm, but injured nevertheless, for something had happened to him as a result of that explosion. He used to say: "I'm dead inside. I don't feel anything any more. I enjoy being with you, but I don't feel any emotion towards you." Gair never struck me as being a handsome man. He had a bulbous nose set crooked in a thin, Scottish face. He had a curiously twisted, cruel smile, and broken, uneven teeth. His walk was gangling and ungainly, as though his bones were not properly articulated. He had no sense of rhythm so that when he danced his shuffling steps seemed wholly unrelated to the music. He was a sensual man with an attraction for women of a power such as I have seen in only one other man. He would break "dates" and behave towards women with utter callousness. He would laugh openly at their sentiments and walk off, leaving them, without a word of reason or apology. Yet they ran after him, seeking him with a hunger that was animalistic. I ought to say that they wanted him even before he had spoken to them just as much as when he had maltreated them. I had the embarrassment more than once of their tears when he had finished with them. It seemed too that his attraction knew no age limits. We stayed together one week-end in a house in Essex. When he went to bed he was visited in the night first by the daughter and then by the mother. They missed each other by only half an hour. Gair felt nothing for the women he slept with, but he made love to them with a passion that satisfied them as obviously as it left him unsatisfied. He sought women promiscuously and moved on to the next as soon as he realized that the previous one had nothing to give him. He was engaged on a search, as reckless as it was greedy, for a woman who could provide the stimulus to "bring him back to life." In the same way he went into the Fleet Air Arm hoping that the sensations of fear and excitement might revitalize him. He never found the stimulus he sought so avidly. In 1946, a few months before I was demobilized, I was working in London at the Admiralty. I had written earlier to Gair suggesting a meeting in London. I had received no reply. I rang up the air station where he was serving. I spoke to one of his fellow-officers there and asked to speak to Gair. "You can't," he said. "He hanged himself in the 'heads' last Saturday night. Damned selfish, I call it, leaving us to clean up his mess."

* * *

I snatched at anything resembling literature or art to keep alive the memory of the kind of life I had glimpsed at Oxford. *Penguin New Writing*, with its strange combination of detachment from, yet involvement in, the war, was a source of great comfort and encouragement. I tried one or two immature pieces on John Lehmann which, very properly, were never published. That magazine, with its self-conscious observation of contemporary experience and with its art plates of paintings and stage designs, was a constant reminder that the mind could survive all this—and "all this" might mean scavenging the roads of Lee-on-Solent barracks, or enduring the stink and obscenity of a sweating barrack-room, the spirit-grinding futilities of square-bashing or the chronic humiliations that were ennobled by their being described as "discipline." The flashes of satire as well as the thunder rolls of soulful solemnities contained in *Penguin New Writing* were as refreshing as a day spent in the country with a girl, away from the shame and self-pity of barracks. The bad, imitative poetry which it inspired, like the florid, extravagant love-letters I seemed to be writing so often to so many different girls, like the acquisition of a cigarette holder in which I smoked Balkan Sobranie cigarettes, could be justi-fied and even commended as exercises necessary to keep the spirit afloat. Whatever I may have said in criticism of John Lehmann else-where, and however I may now question the quality of individual contributions to *Penguin New Writing*, I must here record my grate-ful thanks to him. Without his magazine as a sort of buoy to mark the channel back to civilization and hope, life would have seemed even more bewildering and despondent than it did.

There was no cohesion or continuity about my efforts to keep afloat. For a few days in Portsmouth barracks I collaborated with another man in writing popular songs. At the Fleet Air Arm training establish-ment, H.M.S. *St Vincent*, at Gosport, I wrote sketches and lyrics for a show we put on under the guidance of a lieutenant, formerly pro-fessional actor who did for our shows some really first-class female impersonations in the Douglas Byng manner. In Canada, while await-ing my draft back to England, I managed to persuade some authority or other that half my working days could most profitably be spent in the library studying Spanish. I did try to learn Spanish, but I also found in the library a massive, three-volume work on the History of Art and spent a lot of time with that, comparing notes and opinions with another rating, an ex-art student. I wrote occasionally to David Cecil and received sympathetic and invigorating letters back from him, telling me how the university was beginning to fill up again and how much I should enjoy coming back myself. And then, of course, as the war in Europe was obviously coming to an end, there were the amateurish and reluctantly organized lectures on Current Affairs.

Indolence and disinterest on the part of the officers detailed to organize these lectures meant that any man who was foolhardy enough to volunteer would be allowed to lecture to his heart's content. It also meant, in the event, that lectures on politics assumed an emphatically left-wing bias. I cannot remember a single instance when anyone, officer or rating, objected to this bias. It was more than a correct reflection of a generally-held belief that the first post-war government must be a Socialist one. Young minds at any rate were full of heady phrases like "a Socialist Britain," "planned economy," "public ownership," "equality of opportunity," and so on, all of them deriving from and expressing a common belief that no government other than a Socialist one could prevent a recurrence of the miseries of the Thirties or could build the brave, idealistic world which would justify "all this." I had no vote in the 1945 election because I was too young, but if I had been old enough there is no doubt that I should have voted for the Socialists. There is no recollection now of any counter-propaganda from the Conservative side to all this left-wing bias openly insinuated into Current Affairs lectures and contained in all the magazines I, at least, was reading. But even if there had been I do not think I should have listened to it. The lead weight of "reactionary" was firmly attached to the Tories and it was heavy enough to sink them far beyond rescue in the 1945 election. They never had a hope of winning and the only surprising thing is that anyone was surprised by the result.

Men in uniform, finally ground down to an interest only in personal survival and the discovery of the quickest possible escape route back to Civvy Street, had no room in their minds for adulation of Winston Churchill. That he had rallied the country in 1940 they remembered; that he was now at the head of a fighting machine that was winning the war they knew, but as insignificant, often rusty cogs in the machine they accepted and did not judge. This was especially true, I fancy, of those hundreds of thousands, as they must have been, whose energies were so fatuously misused and wasted that they failed to see themselves as cogs at all. At most it was accepted that Winston Churchill was a great war-leader who would be totally unsuited for leading us to victory in peacetime. But those who talk of ingratitude to

Winston Churchill in the 1945 election should recognize that it was the Tories we wanted to throw out, not Churchill personally. Of course the Prime Minister must have convinced many waverers by his grossly-misjudged "Gestapo" speech. That speech contained sentiment so pot-bellied and distorted, as it seemed then, and so alien to the general mood of men in the Service, that one can still only wonder at the gap it revealed between the minds of the Tory propagandists—or perhaps only Winston Churchill himself—and those of the electorate.

VE Day was celebrated with drunkenness and a vision of release and its hopes confirmed by the return of the Socialists to power. We did not then know that power was being given to a party unprepared for it and that the intoxicating ideals and slogans by which some men had sustained their lives and with which others, like myself, had grown up would be incapable of translation into practical, workaday terms. Nor did we know that the next Prime Minister would go to Potsdam and play his part in the laying of the foundations for the tensions of the next decade.

Even now, I am not sure that prescience would have made me want it otherwise. The six years during which the Socialists ruled this country taught us all the lessons, including those who are still Socialists, which had to be learned if the great delusions were not to persist into another generation. Also, during their time in power, however much of the planning had been done under the Coalition Government, it was they who built the Welfare State and that, with all its imperfections which we can now see, for all that much remains to be done to modify it, is something we wanted and something I do not wish to see wholly undone. When the Tories came back to power they were stronger, the more creative, and properly chastened for their time in the wilderness; they were capable of giving the country good administration when it was most needed as they certainly would not have been ready to do in 1945. As for Potsdam, perhaps it is more the ghost of Roosevelt than the flesh of Clement Atlee that should take the blame for the conclusion of agreements which nourished Soviet Imperialism and made friction in Germany inevitable. But who is to say now that any other group of men would have made any better a job of it?

*   *   *

During the Easter vacation of 1948, before I was due to take Schools, I worked on the *Daily Express* in Fleet Street. I had asked for and had been given a "trial" as a reporter. My wife, Shelagh, joined me in London. We made our first married "home" together in one attic room in a Bayswater boarding house. I paid £5 15s a week for bed and breakfast for the two of us. Neither of us is likely to forget or underestimate the misery of that period of our lives. It was, as elders have insisted on telling us, imprudent for us to have married with less than no money and with six months of separation to follow the wedding before we could be permanently together. I am glad to say that we did not heed that elderly advice. But there were many times in the months to follow when we both wondered whether we should not have waited. A couple of anxious, strained weekends in Oxford when Shelagh came there from Nottingham were all we had been able to manage together before we met in London. Then we came together still virtually strangers, trying each time to accustom ourselves to the strangeness of the married state and to the strangeness of being always with the other person. That Easter vacation was not only a time when I was on trial at the *Express*. It was also a time when we were really trying married life together for the first time. The circumstances were not helpful.

Our room was five flights up. It contained a rusty, narrow, creaking, uncomfortable bed; one small table; a wash-basin (the bathroom could be used only at specified times of the day and the water was never hot); one narrow, shabby arm-chair with the springs protruding; the smell of cabbage always insinuating itself into the room; the seemingly constant sound of a man in a lonely bedroom across the way playing over and over again a record of Vera Lynn singing *Yours*. The boarding-house contained its usual quota of eccentrics including one grey-haired woman who appeared from her room only to descend the stairs in her white flannel nightgown and with wild hair and equally wild eyes abuse anyone in sight, screaming at them and the world in general.

Quite irrationally, for I should blame myself just as much as the times for our situation, I find myself feeling envy to the point of bitterness for those authors who tell of their marriages and say "and then we began our married life in a house at Hampstead which we rented from the So-and-so's." The idea of renting a house in London from anyone in 1948 was impossible of imagination. It was furnished rooms and furnished flats only—and almost always there should have been inverted commas around the furnished.

The "furnished" attic room in a dilapidated, peeling Bayswater square was our first home, then. I went off each morning to the *Express* and Shelagh went to a sweet factory in West London as part of her "practical work" as a social science student. She came back each evening with the stench of the place still in her nostrils, but at least we had plenty of boiled sweets to chew in our room. How far removed was this from the "flat" which, as a boy, I had told my mother and father I should have in London. I could see no grand piano, no butler and no cocktail cabinet here. Just grimy, faded wallpaper; one inadequate electric lamp; creaking floorboards; a gasfire on the shilling-in-the-slot principle; the sound of voices from the next room; the saucer of "butter" and the packet of sugar, which were our closely-guarded rations to be taken each morning to the breakfast table below.

When I record our hunt for a permanent, unfurnished home—it took us three years in all, living in one furnished place after another, including one period of seven months *en famille* with a very kind colleague—and remember that I was earning a good wage the whole of that time, I dread to think of the miseries of other young married people in London. I saw one of them when I covered stories about "squatters" and no matter what the political convictions of some of them and however their conditions were exploited by the Communists, I know that their suffering was appallingly real. And how hopeless it seemed of solution. There were times even for us when we preferred the unhappiness of separation again to the dangerous agonies of living together in such a way that nerves were always being scratched and love was being poisoned by the nag, nag, nag of anxiety to find a way out, to find, in that cosy suburban phrase, somewhere of our own.

After taking Schools in June, 1948, I came to London again to take a job on the staff of the *Express*. Shelagh joined me almost immediately, refusing to do a final spell of "practical work" in Birmingham or somewhere of that sort. Before she arrived, I spent all my spare time poring over the classified columns of the papers and at the squalid noticeboards outside the Bayswater and Notting Hill shops. At last I found somewhere—though hardly of our own. It was a furnished flat on the ground floor of a house in Notting Hill Gate. It had one bed-

room, one sitting-room and one kitchen, to be shared with the landlady. The outside of the house was badly in need of paint while our
flat, on the other hand, could have done with much less. It was furnished with the heaviest and darkest of Victoriana, blacks and browns
and, of course, pictures of moorland dawns and stags at bay. The
kitchen was dreary and primitive, the bedroom was semi-basement.
It cost us four and a half guineas a week. But, or so it seemed at first,
it was heaven after the attic room. Even to be able to unpack all one's
clothes and hang them up, or put them in drawers, was consoling. And
although the landlady had her room at the end of the passage, beyond
the kitchen, in our sitting-room and bedroom we were on our own.
Many contemporaries will understand the extent of the relief.

This was our first acquaintance, however, with landladies who live
on the premises and we had not appreciated the potential menace of
that arrangement. (The five flights of stairs in the boarding-house had
been something of a protection from that kind of intrusion at least.)
She was a woman of about sixty, pathetic when contemplated from
a long distance of years, but her virtues less capable of discernment
at close quarters. She had a large, red bulbous nose stuck in the
middle of a rosy face whose other notable feature was the lips, bluish
and eager to twist in the telling of some particularly revolting story.
Like my landladies in Leeds, she wore flat-heeled shoes with a school-
girl button strap across them. She puddled her way along, flip-flap
with the feet. Her hands were red and ugly; she always stared at them
as she talked. Her stories, and there were many of them, as my wife
discovered when exposed to her in the kitchen, were nearly always of
the evil of people she knew or had known. She told of this evil with
blue-lipped relish. She was a spiritualist and her communications with
those on the "other side" seemed to increase her awareness of evil-doers
and evil deeds.

The climax of her story-telling came one day when she started to
describe to my wife the behaviour of the couple who had had the flat
before us. "They were always quarrelling," she said, "shouting at each
other. I could hear them. Every night. And they were filthy people.
Filthy habits. I went into their bedroom to examine the sheets and
I saw the signs on them. Sex. Filthy." I heard this story when I came
home from work. My wife was almost sick in telling it to me. We felt
we could stand little more of this woman. We knew now that my

wife was pregnant and the thought of having a baby in a house where this woman lived filled us both with horror. One evening soon after this, she pushed a note under the door. It informed me that she would have to put the rent up from four and a half guineas to five and a half. I went to see her immediately. I told her I would not pay the increase. She said I must. I told her I would take her to the Rent Tribunal. At that she trembled and seemed about to burst into tears. I cannot remember being filled with pity and remorse at the sight. I said we would not pay the increase and we would leave within the month. As it was we moved within the week—back to the boarding-house, but this time to a slightly better, slightly bigger room on the second floor.

We went back to the boarding-house and back, also, to the search for a flat. By now I had thrown off romantic memories of Notting Hill Gate as I had known it as a bachelor while awaiting demobilization from the Navy. Now it seemed to me a compound of evil, squalor and frustration. We did not mind any longer whether we lived "in Town" or not. I paid four guineas to an alleged flat-finding agency whose activities proved only how it was possible to defraud people within the law. At last I saw a notice in an estate agent's window for a furnished flat in Thornton Heath. We saw it and we took it. It was on the third floor of a block. It had one bedroom, one sitting-room, one kitchen and one bathroom (with shower attachment) and no landlady on the premises. There was no doubt at all this time; this really was heaven. The furniture was new. The decorations were clean and bright. It cost four guineas a week. I signed the contract undertaking to rent it for the next twelve months. I paid a month's rent in advance. We moved in. Three days later I was called to see Lord Beaverbrook at Arlington House. Thirty-six hours after that I went on board the Queen Elizabeth to sail with him to America. My wife went back to stay with her mother in Oxford. For the next three months our flat was empty and I was paying four guineas a week for it.

When I returned to England just before Christmas, Shelagh was six months' pregnant. Susan was born in March, 1949, and took her place in the one-bedroom flat. She cried a lot. We spent hours pushing her up and down the short hall passage in her pram trying to quieten her. When I came home in the early hours of the morning after working at the *Express* she was sometimes crying or my movements in the bedroom started her crying. There was no room in which to escape.

This was not quite heaven after all. Nor, as I know Mr. Lehmann and Mr. Spender would agree, were the conditions ideal for creative writing. Time and place have considerable influence on our lives, the direction of our talents and the quality of our achievements. Art can have no existence independent of the peculiarities of its creator's environment. Lehmann and Spender and their like wrote, lived and acted as they did because of the time and place in which they were born. They are bound to be strangers to us, as we must be to them, and we are the more likely to understand each other if we acknowledge this from the start than we are if we seek to meet by looking for likenesses.

The anxieties of finding a place to live and bring up our families in post-war Britain have been chronic with many of us. It is only natural therefore that we should tend to emphasize these difficulties and to look with envy upon the writers of the Thirties who, if they often had to work for their living, did not know our particular problems to anything like the same degree. It follows no less naturally that we should also underestimate and misinterpret the anxieties peculiar to them. All this means is that we are bound to be different from them and we shall produce different kinds of writing. That is not an excuse but a simple statement of fact. Just as certainly, no matter how hard we try to understand them and they us, a mutual antagonism will persist.

*   *   *

I cannot mark the time at which I began to admit that the Socialist idea could never be more than a noble illusion; that apart from the bungling of this particular Socialist administration in trying to translate theory into practice there was also the much more comprehensive failure of the human element by which Socialism created not a universal brotherhood but a clogging, spreading weed of bureaucracy, leading logically perhaps to an authoritarian state. And even when this was admitted it was with some shame, for the utterance of the truth impelled one into the use of all those disparaging, "realistic" sentiments previously associated only with blimps. To sound like a blimp was a terrible charge to incur; Socialist propaganda had never been so successful as in making vigorous opposition to Socialist ideas seem discreditable, contemptible, unintelligent. The fashion dies hard and even now there are some who do the Tory cause great harm by their "blimpish" speeches. It is not so much what they are trying to say, for that may well be a compound of truths, but the way they say it: the particular words they use, forever tainted in our minds; the manner of speech, also, in the intonations peculiar to a class of politician condemned to certain ridicule by the parodists and satirists of the Socialist revolution. It may be that the next generation will accept these sentiments at their face value and will not find them contaminated and corrupted by associations from the past. But for us, when a Tory politician stands on a platform and talks about the "Empah" then reason flees and we are possessed again by a childhood image of a Tory, stiff-necked and stiff-brained. We do not need to be told how irrational this may be; the reaction is an amalgam of envy, contempt and second-generation bitterness; but it is a political fact.

In the spring of 1952, I thought much about emigrating to Canada. My wife, my daughter, then aged three, and I went through all the necessary medical examinations. Letters passed to and fro between England and Canada, as I sought the advice of friends out there and tried to get a definite promise of a job before leaving this country. In the end we abandoned the idea, not because the opportunity of Canada suddenly staled—I had seen enough of it during the war and again with Lord Beaverbrook to make me like the country and to know the possibilities of expansion—and not because the thoughts which had driven us towards emigration had altered; but finally for the simple bread-and-butter reason that I had not enough money to secure us there while finding a job. By now it had been made clear to me that journalists were not among the most highly valued members of the community and jobs were not easy to get on newspapers even for someone from Fleet Street. Most Canadian journalists dreamed of getting jobs in New York or even London. I was told I would be able to make a living out there and probably quite soon a good one, but only if I made my mind up that "selling" was the thing to do. I tried to be honest with myself and I realized that my training had not equipped me for the role of salesman; Oxford had corrupted any such straightforward, acquisitive instincts in me. I decided that I was the peculiar kind of parasite Canada could not yet afford to keep in the way to which he would like to be accustomed. The flesh was willing but the spirit was weak.

I left Canada to others with more courage than I and with temperaments more adaptable to the business of selling oil, or motor cars, or vacuum cleaners, or advertising, or insurance. The feelings which drove me to consider emigration and drove others of my generation all the way to new countries were commonly experienced. They persist still, although in my own instance I have found new ways of ignoring them and finding satisfaction in my own country. Frequently enough the impulse to emigrate is accompanied by a feeling that Britain is "finished," that it is subject to an inevitable, if gradual, decline of power and prosperity. The arguments brought forward to sustain this feeling are rarely, if ever, convincing. That idea comes after more complex ones, as a rationalization, a self-justification for emigration.

At the root of the discontent was a paradox of the social revolution. Socialism had fought for some fifty years to achieve a redistribution of income, a fairer share-out of the good things in life, in brief, to see that the sons had a better time of it than the fathers. This was the motive-power behind the working-class revolutionaries and the same ends were desired by the more well-to-do revolutionaries as a means of expiating their sense of guilt. Greater opportunities were demanded for the sons of poor men to enjoy a rich man's education; security from financial anxiety as well as assurance of the best possible treatment were demanded for the sick; an equal chance for the lad from the back streets to compete for success in the professions and for public office; guarantees that the weak should not be driven to the wall, but protected and cosseted by society in the hour of misfortune. These and numerous other aims impelled the revolutionaries of old. They were rebelling against the ancient acceptance of the idea that the few should enjoy luxury while the many knew only squalor and misery.

Inevitably the achievement of these aims meant changing the structure of society and meant also, although it was not realized in the heat of battle, destroying much that was good and valuable. But the revolt grew in strength until it commanded the support of the majority in Britain. This was the triumph of Laski, the Left Book Club, the *New Statesman*, of unemployment and of war. The Socialist state was peacefully evolved. But when victory came to the jubilation of the majority, including the young Servicemen like myself whether we had a vote or not, it was impossible to see what success would really mean. It was not until we had been living in the Socialist state for some three or four years—an imperfect realization of the ideal, but nevertheless fulfilling many of the most desirable conditions—that we began to appreciate what had really happened. Even now, after the Tories have been in power for more than four years, the situation is still fundamentally the same, a situation which grieves great numbers of us.

The terrible truth seems to be that the revolutionaries, in their noble zeal to make the world a better place for their sons, in seeking to maintain the Socialist state and even, as some would still wish, to press it further towards the climax of the collectivist state, are in fact penalizing and trampling on the very people they set out to help. Those "sons of the revolution," those of us who may be considered to have derived most benefit from it, are subjected to constant repression. It is true enough that by various designs or accidents we have been given our ration of the rich man's education and given a smell of his ancient privileges. It is true that this education combined with the breaking down of old barriers, has enabled us to win our places in the professions, in the civil service, in politics. But now we are there, as someone remarked in other circumstances, where are we? Either we are classless, cut off from our roots, but not yet integrated into new environments, or else we are considered members of the vast and amorphous middle class. And it is as the latter that our fortune is most dubious.

The talent in us which has been nourished and developed with such paternal care and public expense is impeded in its efforts to find its full expression by all manner of obstacles and regulations common to the welfare state. Further, we have been dressed up in crisply-laundered white shirts and diddly suits bought on what is called genteely a "subscription scheme," but which is really the old familiar "never-never"; put behind the desks in posts of real as well as apparent responsibility; called upon, as may be our lot, to make policies affecting the future progress of the whole nation; given, in brief, the outward trappings of respectability; but at the same time treated much as though we were the enemies of the people. If the "opportunities" the revolutionaries fought to give us were to stop short at this, then one wonders whether the opportunity was worth having. The predicament of the uprooted man has been known before now, but known as an isolated peculiarity, and then the self-made man had at least the fruits of his success to console him for his removal from old friends. But the most common reward today for success achieved through legitimate,

taxable channels is to find a boot crunching firmly on one's presump-
tuous head; and the boot belongs not to a member of the aristocracy,
keeping presumption in its place, but to the Socialist state, the revolutionaries' state, the state of blessed opportunity.

And so here we are, with our degrees and our posh education, our
prideful positions in the public service, our ambitious names in print,
trying to get on with the work brought home in the bulging brief-case,
while the baby cries in the next room or even in the same room, or
while the mortgage slowly and respectably strangles the life, the love,
the adventure and the talent out of us. This could turn into a tale of
self-pity. But we are the sons of our fathers and we have no intention
of sploshing around in self-pity. Whether they know it or not, and I
fancy they do not, the revolutionaries have bred a generation of
counter-revolutionaries. Some of us will revolt by clearing out of the
country altogether; some may, through expiration of hope, voluntarily
twist that cord a little tighter round their necks, seeking their last
demonstration of education in the delights of masochism; others among
us will search for ways to express our rebellion.

Beaverbrook looked for his rebels among the young men of Socialism; he should look for them today among those in revolt against
the doctrines of equalitarianism carried to such a degree that the
harder you work the more shall you suffer the penalties of repression.
It is not that we want to undo all the good that has been done, to
wreck the welfare state, to let the jungle grow again. Any party which
dared to project a policy calculated to bring about that return of unemployment some clinical economists claim is necessary for economic
health may confidently expect to be thrown out on its neck. We are
looking for a way in which humanitarian instincts may be combined
with the encouragement of ambition, that hard work and talent may
receive its proportionate reward, that old and injurious industrial prejudices may be discarded to make room for those new concepts of
modern society which alone can ensure not merely Britain's survival,
but the common advancement of her people. For the moment it is to
the Tories, a potentially young and vigorous party, that many of these
new rebels look. When I became editor of *Truth* in May, 1954, I
wanted to make an old weekly paper into one fitted for the present
day; I wanted also to gather around me minds like my own, pursuing
a policy aimed at injecting into the Tory Party as a whole what already

existed in one section of it, an urge towards new, creative, imaginative thinking, searching for a programme that would release those energies, now dammed by regulation and high taxation, into creative channels, to provide the country with that coherent lead it needed so badly if Britain were not to be symbolized by the professional man coming home in the Tube at night with his tired face and his future fading behind him. The "rebels" are still fighting. But their doubts about the Conservative Party are growing. After a promising start when they seemed capable of throwing away old ideas and of recognizing that post-war Britain could not be governed according to antiquated formulae, the Tories appear to have regressed. There is, once again, in the selection of candidates and the appointing of Ministers, an alarming tendency to examine only a man's tie, his ancestry and his bank balance. Further, at the time of writing, they seem to be as bankrupt of those new ideas needed to tackle wholly new problems as Socialists who still talk of class-warfare and of Workers versus the Boss. If the Tories continue along this path of reaction and general ineptitude they can look forward to a mass desertion from their ranks of people like me whose attachment to them is temporary and entirely conditional upon their exemplary behaviour.

*   *   *

Few of us can afford the luxury of concerning ourselves with what may happen in the long run. Yet the history of mankind should provide a sense of proportion with which to confront present problems. It is true of course that we have now provided ourselves with the means of universal self-destruction. It is also true that for all his graces civilized man until now has not been able to resist the temptation to war. But if we have come a long way from the bow and arrow in finding ways of killing each other it is no less true that we have come just as far in finding ways of feeding and housing men and generally keeping them alive. Similarly, if we have devised more and more fiendish means of subverting the will and liberty of man we have also shown we permit him a greater personal responsibility than ever before. Man has survived to dominate the earth by his superior capacity to adapt himself to his environment. If we are to survive yet and to improve the general lot we must be ready to adapt ourselves still further. We should not expect to come to J. B. Priestley's promised

City in the next two or three thousand years, but neither should we resign ourselves to extinction in Orwell's *1984*, nor yet to a world built by the Admassites.

In one of his "Thoughts in the Wilderness," Priestley asked:

> Where, in the Madame Tussaud's of the national conscious-ness, are the men of letters? Or, for that matter, the other kind of creative artists? Name ten, widely known and highly re-garded, under fifty years of age. Who and where are the mas-sive talents, the towering personalities, the men of genius? Who represents us abroad as we ought to be represented—by the English mind blazing with art and throwing a light on the world we all share—and not by the assistant secretary to the De-partment of Drains, the vice-chairman of the Busybodies Asso-ciation, the Secretary of the Society of Stuffed Shirts?

Priestley's rhetorical questions are justly framed, although I seem to detect a sulky hint that Priestley's own massive talents have not been properly honoured! I should like to answer him with an impassioned, documented defence of my contemporaries, but all I could do is to reply to Priestley as others have tried to do—by laughing at the sight of him on his tired old hobby-horses again. That would be no answer. In my early days at *Truth* in 1953 I told my readers in general, and Messrs. Spender and Lehmann in particular, that we were witnessing a renaissance of English writing. And so I thought sincerely enough in the fever of the journalistic moment. But it seems to me now that not only do our few swallows not make a summer but they don't even make a timid spring. Of course there is a lot of writing going on again, a quantity of production whose merit was exaggerated in the delight one felt that we were not in a permanent coma after all. None will deny us competence; but as for "massive talents" or minds "blazing with art," well . . . There is a deal of writing about our own time such as the old men cannot produce. So far, so good, but never very good.

For one thing, none of our writers has been able to detach himself sufficiently from the obsessive particulars of personal experience to give us a long-shot of contemporary life. There is much good, sensitive reporting, but the camera is held much too close to the subject matter. Then there is the pervasive scepticism; a phrase like Priestley's "the English mind blazing with art," provokes not only a suspicion of the phoney, it makes us uncomfortable. The escape from discomfort is ridicule. Instead of minds blazing with art there is the Arts Council coking with coy benevolence. By and large it is true, and certainly of our prose, that we have left behind the obscurities and the wilful experiments of earlier generations. Our poets, too, strive for a greater directness, seeking simplicity of expression even if it is too rarely achieved; their work shows an economy which any professional writer ought to commend. But, apart from the few who brazenly appear in public with a romantic flush, the mood is still intolerant of the lushly emotional, the pretentious, the arty-crafty.

The critical disciples of Dr. Leavis, the clinical minds, the tough boys whose kindred characteristics earned them a corporate label of "The Movement," have reaped the rewards of being first in the post-war field. The rest of us were glad enough to see some of our own age nosing their way into fame at last. When John Wain, Kingsley Amis and Iris Murdoch produced, within a short time of each other, their comic novels with striking similarities of attitude and purpose (or lack of it) they were quickly lumped together. On the basis of the work they have published so far Amis seems to me to possess the most genuinely creative talent. He has an acute awareness of comedy in situation and in his second novel, *That Uncertain Feeling*, he showed signs of a capacity for emotional sympathy which may lead him on to much better work. Yet, after the first warm pleasures at the idiocies of *Lucky Jim*, what are we to make of the farcical, schoolboy slapstick of much of his comedy? The humour is often at the level of the boy who throws a firework through someone's letter-box and runs away. Amis showed perception and deep sensitivity in his portrayal of the married relations of a young couple in the present day; he also showed, like Wain, that he must find his comedy not in the everyday but in ribald fantasy. It is difficult to ennoble their humour as "satire"; it has no firm basis, no coherent direction; it is undiscriminating buffoonery and it is in danger of resembling the would-be clown who does not recognize when people have had enough of his grotesque antics. The farcical situations—the hero who burns a hole in his hostess's bedclothes, who gets himself involved in amatory complications as unlikely and absurd in their development as any situation created by Goldsmith or Sheridan—quickly become predictable, then tedious in their repetition.

These novelists' resort to the stock figure of the adolescent imagination, the society nymphomaniac who has the power to aid the hero's ambition as well as gobble him up, suggests both a limit to their inventive powers and also a failure to create credible, normal women who can perform the same function of exposing the hero's weaknesses and provide dramatic contrast with the romantic vision of the "nice girl" who is left behind with the kids. Amis, at any rate, showed in *That Uncertain Feeling* he has no need to rely on such crude inventions to achieve his purposes.

The Movement's heroes are forever running away from some largely imaginary mess, seeking escape in the *graffiti* of their private thoughts. More surprising is the way in which Wain, Amis and Murdoch provide solutions through the intervention of a *deus ex machina* in the shape of a millionaire. Now for "tough" boys and girls who are supposed to despise "success" just as much as they do welfare statism and arty-craftyness it is remarkable to find them giving exemption to the millionaire. Surely their comprehensive derision of modern society should not exclude the man who must contain for them, in most extreme form, all those qualities of commercial thuggery they are supposed to be "agin." And, just to be unpardonably prosaic, I do wonder just how many benign millionaires there are strolling around and whether the Movement novelists are not extending their comic licence just a bit too far in imagining such a convenient multiplicity of them. I have known only one man who seemed to collect millionaires as an accidental hobby. But then he often had to leave Britain to bump into them.

They are always running away. . . . The elderly critics of the Movement quickly spotted this escapism, this social nihilism. The French with their novels of *engagement* scorn this failure to become "involved." If ridicule—or fear—of respectability, success, idealism, welfare statism, do-goodism, is not pointing positively towards creative sterility, it is sure to inhibit any writing on a large scale. We laugh at these novels, these snooks cocked at our contemporary situation; but dare we look back at the history of the novel and offer them up for comparison? What are they but cave-paintings or the first pictures hung so proudly on the schoolroom wall by one's children compared with the work of Tolstoy, Dostoevsky, Turgenev or Henry James? The list of greatness behind us could be extended to encompass all manner of achievement and experiment, but only to the further humiliation of contemporary novels. If such novels are indeed contemporary, in the attitude of mind they express if not always in realistic portraiture, what are we to conclude? We must grant J. B. Priestley his rhetorical questions. We can show him no fiery genius, no blinding vision, no hope that our creative artists will show their fellows the way out of the mess. But we can add a "not yet at any rate" in self-defence.

KINGSLEY AMIS

Socialism and the Intellectuals

A political tract which eschews politics, an expression of "left-wing sympathies" which stops just short of
knocking "at the door of the local
Labour party headquarters," Kingsley
Amis's Socialism and the Intellectuals
has become one of the classic statements of the Angry Young Men. In
it Amis examines the fallacy of such
writers as Auden, Spender, Isherwood and Orwell in establishing a
political base for their thought and
art. He concludes that the intellectual's involvement in politics is inevitably romantic and unconstructive,
and that the only satisfactory political
motive is self-interest.

I

AS WILL SOON BECOME obvious from what I
have to say, I am not a politician, nor am I specially well-
informed about politics. Since most people who write political pamphlets are usually one or the other, this at any
rate will make a change. I read and argue and even sometimes try to think about politics, but I speak with no authority. And I must explain at once that the views I shall
express are very far from being the views of the Fabian
Society. In fact this essay is a tarted-up version of a talk
given to a weekend school, in which my purpose was, if

nothing else, to draw as few hear-hears as possible. In this, if in nothing else, I succeeded. Many of my arguments are likely to be weari-
somely familiar, and any possible interest they hold may well be only
that someone like me is advancing them, that I can give some sort of
low-down on the political character of—how shall I describe myself?
As an elderly young intellectual, perhaps, with connections in the
educational and literary worlds and with left-wing sympathies.

I will begin by explaining how I fit into the class set-up. My father
is an office worker, and I grew up in a modest but comfortable lower-
middle-class home in the London suburbs. I was a scholarship boy at a
large London day school and, also on a scholarship, studied English at
one of the less pretentious Oxford colleges. There I went through the
callow marxist phase that seemed almost compulsory for my generation. Next came the Army, which clears the mind wonderfully. In
1945 I voted Labour by proxy, and have voted Labour at all three
general elections since, as well as in all local elections. I feel that
unless something very unexpected happens I shall vote Labour to the
end of my days, however depraved the Labour candidate may be and
however virtuous his opponent.

These things being so, I often ask myself why I belong to no political organisation, except the Association of University Teachers, one
of the smallest trade unions, if that is the right term, in the country.
Admittedly, I have a poster in my front window at election-time, when
I also lend my car to the local party—but why don't I belong to it, why
don't I go out canvassing like many of my academic acquaintances
(including at least one professor of philosophy)? I hope that some sort
of answer to these questions will emerge as I proceed.

I want next to make a few distinctions and definitions. I take as my
general field of reference the middle-class intellectual, using the
phrase in a pretty wide sense. One could reel off a fairly long list of
the occupations pursued by the kind of people I am discussing, and
this may be helpful in attaining some sort of precision. I mean occupations like those of university, college and school teachers, perhaps the
lower ranks of the civil service, journalists, industrial scientists, li-
brarians, G.P.'s, some of the clergy (predominantly the non-conformist
sects?), and the various brands of literary and artistic, or arty, intellectual. This is by no means an exhaustive list, but it may serve as a
guide. Obviously there will be sub-divisions among these people as

far as their political attitude is concerned, and these divisions may be associated with the lines of demarcation between their various occupations. I think they often are so associated.

THE ACADEMICS

I am going to refer first to a small but important sub-group which I mentioned earlier: the academics. The decline in political activity among intellectuals as a whole must, I think, be taken as a fact in the perspective of the last twenty years, and it is particularly noticeable among our younger novelists and poets. But it does not apply nearly so strongly, in my observation, to academic people. Leaving out the apathetics, whom one might expect to find anyway in the senior common room of a university, we might divide this sub-group into two. The first I could label at once as roughly the sociological academics. They are, of course, comparatively few in number, at the most 5 per cent of college staffs, but for our present purposes they are of particular interest.

To start with, this type of academic tends to be strongly political and as a rule strongly anti-communist. They mostly adhere to the left wing of the Labour Party, although there is a Liberal fraction which is surprisingly, and rather disconcertingly, influential. But Labour and Liberal alike they are active: they work in the local parties between as well as during election campaigns and, for what it is worth, they do a good deal in the lower ranks of the Association of University Teachers. This means, of course, that they are much stronger than their mere numbers would suggest. When I called them "sociological" I meant that they are made up of economists, social scientists, statisticians and the like, and I detect somewhere in the background the sinister hand of the London School of Economics.

But it is not only the reasonably high-powered sociological expert who is concerned here. I wonder whether perhaps such people round about the universities are at all paralleled by similar people outside: social workers, probation officers and so on, though I do not know about this. At any rate, it is in this general direction that we would do well to look when we try to find the sort of person who may help the Labour Party to "re-think," to revise its attitude to the problems of socialism, and I should like to think that the party planners were bearing them in mind. Their potential contribution is large.

MILITANCY AND REALISM

In a place like Swansea, at least, the sociological academic has the chance of working on the rather vague inherited socialism (or radicalism) which many of the students display—it is militant in *attitude* though often not much else—and might help to turn it into something a little better informed. But the great quality of this kind of academic for my purpose is that he is realistic, not romantic: a point to which I shall return later. For the moment I should just like to suggest that this realism can have a short-run effect damaging to Labour interests. I have talked to sociologists who are disturbed about what they regard as the mass-production of welfare schemes, especially in housing. It is felt that these are sometimes applied with too little regard for individual preferences; a kind of blanket of welfare descends indiscriminately. Making a fuss about such things will obviously benefit Labour in the long run, but that day is not yet.

The second of my two academic categories is less definite and less interesting in this connection. They are the people on the fringe of a political party or just inside it, and I should guess that they are pretty equally divided between the two main parties, though there are a few outlandishly left-wing and militant characters here, including my professor-of-philosophy friend. I mention this category only to say that whatever side they may be on they too are not romantic, they are comparatively undeluded. This I think depends simply on having a settled job which, however tenuously, does bring them into contact with reality. From this point of view, as from others, the student is the lifeblood of his teacher.

II

I turn now to a different group, though it has connections with the academic group, especially since the war. I refer to what might be called the intellectual pure and simple (if these terms are appropriate): I mean the literary and arty man, the writer in the widest sense, the critic, the journalist, the self-employed intelligentsia if you like. It is often said that in the Thirties we had a predominantly left-wing intelligentsia, but now it's right-wing if it's anything—and often it isn't anything. For this purpose the Thirties can be stretched on until about

1945. I remember an acquaintance of mine at that period indignantly asserting his working-class background to an audience of sceptical ex-grammar school boys. It was discovered too late that this chap had been to school at Haileybury or somewhere, and his father owned half the Midlands. (This incident was a kind of ludicrous capsule parody of the career of George Orwell, a very significant witness in the case we are discussing.)

THE SELF-EMPLOYED INTELLIGENTSIA

You can see, anyway, that at the time I am speaking of it was the "done" thing to be inclined to the left. A man who was not, and further was not active in the movement, was often regarded with much the same mixture of contempt and unbelief as nowadays, I am told, greets the Oxford undergraduate who wants to be in the swim but fails to go to church. A fascinating paper could be written on that particular shift of fashion, and its conclusion would tell us a lot about the real value of such middle-class progressive sentiment. In the Thirties then we had Mr. W. H. Auden, the idol of the young, talking about the glories of working for the overthrow of capitalism by force. The great point is that it was not only politically desirable, it was also a form of spiritual salvation.

> To think no thought but ours
> To hunger, work illegally,
> And be anonymous.

In Auden's wake we had not only a group of lesser writers but the hopes and aspirations, to coin a phrase, of hundreds of young intellectuals who perhaps could hardly hold a pen but who found, when the Spanish war came along, that they could manage to hold a rifle. This readiness to face death in pursuit of their principles is obviously much to the credit of the young men of the Thirties, and I think this is much too often forgotten today. It is too easy to laugh at them in retrospect, especially if one is a comfortably-off right-wing journalist who knows quite well that whatever happens he won't get his hands dirty. (Not that I myself would fancy getting mine dirty if it meant the chance of being killed.) But there are other things about this group which do link them with the intelligentsia of the Fifties.

ATTITUDES IN THE THIRTIES

The first point is that although the political colouring in the work of writers like Auden, Spender, Day Lewis and so on was widespread, it was not the only form of colouring, and it did not go at all deep. Even in a comparatively straightforward political play like *The Dog Beneath the Skin* the actual political content, even the anti-fascist content, is very small. It is jostled by a whole lot of other interests, in which the desire to shock the *bourgeoisie* was important. And that *bourgeoisie* which Auden and his friends were so interested in ridiculing and denouncing was the *bourgeoisie* of Flaubert rather than that of Marx, from whom they merely borrowed a few technical-sounding terms to use about it.

In some ways these people were only conducting in public a personal vendetta against their parents (see *The Ascent of F6*) and one or two unsympathetic headmasters. This notion of political writing and other activity as a kind of self-administered therapy for personal difficulties rather than as a contribution towards the reform of society—this I think is an important key to the whole intellectual approach to politics, not just to that of the Thirties. Indeed I sometimes think that the whole middle stratum of Britain, not just the intelligentsia, chooses its politics by temperament only. Loving what is established and customary pulls you to the right: hating it pulls you to the left. And behind that again lies perhaps your relations with your parents: your family environment can seem a warm nest, or it can seem, in Isherwood's phrase, "the enormous bat-shadow of home," something to be fled from and rebelled against. But this is speculation.

MARXISM AND WHAT IT MEANT

I should like now to look a little more closely at the marxist element in the thought of these intellectuals of the Thirties. My own experience at the university in 1941–2—at the tail-end of the movement—suggests to me that of several possible ways of distinguishing between the marxist and the non-marxist, one is especially interesting from our viewpoint. The marxist wing included a strong faction of the more specifically literary and artistic intellectual which did not appear to the same degree in the democratic-socialist wing: a budding schoolmaster, let us say, was far less likely to be a marxist than a budding poet was. The same sort of thing held true, I feel, in the world outside the university. The actual amount of knowledge of marxism, and in particular of what it meant when applied in practical politics, was, as I have said, very small indeed.

This lack of knowledge—or this refusal to recognise what was plainly evident—can be seen in another significant example from Auden, a stanza from his poem *Spain 1937*:

> To-day the deliberate increase in the chances of death,
>   The conscious acceptance of guilt in the necessary murder;
>   To-day the expending of powers
>   On the flat ephemeral pamphlet and the boring meeting.*

George Orwell has an interesting and highly characteristic comment on this, less known than it might be because it occurs for some reason in his essay on Henry Miller. Orwell says:

> The stanza is intended as a sort of thumb-nail sketch in the life of a "good party man." In the morning a couple of political murders, a ten-minute interval to stifle "bourgeois" remorse, and then a hurried luncheon and a busy afternoon and evening chalking walls and distributing leaflets. All very edifying. But notice the phrase "necessary murder." It could only be written by a person to whom murder is at most a *word*. Mr. Auden's brand of amoralism is only possible if you are the kind of person who is always somewhere else when the trigger is pulled. So much of left-wing thought is a kind of playing with fire by people who do not even know that fire is hot.

We have now reached the point where I can connect the Auden outlook both with the intellectual climate of the Fifties and with what I was saying earlier about romanticism. To Orwell, what Auden and his various allies were doing and saying was wicked; if not deliberately so, then wicked out of a kind of criminal folly. Folly it no doubt was;

---

* This is the stanza as Orwell quotes it. All the texts I have seen read "the *inevitable* increase" and the "*fact of* murder." It would be unlike Orwell to misquote, and my assumption is that in this extract he has preserved an earlier reading, afterwards touched up by Auden to give it a less ruthless implication. I have not been able to consult the first edition of the poem.

but we have to remember that a few dozen intellectuals of the Auden school, if no more, had been to Spain at the time when Orwell was writing and had certainly got to know that fire is hot. Mr. Auden was not I think present in person on that occasion; Orwell was. But my point here is that it is getting the emphasis wrong to denounce the pre-1940 intellectual as wicked. What you had there, I think, was a quality as characteristic of the Fifties intellectual as of his predecessor in the Thirties: romanticism.

III

Romanticism in a political context I would define as an irrational capacity to become inflamed by interests and causes that are not one's own, that are outside oneself. If this sounds hostile or bad-tempered, I had better say at once that I see myself as a sufferer from political romanticism just as much as the next man. Anyway, by his station in society the member of the intelligentsia really has no political interests to defend, except the very general one (the one he most often forgets) of not finding himself bossed around by a totalitarian government. But compared with, say, a steelworker or a banker he is politically in a void. Furthermore, he belongs to no social group which might lend him stability; his only group is the intelligentsia itself, where stability is associated mainly with alcoholic coma. In these circumstances our intellectual shops around for a group and for a cause to get excited about.

POLITICAL ROMANTICISM

At some periods these things are readily available: Spain and its committees, Abyssinia, unemployment, the rise of Fascism and so on. (I shall have something to say later about Hungary and Suez.) The Communist solution to such problems has at least two well-known attractions. First, it offers certainty in the baffling flux not only of politics but of life in general. And the intellectual, although presumably trained to look for truth, has recently shown a paradoxical preference for certainty. This, obviously enough, is the link between marxism and that other system of answers to all the intellectual's questions, dogmatic Christianity. Marxism, however, has a second attraction not offered by the Church: it involves violence. Violence has a good deal of charm for some sections of the intelligentsia (as the cult of bullfighting shows), or at any rate the thought of violence is attractive. It provides a way of getting one's own back by proxy on one's parents and one's old headmaster; one can work off the guilt of having been to a public school and so on by chatting about blowing up the class one was born into; one can compensate with some dash for one's thwarted desire for power, which is often obsessive in these circles. Quite soon it becomes natural to write airily about political murders and read about them with appreciation.

We were nicely fixed up, the romantics might say, in 1937; but what about 1957? When we shop around for an outlet we find there is nothing in stock: no Spain, no Fascism, no mass unemployment. (No Hungary? I should not like to venture a prediction.) We still read the good old *New Statesman* regularly, but we never find enough in it about Mr. Bevan, the one man with the touch of violence that will appeal to us. Mr. Gaitskell is running the show now, and he isn't violent, in fact—despite a pretty good effort over Suez—not at all the sort of man one expects to see at the head of a Labour Party. (I would not be understood, by the way, as disagreeing with all points in the romantic case.) Did somebody mention *Tribune?* But, my dear, the book reviews are perfectly appalling. Perhaps politics is a thing that only the unsophisticated can really go for.

WHAT ARE WE TO DO?

So what on earth, the complaint might continue, are we to do? We can show how wrong the Thirties people were by turning right round and fanatically hating the Russians instead. We can buy *The European* and listen to Sir Oswald Mosley and his little friends telling us what we've been missing all these years. Or we can join the Church. Apart from giving us authoritative answers to all our problems, it gives us a sense of tradition. This is extra comforting at a time when everyone, from Dr. Leavis at Cambridge to Mr. Priestley in *Reynolds News*, is saying that our values are perishing before the New Barbarism—which used to mean Hitlerism, but now it means the Welfare State and commercial television.

The Welfare State, indeed, is notoriously unpopular with intellectuals. It was all very well to press for higher working-class wages in the old days, but now that the wages have risen the picture is less

attractive; why, some of them are actually better off than we are ourselves. We never contemplated *that*. And now the Labour Party have
the confounded cheek to press for more equality still. They are out to
make everyone the same, you see. Levelling down. The Tories were
right after all. (The argument that equal incomes, and/or the de-
struction of the class system, would turn everyone into replicas of
everyone else is an interesting one, and although totally erroneous—
as can at once be seen by noting the wild range of idiosyncrasy in
even a homogeneous environment like a senior common room—it is
nevertheless extremely widespread.)

IV

The foregoing is, of course, an exaggerated portrait, but if you will
not meet one man who corresponds to all of it, you would meet many
to whom a fair-sized fraction is applicable. What I have said is at any
rate strikingly different from the account given by Orwell in his long
series of denunciations of the British intellectual, which culminated,
of course, in *Nineteen Eighty-Four*. I take this as a political pamphlet
with a warning about totalitarianism addressed to the intelligentsia.
Orwell was in fact warning the late Forties of something that had already been averted in the late Thirties, for he had not noticed the huge
revision of feeling and opinion that began in 1940. He was a sick man;
he had also completed his long-impending development into a hysterical neurotic with a monomania about the depravity of British
intellectuals. For him there could be no changes. I doubt if he ever
recovered from the experience, brilliantly retailed in his *Homage to
Catalonia*, of seeing how Communists can treat their allies when
"necessity" demands. After that he must concentrate on warning, on
denouncing, on stopping the rot in Britain.

This development in Orwell has had some curious consequences. Of
all the writers who appeal to the post-war intelligentsia, he is far and
away the most potent. Apart from incessantly hearing his name
spoken, we can hardly pass a month without reading an article on him.
I seem to have counted no less than three critical biographies of him.
At least one more is, I believe, on the way. In many ways this is encouraging. No modern writer has his air of passionately believing what
he has to say and of being passionately determined to say it as force-

fully and simply as possible. Most passionately he believed that left-wing politics are a trap for what I have called the political romantic; so passionately, indeed, that the trap becomes a trap and nothing else. Orwell's insistence that the political game *can* be dirty and dishonest and treacherous, that it *often* is, betrays him into implying that it *must* be a dirty game, that it *always* is. And his warnings were always delivered at the top of his voice.

GEORGE ORWELL AND CLASS-CONSCIOUSNESS

In another way Orwell cut at the root of things by his famous attempt to stop being a typical middle-class intellectual and to start being a member of the working class. Hence his perfectly voluntary spell as a down-and-out and such painful tricks as his habit of sucking his tea noisily out of the saucer—which few workmen would take as a gesture of solidarity, I imagine. Changing one's class *downwards* is more difficult than changing one's sex, and we really have Orwell to thank for demonstrating this. After reading him, the only influential writer of his generation to have an honest shot at it, no romantic could believe that "identification with the working classes" was anything but a mug's game.

I may have shown a certain animus towards Orwell, and I have not had occasion to do more than mention some of his many fine qualities. But animus remains, and the reason for it is this. He was the man above all others who was qualified to become the candid friend the Labour party needed so much in the years after 1945. But what he did was to become a right-wing propagandist by negation, or at any rate a supremely powerful—though unconscious—advocate of political quietism. Had he lived to see the Fifties he might have realised this, but I rather doubt it. In his own highly individual way he was, I suspect, a romantic like the rest, and that "indifference to reality" which he so cogently attributes to the intellectual's interest in politics was a leading characteristic of his own tortured prophecies.

V

It would be unfair, and also perhaps rather unconvincing, to blame Orwell alone for the present political apathy of the intelligentsia, though I do think him important. I should say that Mr. Arthur Koestler, whose name might be coupled with his in this connection, has exerted far less of a pull. *Darkness at Noon* was undoubtedly an important anti-Soviet novel, but our intellectual, however excessively internationalist he may be in his literary tastes, can still be insular enough to feel that British politics are too special ever to be properly understood by a foreigner. The fact that Mr. Koestler has been a continental socialist thus works against him instead of for him. This may well be far too facile an explanation, but the relative standing I have assigned to these two jeremiahs, is not, I think, far out.

CAUSES OF APATHY

What are the other causes of apathy? Some have been often enough rehearsed as explanations of left-wing apathy in general, but one or two of them apply with a different emphasis in our field. The widespread loss of confidence in Russia, which Mr. Crossman has mentioned as pushing the independent voter away from the left, comes in with special force here. Some extreme romantics, it is true, could still (until very recently anyway) acclaim Russia as a cultural wonderland even after going behind the Iron Curtain, and some months ago I spent a stimulating evening with a marxist friend who described to me the touching scene he claimed to have witnessed in rural Czechoslovakia, with peasants playing a social-realist pastoral on their pipes while the local party member—the only one in the province, apparently—looked on with a benign smile. To anyone who can believe this, the events in Hungary may well seem the outcome of a Western plot.

But apart from the lunatic fringe, who must I think have ceased to become recruited to Communism after about 1940, Russia's spiritual defection seems taken for granted. This has had the agreeable effect of stifling some of the flatulence of parlour marxism, but it has also had the corresponding effect of closing one of the traditional golden gates into the Labour Movement. It has always been an intellectual axiom that Britain is half-dead, and if there is no rallying-point abroad, some people are going to do no rallying at all. It would not occur to them that the Welfare State is worth rallying to.

At home, indeed, very few causes offer themselves to the cruising rebel. No more millions out of work, no more hunger-marches, no more strikes; none at least that the rebel can take an interest in, when the strike pay-packet is likely to be as much as he gets himself for a review of Evelyn Waugh or a talk about basset-horns on the Third Programme—so he imagines, at any rate. One can "identify" oneself with a miner who washes in front of the kitchen fire and is paid something under the national average. It is less easy in the days of pit-head baths and £20 a week—of course only a minority pull in as much as that, but that escapes notice in romantic circles, in the same way as a few hundred thousand unemployed are too few to get noticed. Your intellectual has never been the man for subtleties of this sort; it is the broad picture he cares about; and indeed to be fair to him for a change, it is hard at the moment to quarrel with that view of the broad picture; individual hardship—hardship for one person in thirty or forty, say— but general prosperity, however unequally it may be distributed.

THE DIRECTION OF A CHANGE

Another matter which weighs against the left is the vague and *sotto voce*, but fairly general, disquiet about the direction in which our society (and the Labour party) is moving, insofar as a direction can be discerned. There is some uneasiness, for example, about nationalisation, or about the Labour party's form of it; it is felt that there are monopolistic tendencies, that workers are finding it harder to change their jobs than they should, that power-hunters and organisation-maniacs are coming into their own. Now I don't know whether these fears are justified or not, and if they are they may well be laid to rest by the "new look" which Labour is devising for nationalism, though it will be long before the influence of this can be felt. But, I will repeat, for our purposes it matters very little whether or not the fears I have mentioned are justified: the intelligentsia—and once more I include myself—doesn't understand economics and it doesn't work in the nationalised industries.

These feelings are only feelings, and they may well be only the result of successful right-wing propaganda; but they are there just the same. I think in fact that the younger Tories have been pretty astute in this department. People like the late political commentator of the *Spectator*, Mr. Charles Curran—who I may say stirs my emotions as they have not been stirred for many a long year—have made a very good thing out of the technique of the advertising copy-writer whereby the effect you want to produce is stated as a fact: compare "The in-

telligent modern hostess buys Higgens's soups" and "The Unions have
long rejected the Socialist solution."

NON-POLITICAL ISSUES

To resume: it is worth noticing that the issues which will attract our
contemporary romantic are non-political ones, or ones that are not in
the first place political: the colour bar, horror-comics, juvenile delinquency, the abolition of capital punishment, the reform of the laws
relating to divorce and homosexuality. It may be in place to say a little
more about this last one. One feels that a progressive party should
have this reform on its programme, but to adopt it in an election campaign, which would undoubtedly attract many romantics, would be
likely to have the opposite effect on the rank and file. I cannot see
myself explaining, to an audience of dockers, say, just why homosexual relations between consenting adults should be freed from legal
penalty. It is a truism, but in the ways of truisms a most important fact,
that what will appeal to the romantic, with his emotional substitute
for political interests, will alienate the ordinary party man. And, as I
suggested in my remarks about equality at the end of Section 3, the
converse is just as true.

We see this clash of attitudes clearly over the question of relations
with undeveloped territories. Here the romantic is surely right in
agreeing that if the British working man has climbed up to some sort
of prosperity, then his next job, a vital one, is to pull the African and
Asian worker up the ladder after him. But if a new steel-mill is to go
up at either Calcutta or Llanelly there are obviously not going to be
many interested parties in Britain who will insist it must go up at
Calcutta. The romantic will, if he hears about it and gets a chance of
insisting, but it's easy for him: he isn't an interested party.

Until very recently there has really been only one political issue of
anything like the same proportions and of the same kind as the
Abyssinias and the Spains of the Thirties: I mean, of course, Cyprus.
Here at any rate is something which potentially unites the romantic
with the practical man. But what gets done about it? Compare what
does get done about it with what would have got done about it in the
Thirties. In my innocence I asked one of my Labour party sociological
friends why there weren't protest meetings all over the place, why

people weren't organising something. "We run meetings all right," he said, "but nobody turns up. Have you ever tried protesting to an empty hall?"

SUEZ AND HUNGARY

But now—I am writing just three weeks after the Russian assault on Hungary and the Anglo-Franco-Israeli assault on Egypt—we have a couple of first-class political issues confronting us. The intellectuals have been up in arms, protesting, helping to pass resolutions, sending letters and telegrams, even demonstrating. It is too early to say what long-term effect, if any, the Hungarian and Egyptian crises will have on the behaviour of our romantics, but I imagine (hoping to be proved wrong) that such effect will be slight. If the crises settle down quickly, as at the moment they show signs of doing, they will soon slip the minds of most people, intellectuals and non-intellectuals alike. What is needed is a good, long, steadily-worsening crisis out in the open where everyone can see it. The events likely to follow upon the oil shortage are from this point of view very "promising," as a marxist might put it.

On the whole, though, politics have become, and seem all too likely to remain, unromantic. When the immediate excitement of a demonstration is over, they quickly fall away into Auden's flat ephemeral pamphlet (no rudeness, please) and boring meeting. And while we are on boring meetings, let me complain as savagely as possible about the local Labour party meeting on Suez which, breaking a habit of nearly fifteen years' standing, I went so far as to attend, vowing to join the party immediately afterwards. Within a quarter of an hour I had silently released myself from my vow. I had forgotten what political meetings were like. Out they poured from speaker after speaker, all the vile old sick-and-tired thought-savers: "I am sure I speak for all of us here when I say that we deeply deplore . . . act of wanton aggression . . . policy based on international justice . . . extend the hand of friendship . . . spirit in the country today . . . united as never before . . . go forward to victory." In my undisciplined way I could not, or anyhow did not, refrain from groaning slightly at some of this. Indignant glances were turned on me, as on a self-confessed Suez Grouper. And I saw that those who call for a war on clichés in popular political writing and speechifying are wasting their time. It is on clichés that majorities are and must be fed.

And so, as I said at the beginning, I put up my poster, lend my car, cast my vote, demonstrate once in ten years and the rest of the time fall back on chatting about politics with my friends. But it is never really honest to plead boredom and leave it at that. Obviously the reasons for mine are that I feel my security is not threatened—perhaps it really is, but no matter, it doesn't *seem* to be—or in other words I have no political interests to defend, and I have no desire for any kind of political career whatever. If I were shaken up I should act, at least I hope I should, but not until then. And what use should I be if I did?

VI

I might re-phrase that last question by asking what, if anything, the intellectual has to give to the Labour Movement. I wonder very much if he has anything. I often feel that even the intellectual who takes up some sort of political career, attains some power or influence in that field, stands a good chance of being wrong on any given issue, a rather better chance than the ordinary Labour party or trade union man. In actual relationships within party politics he will be distrusted for the middle-class habits he is likely to have, particularly his middle-class or public-school accent. It may sound absurd or ill-natured to mention this at all, but I am sure that here we have a tremendously important badge of class-difference, one which probably did more than anything else to negate Orwell's efforts to become a working man.

In the field of political theory your intellectual is likely to be a pure theorist, much too indifferent to changing conditions, not nearly empirical enough, without a quarter of the tactical sense that your trade union official will have picked up without noticing. (I am aware that this too has its dangers.) The intellectual's love of the broad picture, which I mentioned earlier, led him to tell us in the Thirties that rational methods of distribution would solve world food problems, without bothering with the tedious checking-up process which would have told him how few bellies all that burnt coffee would have filled. I should like to see this gone into in detail, for I have not the knowledge.

SELF-INTEREST—OR GUILT?

On the whole I may seem to have shown a certain amount of acrimony towards the intelligentsia, which is rather unfair, because some of my best friends are intellectuals. Nor can I ever pretend that I am not one myself. But I do sometimes feel that if, as the evidence seems to show, many of them have moved over to the right, or at least away from the left, then this is not necessarily unmixed loss to the left. These fellows represent after all only a tiny fraction of the voting strength and we can well afford to do without a great deal of their conversation. And even assuming it is desirable to entice them back I am too much too little of a politician to begin suggesting how this is to be done. All I can think of is that the obvious place to start would be, not the literary cocktail party, but the university junior common room.

There is another reason why I do not grieve overmuch at all this defection or apathy, even though any right-wing sentiment in the mouth of an intellectual (or anywhere else) is likely to annoy me. The reason is that I think the best and most trustworthy political motive is self-interest. I share a widespread suspicion of the professional espouser of causes, the do-gooder, the archetypal social worker who knows better than I do what is good for me. (The only edge the Tories have over the socialists from my point of view is that they at least are not out to do anybody any good except themselves.)

It will come as no surprise if I confess in conclusion that I feel very little inclination to go and knock at the door of the local Labour party headquarters. My only reason for doing so, apart from mere vulgar curiosity, would be a sense of guilt. And this is not enough. How agreeable it must be to have a respectable motive for being politically active.

JOHN OSBORNE

Sex and Failure*

A playwright's criticism of the work of another, writes John Osborne, will "merely tell you how he would have written the same play. He will usually manage to tell you something about himself."

In this important discussion of the contemporary dramatist who has exercised perhaps the strongest influence on his own work, the author of Look Back in Anger and The Entertainer sets forth, more clearly than anywhere else to date, his views on character, the theater and the function of the playwright in the present-day world.

*Review of Tennessee Williams's FOUR PLAYS, CAT ON A HOT TIN ROOF and BABY DOLL.

THERE ARE TOO MANY CRITICS. I have no intention of setting up in the appraisal business. A playwright should never try to make—or pretend to make—objective critical judgments on the work of another. He can't. He will merely tell you how he would have written the same play. He will usually manage to tell you something about himself. Having said this, what are my reactions to the plays of Tennessee Williams?

To ignore these plays is to ignore the world we live in. Every serious British dramatist is indebted to them. Firstly, they are a kick in the face of the common belief among playgoers in this country that suffering is some form of inferiority. They are an assault on the army of the tender-minded and tough-hearted, the emotion snobs who believe that protest is vulgar, and to be articulate is to be sorry for oneself; the milk-in-first and phleghm boys who will mine meanings from seams that fell apart years ago, but will summon up all their disengaged hostility, all their slicked-up tired old journalistic attitudes, and get into a pedantic, literal-minded flap over inessentials when they are forced to look at a slum or a bombed site (these two really seem to hurt for some reason) all the evening—or, worse, at the kind of homes millions of people have to live in.

These are the people who will tell you that Blanche Dubois is just a whore, anyway, and can't understand what all the nasty, sordid fuss is about. This is the adjustment school of criticism, who even look like packing off their own Hedda Gabler to the Marriage Guidance Clinic sometimes.

These plays are about failure. That is what makes human beings interesting. So what do they want? To give Brick a cold bath and Blanche a bromide somewhere before the first interval so that we can all go home and watch a decent, straightforward documentary about mental illness on television? Each one of these plays is an assault on this school of criticism ("Why doesn't he stop loafing about and try a good job of work?" "Why doesn't she face up to her responsibilities and snap out of it?"). These are the people who don't care much about what you say as long as you say it nicely, who believe that playwrights should be like the Royal Family, above the brawl and conflict of life as we know it. I rejoice in Tennessee Williams because I'm sure he never took a cold bath in his life, and he wouldn't have the almighty nerve to suggest it to anyone else.

The argument of the adjustment school is that characters like Blanche and Brick are not "normal," and they aren't like *us*. In fact, they are, yes—neurotics. Now this attitude is, I believe, built on a complete misconception of what theatre—or, indeed, art—is about. Adler said somewhere that the neurotic is like the normal individual only more so. A neurotic is not less adequate than an auditorium full of "normals." Every character trait is a neurosis writ small. I like my plays writ large, and that is how these are written. Those who complain of people like Blanche being neurotic are objecting to theatrical method itself. When one reads that one person in twenty in this country will at some time in his, or her, life enter a mental institution (and what are the other nineteen doing? Going to see "Salad Days," I suppose) one wonders how the adjustment school manages to keep so magnificently fit.

These plays tell us something about what is happening in America, and that is something we must know about. Lacking a live culture of our own, we are drawing more heavily than ever on that of the United States. This will turn out to be the most expensive and burdensome of the American loans, but we can't expect to put some kind of tariff barrier when they start sending over their own particular anxieties and neuroses. America is as sexually obsessed as a medieval monastery. That is what these plays are about—sex. Sex and failure. The moral failure of Protestant Capitalism has produced the biggest sexual nut-house since the Middle Ages. And let us remember, sex is everybody's problem. Even Aunt Edna has an itch under the tea tray.

Williams's women—Blanche, Maggie the Cat, Alma in "Summer and Smoke," Baby Doll—they all cry out for defilement, and most of them get it. In Baby Doll, Williams has hit off the American Girl-Woman of the last hundred years—spoilt, ignorant, callous, resentful. But no more resentful than the American male. Make no mistake about it—this Baby Doll kid is a killer. She would eat a couple of guys and spit them out before breakfast. When Archie Lee says, "You'll get your birthday present all right," every male from Houston to Boston must want to throw his hat in the air and cheer. "You and me have had this date right from the beginning," says Stanley. The female must come toppling down to where she should be—on her back. The American male must get his revenge sometime.

Each one of these plays is more interesting than anything written in this country during the same period, with the exception of "Camino Real," which is a ragbag of—often exciting—tricks. Now, I have no objection to tricks. If one accepts that theatre is some kind of magic, a dramatist without tricks is like a conjurer without a top hat. But "Camino Real" is full of tedious symbols and deadbeat intellectualism. If it were in a mean kind of verse, it would almost certainly fool somebody—in the West End, anyway.

This play is the sore thumb on this hand of five plays. It is a fine hand, sensitive, compassionate, gifted, extended. But a little plump and soft, and, occasionally, slightly clammy. The softness does not lie in the pity ("Streetcar"—still his best play—throbs with compassion). I believe it lies buried deep in Williams's personality as a writer, which seems to me to be feminine—with its set mouth of female cunning, its unsure attitudes and moral inconsistency, sedentary, exposed, *underneath*. But this may be a failure of my own vision.

These five plays and one film script make up most of Tennessee Williams's statement to date. It is one worth making, full of private fires and personal visions. It is worth a thousand statements of a thousand politicians.

part three

CRITICISM AND COMMENTARY

KENNETH REXROTH

Disengagement: The Art of the Beat Generation

"Against the ruin of the world, there is only one defense—the creative act." Poet and critic, Kenneth Rexroth has stood almost alone in perceiving the relevance and prophesy of the art of "disaffiliation." Instrumental in establishing the Beat Generation as a potent literary force, he has found himself projected into the role of its elder statesman. Not an apologist for its excesses of perception, but rather an eloquent spokesman for the validity of its attitudes in this time and place, Rexroth penned the following observations before either "Howl" or On the Road *had been published.*

LITERATURE GENERALLY, but literary criticism in particular, has always been an area in which social forces assume symbolic guise, and work out—or at least exemplify—conflicts taking place in the contemporary, or rather, usually the just-past wider arena of society. Recognition of this does not imply the acceptance of any general theory of social or economic determinism. It is a simple, empirical fact. Because of the pervasiveness of consent in American society generally, that democratic leveling up or down so often bewailed since de Tocqueville, American

literature, especially literary criticism, has usually been ruled by a
"line." The fact that it was spontaneously evolved and enforced only
by widespread consent has never detracted from its rigor—but rather
the opposite. It is only human to kick against the prodding of an Erich
Auerbach or an Andrey Zhdanov. An invisible, all-enveloping com-
pulsion is not likely to be recognized, let alone protested against.

After World War I there was an official line for general consumption: "Back to Normalcy." Day by day in every way, we are getting
better and better. This produced a literature which tirelessly pointed
out that there was nothing whatsoever normal about us. The measure
of decay in thirty years is the degree of acceptance of the official myth
today—from the most obscure hack on a provincial newspaper to the
loftiest metaphysicians of the literary quarterlies. The line goes: "The
generation of experimentation and revolt is over." This is an ethereal-
ized corollary of the general line: "The bull market will never end."

I do not wish to argue about the bull market, but in the arts nothing
could be less true. The youngest generation is in a state of revolt so
absolute that its elders cannot even recognize it. The disaffiliation,
alienation, and rejection of the young has, as far as their elders are
concerned, moved out of the visible spectrum altogether. Critically
invisible, modern revolt, like X-rays and radioactivity, is perceived
only by its effects at more materialistic social levels, where it is called
delinquency.

"Disaffiliation," by the way, is the term used by the critic and poet,
Lawrence Lipton, who has written several articles on this subject, the
first of which, in the *Nation,* quoted as epigraph, "We disaffiliate . . ."
—John L. Lewis.

Like the pillars of Hercules, like two ruined Titans guarding the
entrance to one of Dante's circles, stand two great dead juvenile
delinquents—the heroes of the post-war generation: the great saxo-
phonist, Charlie Parker, and Dylan Thomas. If the word deliberate
means anything, both of them certainly deliberately destroyed themselves.

Both of them were overcome by the horror of the world in which
they found themselves, because at last they could no longer overcome
that world with the weapon of a purely lyrical art. Both of them were
my friends. Living in San Francisco I saw them seldom enough to see
them with a perspective which was not distorted by exasperation or

fatigue. So as the years passed, I saw them each time in the light of an accelerated personal conflagration.

The last time I saw Bird, at Jimbo's Bob City, he was so gone—so blind to the world—that he literally sat down on me before he realized I was there. "What happened, man?" I said, referring to the pretentious "Jazz Concert." "Evil, man, evil," he said, and that's all he said for the rest of the night. About dawn he got up to blow. The rowdy crowd chilled into stillness and the fluent melody spiraled through it.

The last time I saw Dylan, his self-destruction had not just passed the limits of rationality. It had assumed the terrifying inertia of inanimate matter. Being with him was like being swept away by a torrent of falling stones.

Now Dylan Thomas and Charlie Parker have a great deal more in common than the same disastrous end. As artists, they were very similar. They were both very fluent. But this fluent, enchanting utterance had, compared with important artists of the past, relatively little content. Neither of them got very far beyond a sort of entranced rapture at his own creativity. The principal theme of Thomas's poetry was the ambivalence of birth and death—the pain of blood-stained creation. Music, of course, is not so explicit an art, but anybody who knew Charlie Parker knows that he felt much the same way about his own gift. Both of them did communicate one central theme: Against the ruin of the world, there is only one defense—the creative act. This, of course, is the theme of much art—perhaps most poetry. It is the theme of Horace, who certainly otherwise bears little resemblance to Parker or Thomas. The difference is that Horace accepted his theme with a kind of silken assurance. To Dylan and Bird it was an agony and terror. I do not believe that this is due to anything especially frightful about their relationship to their own creativity. I believe rather that it is due to the catastrophic world in which that creativity seemed to be the sole value. Horace's column of imperishable verse shines quietly enough in the lucid air of Augustan Rome. Art may have been for him the most enduring, orderly, and noble activity of man. But the other activities of his life partook of these values. They did not actively negate them. Dylan Thomas's verse had to find endurance in a world of burning cities and burning Jews. He was able to find meaning in his art as long as it was the answer to air raids and gas ovens. As the world began to take on the guise of an immense air raid or gas oven, I believe his art became meaningless to him. I think all this could apply to Parker just as well, although, because of the nature of music, it is not demonstrable—at least not conclusively.

Thomas and Parker have more in common than theme, attitude, life pattern. In the practice of their art, there is an obvious technical resemblance. Contrary to popular belief, they were not great technical innovators. Their effects are only superficially startling. Thomas is a regression from the technical originality and ingenuity of writers like Pierre Reverdy or Apollinaire. Similarly, the innovations of bop, and of Parker particularly, have been vastly overrated by people unfamiliar with music, especially by that ignoramus, the intellectual jitterbug, the jazz aficionado. The tonal novelties consist in the introduction of a few chords used in classical music for centuries. And there is less rhythmic difference between progressive jazz, no matter how progressive, and Dixieland, than there is between two movements of many conventional symphonies.

What Parker and his contemporaries—Gillespie, Davis, Monk, Roach (Tristano is an anomaly), etc.—did was to absorb the musical ornamentation of older jazz into the basic structure, of which it then became an integral part, and with which it then developed. This is true of the melodic line which could be put together from selected passages of almost anybody—Benny Carter, Johnny Hodges. It is true of the rhythmic pattern in which the beat shifts continuously, or at least is continuously sprung, so that it becomes ambiguous enough to allow the pattern to be dominated by the long pulsations of the phrase or strophe. This is exactly what happened in the transition from baroque to rococo music. It is the difference between Bach and Mozart.

It is not a farfetched analogy to say that this is what Thomas did to poetry. The special syntactical effects of a Rimbaud or an Edith Sitwell—actually ornaments—become the main concern. The metaphysical conceits, which fascinate the Reactionary Generation still dominant in backwater American colleges, were embroideries. Thomas's ellipses and ambiguities are ends in themselves. The immediate theme, if it exists, is incidental, and his main theme—the terror of birth—is simply reiterated.

This is one difference between Bird and Dylan which should be pointed out. Again, contrary to popular belief, there is nothing crazy or frantic about Parker either musically or emotionally. His sinuous melody is a sort of naïve transcendence of all experience. Emotionally it does not resemble Berlioz or Wagner; it resembles Mozart. This is true also of a painter like Jackson Pollock. He may have been eccentric in his behavior, but his paintings are as impassive as Persian tiles. Partly this difference is due to the nature of verbal communication. The insistent talk-aboutiveness of the general environment obtrudes into even the most idyllic poetry. It is much more a personal difference. Thomas certainly wanted to tell people about the ruin and disorder of the world. Parker and Pollock wanted to substitute a work of art for the world.

Technique pure and simple, rendition, is not of major importance, but it is interesting that Parker, following Lester Young, was one of the leaders of the so-called saxophone revolution. In modern jazz, the saxophone is treated as a woodwind and played with conventional embouchure. Metrically, Thomas's verse was extremely conventional, as was, incidentally, the verse of that other tragic enragé, Hart Crane.

I want to make clear what I consider the one technical development in the first wave of significant post-war arts. Ornament is confabulation in the interstices of structure. A poem by Dylan Thomas, a saxophone solo by Charles Parker, a painting by Jackson Pollock—these are pure confabulations as ends in themselves. Confabulation has come to determine structure. Uninhibited lyricism should be distinguished from its exact opposite—the sterile, extraneous invention of the corn-belt metaphysicals, our present blight of poetic professors.

Just as Hart Crane had little influence on anyone except very reactionary writers—like Allen Tate, for instance, to whom Valéry was the last word in modern poetry and the felicities of an Apollinaire, let alone a Paul Éluard were nonsense—so Dylan Thomas's influence has been slight indeed. In fact, his only disciple—the only person to imitate his style—was W. S. Graham, who seems to have imitated him without much understanding, and who has since moved on to other methods. Thomas's principal influence lay in the communication of an attitude—that of the now extinct British romantic school of the New Apocalypse—Henry Treece, J. F. Hendry, and others—all of whom were quite conventional poets.

Parker certainly had much more of an influence. At one time it was the ambition of every saxophone player in every high school band in America to blow like Bird. Even before his death this influence had begun to ebb. In fact, the whole generation of the founding fathers of bop—Gillespie, Monk, Davis, Blakey, and the rest—are just now at a considerable discount. The main line of development today goes back to Lester Young and by-passes them.

The point is that many of the most impressive developments in the arts nowadays are aberrant, idiosyncratic. There is no longer any sense of continuing development of the sort that can be traced from Baudelaire to Éluard, or for that matter, from Hawthorne through Henry James to Gertrude Stein. The cubist generation before World War I, and, on a lower level, the surrealists of the period between the wars, both assumed an accepted universe of discourse, in which, to quote André Breton, it was possible to make definite advances, exactly as in the sciences. I doubt if anyone holds such ideas today. Continuity exists, but like the neo-swing music developed from Lester Young, it is a continuity sustained by popular demand.

In the plastic arts, a very similar situation exists. Surrealists like Hans Arp and Max Ernst might talk of creation by hazard—of composing pictures by walking on them with painted soles, or by tossing bits of paper up in the air. But it is obvious that they were self-deluded. Nothing looks anything like an Ernst or an Arp but another Ernst or Arp. Nothing looks less like their work than the happenings of random occasion. Many of the post-World War II abstract expressionists, apostles of the discipline of spontaneity and hazard, look alike, and do look like accidents. The aesthetic appeal of pure paint laid on at random may exist, but it is a very impoverished appeal. Once again what has happened is an all-consuming confabulation of the incidentals, the accidents of painting. It is curious that at its best, the work of this school of painting—Mark Rothko, Jackson Pollock, Clyfford Still, Robert Motherwell, Willem deKooning, and the rest—resembles nothing so much as the passage painting of quite unimpressive painters: the mother-of-pearl shimmer in the background of a Henry McFee, itself a formula derived from Renoir; the splashes of light and black which fake drapery in the fashionable imitators of Hals and Sargent. Often work of this sort is presented as calligraphy—the pure utterance of the brush stroke seeking only absolute painteresque values. You have only to compare such painting with the work of, say, Sesshu, to realize that someone is using words and brushes carelessly.

At its best the abstract expressionists achieve a simple rococo decorative surface. Its poverty shows up immediately when compared with Tiepolo, where the rococo rises to painting of extraordinary profundity and power. A Tiepolo painting, however confabulated, is a universe of tensions in vast depths. A Pollock is an object of art—bijouterie—disguised only by its great size. In fact, once the size is big enough to cover a whole wall, it turns into nothing more than extremely expensive wallpaper. Now there is nothing wrong with complicated wallpaper. There is just more to Tiepolo. The great Ashikaga brush painters painted wallpapers, too—at least portable ones, screens.

A process of elimination which leaves the artist with nothing but the play of his materials themselves cannot sustain interest in either artist or public for very long. So, in the last couple of years, abstract expressionism has tended toward romantic suggestion—indications of landscape or living figures. This approaches the work of the Northwest school—Clayton Price, Mark Tobey, Kenneth Callahan, Morris Graves—who have of all recent painters come nearest to conquering a territory which painting could occupy with some degree of security. The Northwest school, of course, admittedly is influenced by the ink painters of the Far East, and by Tintoretto and Tiepolo. The dominant school of post-World War II American painting has really been a long detour into plastic nihilism. I should add that painters like Ernie Briggs seem to be opening up new areas of considerable scope within the main traditional abstract expressionism—but with remarkable convergence to Tobey or Tintoretto, as you prefer.

Today American painting is just beginning to emerge with a transvaluation of values. From the mid-nineteenth century on, all ruling standards in the plastic arts were subject to continual attack. They were attacked because each on-coming generation had new standards of their own to put in their place. Unfortunately, after one hundred years of this, there grew up a generation ignorant of the reasons for the revolt of their elders, and without any standards whatever. It has been necessary to create standards anew out of chaos. This is what modern education purports to do with finger painting in nursery schools. This is why the Northwest school has enjoyed such an advantage over the abstract expressionists. Learning by doing, by trial and error, is learning by the hardest way. If you want to overthrow the cubist tradition of architectural painting, it is much easier to seek out its opposites in the history of culture and study them carefully. At least it saves a great deal of time.

One thing can be said of painting in recent years—its revolt, its rejection of the classic modernism of the first half of the century, has been more absolute than in any other art. The only ancestor of abstract expressionism is the early Kandinsky—a style rejected even by Kandinsky himself. The only painter in a hundred years who bears the slightest resemblance to Tobey or Graves is Odilon Redon (perhaps Gustave Moreau a little), whose stock was certainly not very high with painters raised in the cubist tradition.

The ready market for prose fiction—there is almost no market at all for modern painting, and very much less for poetry—has had a decisive influence on its development. Sidemen with Kenton or Herman may make a good if somewhat hectic living, but any novelist who can write home to mother, or even spell his own name, has a chance to become another Brubeck. The deliberately and painfully intellectual fiction which appears in the literary quarterlies is a by-product of certain classrooms. The only significant fiction in America is popular fiction. Nobody realizes this better than the French. To them our late-born imitators of Henry James and E. M. Forster are just *chiens qui fument*, and arithmetical horses and bicycling seals. And there is no more perishable commodity than the middle-brow novel. No one today reads Ethel L. Voynich or Joseph Hergesheimer, just as no one in the future will read the writers' workshop pupils and teachers who fill the literary quarterlies. Very few people, except themselves, read them now.

On the other hand, the connection between the genuine high-brow writer and the genuinely popular is very close. Hemingway had hardly started to write before his style had been reduced to a formula in *Black Mask*, the first hard-boiled detective magazine. In no time at all he had produced two first-class popular writers, Raymond Chandler and Dashiell Hammett. Van Vechten, their middle-brow contemporary, is forgotten. It is from Chandler and Hammett and Hemingway that the best modern fiction derives; although most of it comes out in hard covers, it is always thought of as written for a typical pocketbook audience. Once it gets into pocketbooks it is sometimes difficult to draw the line between it and its most ephemeral imitators. Even the most *précieux* French critics, a few years ago, considered

Horace McCoy America's greatest contemporary novelist. There is not only something to be said for their point of view; the only thing to be said against it is that they don't read English.

Much of the best popular fiction deals with the world of the utterly disaffiliated. Burlesque and carnival people, hipsters, handicappers and hop heads, wanted men on the lam, an expendable squad of soldiers being expended, anyone who by definition is divorced from society and cannot afford to believe even an iota of the social lie—these are the favorite characters of modern post-war fiction, from Norman Mailer to the latest ephemerid called *Caught*, or *Hung Up*, or *The Needle*, its bright cover winking invitingly in the drugstore. The first, and still the greatest, novelist of total disengagement is not a young man at all, but an elderly former I.W.W. of German ancestry, B. Traven, the author of *The Death Ship* and *The Treasure of Sierra Madre*.

It is impossible for an artist to remain true to himself as a man, let alone an artist, and work within the context of this society. Contemporary mimics of Jane Austen or Anthony Trollope are not only beneath contempt. They are literally unreadable. It is impossible to keep your eyes focused on the page. Writers as far apart as J. F. Powers and Nelson Algren agree in one thing—their diagnosis of an absolute corruption.

This refusal to accept the mythology of press and pulpit as a medium for artistic creation, or even enjoyable reading matter, is one explanation for the popularity of escapist literature. Westerns, detective stories and science fiction are all situated beyond the pale of normal living. The slick magazines are only too well aware of this, and in these three fields especially exert steady pressure on their authors to accentuate the up-beat. The most shocking example of this forced perversion is the homey science fiction story, usually written by a woman, in which a one-to-one correlation has been made for the commodity-ridden tale of domestic whimsey, the stand-by of magazines given away in the chain groceries. In writers like Judith Merrill the space pilot and his bride bat the badinage back and forth while the robot maid makes breakfast in the jet-propelled lucite orange squeezer and the electronic bacon rotobroiler, dropping pearls of dry assembly plant wisdom (like plantation wisdom but drier), the whilst. Still, few yield to these pressures, for the obvious reason that fiction indistinguishable from the advertising columns on either side of the page defeats its own purpose, which is to get the reader to turn over the pages when he is told "continued on p. 47."

Simenon is still an incomparably better artist and psychologist than the psychological Jean Stafford. Ward Moore is a better artist than Eudora Welty, and Ernest Haycox than William Faulkner, just as, long ago, H. G. Wells was a better artist, as artist, than E. M. Forster, as well as being a lot more interesting. At its best, popular literature of this sort, coming up, meets high-brow literature coming down. It has been apparent novel by novel that Nelson Algren is rising qualitatively in this way. In his latest novel, thoroughly popular in its materials, *A Walk on the Wild Side,* he meets and absorbs influences coming down from the top, from the small handful of bona fide highbrow writers working today—Céline, Jean Genêt, Samuel Beckett, Henry Miller. In Algren's case this has been a slow growth, and he has carried his audience with him. Whatever the merits of his subject matter or his thesis—"It is better to be out than in. It is better to be on the lam than on the cover of *Time* Magazine"—his style started out as a distressing mixture of James Farrell and Kenneth Fearing. Only recently has he achieved an idiom of his own.

There is only one thing wrong with this picture, and that is that the high-brow stimulus still has to be imported. Algren, who is coming to write more and more like Céline, has no difficulty selling his fiction. On the other hand, an author like Jack Kerouac, who is in his small way the peer of Céline, Destouches or Beckett, is the most famous "unpublished" author in America. Every publisher's reader and adviser of any moment has read him and is enthusiastic about him. In other words, anybody emerging from the popular field has every advantage. It is still extremely difficult to enter American fiction from the top down.

The important point about modern fiction is that it is salable, and therefore viable in our society, and therefore successful in the best sense of the word. When a novelist has something to say, he knows people will listen. Only the jazz musician, but to a much lesser degree, shares this confidence in his audience. It is of the greatest social significance that the novelists who say, "I am proud to be delinquent" are nevertheless sold in editions of hundreds of thousands.

Nobody much buys poetry. I know. I am one of the country's most successful poets. My books actually sell out—in editions of two thousand. Many a poet, the prestige ornament of a publisher's list, has more charges against his royalty account than credits for books sold. The problem of poetry is the problem of communication itself. All art is a symbolic criticism of values, but poetry is specifically and almost exclusively that. A painting decorates the wall. A novel is a story. Music . . . soothes a savage breast. But poetry you have to take straight. In addition, the entire educational system is in a conspiracy to make poetry as unpalatable as possible. From the seventh grade teacher who rolls her eyes and chants H.D. to the seven types of ambiguity factories, grinding out little Donnes and Hopkinses with hayseeds in their hair, everybody is out to de-poetize forever the youth of the land. Again, bad and spurious painting, music, and fiction are not really well-organized, except on obvious commercial levels, where they can be avoided. But in poetry Gresham's Law is supported by the full weight of the powers that be. From about 1930 on, a conspiracy of bad poetry has been as carefully organized as the Communist Party, and today controls most channels of publication except the littlest of the little magazines. In all other departments of American culture, English influence has been at a steadily declining minimum since the middle of the nineteenth century. In 1929, this was still true of American poetry. Amy Lowell, Sandburg, H.D., Pound, Marianne Moore, William Carlos Williams, Wallace Stevens—all of the major poets of the first quarter of the century owed far more to Apollinaire or Francis Jammes than they did to the whole body of the English tradition. In fact, the new poetry was essentially an anti-English, pro-French movement—a provincial but clear echo of the French revolt against the symbolists. On the other hand, Jules Laforgue and his English disciples, Ernest Dowson and Arthur Symons, were the major influence on T. S. Eliot. Unfortunately Mr. Eliot's poetic practice and his thoroughly snobbish critical essays which owed their great cogency to their assumption, usually correct, that his readers had never heard of the authors he discussed—Webster, Crashaw, or Lancelot Andrewes—lent themselves all too easily to the construction of an academy and the production of an infinite number of provincial academicians—policemen entrusted with the enforcement of Gresham's Law.

Behind the façade of this literary Potemkin village, the main stream of American poetry, with its sources in Baudelaire, Lautréamont, Rimbaud, Apollinaire, Jammes, Reverdy, Salmon, and later Breton and Éluard, has flowed on unperturbed, though visible only at rare intervals between the interstices of the academic hoax. Today the class magazines and the quarterlies are filled with poets as alike as two bad pennies. It is my opinion that these people do not really exist. Most of them are androids designed by Ransom, Tate, and Co., and animated by Randall Jarrell. They are not just counterfeit; they are not even real counterfeits, but counterfeits of counterfeits. On these blurred and clumsy coins the lineaments of Mr. Eliot and I. A. Richards dimly can be discerned, like the barbarized Greek letters which nobody could read on Scythian money.

This is the world in which over every door is written the slogan: "The generation of experiment and revolt is over. Bohemia died in the twenties. There are no more little magazines." Actually there have never been so many little magazines. In spite of the fantastic costs of printing, more people than ever are bringing out little sheets of free verse and making up the losses out of their own pockets. This world has its own major writers, its own discoveries, its own old masters, its own tradition and continuity. Its sources are practically exclusively French, and they are all post-symbolist, even anti-symbolist. It is the Reactionary Generation who are influenced by Laforgue, the symbolists, and Valéry. Nothing is more impressive than the strength, or at least the cohesion, of this underground movement. Poets whom the quarterlies pretend never existed, like Louis Zukovsky and Jack Wheelwright, are still searched out in large libraries or obscure bookshops and copied into notebooks by young writers. I myself have a complete typewritten collection of the pre-reactionary verse of Yvor Winters. And I know several similar collections of "forgotten modernists" in the libraries of my younger friends. People are aways turning up who say something like, "I just discovered a second-hand copy of Parker Tyler's The Granite Butterfly in a Village bookshop. It's great, man." On the other hand, I seriously doubt whether The Hudson Review would ever consider for a moment publishing a line of Parker Tyler's verse. And he is certainly not held up as an example in the Iowa Writers' Workshop. There are others who have disappeared entirely—Charles Snider, Sherry Mangan, R. E. F. Larsson, the early Winters, the last poems of Ford Madox Ford. They get back into circulation, as far as I know, only when I read them to somebody at home or on the air, and then I am always asked for a copy. Some of the old avant garde seem to have written themselves out, for instance, Mina Loy. There are a few established old masters, outstanding of whom are, of course, Ezra Pound and William Carlos Williams. I am not a passionate devotee of Pound myself. In fact, I think his influence is largely pernicious. But no one could deny its extent and power amongst young people today. As for Williams, more and more people, even some of the Reactionary Generation, have come to think of him as our greatest living poet. Even Randall Jarrell and R. P. Blackmur have good words to say for him.

Then there is a middle generation which includes Kenneth Patchen, Jean Garrigue, myself, and a few others—notably Richard Eberhart, who looks superficially as if he belonged with the Tates and Blackmurs but who is redeemed by his directness, simplicity, and honesty, and Robert Fitzgerald and Dudley Fitts. Curiously enough, in the taste of the young, Kenneth Fearing is not included in this group, possibly because his verse is too easy. It does include the major work, for example, *Ajanta*, of Muriel Rukeyser.

I should say that the most influential poets of the youngest established generation of the avant garde are Denise Levertov, Robert Creeley, Charles Olson, Robert Duncan, and Philip Lamantia. The most influential avant garde editor is perhaps Cid Corman, with his magazine *Origin*. Richard Emerson's *Golden Goose* and Robert Creeley's *Black Mountain Review* seem to have suspended publication temporarily. Jonathan Williams, himself a fine poet, publishes the Jargon Press.

All of this youngest group have a good deal in common. They are all more or less influenced by French poetry, and by Céline, Beckett, Artaud, Genêt, to varying degrees. They are also influenced by William Carlos Williams, D. H. Lawrence, Whitman, Pound. They are all interested in Far Eastern art and religion; some even call themselves Buddhists. Politically they are all strong disbelievers in the State, war, and the values of commercial civilization. Most of them would no longer call themselves anarchists, but just because adopting such a label would imply adherence to a "movement." Anything in the way of an explicit ideology is suspect. Contrary to gossip of a few years back, I have never met anybody in this circle who was a devotee of the dubious notions of the psychologist, Wilhelm Reich; in fact, few of them have ever read him, and those who have consider him a charlatan.

Although there is wide diversity—Olson is very like Pound; Creeley resembles Mallarmé; Denise Levertov in England was a leading New Romantic, in America she has come under the influence of William Carlos Williams; Robert Duncan has assimilated ancestors as unlike as Gertrude Stein and Éluard, and so on—although this diversity is very marked, there is a strong bond of aesthetic unity too. No avant garde American poet accepts the I. A. Richards-Valéry thesis that a poem is an end in itself, an anonymous machine for providing aesthetic experiences. All believe in poetry as communication, statement from one person to another. So they all avoid the studied ambiguities and metaphysical word play of the Reactionary Generation and seek clarity of image and simplicity of language.

In the years since the war, it would seem as though more and more of what is left of the avant garde has migrated to Northern California. John Berryman once referred to the Lawrence cult of "mindless California," and Henry Miller and I have received other unfavorable publicity which has served only to attract people to this area. Mr. Karl Shapiro, for instance, once referred to San Francisco as "the last refuge of the Bohemian remnant"—a description he thought of as invidious. Nevertheless it is true that San Francisco is today the seat of an intense literary activity not unlike Chicago of the first quarter of the century. A whole school of poets has grown up—almost all of them migrated here from somewhere else. Some of them have national reputations, at least in limited circles. For example, Philip Lamantia among the surrealists; William Everson (Br. Antoninus, O.P)—perhaps the best Catholic poet. Others have come up recently, like Lawrence Ferlinghetti, Allen Ginsberg, Gary Snyder, Philip Whalen, James Harmon, Michael McClure, and still have largely local reputations. But the strength of these reputations should not be underestimated. The Poetry Center of San Francisco State College, directed by Ruth Witt-Diamant, gives a reading to a large audience at least twice a month. And there are other readings equally well attended every week in various galleries and private homes.

This means that poetry has become an actual social force—something which has always sounded hitherto like a Utopian dream of the

William Morris sort. It is a very thrilling experience to hear an audience of more than three hundred people stand and cheer and clap, as they invariably do at a reading by Allen Ginsberg, certainly a poet of revolt if there ever was one.

There is no question but that the San Francisco renaissance is radically different from what is going on elsewhere. There are hand presses, poetry readings, young writers elsewhere—but nowhere else is there a whole younger generation culture pattern characterized by total rejection of the official high-brow culture—where critics like John Crowe Ransom or Lionel Trilling, magazines like the *Kenyon*, *Hudson* and *Partisan* reviews, are looked on as "The Enemy"—the other side of the barricades.

There is only one trouble about the renaissance in San Francisco. It is too far away from the literary market place. That, of course, is the reason why the Bohemian remnant, the avant garde have migrated here. It is possible to hear the story about what so-and-so said to someone else at a cocktail party twenty years ago just one too many times. You grab a plane or get on your thumb and hitchhike to the other side of the continent for good and all. Each generation, the great Latin poets came from farther and farther from Rome. Eventually, they ceased to even go there except to see the sights.

Distance from New York City does, however, make it harder to get things, if not published, at least nationally circulated. I recently formed a collection for one of the foundations of avant garde poetry printed in San Francisco. There were a great many items. The poetry was all at least readable, and the hand printing and binding were in most cases very fine indeed. None of these books were available in bookstores elsewhere in the country, and only a few of them had been reviewed in newspapers or magazines with national circulation.

Anyway, as an old war horse of the revolution of the word, things have never looked better from where I sit. The avant garde has not only not ceased to exist. It's jumping all over the place. Something's happening, man.

The disengagement of the creator, who, as creator, is necessarily judge, is one thing, but the utter nihilism of the emptied-out hipster is another. What is going to come of an attitude like this? It is impossible to go on indefinitely saying: "I am proud to be a delinquent," without destroying all civilized values. Between such persons no **true** enduring interpersonal relationships can be built, and of course, nothing resembling a true "culture"—an at-homeness of men with each other, their work, their loves, their environment. The end result must be the desperation of shipwreck—the despair, the orgies, ultimately the cannibalism of a lost lifeboat. I believe that most of an entire generation will go to ruin—the ruin of Céline, Artaud, Rimbaud, voluntarily, even enthusiastically. What will happen afterwards I don't know, but for the next ten years or so we are going to have to cope with the youth we, my generation, put through the atom smasher. Social disengagement, artistic integrity, voluntary poverty—these are powerful virtues and may pull them through, but they are not the virtues we tried to inculcate—rather they are the exact opposite.

WALTER ALLEN

Review of Lucky Jim

What Gertrude Stein's celebrated remark to Hemingway was to "the lost generation" Walter Allen's review of Lucky Jim *has become to the Angry Young Men. Allen precociously recognized that the English novel was making a turn, and in doing so he helped it move faster along its new way. His opening pronouncement is still the theme of much discussion in British literary circles.*

A NEW HERO HAS RISEN AMONG US. Is he the intellectual tough or the tough intellectual? He is consciously, even conscientiously, graceless. His face, when not dead pan, is set in a snarl of exasperation. He has one skin too few, but his is not the sensitiveness of the young man in earlier twentieth-century fiction: it is the phoney to which his nerve-ends are tremblingly exposed, and at the least suspicion of the phoney he goes tough. He is at odds with his conventional university education, though he comes generally from a famous university: he has seen through the academic racket as he sees through all the others. A racket is phoneyness organised, and in contact with phoneyness he turns just as red as litmus paper does in contact with an acid. In life he has been among us for some little time. One may speculate whence he derives. The Services, certainly, helped to make him; but George Orwell, Dr. Leavis and the Logical Positivists—or, rather, the attitudes these represent—all contributed to his genesis. In fiction I think he first arrived last year, as the central character of Mr. John Wain's novel *Hurry On Down*. He turns up again in Mr. Amis's *Lucky Jim.*

Mr. Wain's character was the picaresque hero, and the picaresque has commonly been a vehicle for satire. Mr. Amis isn't writing picaresque or even satire. He comes at times very close to farce, yet not farce as we normally think of it. His hero, Jim Dixon, is in his first term as an assistant lecturer in history in a provincial university. Everything goes wrong for him. He has the gift of precipitating the most impossible situations, situations which cannot be explained away. Thus, on his first appearance in the university, he appears to have gratuitously assaulted the Professor of English. He goes for an arty week-end at the Professor of History's, quarrels with the Professor's son, gets drunk and sets his bed on fire with a forgotten cigarette. Towards the end of the term, when he has to deliver the popular public lecture which may reinstate him in the eyes of the Faculty and save his job, he finds himself involuntarily parodying the manner first of the Principal and then of his Professor, and finally embarked on a wild burlesque of all such popular lectures on his theme—"Merrie England," which he is supposed to praise.

This may suggest that he is, as it were, remotely a Chaplin-figure, the *naif* who, from his very innocence, exposes the sham. Jim Dixon is far from that: he is, in his anxious way, playing the racket. If he were less anxious, he would play it better: the impossible situations arise from the fact he can never wholly kid himself that the racket is worth playing. He is not the dumb ox with the heart of gold at all; his attitude, even as he compromises, is much more that of Mr. Lewis's Soldier of Humor.

Lucky Jim is an extremely interesting first novel, and parts of it are very funny indeed: the episodes of the bed-burning and Jim's public lecture, for instance, mount to the complexity and tension of certain passages in the Marx Brothers' films or in the paper-hanging act one still sees from time to time in pantomime. And Mr. Amis has an unwaveringly merciless eye for the bogus: some aspects of provincial culture—the madrigals and recorders of Professor Welch, for instance —are pinned down as accurately as they have ever been; and he has, too, an eye for character—the female lecturer Margaret, who battens neurotically on Jim's pity, is quite horribly well done. Mr. Amis is a novelist of formidable and uncomfortable talent.

NORMAN MAILER

The White Negro

*The American existentialist par ex-
cellence—the new hero of the Beat
Generation—is the hipster, the man
who rejects permanence, order and
continuity, and all truths except "instantaneous" ones. These he seeks
with a religious ardor that plunges
him continually into the very vortex
of the moment's colliding sensations.
As Hip is a way of life, so it has
its rationale: in this brilliant, complex essay Norman Mailer explores
the philosophy of Hip—what it is,
whence it comes, its virtues and potential dangers.*

I

PROBABLY, WE WILL never be able to determine
the psychic havoc of the concentration camps and the atom
bomb upon the unconscious mind of almost everyone alive
in these years. For the first time in civilized history, perhaps for the first time in all of history, we have been forced
to live with the suppressed knowledge that the smallest
facets of our personality or the most minor projection of
our ideas, or indeed the absence of ideas and the absence
of personality, could mean equally well that we might still
be doomed to die as a cipher in some vast statistical opera-

tion in which our teeth would be counted, and our hair would be saved, but our death itself would be unknown, unhonored, and unremarked, a death which could not follow with dignity as a possible consequence to serious actions we had chosen, but rather a death by *deus ex machina* in a gas chamber or a radioactive city; and so if in the midst of civilization—that civilization founded upon the Faustian urge to dominate nature by mastering time, mastering the links of social cause and effect—in the middle of an economic civilization founded upon the confidence that time could indeed be subjected to our will, our psyche was subjected to the intolerable anxiety that death being causeless, life was causeless as well, and time deprived of cause and effect had come to a stop.

The Second World War presented a mirror to the human condition which blinded anyone who looked into it. For if tens of millions were killed in concentration camps out of the inexorable agonies and contractions of super-states founded upon the always insoluble contradictions of injustice, one was then obliged also to see that no matter how crippled and perverted an image of man was the society he had created, it was nonetheless his creation, his collective creation (at least his collective creation from the past) and if society was so murderous, then who could ignore the most hideous of questions about his own nature?

Worse. One could hardly maintain the courage to be individual, to speak with one's own voice, for the years in which one could complacently accept oneself as part of an elite by being a radical were forever gone. A man knew that when he dissented, he gave a note upon his life which could be called in any year of overt crisis. No wonder then that these have been the years of conformity and depression. A stench of fear has come out of every pore of American life, and we suffer from a collective failure of nerve. The only courage, with rare exceptions, that we have been witness to, has been the isolated courage of isolated people.

II

It is on this bleak scene that a phenomenon has appeared: the American existentialist—the hipster, the man who knows that if our collective condition is to live with instant death by atomic war, relatively quick death by the State as *l'univers concentrationnaire,* or with a slow death by conformity with every creative and rebellious instinct stifled (at what damage to the mind and the heart and the liver and the nerves no research foundation for cancer will discover in a hurry), if the fate of twentieth century man is to live with death from adolescence to premature senescence, why then the only life-giving answer is to accept the terms of death, to live with death as immediate danger, to divorce oneself from society, to exist without roots, to set out on that uncharted journey into the rebellious imperatives of the self. In short, whether the life is criminal or not, the decision is to encourage the psychopath in oneself, to explore that domain of experience where security is boredom and therefore sickness, and one exists in the present, in that enormous present which is without past or future, memory or planned intention, the life where a man must go until he is beat, where he must gamble with his energies through all those small or large crises of courage and unforeseen situations which beset his day, where he must be with it or doomed not to swing. The unstated essence of Hip, its psychopathic brilliance, quivers with the knowledge that new kinds of victories increase one's power for new kinds of perception; and defeats, the wrong kind of defeats, attack the body and imprison one's energy until one is jailed in the prison air of other people's habits, other people's defeats, boredom, quiet desperation, and muted icy self-destroying rage. One is Hip or one is Square (the alternative which each new generation coming into American life is beginning to feel), one is a rebel or one conforms, one is a frontiersman in the Wild West of American night life, or else a Square cell, trapped in the totalitarian tissues of American society, doomed willy-nilly to conform if one is to succeed.

A totalitarian society makes enormous demands on the courage of men, and a partially totalitarian society makes even greater demands for the general anxiety is greater. Indeed if one is to be a man, almost any kind of unconventional action often takes disproportionate courage. So it is no accident that the source of Hip is the Negro for he has been living on the margin between totalitarianism and democracy for two centuries. But the presence of Hip as a working philosophy in the sub-worlds of American life is probably due to jazz, and its knife-like entrance into culture, its subtle but so penetrating influence on an avant-garde generation—that post-war generation of adventurers who (some consciously, some by osmosis) had absorbed the lessons of disillusionment and disgust of the Twenties, the Depression, and the War. Sharing a collective disbelief in the words of men who had too much money and controlled too many things, they knew almost as powerful a disbelief in the socially monolithic ideas of the single mate, the solid family and the respectable love life. If the intellectual antecedents of this generation can be traced to such separate influences as D. H. Lawrence, Henry Miller, and Wilhelm Reich, the viable philosophy of Hemingway fits most of their facts: in a bad world, as he was to say over and over again (while taking time out from his parvenu snobbery and dedicated gourmandise), in a bad world there is no love nor mercy nor charity nor justice unless a man can keep his courage, and this indeed fitted some of the facts. What fitted the need of the adventurer even more precisely was Hemingway's categorical imperative that what made him feel good became therefore The Good.

So no wonder that in certain cities of America, in New York of course, and New Orleans, in Chicago and San Francisco and Los Angeles, in such American cities as Paris and Mexico, D.F., this particular part of a generation was attracted to what the Negro had to offer. In such places as Greenwich Village, a ménage-a-trois was completed— the bohemian and the juvenile delinquent came face-to-face with the Negro, and the hipster was a fact in American life. If marijuana was the wedding ring, the child was the language of Hip for its argot gave expression to abstract states of feeling which all could share, at least all who were Hip. And in this wedding of the white and the black it was the Negro who brought the cultural dowry. Any Negro who wishes to live must live with danger from his first day, and no experience can ever be casual to him, no Negro can saunter down a street with any real certainty that violence will not visit him on his walk. The cameos of security for the average white: mother and the home, job and the family, are not even a mockery to millions of Negroes; they are impossible. The Negro has the simplest of alternatives: live a life of constant humility or ever-threatening danger. In such a pass where paranoia is as vital to survival as blood, the Negro had stayed alive and begun to grow by following the need of his body where he could. Knowing in the cells of his existence that life was war, nothing but war, the Negro (all exceptions admitted) could rarely afford the sophisticated inhibitions of civilization, and so he kept for his survival the art of the primitive, he lived in the enormous present, he subsisted for his Saturday night kicks, relinquishing the pleasures of the mind for the more obligatory pleasures of the body, and in his music he gave voice to the character and quality of his existence, to his rage and the infinite variations of joy, lust, languor, growl, cramp, pinch, scream and despair of his orgasm. For jazz is orgasm, it is the music of orgasm, good orgasm and bad, and so it spoke across a nation, it had the communication of art even where it was watered, perverted, corrupted, and almost killed, it spoke in no matter what laundered popular way of instantaneous existential states to which some whites could respond, it was indeed a communication by art because it said, "I feel this, and now you do too."

So there was a new breed of adventurers, urban adventurers who drifted out at night looking for action with a black man's code to fit their facts. The hipster had absorbed the existentialist synapses of the Negro, and for practical purposes could be considered a white Negro.

To be an existentialist, one must be able to feel oneself—one must know one's desires, one's rages, one's anguish, one must be aware of the character of one's frustration and know what would satisfy it. The over-civilized man can be an existentialist only if it is chic, and deserts it quickly for the next chic. To be a real existentialist (Sartre admittedly to the contrary) one must be religious, one must have one's sense of the "purpose"—whatever the purpose may be—but a life which is directed by one's faith in the necessity of action is a life committed to the notion that the substratum of existence is the search, the end meaningful but mysterious; it is impossible to live such a life unless one's emotions provide their profound conviction. Only the French, alienated beyond alienation from their unconscious could welcome an existential philosophy without ever feeling it at all; indeed only a Frenchman by declaring that the unconscious did not exist could then proceed to explore the delicate involutions of consciousness, the microscopically sensuous and all but ineffable *frissons* of mental becoming, in order finally to create the theology of atheism and so submit that in a world of absurdities the existential absurdity is most coherent.

In the dialogue between the atheist and the mystic, the atheist is on the side of life, rational life, undialectical life—since he conceives of death as emptiness, he can, no matter how weary or despairing, wish for nothing but more life; his pride is that he does not transpose his weakness and spiritual fatigue into a romantic longing for death, for such appreciation of death is then all too capable of being elaborated by his imagination into a universe of meaningful structure and moral orchestration.

Yet this masculine argument can mean very little for the mystic. The mystic can accept the atheist's description of his weakness, he can agree that his mysticism was a response to despair. And yet . . . and yet his argument is that he, the mystic, is the one finally who has chosen to live with death, and so death is his experience and not the atheist's, and the atheist by eschewing the limitless dimensions of profound despair has rendered himself incapable to judge the experience. The real argument which the mystic must always advance is the very intensity of his private vision—his argument depends from the vision precisely because what was felt in the vision is so extraordinary that no rational argument, no hypotheses of "oceanic feelings" and certainly no skeptical reductions can explain away what has become for him the reality more real than the reality of closely reasoned logic. His inner experience of the possibilities within death is his logic. So, too, for the existentialist. And the psychopath. And the saint and the bullfighter and the lover. The common denominator for all of them is their burning consciousness of the present, exactly that incandescent consciousness which the possibilities within death has opened for them. There is a depth of desperation to the condition which enables one to remain in life only by engaging death, but the reward is their knowledge that what is happening at each instant of the electric present is good or bad for them, good or bad for their cause, their love, their action, their need.

It is this knowledge which provides the curious community of feeling in the world of the hipster, a muted cool religious revival to be sure, but the element which is exciting, disturbing, nightmarish perhaps, is that incompatibles have come to bed, the inner life and the violent life, the orgy and the dream of love, the desire to murder and the desire to create, a dialectical conception of existence with a lust for power, a dark, romantic, and yet undeniably dynamic view of existence for it sees every man and woman as moving individually through each moment of life forward into growth or backward into death.

III

It may be fruitful to consider the hipster a philosophical psycho-path, a man interested not only in the dangerous imperatives of his psychopathy but in codifying, at least for himself, the suppositions on which his inner universe is constructed. By this premise the hipster is a psychopath, and yet not a psychopath but the negation of the psycho-path for he possesses the narcissistic detachment of the philosopher, that absorption in the recessive nuances of one's own motive which is so alien to the unreasoning drive of the psychopath. In this country where new millions of psychopaths are developed each year, stamped with the mint of our contradictory popular culture (where sex is sin and yet sex is paradise), it is as if there has been room already for the development of the antithetical psychopath who extrapolates from his own condition, from the inner certainty that his rebellion is just, a radical vision of the universe which thus separates him from the gen-eral ignorance, reactionary prejudice, and self-doubt of the more con-ventional psychopath. Having converted his unconscious experience into much conscious knowledge, the hipster has shifted the focus of his desire from immediate gratification toward that wider passion for future power which is the mark of civilized man. Yet with an irreduci-ble difference. For Hip is the sophistication of the wise primitive in a giant jungle, and so its appeal is still beyond the civilized man. If there are ten million Americans who are more or less psychopathic (and the figure is most modest), there are probably not more than one hundred thousand men and women who consciously see them-selves as hipsters, but their importance is that they are an elite with the potential ruthlessness of an elite, and a language most adolescents can understand instinctively for the hipster's intense view of existence matches their experience and their desire to rebel.

Before one can say more about the hipster, there is obviously much to be said about the psychic state of the psychopath—or, clinically, the psychopathic personality. Now, for reasons which may be more curious than the similarity of the words, even many people with a psycho-analytical orientation often confuse the psychopath with the psychotic. Yet the terms are polar. The psychotic is legally insane, the psychopath is not; the psychotic is almost always incapable of discharging in physical acts the rage of his frustration, while the psychopath at his extreme is virtually as incapable of restraining his violence. The psychotic lives in so misty a world that what is happening at each moment of his life is not very real to him whereas the psychopath seldom knows any reality greater than the face, the voice, the being of the particular people among whom he may find himself at any moment. Sheldon and Eleanor Glueck describe him as follows:

> The psychopath . . . can be distinguished from the person sliding into or clambering out of a "true psychotic" state by the long tough persistence of his anti-social attitude and behaviour and the absence of hallucinations, delusions, manic flight of ideas, confusion, disorientation, and other dramatic signs of psychosis.

The late Robert Lindner, one of the few experts on the subject, in his book *Rebel Without A Cause—The Hypnoanalysis of a Criminal Psychopath* presented part of his definition in this way:

> . . . the psychopath is a rebel without a cause, an agitator without a slogan, a revolutionary without a program: in other words, his rebelliousness is aimed to achieve goals satisfactory to himself alone; he is incapable of exertions for the sake of others. All his efforts, hidden under no matter what disguise, represent investments designed to satisfy his immediate wishes and desires . . . The psychopath, like the child, cannot delay the pleasures of gratification; and this trait is one of his underlying, universal characteristics. He cannot wait upon erotic gratification which convention demands should be preceded by the chase before the kill: he must rape. He cannot wait upon the development of prestige in society: his egoistic ambitions lead him to leap into headlines by daring performances. Like a red thread the predominance of this mechanism for immediate satisfaction runs through the history of every psychopath. It explains not only his behaviour but also the violent nature of his acts.

Yet even Lindner, who was the most imaginative and most sympathetic of the psychoanalysts who have studied the psychopathic personality, was not ready to project himself into the essential sympathy—which is that the psychopath may indeed be the perverted and dangerous front-runner of a new kind of personality which could become the central expression of human nature before the twentieth century is over. For the psychopath is better adapted to dominate those mutually contradictory inhibitions upon violence and love which civilization has exacted of us, and if it be remembered that not every psychopath is an extreme case, and that the condition of psychopathy is present in a host of people including many politicians, professional soldiers, newspaper columnists, entertainers, artists, jazz musicians, call-girls, promiscuous homosexuals and half the executives of Hollywood, television, and advertising, it can be seen that there are aspects of psychopathy which already exert considerable cultural influence.

What characterizes almost every psychopath and part-psychopath is that they are trying to create a new nervous system for themselves. Generally we are obliged to act with a nervous system which has been formed from infancy, and which carries in the style of its circuits the very contradictions of our parents and our early milieu. Therefore, we are obliged, most of us, to meet the tempo of the present and the future with reflexes and rhythms which come from the past. It is not only the "dead weight of the institutions of the past" but indeed the inefficient and often antiquated nervous circuits of the past which strangle our potentiality for responding to new possibilities which might be exciting for our individual growth.

Through most of modern history, "sublimation" was possible: at the expense of expressing only a small portion of oneself, that small portion could be expressed intensely. But sublimation depends on a reasonable tempo to history. If the collective life of a generation has moved too quickly, the "past" by which particular men and women of that generation may function is not, let us say, thirty years old, but relatively a hundred or two hundred years old. And so the nervous system is overstressed beyond the possibility of such compromises as sublimation, especially since the stable middle-class values so prerequisite to sublimation have been virtually destroyed in our time, at least as nourishing values free of confusion or doubt. In such a crisis of accelerated historical tempo and deteriorated values, neurosis tends to be replaced by psychopathy, and the success of psychoanalysis (which even ten years ago gave promise of becoming a direct major force) diminishes because of its inbuilt and characteristic incapacity to handle patients more complex, more experienced, or more adventurous than the analyst himself. In practice, psychoanalysis has by now become all too often no more than a psychic blood-letting. The patient is not so much changed as aged, and the infantile fantasies which he is encouraged to express are condemned to exhaust themselves against the analyst's non-responsive reactions. The result for all too many patients is a diminution, a "tranquilizing" of their most interesting qualities and vices. The patient is indeed not so much altered as worn out—less bad, less good, less bright, less willful, less destructive, less creative. He is thus able to conform to that contradictory and unbearable society which first created his neurosis. He can conform to what he loathes because he no longer has the passion to feel loathing so intensely.

The psychopath is notoriously difficult to analyze because the fundamental decision of his nature is to try to live the infantile fantasy, and in this decision (given the dreary alternative of psychoanalysis) there may be a certain instinctive wisdom. For there is a dialectic to changing one's nature, the dialectic which underlies all psychoanalytic method: it is the knowledge that if one is to change one's habits, one must go back to the source of their creation, and so the psychopath exploring backward along the road of the homosexual, the orgiast, the drug-addict, the rapist, the robber and the murderer seeks to find those violent parallels to the violent and often hopeless contradictions he knew as an infant and as a child. For if he has the courage to meet the parallel situation at the moment when he is ready, then he has a chance to act as he has never acted before, and in satisfying the frustration—if he can succeed—he may then pass by symbolic substitute through the locks of incest. In thus giving expression to the buried infant in himself, he can lessen the tension of those infantile desires and so free himself to remake a bit of his nervous system. Like the neurotic he is looking for the opportunity to grow up a second time, but the psychopath knows instinctively that to express a forbidden impulse actively is far more beneficial to him than merely to confess the desire in the safety of a doctor's room. The psychopath is ordinately ambitious, too ambitious ever to trade his warped brilliant conception of his possible victories in life for the grim if peaceful attrition of the analyst's couch. So his associational journey into the past is lived out in the theatre of the present, and he exists for those charged situations where his senses are so alive that he can be aware actively (as the analysand is aware passively) of what his habits are, and how he can change them. The strength of the psychopath is that he knows (where most of us can only guess) what is good for him and what is bad for him at exactly those instants when an old crippling habit has become so attacked by experience that the potentiality exists to change it, to replace a negative and empty fear with an outward action, even if— and here I obey the logic of the extreme psychopath—even if the fear is of himself, and the action is to murder. The psychopath murders— if he has the courage—out of the necessity to purge his violence, for if he cannot empty his hatred then he cannot love, his being is frozen with implacable self-hatred for his cowardice. (It can of course be suggested that it takes little courage for two strong eighteen-year old hoodlums, let us say, to beat in the brains of a candy-store keeper, and indeed the act—even by the logic of the psychopath—is not likely to prove very therapeutic for the victim is not an immediate equal. Still, courage of a sort is necessary, for one murders not only a weak fifty-year old man but an institution as well, one violates private property, one enters into a new relation with the police and introduces a dangerous element into one's life. The hoodlum is therefore daring the unknown, and so no matter how brutal the act, is not altogether cowardly.)

At bottom, the drama of the psychopath is that he seeks love. Not love as the search for a mate, but love as the search for an orgasm more apocalyptic than the one which preceded it. Orgasm is his therapy— he knows at the seed of his being that good orgasm opens his possibilities and bad orgasm imprisons him. But in this search, the psychopath becomes an embodiment of the extreme contradictions of the society which formed his character, and the apocalyptic orgasm often remains as remote as the Holy Grail, for there are clusters and nests and ambushes of violence in his own necessities and in the imperatives and retaliations of the men and women among whom he lives his life, so that even as he dreams his hatred in one act or another, so the conditions of his life create it anew in him until the drama of his movements bears a sardonic resemblance to the frog who climbed a few feet in the well only to drop back again.

Yet there is this to be said for the search after the good orgasm: when one lives in a civilized world, and still can enjoy none of the cultural nectar of such a world because the paradoxes on which civilization is built demands that there remain a cultureless and alienated

bottom of exploitable human material, then the logic of becoming a
sexual outlaw (if one's psychological roots are bedded in the bottom)
is that one has at least a running competitive chance to be physically
healthy so long as one stays alive. It is therefore no accident that
psychopathy is most prevalent with the Negro. Hated from outside
and therefore hating himself, the Negro was forced into the position
of exploring all those moral wildernesses of civilized life which the
Square automatically condemns as delinquent or evil or immature or
morbid or self-destructive or corrupt. (Actually the terms have equal
weight. Depending on the telescope of the cultural clique from which
the Square surveys the universe, "evil" or "immature" are equally
strong terms of condemnation.) But the Negro, not being privileged
to gratify his self-esteem with the heady satisfactions of categorical
condemnation, chose to move instead in that other direction where all
situations are equally valid, and in the worst of perversion, promis-
cuity, pimpery, drug addiction, rape, razor-slash, bottle-break, what-
have-you, the Negro discovered and elaborated a morality of the bottom, an ethical differentiation between the good and the bad in every
human activity from the go-getter pimp (as opposed to the lazy one)
to the relatively dependable pusher or prostitute. Add to this, the
cunning of their language, the abstract ambiguous alternatives in
which from the danger of their oppression they learned to speak.
("Well, now, man, like I'm looking for a cat to turn me on . . ."), add
even more the profound sensitivity of the Negro jazzman who was the
cultural mentor of a people, and it is not too difficult to believe that
the language of Hip which evolved was an artful language, tested
and shaped by an intense experience and therefore different in kind
from white slang, as different as the special obscenity of the soldier
which in its emphasis upon "ass" as the soul and "shit" as circum-
stance, was able to express the existential states of the enlisted men.
What makes Hip a special language is that it cannot really be taught
—if one shares none of the experiences of elation and exhaustion
which it is equipped to describe, then it seems merely arch or vulgar
or irritating. It is a pictorial language, but pictorial like non-objective
art, imbued with the dialectic of small but intense change, a language
for the microcosm, in this case, man, for it takes the immediate experiences of any passing man and magnifies the dynamic of his movements, not specifically but abstract so that he is seen more as a vector

in a network of forces than as a static character in a crystallized field. (Which, latter, is the practical view of the snob.) For example, there is real difficulty in trying to find a Hip substitute for "stubborn." The best possibility I can come up with is: "That cat will never come off his groove, dad." But groove implies movement, narrow movement but motion nonetheless. There is really no way to describe someone who does not move at all. Even a creep does move—if at a pace exasperatingly more slow than the pace of the cool cats.

IV

Like children, hipsters are fighting for the sweet, and their language is a set of subtle indications of their success or failure in the competition for pleasure. Unstated but obvious is the social sense that there is not nearly enough sweet for everyone. And so the sweet goes only to the victor, the best, the most, the man who knows the most about how to find his energy and how not to lose it. The emphasis is on energy because the psychopath and the hipster are nothing without it since they do not have the protection of a position or a class to rely on when they have overextended themselves. So the language of Hip is a language of energy, how it is found, how it is lost.

But let us see. I have jotted down perhaps a dozen words, the Hip perhaps most in use and most likely to last with the minimum of variation. The words are man, go, put down, make, beat, cool, swing, with it, crazy, dig, flip, creep, hip, square. They serve a variety of purposes, and the nuance of the voice uses the nuance of the situation to convey the subtle contextual difference. If the hipster moves through his night and through his life on a constant search with glimpses of Mecca in many a turn of his experience (Mecca being the apocalyptic orgasm) and if everyone in the civilized world is at least in some small degree a sexual cripple the hipster lives with the knowledge of how he is sexually crippled and where he is sexually alive, and the faces of experience which life presents to him each day are engaged, dismissed or avoided as his need directs and his lifemanship makes possible. For life is a contest between people in which the victor generally recuperates quickly and the loser takes long to mend, a perpetual competition of colliding explorers in which one must grow or else pay more for remaining the same, (pay in sickness, or depression, or anguish for the lost opportunity) but pay or grow.

Therefore one finds words like go, and make it, and with it, and swing: "Go" with its sense that after hours or days or months or years of monotony, boredom, and depression one has finally had one's chance, one has amassed enough energy to meet an exciting opportunity with all one's present talents for the flip (up or down) and so one is ready to go, ready to gamble. Movement is always to be preferred to inaction. In motion a man has a chance, his body is warm, his instincts are quick, and when the crisis comes, whether of love or violence, he can make it, he can win, he can release a little more energy for himself since he hates himself a little less, he can make a little better nervous system, make it a little more possible to go again, to go faster next time and so make more and thus find more people with whom he can swing. For to swing is to communicate, is to convey the rhythms of one's own being to a lover, a friend, or an audience, and—equally necessary—be able to feel the rhythms of their response. To swing with the rhythms of another is to enrich oneself—the conception of the learning process as dug by Hip is that one cannot really learn until one contains within oneself the implicit rhythm of the subject or the person. As an example, I remember once hearing a Negro friend have an intellectual discussion at a party for half an hour with a white girl who was a few years out of college. The Negro literally could not read or write, but he had an extraordinary ear and a fine sense of mimicry. So as the girl spoke, he would detect the particular formal uncertainties in her argument, and in a pleasant (if slightly Southern) English accent, he would respond to one or another facet of her doubts. When she would finish what she felt was a particularly well-articulated idea, he would smile privately and say, "Other-direction . . . do you really believe in that?"

"Well . . . No," the girl would stammer, "now that you get down to it, there is something disgusting about it to me," and she would be off again for five more minutes.

Of course the Negro was not learning anything about the merits and demerits of the argument, but he was learning a great deal about a type of girl he had never met before, and that was what he wanted. Being unable to read or write, he could hardly be interested in ideas nearly as much as in lifemanship, and so he eschewed any attempt to obey the precision or lack of precision in the girl's language, and instead sensed her character (and the values of her social type) by swinging with the nuances of her voice.

So to swing is to be able to learn, and by learning take a step toward making it, toward creating. What is to be created is not nearly so important as the hipster's belief that when he really makes it, he will be able to turn his hand to anything, even to self-discipline. What he must do before that is find his courage at the moment of violence, or equally make it in the act of love, find a little more of himself, create a little more between his woman and himself, or indeed between his mate and himself (since many hipsters are bisexual), but paramount, imperative, is the necessity to make it because in making it, one is making the new habit, unearthing the new talent which the old frustration denied.

Whereas if you goof (the ugliest word in Hip), if you lapse back into being a frightened stupid child, or if you flip, if you lose your control, reveal the buried weaker more feminine part of your nature, then it is more difficult to swing the next time, your ear is less alive, your bad and energy-wasting habits are further confirmed, you are farther away from being with it. But to be with it is to have grace, is to be closer to the secrets of that inner unconscious life which will nourish you if you can hear it, for you are then nearer to that God which every hipster believes is located in the senses of his body, that trapped, mutilated and nonetheless megalomaniacal God who is It, who is energy, life, sex, force, the Yoga's *prana*, the Reichian's orgone, Lawrence's "blood," Hemingway's "good," the Shavian life-force; "It"; God; not the God of the churches but the unachievable whisper of mystery within the sex, the paradise of limitless energy and perception just beyond the next wave of the next orgasm.

To which a cool cat might reply, "Crazy, man!"

Because, after all, what I have offered above is an hypothesis, no more, and there is not the hipster alive who is not absorbed in his own tumultuous hypotheses. Mine is interesting, mine is way out (on the avenue of the mystery along the road to "It") but still I am just one cat in a world of cool cats, and everything interesting is crazy, or at least so the Squares who do not know how to swing would say.

(And yet crazy is also the self-protective irony of the hipster. Living with questions and not with answers, he is so different in his isolation and in the far reach of his imagination from almost everyone with whom he deals in the outer world of the Square, and meets generally so much enmity, competition, and hatred in the world of Hip, that his isolation is always in danger of turning upon itself, and leaving him indeed just that, crazy.)

If, however, you agree with my hypothesis, if you as a cat are way out too, and we are in the same groove (the universe now being glimpsed as a series of ever-extending radii from the center) why then you say simply, "I dig," because neither knowledge nor imagination comes easily, it is buried in the pain of one's forgotten experience, and so one must work to find it, one must occasionally exhaust oneself by digging into the self in order to perceive the outside. And indeed it is essential to dig the most, for if you do not dig you lose your superiority over the Square, and so you are less likely to be cool (to be in control of a situation because you have swung where the Square has not, or because you have allowed to come to consciousness a pain, a guilt, a shame or a desire which the other has not had the courage to face). To be cool is to be equipped, and if you are equipped it is more difficult for the next cat who comes along to put you down. And of course one can hardly afford to be put down too often, or one is beat, one has lost one's confidence, one has lost one's will, one is impotent in the world of action and so closer to the demeaning flip of becoming a queer, or indeed closer to dying, and therefore it is even more difficult to recover enough energy to try to make it again, because once a cat is beat he has nothing to give, and no one is interested any longer in making it with him. This is the terror of the hipster—to be beat—because once the sweet of sex has deserted him, he still cannot give up the search. It is not granted to the hipster to grow old gracefully—he has been captured too early by the oldest dream of power, the gold fountain of Ponce de Leon, the fountain of youth where the gold is in the orgasm.

To be beat is therefore a flip, it is a situation beyond one's experience, impossible to anticipate—which indeed in the circular vocabulary of Hip is still another meaning for flip, but then I have given just a few of the connotations of these words. Like most primitive vocabularies each word is a prime symbol and serves a dozen or a hundred functions of communication in the instinctive dialectic through which the hipster perceives his experience, that dialectic of the instantaneous differentials of existence in which one is forever moving forward into more or retreating into less.

V

It is impossible to conceive a new philosophy until one creates a new language, but a new popular language (while it must implicitly contain a new philosophy) does not necessarily present its philosophy overtly. It can be asked then what really is unique in the life-view of Hip which raises its argot above the passing verbal whimsies of the bohemian or the lumpenproletariat.

The answer would be in the psychopathic element of Hip which has almost no interest in viewing human nature, or better, in judging human nature, from a set of standards conceived a priori to the experience, standards inherited from the past. Since Hip sees every answer as posing immediately a new alternative, a new question, its emphasis is on complexity rather than simplicity (such complexity that its language without the illumination of the voice and the articulation of the face and body remains hopelessly incommunicative). Given its emphasis on complexity, Hip abdicates from any conventional moral responsibility because it would argue that the result of our actions are unforeseeable, and so we cannot know if we do good or bad, we cannot even know (in the Joycean sense of the good and the bad) whether unforeseeable, and so we cannot know if we do good or bad, we cannot be certain that we have given them energy, and indeed if we could, there would still be no idea of what ultimately they would do with it.

Therefore, men are not seen as good or bad (that they are good-and-bad is taken for granted) but rather each man is glimpsed as a collection of possibilities, some more possible than others (the view of character implicit in Hip) and some humans are considered more capable than others of reaching more possibilities within themselves in less time, provided, and this is the dynamic, provided the particular character can swing at the right time. And here arises the sense of context which differentiates Hip from a Square view of character. Hip sees the context as generally dominating the man, dominating him because his character is less significant than the context in which he must function. Since it is arbitrarily five times more demanding of one's energy to accomplish even an inconsequential action in an unfavorable context than a favorable one, man is then not only his character but his context, since the success or failure of an action in a given context reacts upon the character and therefore affects what the character will be in the next context. What dominates both character and context is the energy available at the moment of intense context.

Character being thus seen as perpetually ambivalent and dynamic enters then into an absolute relativity where there are no truths other than the isolated truths of what each observer feels at each instant of his existence. To take a perhaps unjustified metaphysical extrapolation, it is as if the universe which has usually existed conceptually as a Fact (even if the Fact were Berkeley's God) but a Fact which it was the aim of all science and philosophy to reveal, becomes instead a changing reality whose laws are remade at each instant by everything living, but most particularly man, man raised to a neo-medieval summit where the truth is not what one has felt yesterday or what one expects to feel tomorrow but rather truth is no more nor less than what one feels at each instant in the perpetual climax of the present.

What is consequent therefore is the divorce of man from his values, the liberation of the self from the Super-Ego of society. The only Hip morality (but of course it is an ever-present morality) is to do what one feels whenever and wherever it is possible, and—this is how the war of the Hip and the Square begins—to be engaged in one primal battle: to open the limits of the possible for oneself, for oneself alone because that is one's need. Yet in widening the arena of the possible, one widens it reciprocally for others as well, so that the nihilistic fulfillment of each man's desire contains its antithesis of human cooperation.

If the ethic reduces to Know Thyself and Be Thyself, what makes it radically different from Socratic moderation with its stern conservative respect for the experience of the past, is that the Hip ethic is immoderation, child-like in its adoration of the present (and indeed to respect the past means that one must also respect such ugly consequences of the past as the collective murders of the State). It is this adoration of the present which contains the affirmation of Hip, be- cause its ultimate logic surpasses even the unforgettable solution of the Marquis de Sade to sex, private property, and the family, that all men and women have absolute but temporary rights over the bodies

of all other men and women—the nihilism of Hip proposes as its final
tendency that every social restraint and category be removed, and the
affirmation implicit in the proposal is that man would then prove to
be more creative than murderous and so would not destroy himself.
Which is exactly what separates Hip from the authoritarian philoso-
phies which now appeal to the conservative and liberal temper—what
haunts the middle of the Twentieth Century is that faith in man has
been lost, and the appeal of authority has been that it would restrain
us from ourselves. Hip, which would return us to ourselves, at no
matter what price in individual violence, is the affirmation of the
barbarian for it requires a primitive passion about human nature to
believe that individual acts of violence are always to be preferred to
the collective violence of the State; it takes literal faith in the creative
possibilities of the human being to envisage acts of violence as the
catharsis which prepares growth.

Whether the hipster's desire for absolute sexual freedom contains
any genuinely radical conception of a different world is of course another matter, and it is possible, since the hipster lives with his hatred,
that many of them are the material for an elite of storm troopers ready
to follow the first truly magnetic leader whose view of mass murder
is phrased in a language which reaches their emotions. But given the
desperation of his condition as a psychic outlaw, the hipster is equally
a candidate for the most reactionary and most radical of movements,
and so it is just as possible that many hipsters will come—if the crisis
deepens—to a radical comprehension of the horror of society, for even
as the radical has had his incommunicable dissent confirmed in his experience by precisely the frustration, the denied opportunities, and the
bitter years which his ideas have cost him, so the sexual adventurer
deflected from his goal by the implacable animosity of a society constructed to deny the sexual radical as well, may yet come to an equally
bitter comprehension of the slow relentless inhumanity of the conservative power which controls him from without and from within.
And in being so controlled, denied, and starved into the attrition of
conformity, indeed the hipster may come to see that his condition is no
more than an exaggeration of the human condition, and if he would
be free, then everyone must be free. Yes, this is possible too, for the
heart of Hip is its emphasis upon courage at the moment of crisis, and
it is pleasant to think that courage contains within itself (as the ex-

planation of its existence) some glimpse of the necessity of life to become more than it has been.

It is obviously not very possible to speculate with sharp focus on
the future of the hipster. Certain possibilities must be evident, however, and the most central is that the organic growth of Hip depends
on whether the Negro emerges as a dominating force in American life.
Since the Negro knows more about the ugliness and danger of life
than the White, it is probable that if the Negro can win his equality,
he will possess a potential superiority, a superiority so feared that the
fear itself has become the underground drama of domestic politics.
Like all conservative political fear it is the fear of unforeseeable consequences, for the Negro's equality would tear a profound shift into the
psychology, the sexuality, and the moral imagination of every White
alive.

With this possible emergence of the Negro, Hip may erupt as a
psychically armed rebellion whose sexual impetus may rebound
against the anti-sexual foundation of every organized power in
America, and bring into the air such animosities, antipathies, and
new conflicts of interest that the mean empty hypocrisies of mass conformity will no longer work. A time of violence, new hysteria, confusion and rebellion will then be likely to replace the time of conformity. At that time, if the liberal should prove realistic in his belief
that there is peaceful room for every tendency in American life, then
Hip would end by being absorbed as a colorful figure in the tapestry.
But if this is not the reality, and the economic, the social, the psychological, and finally the moral crises accompanying the rise of the Negro
should prove insupportable, then a time is coming when every political
guide post will be gone, and millions of liberals will be faced with
political dilemmas they have so far succeeded in evading, and with a
view of human nature they do not wish to accept. To take the desegregation of the schools in the South as an example, it is quite likely
that the reactionary sees the reality more closely than the liberal when
he argues that the deeper issue is not desegregation but miscegenation
(As a radical I am of course facing in the opposite direction from the
White Citizen's Councils—obviously I believe it is the absolute human
right of the Negro to mate with the White, and matings there will
undoubtedly be, for there will be Negro high school boys brave
enough to chance their lives.) But for the average liberal whose mind

has been dulled by the committee-ish cant of the professional liberal, miscegenation is not an issue because he has been told that the Negro does not desire it. So, when it comes, miscegenation will be a terror, comparable perhaps to the derangement of the American Communists when the icons to Stalin came tumbling down. The average American Communist held to the myth of Stalin for reasons which had little to do with the political evidence and everything to do with their psychic necessities. In this sense it is equally a psychic necessity for the liberal to believe that the Negro and even the reactionary Southern White are eventually and fundamentally people like himself, capable of becoming good liberals too if only they can be reached by good liberal reason. What the liberal cannot bear to admit is the hatred beneath the skin of a society so unjust that the amount of collective violence buried in the people is perhaps incapable of being contained, and therefore if one wants a better world one does well to hold one's breath, for a worse world is bound to come first, and the dilemma may well be this: given such hatred, it must either vent itself nihilistically or become turned into the cold murderous liquidations of the totalitarian state.

VI

No matter what its horrors the Twentieth Century is a vastly exciting century for its tendency is to reduce all of life to its ultimate alternatives. One can well wonder if the last war of them all will be between the blacks and the whites, or between the women and the men, or between the beautiful and ugly, the pillagers and managers, or the rebels and the regulators. Which of course is carrying speculation beyond the point where speculation is still serious, and yet despair at the monotony and bleakness of the future have become so engrained in the radical temper that the radical is in danger of abdicating from all imagination. What a man feels is the impulse for his creative effort, and if an alien but nonetheless passionate instinct about the meaning of life has come so unexpectedly from a virtually illiterate people, come out of the most intense conditions of exploitation, cruelty, violence, frustration, and lust, and yet has succeeded as an instinct in keeping this tortured people alive, then it is perhaps possible that the Negro holds more of the tail of the expanding elephant of truth than the radical, and if this is so, the radical humanist could do worse than to brood upon the phenomenon. For if a revolutionary time should come again, there would be a crucial difference if someone had already delineated a neo-Marxian calculus aimed at comprehending every circuit and process of society from ukase to kiss as the communications of human energy—a calculus capable of translating the economic relations of man into his psychological relations and then back again, his productive relations thereby embracing his sexual relations as well, until the crises of capitalism in the Twentieth Century would yet be understood as the unconscious adaptations of a society to solve its economic imbalance at the expense of a new mass psychological imbalance. It is almost beyond the imagination to conceive of a work in which the drama of human energy is engaged, and a theory of its social currents and dissipations, its imprisonments, expressions, and tragic wastes are fitted into some gigantic synthesis of human action where the body of Marxist thought, and particularly the epic grandeur of *Das Kapital* (that first of the major *psychologies* to approach the mystery of social cruelty so simply and practically as to say that we are a collective body of humans whose life-energy is wasted, displaced, and procedurally stolen as it passes from one of us to another)—where particularly the epic grandeur of *Das Kapital* would find its place in an even more God-like view of human justice and injustice, in some more excruciating vision of those intimate and institutional processes which lead to our creations and disasters, our growth, our attrition, and our rebellion.

JOHN HOLLOWAY

Tank in the Stalls: Notes on the "School of Anger"

Even more than the Beat Generation, whose novelty was sure to have its effect in the United States, the Angry Young Men have found themselves attacked or ridiculed. There is an almost universal insensibility among British highbrow critics to the relevance and validity of The Movement writers. John Holloway's "Tank in the Stalls" attempts to relate the Angry Young Men to a tradition of the English novel. But in equating Jimmy Porter with Mr. Polly, and Larry Vincent with Thomas Hardy's Jude, Holloway demonstrates a typical inability—or an unwillingness—to engage his subject on its most essential level, as a criticism of existence in a time and place which is also his own.

ANYONE IN BRITAIN who has anything to say about Angry Young Men had better say it quickly: the field is now trampled over so often, it is rapidly becoming contaminated. I must therefore snap up a passing reference in the London Letter of the current *Manchester Guardian Weekly* (July 4th), since this may be my last reputable chance. No one, by now, need be surprised to find passing references in the weeklies. The surprise would be not to. The trend seems to have begun with John Wain's *Hurry on Down* (1953); although the name is taken from an in essence quite irrelevant context, Leslie Paul's *Angry Young Man* (1951) which is about angry youth in politics, left-wingism and unemployment during the 1930's. It is just accident that this originally political label is attached to the string now so often wrapped around Kingsley Amis's *Lucky Jim*, John Osborne's *Look Back in Anger*, George Scott's part-autobiography *Time and Place* and the rest. Although the chief danger may be facile generalization, it is a nominal risk to say that these take less of a political stand than a stand against having any political stand. This, indeed, is explicitly the gist of Mr. Amis's recent Fabian pamphlet. I hope in a moment to offer a hint as to why this attitude should have developed. The first thing to notice is how frequently these books and their authors are now made into a shuttlecock by the press and the weeklies and in conversation. (The latest is a strip cartoon in the *Daily Mirror*.) The second, to trace if one can the curious way in which this interest in them has been limited.

"A new kind of 'hero' ": (quotation marks multiply as mark of one's embarrassment) this is what one is now so often told has arrived. Since every event has a cause, it must be proper to ask what has brought him. K. W. Gransden (*Twentieth Century*, March 1957) hints that he is the product of a generation of writers who are having it both ways, or nearly: trying to run with the establishment and hunt with the "creative opposition"—enjoying both the sweets and the bitters of success. Geoffrey Gorer (*New Stateman*, May 4th) offers sociology: young men who pass through the present educational system of state school and grant-aided university (more like the sweeping steps of the British Museum than an educational "ladder": and so it should be), marry into a higher class than they come from—"male hypergamy"— and get adopted into it. The price they pay is psychological strain which they or their representatives then put into plays or novels. Hence "the new hero": tough, rude, clumsy, ill-dressed, ill-washed, an enemy of phoney 'culture' and phoney everything—and successful with that unexplained but decisive success which usually belongs to Zeitgeist figures.

I have not forgotten the *Manchester Guardian Weekly*; but why it justified re-opening this question must wait for a moment. There is no "new kind of hero" at all. No one kind. This becomes clear as soon as the investigation turns to cases. There may be a simplification or a generalization to be made: this isn't it. The hero of *Lucky Jim* may be rude and ill-dressed; but all in all he is human and considerate in a world mainly of paper cut-outs, he gets the livelier job and the superior girl, and his clumsiness is the formidable kind: it is a true driving force, it arrives. Charles Lumley (*Hurry on Down*) ends with more money, but by chance, not by drive; at the end of the book "he valued his niche simply because it gave him the means, through his new wealth, to put himself beyond the struggle." The social aim is "neutrality," opting out from a social war: "his demands on life had grown smaller and smaller." Jimmy Porter of *Look Back in Anger* ("Lucky Jimmy Porter" I have heard him called: there are no on-the-spot fines in Britain, but we need them for such bad and misleading jokes as that) isn't successful at all, doesn't want success, and couldn't but destroy it if he got it. No one, on the other hand, could be less of a rubber-boat-always-knocked-about-but-always-comes-up figure. Joe Lampton (in John Braine's *Room at the Top*) is remarkably competent and remarkably successful: but finds (or so we are told, for the end of the story is thin) that success, wealth, marriage up the ladder, prove a sham. Thomas Hinde's *Happy as Larry* seems relevant here. Larry Vincent too is just as much a hypergamist as Jimmy Porter. He and his wife also live in an attic flat. He too is always out of a job and into a pub. But he is totally ineffective instead of successful, a feeble-minded trouble-making intolerable saint instead of an overbearing bully, and a Londoner instead of a Midlander or a Northerner. Kingsley Amis's second novel (*That Uncertain Feeling*) is perhaps a minor document in the case. Lewis, its hero, is somewhere between Jim Dixon and Joe Lampton. John Wain's *Living in the Present* seems not to be in the genre at all.

This is the merest sketch: but clearly, the differences between these characters are as clear as the similarities or clearer. Of course these books reflect contemporary social pressures and tensions. Of course one can see in them some of the social and psychological difficulties which confront successful risers in the educational system (and these were by no means many until the very recent past); or the spread of south-of-England subutopian amenities or pseudo-amenities to the industrial north (this I suspect to be one of our most important recent changes); or the garish drabness, rootlessness and money-making cynicism which have been common (and their opposites have been common too) in post-war England. What does all this amount to? It amounts to a very simple fact, the simplicity of which we seem rather to have forgotten: various aspects of the total social spectrum have been turning up in novels. New ones have to turn up for the first time.

The *Manchester Guardian Weekly* was simply reporting that Siegfried Sassoon had been awarded the 1957 Queen's Medal for Poetry: "today's angry young man is notoriously tomorrow's recipient of honours," it said. The completely casual reference is index of how familiar the idea has grown. "Today" and "tomorrow" were being used somewhat freely, since the reference back was to Sassoon's savagely ironical war poems, the jolly general who fraternized with the troops and "did for them all with his plan of campaign," or the silly audiences at shows:

> I'd like to see a tank come down the stalls
> > Lurching to ragtime tunes, or "Home Sweet Home,"
> And there'd be no more jokes in music-halls
> > To mock the riddled corpses round Bapaume.

The anger of Sassoon's war poems was not, of course, the kind with which my note is concerned. Were there no earlier analogy whatever to the situations and attitudes of Amis, Wain, Osborne, etc., then the problem might be other than it is and harder than it is. By good luck, however, that earlier analogy is ready to hand:

> Acting on Chitterlow's advice to have a bit of a freshener before returning to the Emporium, K— walked some way along the Leas and back, and then went down to a shop near the Harbour to get a cup of coffee. He found that extremely invigorating, and he went on up the High Street to face the inevitable terrors of the office. . . . After all, it was not an unmanly headache; he had been out all night, and he had been drinking, and his physical disorder was there to witness the fact . . . he pulled his spirits together, put his hat back from his pallid brow, thrust his hands into his trousers pockets, and adopted an altogether dissipated carriage. . . . Just for a moment he was glad that his patch at the knee was, after all, visible, and that some, at least, of the mud on his clothes had refused to move at Chitterlow's brushing. What wouldn't they think he'd been up to? He passed them without speaking.

"K—" is not Kafka, it is *Kipps*. H. G. Wells in 1905 was already busy with such topics as rising in the world, the petty Jack-in-Office, phoney middle-class culture—Miss Walshingham and her wood-carving class. *Mr. Polly* (1910) had less education than Jimmy Porter got from his white-tile university or Joe Lampton from a correspondence course in a PW camp; but he still had some. There are other resemblances. "At first there were attempts to bully him (Polly) on account of his refusal to consider face-washing a diurnal duty, but two fights with the apprentices next above him established a useful reputation for choler, and the presence of girl apprentices in the shop somehow raised his standard of cleanliness to a more acceptable level." The futile, angry scene with which the book opens does not occur until Polly is thirty-seven; but it is like the opening scene of *Look Back in Anger* in that it too displays a cosmic disgust which is focussed upon the speaker's squalid home life, and which is provoked by what, in 1905, was no bad shot at a psychological malaise:

> He suffered from *indigestion* now nearly every afternoon in his life, but as he lacked introspection he projected the associated discomfort upon the world.

Wells' dialogue dates, of course. "Hole! . . . 'Ole! . . . Oh! *Beastly* silly Wheeze of a hole!" is not mid-century conversation and is not mid-century humour. What Jimmy Porter says is "Let's pretend that we're human beings, that we're actually alive" (which is not mid-century humour either). Wells may be different (in ways not relevant at present, he is profoundly so), but Wells is what, in anger or oblivion doesn't matter, John Osborne is looking back to.

Nor Wells only. Given that we are concerned not with one unique thing, but with a related variety of things which have been getting into English novels in recent years; and given also that to trace a partial resemblance is not to claim a total identity, the parallels go further. *Jude the Obscure* is one:

> "If that can be done," said Jude, "at college gates in the most religious and educational city in the world, what shall we say as to how far we've got?"
> "Order," said one of the policemen, who had been engaged with a comrade in opening the huge doors opposite the col-

lege. "Keep yer tongue quiet, my man, while the procession passes."

. . . "Well. *I'm an outsider* to the end of my days" (Jude) sighed after a while.

—or Bob Sawyer, sixty years earlier still, giving a party which included a young gentleman "in a shirt emblazoned with pink anchors": certainly no happier than Larry about his landladies, and clearly looking in anger at them:

"That's her malevolence, that's her malevolence," returned Mr. Bob Sawyer, vehemently. "She says that if I can afford to give a party I ought to be able to pay her confounded 'little bill'."

Perhaps there is no need to go back along this tightrope any further. The shifts and differences are of course great. The 1950's have their distinctive features. Some of them get into these novels. Others elsewhere. The essence of the matter is that these novels merely illustrate, in varied detail, local or transient forms of permanent social stresses in English life up and down the country; and that to do so has been a recurrent feature of the English novel. If the heroes have something new in common, they have something old in common too. If the plots centre on details of jobs, money, sex and success, they centre on what the English novel centred on throughout the nineteenth century.

The surprise, in fact, is not that this should be so, but rather that readers should be surprised and intrigued when they find the details of obscure middle-class provincial life occupying the substance of what make a claim to be serious and ambitious novels (Amis and Wain have standing as poets, critics, and commentators in general upon the current cultural scene).

Why should work of this kind be a source of surprise and intrigue? I can only venture a very long shot at this, because to give the full answer would be to write the history of literature and of thought about it in Britain this century. But several things afford clues. Among them are Virginia Woolf's essay on "Modern Fiction" (included in *The Common Reader*, 1925), with its attack on Wells and eulogy of Russian fiction. The counterpart of this is Amis's depreciation of Virginia Woolf in a recent issue of the weekly *Spectator*. The best clue to what has been going on, though, may possibly be John Wain's verse. On the surface, this is cool, self-depreciatory, ironical: it follows on from William Empson, and Wain has claimed more than once that he was the first to work the Empson line, as it were. In so far as this is so, it would have its relation to the poetic revolution of Eliot and Pound (largely, as everyone knows, on French models) and would continue their reaction against the English poetic tradition of the Romantics and the Nineteenth Century. Yet in these characteristic lines from a poem characteristically entitled *Eighth Type of Ambiguity*, is that really what one finds?—

> When love as germ invades the purple stream
> It splashes round the veins and multiplies
> Till objects of desire are what they seem;
> Then *all creation wears a chic disguise* . . .

"Chic" is an unkind and perhaps unnecessary word in my context, but the words I have italicized bear an illuminating relation to Wain's own verse. Take *Don't Let's Spoil It All*:

> She had to *leave him choking in his fear* . . .
> The lesson is that *dying hearts must die.*

Or take *Reasons for Not Writing Nature Poetry*. One can imagine Pound, or conceivably Eliot, endorsing that subject. But treated this way?—

> Content, without embellishment, to note
> How little beauty *bids the heart rejoice*,
> How little beauty *catches at the throat*.
> *Simply, I love this mountain and this bay*
> With love that I can *never speak* by rote . . .

This is exactly the reason against writing nature poetry which would have least appealed to them. We know, however, where to look for poetry which sees the cosmos essentially as fringe for the ego, or which claims that there are thoughts (especially about mountains and what goes with them) that lie too deep for tears or words. It is not in the work of Eliot and Pound, it is in what they reacted from.

My last port of call would be, with Virginia Woolf's praise for the Russians and depreciation of Wells in mind, the well-known letter of D. H. Lawrence (5 June, 1914) in which he expresses his new conception of personality as it concerns the novelist ("you musn't look in my novel for the old stable *ego* of the character"), and starts by saying that this is something he has partly learnt from Marinetti. Everyone is agreed, I suppose, that literature in England, in the two decades after 1910, received the biggest impact of avant-garde ideas, interests and techniques from the continent of Europe that it had had since the later seventeenth century. This relates not only to Pound and Eliot, but also to Joyce, to Lawrence ("I believe that, just as an audience was found in Russia for Tchekhov, so an audience might be found in England for some of my stuff": letter of 1 Feb., 1913), Yeats, and (one should have Bergson in mind besides the Russians) Virginia Woolf.

The present fact is that in Britain this great impulse has largely spent itself; just as the not altogether dissimilar impulse spent itself by the mid-eighteenth century. One could go even further, and say that rather as mid-eighteenth century writers were veering round towards Spenser's and our other early poetry, but at the same time were inclined to patronize these things, so there are writers today who disparage Romantic poets while standing far nearer to them than they think.

Here I revert to provincial young men who grow up, get grants and girls, and struggle to climb up in or out of the career stream. What John Wain's verse shows so clearly, his novels and those of the others show not much less so. The Great Continental Impact (we were in for it when two American college teachers got off their boats around 1910), is no longer the decisive force; and English writing, for good or ill, is reverting to some of its more indigenous traditions. In poetry the situation is complex by virtue partly of the fact that the continental, Symbolist influence was deeply and in large part rightly linked with a recovery of what had been forgotten in our own Elizabethan-Jacobean period. In the novel, we are reverting to our well-established nineteenth century preoccupations: the detail of our provincial and local life; our elaborate and multiple gradations of money, influence or power; and what has perhaps always been intimately linked with these, our processes of sexual selection. To be surprised or especially intrigued by the Angry Young Man school (to speak in labels for a moment) is merely to take the admirable, but special and indeed esoteric fictional preoccupations of the last thirty years as not special, but normal; and to find the familiar unfamiliar when one sees it again after, in more than one sense, a Period.

That the Continental Injection has worn off seems to me to be a plain fact. True, the work I have been discussing makes one say that this is a major loss and very little gain with it. Whether that must always be the verdict remains to be seen. What may even now be added, though, is that the fully effective recovery of some of the indigenous resources of our literature, and at the same time the enrichment of them with at least something from the last forty years, is one of the major tasks now confronting the writer in Britain.

GEOFFREY GORER

The Perils of Hypergamy

We see what we have been trained to see. Geoffrey Gorer, one of England's leading anthropologists, observes a sociological phenomenon at the heart of most of the Angry Young Men novels and plays. He speculates on the causes of the phenomenon and the reasons why its consequences are usually so distressful. If Gorer seems to oversimplify the case, it is, in part, because he fails to explore the particular extensions in each work of what he labels male hypergamy. Jim Dixon-Christine is not Jimmy Porter-Alison is not Joe Lampton-Susan Brown. Nevertheless, Gorer's analysis is valuable in establishing one of the central symbols of The Movement.

NOW I'M PRACTICALLY SURE OF IT. *Lucky Jim, Look Back in Anger* and all that lot roused my suspicions; and the clincher has come with John Braine's *Room at the Top*, which tells much the same story all over again, brilliantly and bitterly. The curse which is ruining, in fantasy if not in their own lives, these brilliant young men of working-class origin and welfare-state opportunity is what anthropologists have dubbed male hypergamy. It is a new pattern in English life, and apparently a very distressing one.

In any society stratified by caste or class—and this means all complex societies, all societies composed of more than one ethnic group when the groups are distinguishable by appearance or speech, and all societies colonised or missionised by Hinduism—the great majority of marriages or socially recognised sexual relationships take place within the caste or class. This is to say that the caste or class tends to be endogamous, by definition where caste is concerned, by custom with class. But even in the most rigid societies, even in Hindu India or the southern United States or South Africa, some marriages across class or caste barriers do occur or, where such marriages are forbidden by civil law, become established and public irregular unions.

When such cross-class or cross-caste unions do occur, the society has to decide to which social position the couple shall be assigned. Probably the more common is for the higher status partner to be degraded to the lower status, to "lose caste" or "become *déclassé*" in the precise meaning of the common phrases; but there are situations where the lower class or caste partner is raised to the higher status of the spouse, and this is technically called hypergamy, marrying upwards.

In most societies status or prestige tends to be connected with one of the sexes rather than the other, a facet of what is popularly (and inaccurately) called patriarchy or matriarchy; in "male prestige" societies a woman's status is derived from her father and her husband; in "female prestige" societies a man's status will be related to that of his mother, his sister and his wife. It seems fairly simple for the person of the sex which carries esteem to give status to a lower-class partner; King Cophetua could raise the beggar maid; or, to come nearer to our own time, any number of chorus girls could be raised to the peerage. Female hypergamy fits fairly well into English society, and has informed the dreams of any number of unprivileged girls, from *Jane Eyre* to most of the serials in most of the current women's magazines.

As far as we know, male hypergamy has always been a relatively uncommon arrangement, though it has taken place regularly in some matrilineal societies, notably some of the tribes and castes of southern India. There seem to be two general, though not universal, reasons for this; in most societies property (other than title to land) is usually gained and held by men, and although wealth and high status never completely coincide, the former is very often a prerequisite for the latter; and leisured men seem to find the manipulation of symbols more congenial than do leisured women; and status, as much as the arts, is to a very great extent dependent on the proper manipulation of symbols.

These are generalizations, not universals. In the contemporary United States, the symbols of high status have been almost entirely left in women's hands—an application for inclusion in the *Social Register* must be accompanied by letters of recommendation from two women who are already included; and in the United States male hypergamy is a recognised technique for the advancement of an able, ambitious but lower status man; "marrying the boss's daughter" is the way this step is usually described. In the novels and films elaborating this theme, the hero's happiness is rarely shadowed.

In *Lucky Jim, That Uncertain Feeling, Look Back in Anger, Room at the Top* (to mention no others) the hero, of working-class origin, is married to, or involved in a public liaison with, a middle to upper-middle-class woman and doesn't really enjoy it at all, in the long run. He thinks he is "destroyed" by her, or would be "destroyed" by her if he didn't return to his proper working-class environment, or both are reduced to mutual misery and recrimination. These cross-class unions, with male hypergamy, don't work out, we are told with humour and anger and passion and sentimentality; and yet it is implied, if not stated, that it is only among women of this higher social class that these bright young men can expect to find wives or mistresses.

It is perhaps necessary to enter a *caveat* that I am talking about works of fiction, not about the authors, of whose personal lives I know nothing at all. The fantasies underlying these fictions are realistic enough and coherent enough so that they can be treated as referring to contemporary English life, even if it be impossible, or at least very ill-mannered, to identify specific instances of such unions.

The records are sparse, but it seems as if, before 1939, the higher-status Englishwoman was declassed to her lower-status spouse; when a school teacher married a miner, she became a miner's wife, not he a teacher's husband; the fictions of D. H. Lawrence have several examples of the lady marrying downwards (hypogamy, in anthropological vocabulary). The problem, therefore, is why male hypergamy has suddenly become at the least a possibility to be considered, and why it is felt to be so inevitably destructive by the young men to whom it might occur?

The English class structure has never been really rigid or impermeable; but, in the past, upward mobility—the moving from a lower class to a higher one—was a relatively slow process, the penetration of the upper middle or upper classes usually taking more than one generation. Typically, a man of the middle or working classes made a fortune and provided his children with the type of education which would train them to move in a social class in which he and his wife would never be at ease. Both real life and fiction abound with examples; it was one of Thackeray's favourite themes (the Osbornes in *Vanity Fair* make all the points).

The 1944 Education Act, and its sequels, have enormously speeded up this process, so that the university education which was formerly the culmination of two or three generations of earnest striving on the part of the whole family, is now available to the sons (apparently much less to the daughters) of working-class families if they are bright enough, persistent enough, and tough enough. Although higher social class has not been determined entirely by education in England, it is probably the single most important component of class position between the ranges of the upper working- and upper middle-classes, that is to say for something like a quarter of the English population; and anybody who completes a university education has the qualifications for a profession in which most of his colleagues will be of middle- or upper middle-class status.

These bright young working-class lads jump three or four social classes (in the English seven-class social hierarchy) in the second decade of their lives. At the end of that period their intellectual interests, their social horizons, and almost certainly their accent and vocabulary—the chief stigmata of social class—are much nearer to those of their fellow graduates than they are to those of their parents or their less bright brothers and sisters. But because this process of social mobility has started so relatively late (probably after the 11-plus examination) when the main lines of their character are already established, their emotional values, their type of sex identification and their patterns of domestic life are all rooted in the sub-culture of the English working class, nostalgically for Mr. Richard Hoggart, more or less defiantly for the heroes of the novels and plays I am discussing. They are, quite inevitably, divided men unless (as in *That Uncertain Feel-*

ing) they decide to reject all the opportunities a grateful state has given them.

The further you go down the English social scale the greater the contrast made between the typical and expected behaviour, and even voice pitch, of male and female. It is very much easier for a working-class man to imperil his status as a male than it is for one of the upper middle-class. A light tenor voice, a la-di-da (B.B.C. standard English) accent, an extended vocabulary, restraint in the use of expletives, all carry the stigma of being cissy or pansy; and not one working man in a hundred but would be ashamed of being caught by a mate in doing the sort of housework and child-tending which is taken for granted by young fathers of the professional classes today.

In their secondary school days the future university students are likely to have undergone a good deal of mockery and self-questioning for their studious abstention from the pursuit of money and pleasure which their mates enjoy from the age of 15; and consequently they feel driven to emphasise their manliness in such ways as are open to them, perhaps by surliness or pugnacity, but certainly by frequent copulation or attempts thereat. There is no reason to suppose their physiological urges are stronger, or less strong, than those of their contemporaries who have not moved in social class; but their psychological urges are much more over-determined.

This is where the trap of hypergamy opens. Casual intercourse with tarts is likely to be inadequately satisfying (to say nothing of the expense). One wants to be able to talk to the girl as well; and girls still in the working-class have no conversation which is satisfying for any length of time to a newly-educated man. Presumably the happiest marry girls as mobile as themselves or foreigners, but they haven't so far written books or plays, or even appeared in them. The others get involved with upper middle-class girls, with the comically tragic results we read about.

The assured status of the upper middle-class girl is intellectually seen as desirable, indeed as an emotional reward for all the hard work, so that it would not be satisfactory if she abandoned her manners and habits and became a working-class wife; but the upper middle-classes and the working-classes have very different models of ideal masculine and feminine, husbandly and wifely behaviour, and each is seen as destructive to integrity and self respect by the member of the other sex and class. The working-class husband expects, and most of the time gets, far more service and subservience from his wife than does a man of the upper middle-class (whose wife would complain that she is being turned into a drudge); an upper middle-class wife gets far more consideration and physical help, where there is no money for servants, from her husband than does a woman of the working-class (whose husband would complain that he is being unmanned, turned into a cissy). If both are strong characters—and both are likely to be, the man to have fought his way to his present position, the girl to have defied conventions so far—conflict would appear theoretically almost inevitable; and the books and plays tell us what forms these conflicts take.

In this English pattern, there is a much better fit with female hypergamy, for both sexes feel themselves indulged; and, as far as I know, chorus girls were happy, and made their well-born husbands happy, in the old Gaiety days.

BIOGRAPHICAL NOTES

Critic WALTER ALLEN was born in Birmingham, England, in 1911 and educated at Birmingham University. His works include a study of *Arnold Bennett, Reading a Novel, The English Novel* and *Six Great Novelists*. A frequent reviewer of fiction for the *New Statesman and Nation* and the London *Times*, Allen makes his home in Exmouth, Devon.

KINGSLEY AMIS was born in London in 1922 and educated at St. John's College, Oxford. His verse, clean of diction, tough of mind, had already established him firmly among the so-called University Wits, when *Luck Jim* appeared. This highly successful first novel—unexpectedly—set off The Movement, and Amis was recognized as one of the foremost younger intellectuals of post-war England. He has written another novel, *That Uncertain Feeling*. His poetry has been collected in *Bright November, A Case of Samples,* and *A Frame of Mind*. Amis is presently a Lecturer in English at the University College in Swansea, where he lives with his wife and two children.

JOHN BRAINE was born in 1922 in Bradford, Yorkshire. He quit school to work at various jobs, but managed later to qualify for a certificate from a correspondence school. *Room at the Top,* a first novel, dealt with the efforts of an Angry Young Man to assimilate into provincial upper-middle-class society—a betrayal of self which ended in tragedy and spiritual defeat. Braine is now a librarian in Yorkshire.

Born in Idaho Falls, Idaho, in 1922, CHANDLER BROSSARD spent his early years in Washington, D.C., and in other cities along the eastern seaboard; he also lived for extended periods in Europe. He has been a reporter on the *Washington Post* and a member of the editorial staff of the *New Yorker*. In 1950 and 1951 he was executive editor of the *American Mercury*. His first novel, *Who Walk in Darkness*, was among the earliest works dealing with the American hipster. In addition to writing four other published novels, Brossard has edited and contributed to a collection of essays, *The Scene Before You*. He is presently a department editor on *Look*.

ANATOLE BROYARD was born in New Orleans. He was seven years old when his family moved to Brooklyn and eighteen when he moved to

Greenwich Village. He was a captain in the Army during World War II. After the war he attended the New School for Social Research, where he now teaches and lectures on popular culture. *Partisan Review, discovery, Commentary,* and other periodicals have published his stories and articles. He presently works for *The Reporter.*

R. V. CASSILL was born in 1919 in Cedar Falls, Iowa. After service with the Army in the South Pacific, he returned to his native state and received an M.A. from the University of Iowa in 1947. He remained for several years to teach in the Writers' Workshop there. Following a year in Paris on a Fulbright grant, he settled in New York. He has published *The Eagle on the Coin* and other novels. His short stories have appeared in numerous anthologies, including, most recently, *Fifteen by Three,* and in several O. Henry Prize collections. Cassill is married and has one child.

J. P. DONLEAVY was born in 1926 in Brooklyn and raised in the Bronx. He attended Fordham Prep and Manhattan Prep, spent two years in the Navy, and then emigrated to Europe in 1946, where he has lived ever since. After studying bacteriology at Trinity College, Dublin, in which city he also had four exhibitions of paintings, he bought a farm in Kilcoole, County Wicklow, Ireland. Here he wrote his instantaneously popular first novel, *The Ginger Man,* soon to be published in this country. He has completed a second novel, *Helen,* and is presently at work on a third, *A Singular Man.* With his English wife and two children Donleavy now lives in London.

ALLEN GINSBERG was born in Newark, New Jersey, in 1926. Upon graduation from Columbia University, he held various jobs before entering the merchant marine. He knocked around the country for several years, settling for a while in San Francisco. His first book of poems *Howl and Other Poems,* published by the City Lights Bookshop in San Francisco, created a sensation and a court case. In a preface to the book, William Carlos Williams wrote, "This poet sees through and all around the horrors he partakes of in the very intimate details of his poem. He avoids nothing but experiences it to the hilt." Of "Howl," Kenneth Rexroth said: "It is probably the most remarkable single poem published by a young man since the second war." Ginsberg is now living in Paris.

Author and anthropologist, GEOFFREY GORER was born in London in 1905 and educated at Charterhouse, Cambridge, the Sorbonne and the University of Berlin. His wide range of interests and his extensive travels are reflected in numerous books, including *Africa Dances, The American People, Bali and Angkor, Exploring English Character, Himalayan Village, Hot Strip Tease and Other Notes on American Culture* and *The Marquis de Sade.* Gorer now lives on a farm in Sussex, where he divides his time between farming, gardening and writing.

Born in 1928, THOMAS HINDE attended an English public school and then joined the Royal Navy, which he served in various parts of England and on the continent, as well as off the coasts of Burma and India. After being permitted to resign, he went for three years to Oxford, where he read history. He has, at various times, been a private tutor, a circus hand and a temporary civil service employee. Hinde is the author of two novels: *Mr. Nicholas,* not usually associated with The Movement, and *Happy as Larry.*

JOHN HOLLOWAY was born in 1920 on the Kentish edge of London, attended a local grammar school and then went to Oxford. During the war he was an artillery officer. In 1946 he became a prize fellow at All Souls College, Oxford, where he taught philosophy for a short time before transferring to English studies. In 1948 he was appointed lecturer in English at Aberdeen University, and in 1954 was made a lecturer at Cambridge and a Fellow of Queens' College. Holloway is the author of *Language and Intelligence, The Victorian Sage,* and *The Minute* (poems). Married, he presently lives in Cambridge.

CLELLON HOLMES was born in 1926 in Holyoke, Massachusetts. He attended Columbia University and the New School. During the war he served in the Hospital Corps of the Navy. His novel, *Go,* the first volume of a trilogy, was published in 1952. It did much to spread the concept of a Beat Generation. Holmes' second novel will be brought out shortly, and he is presently at work in Connecticut, where he lives, on his third.

JACK KEROUAC was born in Lowell, Massachusetts, in 1922, attended Columbia University and worked as a merchant seaman during World War II. His first novel, *The Town and the City,* was published in 1950. After being rejected by numerous publishers, his second novel was brought out seven years later. It was *On the Road.* Here, for the first time, a large reading public encountered the Beat Generation, and the phrase, coined by Kerouac years before, came into national prominence. There followed newspaper and magazine articles, television interviews—and this anthology. Kerouac's most recently published novel is *The Subterraneans.*

"WILLIAM LEE" is the pseudonym of the author of *Junkie,* which was published as a paperback. During the early post-war years "Lee" was a key figure in the Beat Generation movement, then developing in New York. Thinly-veiled characterizations of him appear in Holmes' *Go* and Kerouac's *The Town and the City* and *On the Road.* He is now living

abroad and is at work on an autobiography which already runs to several
volumes.

NORMAN MAILER was born in Long Branch, New Jersey, in 1923
and raised in Brooklyn. He entered the Army after his graduation from
Harvard. His short story "The Greatest Thing in the World" won the
Story magazine prize in 1941, and in 1944 his novelette A Calculus at
Heaven was published in Cross-section 1944. But it was in 1948, with the
publication of The Naked and the Dead, that the entire nation became
aware of Mailer. This novel, hailed as "the finest work of fiction to come
out of the war," placed him at the forefront of contemporary American
novelists. His subsequent novels have been Barbary Shore and, most recently, The Deer Park. The latter because of its close examination of
sexual activity stirred considerable controversy. Mailer is married and lives
in Connecticut.

GEORGE MANDEL was born in New York City in 1920. Before
entering the Army, he studied art at Pratt Institute and the Art Students
League. He saw service in France, Belgium, Holland and Germany and
was wounded twice in action. After the war he attended the New School.
In 1952 his first novel, Flee the Angry Strangers, was published. He has
edited several anthologies and his short stories have appeared in numerous
collections. He lives in New York City with his wife and two children and
is at work on a novel.

JOHN OSBORNE was born in 1929 in a London tenement district to
working-class parents. He quit school at sixteen to take his first full-time
job, wrote for a number of trade magazines, and then turned to acting.
As an unknown performer, he experienced long periods of unemployment,
during one of which he wrote Look Back in Anger. In spite of mixed
notices, the Royal Court Theatre production of this play was an instantaneous triumph, and it was bought for performance in Paris and New
York and at the Berlin Festival. Osborne's second play, The Entertainer,
no less successful, opened in New York on February 12, 1958, with Sir
Laurence Olivier in the title role.

KENNETH REXROTH, a native of South Bend, Indiana, has lived for
a number of years in San Francisco, where he directed a radio book program on KDFA and did much to bring national prominence to a group of
poets headquartering in San Francisco. Winner of the 1957 Shelley Memorial Award presented by the Poetry Society of America, Rexroth has
published numerous books of poetry. Among them are In What Hour,
The Phoenix and the Tortoise, The Art of Worldly Wisdom, and The
Dragon and the Unicorn. In 1956, New Directions published his volume

In Defense of Earth. He has recently been active in San Francisco and elsewhere giving poetry readings in cafés to the accompaniment of jazz.

Previously unpublished in this country, GEORGE SCOTT supplied this biographical note: "I was one of the immediate post-war generation of writers at Oxford. Educated at State schools, I began work on a local newspaper in Yorkshire at 15. Served in the Navy and joined Lord Beaverbrook's *Daily Express* in 1948 after taking honours degree in English at Oxford. Was editor for four years of *Truth*, the old political and literary review, until its death at Christmas, 1957. *Time and Place*, an autobiographical survey of the background and prejudices of a lower-middle-class boy growing up in the Thirties, was my first book. Affinities with Kingsley Amis, John Wain and John Osborne in my scepticism, my self-mockery, my attacks on Establishment figures and attitudes of mind. Now 32, married with two children, working in journalism and television for a living and on a novel with contemporary political background for the sake of my sanity."

Born in the Bronx in 1928, CARL SOLOMON was proclaimed a "child prodigy" at the age of seven. His ability then to memorize the batting averages of all players in the National and American Leagues won him stories in many New York newspapers. He studied at CCNY, Brooklyn College, and the Sorbonne. Then followed a stint in the merchant marine and as an editor with a New York publishing house. One phase of Solomon's life forms an important part of "Howl," and Solomon appears under other names in other Beat Generation works. His own literary output has been as small as it is distinguished. He now lives in New York, where he is at work on an extended memoir of the Beat Generation.

A former lecturer in English Literature at Reading University, JOHN WAIN was born in 1925 in Stoke-on-Trent, Staffordshire, and educated at St. John's College, Oxford. He began his writing career as one of the University Wits, but at the end of 1955 he left teaching to devote full time to free-lance writing and criticism. Only thirty-three, Wain has an already impressive bibliography, which includes two novels, *Hurry on Down* and *Living in the Present*; two volumes of poetry, *Mixed Feelings* and *A Word Carved on a Sill*; a volume of criticism, *Preliminary Essays*; and an anthology, *Contemporary Reviews of Romantic Poetry*. He is presently engaged in writing three novels.

Son of a Leicester boot and shoe factory worker, COLIN WILSON was born in 1931. Following brief stints in the R.A.F. and the Leicester income tax office, he went to Paris in 1950. Here he wrote plays, poetry and short stories, attended Raymond Duncan's "Akademia" and served on

Merlin and *The Paris Review*. Back in England in 1954, he began *The Outsider*, writing in the British Museum during the day, washing dishes at night to earn money, and living in a sleeping bag on Hampstead Heath. *Religion and the Rebel*, a sequel to *The Outsider*, was published in 1957.